D1483147

THE CITY IN RUSSIAN HISTORY

THE CITY IN RUSSIAN HISTORY

MICHAEL F. HAMM,
EDITOR

The University Press of Kentucky

The Library of Congress system of transliteration has been used throughout this book except in cases where another form of transliteration is more commonly accepted.

ISBN: 0-8131-1328-8

Library of Congress Catalog Card Number: 75-3544

Copyright © 1976 by The University Press of Kentucky

A statewide cooperative scholarly publishing agency serving Berea College, Centre College of Kentucky, Eastern Kentucky University, Georgetown College, Kentucky Historical Society, Kentucky State University, Morehead State University, Murray State University, Northern Kentucky State College, Transylvania University, University of Kentucky, University of Louisville, and Western Kentucky University.

Editorial and Sales Offices: Lexington, Kentucky 40506

For JoAnn, Sarah, and Jill

CONTENTS

ACKNOWLEDGMENTS

I should begin by thanking the scholars who contributed to this volume for their enthusiasm and cooperation. The high quality of their work expedited my editorial efforts. The suggestions of Professor S. Frederick Starr of Princeton University were especially helpful on the matter of developing a theme for the collection. Above all, I thank Professor William L. Blackwell of New York University who undertook the difficult task of writing a concluding chapter. His seasoned perspective adds a particularly valuable dimension to the book.

I also wish to thank Centre College and its president, Thomas A. Spragens, for supporting the project. I extend appreciation as well to Professor Charles T. Hazelrigg of Centre College for his encouragement.

Michael F. Hamm

INTRODUCTION

This collection of original essays is the first attempt outside of the Soviet Union to examine the character of the Russian town through time, specifically from the medieval period to the present. In general, the collection embraces the ideas of a new generation of specialists for, with a few exceptions, only recently have Western scholars turned their attention to the Russian city, particularly prior to the Soviet period. Many of the contributors to this volume have used the archival and library facilities available in the Soviet Union and/or Finland. They represent five academic disciplines—history, geography, political science, architecture, and sociology—and consequently a variety of perspectives and research techniques. As one Soviet urban specialist has stated, the city "embodies the highest achievements of our material and spiritual culture." Inherently complex, the city "connects residence and factory, past and future, individual and society." It is a "tangle of contradictions."[1] I hope that the variety of approaches and analytical tools employed in the creation of this volume, as well as the broad historical perspective it encompasses, will help to untangle the complexities of the Russian city, past and present, and clarify the historical dynamics of Russia's urban development.

A good collection of essays says collectively what no individual scholar could have said by himself. A good collection requires originality of scholarship and approach. But it also needs at least a degree of internal cohesion and continuity—chronological, thematic, or both. Cohesion and continuity must not, however, be stressed to the point that they impose artificial constraints upon the contributor and thereby distort his analysis or conclusions. In examining the complex and multifaceted nature of the city the

1

words of sociologist Amos Hawley bear repeating. "The city represents a cross-section—kaleidoscopic, to be sure—of the whole of life. Hence it lends itself to as many interpretations as there are predilections among its observers."[2]

Selecting a single theme for the collection was consequently not an easy task. The city is an intricate complex of elements, and the historical scope of this collection is intentionally broad. Furthermore, within a given state or region, cities frequently differ in character in accordance with size, function, and other factors. The history of Moscow *may* differ in some ways from that of Minsk, Odessa, or Tashkent, at least during some phases of its development. The great expanse and the ethnic diversity of the Russian empire and Soviet Union further compound this problem.

Nevertheless, many continuities and similarities exist throughout Russian history, particularly because of the preponderant role of the state, whether princely, tsarist, or communist, in determining the basic nature and organization of the city and its role in national life. Highly centralized authoritarianism and bureaucratism have characterized all aspects of Russian development. The state has been virtually omnicompetent; as B. H. Sumner points out, throughout much of Russian history, it has been "the creator and not merely the regulator of all associations within it, other than the church."[3]

Nineteenth-century and early twentieth-century Russian scholars, many of them writing with reform objectives in mind, underscored and at times exaggerated the role of the state in Russian urban development. G. I. Shreider believed that prior to the era of reform in the 1860s the most noteworthy characteristic of the Russian city was its insignificance of size. In many cases the city was merely an administrative unit designed not to fulfill local needs but to serve the needs of the state. I. I. Ditiatin believed that the history of the Russian city was little more than the history of regulations governing the merchant class. Paul Miliukov argued that in contrast to western Europe, and since state needs "outstripped" natural factors, the urban population "had to be created by force."[4]

At least one nineteenth century historian, however, N. D. Chechulin, criticized the tendency to treat the city as an unimportant, accidental growth upon essential Russia. Chechulin presaged modern Soviet specialists in faulting his contemporaries for failing to use sufficient source materials and to draw proper distinction between types of cities and between types of urban growth from region to region.[5] Soviet scholars have stressed that Russian urban development was a natural result of the growth of capitalism, as in the West. Historian P. G. Ryndziunskii, for example, believes that the Russian city may have been unique in the relatively minor influence it exerted and in its lack of "intensive development," but these, he states, are differences from the West only in degree and not in essence.[6] Soviet scholars have also emphasized regional and case studies of cities, including those in the Caucasus, Siberia, and other outlying areas.

Historiography aside, the critical role of the state in shaping the nature of the Russian city has made this theme a unifying constant in all periods. Therefore, wherever possible, the contributors to this collection have addressed themselves to this theme.

The character of the city has grown more complex, quite naturally, during periods of rapid urbanization. In fact, urbanization is a term which often denotes a whole process of social change and not merely urban growth. I have therefore allocated more space to the nineteenth and twentieth centuries than to the preceding era. Hence, in Part I, "The Early Russian Town," the essays are relatively comprehensive, especially with regard to the dimension of time. Since there are almost no studies of early urban life in print, at least in Western languages, the primary purpose of this section is to provide a basic examination of the nature of the early city and its role in national life, with particular emphasis on the relationship between state and city.

In Part II, which encompasses roughly the period from 1800 to 1917, I have combined relatively comprehensive essays—(for example, on nineteenth-century statutory regulation of the city)—with what might be called case studies: of one boom town,

Odessa; of urbanization in a single region, New Russia; and of the geography of Moscow's trade. Aspects of the nineteenth-century city generally can be probed more deeply because of greater and more accessible source materials, both statistical and verbal. One significant phase of city development in this period, the question of proletarian growth and social stability, was omitted partly because of limitations of space, but also because several historians, most notably Reginald Zelnik and Leopold Haimson, have already addressed themselves to this problem. But in sum, I hope that the topical approach to the nineteenth-century city, and the inclusion therein of several analytical techniques, will serve to clarify the nature of the Russian city during this period of industrial growth and change.

The Bolshevik Revolution in 1917 marked the triumph of an urban-based and urban-oriented party. Although land reform, together with the economic disruption and food shortages caused by the Civil War, resulted in temporary migration away from the cities, from 1923 urban Russia again began to grow. With the initiation of collectivization, one purpose of which was to force labor from the rural to the urban sector, and the five-year plans, Russia was rapidly transformed from a predominantly rural to a predominantly urban society. With an urban population of 56 percent in 1969, compared with 18 percent in 1926, the Soviet Union today has more than 200 cities of 100,000 or more inhabitants.

During the past decade considerable debate has emerged within the Soviet Union over certain problems stemming from growth; for instance, how to determine optimal city size, curb excessive growth, and preserve a sense of community in a modern municipal environment. The old question of the distribution of authority between city government and central bureaucracy has surfaced again with renewed vigor. Even the problem of the low birth rate among the Slavs, so worrisome to Soviet demographers, has an urban aspect. For example, ethnic Russians who live in the industrial cities of the RSFSR have fewer children than those who migrate to less urbanized areas. Some Soviet analysts have even looked to "urbanization as a means of equalizing the birth rate throughout the republics of the USSR or, perhaps more precisely, of serving as a birth control factor in the central Asian republics,"[7] which have one of the highest birth rates in the world.

Part III examines this era of intense urbanization and, more specifically, concentrates on several facets of the city planning that accompanied this growth. While very few studies of pre-Revolutionary urban life exist, several good assessments of aspects of the Soviet city have recently been published. In general, however, these focus on the performance and politics of city government and on the growth and typology of the Soviet city. Part III is intended to complement these studies.

The city may or may not be a "tangle of contradictions," but it is certainly a vast complex of factors intricately arranged within the dimensions of space and time. Because of its complicated nature, examination of the city requires a variety of analytical approaches and *The City in Russian History* encompasses this variety. The collection is written from the perspective of the Russian specialist rather than that of the "urbanologist." Nevertheless, it should prove valuable to the student of comparative urban development as well as to the student of Russian history. In fact, William Blackwell attempts the difficult task of providing a comparative perspective in his conclusion.

Leonard Reissman has admonished that "there is a need for a sense of history if one wishes to consider social change and urbanization."[8] This volume is intended to help supply that sense of history for the Russian city. The contributors believe that the book provides a new dimension in Russian historical scholarship and hope it will stimulate further inquiry into a field that is only now beginning to bloom.

Michael F. Hamm

1. Alexei Gutnov *et al., The Ideal Communist City,* trans. Renee Neu Watkins (New York: George Braziller, 1968), p. 5.

2. Amos Hawley, *Urban Society: An Ecological Approach* (New York: Ronald Press, 1972), pp. 3-4.

3. B. H. Sumner, *A Short History of Russia* (New York: Harcourt, Brace, 1949), p.85.

4. G. I. Shreider, "Gorod i gorodovoe polozhenie 1870 g.," in *Istoriia Rossii v XIX v.,* 9 vols. (St. Petersburg, n.d.), 4:4; I. I. Ditiatin, *Ustroistvo i upravlenie gorodov Rossii* (St. Petersburg, 1875); P. Miliukov, *Ocherki po istorii russkoi kul'tury. Chast' pervaia* (St. Petersburg, 1896), p. 237.

5. N. D. Chechulin *Goroda Moskovskago gosudarstva v XVI veke* (St. Petersburg, 1889; reprinted The Hague: Mouton, 1969), pp. 1-13.

6. P. G. Ryndziunskii, *Gorodskoe grazhdanstvo doreformennoi Rossii* (Moscow, 1958), p. 556.

7. See D. I. Valentei *et al., Problemy Urbanizatsii v SSSR* (Moscow, 1971), pp. 53-62; and Helen Desfosses Cohn, "Population Policy in the USSR," *Problems of Communism* 4 (1973): 47.

8. Leonard Reissman, *The Urban Process: Cities in Industrial Societies* (New York: Free Press, 1970), p. 155.

PART 1
THE EARLY RUSSIAN TOWN

The first Russian towns probably emerged in the ninth century as widely scattered military centers, administrative bases for local rulers, and commercial centers tied particularly to river trade. As in western Europe, the church or monastery often served as the keystone of the town's system of fortification. The market square (*torg*) emerged as the civic center of the town, although it was usually located outside the city walls in the adjacent quarters of the tradesmen and craftsmen.[1] In his survey of the physical development of the early Russian town, E. A. Gutkind has noted that "no designs for Ideal Cities—as we know them from Italy, France, and Germany—were conceived. The towns of Old Russia developed unsystematically, and the imposition of a rigid pattern theoretically worked out on the drawing board was totally alien to Russian authorities and architects."[2]

Lawrence Langer begins Part I by examining the medieval Russian town, the composition of its populace, and the impact of the Mongol wars on urban life. Langer observes that "although Russian towns fully recovered from the Mongol invasions by 1500 they did not develop into communes. They lacked the feudal nexus of the medieval West and models of medieval urban development constructed by [Henri] Pirenne and [Max] Weber are not applicable to Russia."

As in medieval Russia, the role of the seventeenth-century city was to provide service and revenue for the state. David Miller observes that this role was accepted by both townsmen and government and was secured by the legislative acts of the century, including the Law Code of 1649 and the urban administrative reforms of 1699.

J. Michael Hittle and Gilbert Rozman examine the eighteenth-century city. Hittle contends that change during this period must be evaluated against "the yardstick of the service city." And while Catherine redefined the functional role of cities in the state order and better equipped them institutionally, urban Russia remained beneath the heavy hand of bureaucratic tutelage.

Rozman asserts that the assumption of urban backwardness in the eighteenth century is generally made without proper reference to the best available evidence. He examines the methodology of various approaches to comparative urban development and offers what he considers to be "the essential first steps for detailed study of Russian cities" during this period.

Notes

1. E. A. Gutkind, *Urban Development in Eastern Europe: Bulgaria, Romania, and the U.S.S.R.*, vol. 8 (New York: Free Press, 1972): 218, 228. For a well-illustrated discussion of the physical development of the Russian town from the tenth to the nineteenth centuries, see Gutkind's chapter 16.

2. Ibid, p. 218.

THE MEDIEVAL RUSSIAN TOWN

Lawrence N. Langer

The Russian word for town, *gorod,* or *grad* in Old Slavic, means citadel, although the chroniclers often employed the term to designate both the fortress and the surrounding population of the suburb (*posad*).[1] Soviet scholarship, while recognizing a modicum of urban trade and handicraft production, has generally defined the town in terms of its military and administrative functions.[2] This definition, even if expanded to include concepts of permanency and size, is not sufficient to distinguish a town from a village. There were many large villages in both medieval Russia and the medieval West, and to surround them with walls or ascribe administrative functions to them did not make them towns. To be sure, the town was more densely populated than the village, but this was not its most distinctive feature.

The essential characteristic of the town was that its inhabitants earned the majority of their livelihood by engaging in nonagricultural pursuits. Many towns, of course, were not completely independent of village industry, and many contained pasture and wooded lands which were used by the populace. Nevertheless, the townsmen satisfied their economic needs within the market. No town could function as a viable economic entity unless it possessed a permanent market.

The town did fulfill the defensive needs of the countryside and, since it was usually located on an important land or water route, was the center of communications. It also served as a center of princely and ecclesiastical administration, but these characteristics were secondary to that of the market.

According to Henri Pirenne and Max Weber, the "true" Western medieval town was a commune, a community or legal personality with related forms of association (such as guilds) and autonomous laws and political institutions, which clearly differentiated the townsmen from the peasantry.[3] The key to the development of the Western town was the fusion of the fortress and the market into a stable urban economy, and the emergence of a merchant class eager to protect its wealth and social status within the framework of an urban community free from the manorial jurisdiction of the feudal nobility. Thus, the town became the byword for personal freedom, *Stadtluft macht frei*.

While it may be admitted that the economy dominated the pulse of urban life, it would seem that Pirenne, in linking the bourgeoisie with urban democracy, has oversimplified the sociology of the town, overstated the importance of economic life, and neglected the other functions which the town provided.[4] In the twelfth and thirteenth centuries, the Western town was primarily a merchant oligarchy, and town freedom meant privilege and power for the guilds. While the Russian town never evolved into a commune, this does not mean that it lacked commerce or industry. The Russian town possessed a stable market and fulfilled as well the other characteristics associated with urban life: defense, secular and ecclesiastical administration, and centers of communication and artistic endeavor.

M. N. Tikhomirov has estimated that on the eve of the Mongol invasions there were approximately 300 towns in Kievan Rus'. Of these towns, nearly 134 are named in twelfth-century written sources and an additional 47 in the first four decades of the thirteenth century.[5] This estimate has been challenged by P. A. Rappoport who has concluded that many of the so-called towns listed by Tikhomirov were minor fortresses and not towns in the sense of possessing a differentiation of labor and an economy based upon trade and manufacture rather than agriculture. Many of these towns served no administrative function and contained few people. They were little more than villages, often less than 15 hectares in size. Rappoport believes that only 100 of these may be classified as towns, but unfortunately he does not list them.[6]

Despite the Mongol invasions of 1237-1241, the number of Russian towns remained substantially unchanged. According to a list compiled between 1387 and 1406, there were 358 Russian towns (a later edition adds 8 Tverite towns), a figure which approximates that of Tikhomirov in his calculations for Kievan Rus'.[7] But excluding the towns which fell under Lithuanian control, the number of Russian towns in the fourteenth and fifteenth centuries was about 130. Of these, A. M. Sakharov has estimated that there were 75 towns in northeast Russia, although he believes that only 29 may be considered economically significant: Rostov, Pereiaslavl'-Zalesskii, Iur'ev-Pol'skii, Suzdal', Vladimir, Uglich, Mologa, Iaroslavl', Kostroma, Gorodets, Nizhnii Novgorod, Galich, Ustiug, Vologda, Beloozero, Moscow, Dmitrov, Zvenigorod, Volok Lamskii, Mozhaisk, Vereia, Serpukhov, Kolomna, Tver', Kashin, Staritsa, Mikulin, Rzheva, and Torzhok.[8] This list, however, excludes the areas of Riazan', Murom, Smolensk, Novgorod, and Pskov, and such towns as Pronski, Viaz'ma, and Ladoga.

Because of the absence of statistical information it is extremely difficult to determine the population of these towns.[9] Novgorod may possibly have numbered between 25,000 and 50,000 and Moscow in the fifteenth century may have had 50,000 to 100,000 inhabitants. The chronicles record that Kostroma fielded an urban militia of more than 5,000 men in 1375 to meet an attack of plunderers from Novgorod. Even if this figure is inflated, it is quite probable that Nizhnii Novgorod and Tver', which were both larger than Kostroma, numbered in all likelihood 10,000 or more. Most of the Russian towns, however, were considerably smaller.

By modern standards these towns do not seem large; but the Russian town from the twelfth through the fifteenth century did not vary greatly from its Western counterpart. By the end of the fifteenth century Moscow had expanded to the huge size of 1,900 hectares. In the twelfth century Novgorod had an area of 410 hectares, while Nizhnii Novgorod in the fourteenth and fifteenth centuries covered 310 hectares within the area of the older fortifications. Pskov, excluding the area beyond the Velikaia River and the suburban area opposite the fortress, measured 220 hectares in the second half of the fifteenth century. At the end of the sixteenth century, the walls of Smolensk contained 190 hectares. These figures compare favorably with the West: Pisa, 185 in 1300; Lübeck, 200 in 1350; London, 288 in 1377; Frankfurt-am-Main, 128 in 1387. Indeed, most Western towns from the tenth through the fourteenth century rarely exceeded 50 to 60 hectares, and any town above 100 hectares was considered large.

Many historians believe that the German territories contained some 3,000 towns, but of these, 2,800 had populations of less than 1,000. Of the remaining 200 towns, at least 150 were smaller than 2,000 and only 50 were important economically. Only 15 towns could boast a population of more than 10,000. Cologne had 30,000 or more, while Lübeck had perhaps as many as 25,000 inhabitants. Frankfurt-am-Main, Wroclaw, Zurich, Strasbourg, Nuremberg, Augsburg, and others had fewer than 20,000 each. In England, only London exceeded 10,000 people, reaching as many as 30,000 to 40,000. Paris had considerably more, while Ypres held barely 10,000. The greatest concentration of urban population was in Italy; before the Black Death, Florence numbered 85,000 and Venice, Naples, and Palermo each had 100,000 or more by the sixteenth century.[10]

In the fourteenth and fifteenth centuries, a town of 10,000 people represented a huge concentration within the confines of a walled area. The size of an urban population was determined by several factors. Generally the most important were the effectiveness of the town in providing protection; the economic, political, and cultural advantages it provided an immigrant; the incidence of famine and plague; and the infant mortality rate, which was high.

The Mongol Invasions

Historians have generally assumed that the Mongol invasions had a disastrous impact upon urban life in Russia. After devastating the Bulgar state on the Volga River, the Mongols razed Pronsk and Riazan', where the carnage was particularly brutal. In the winter

The Early Russian Town

of 1237-1238 they swept into northeast Russia, destroying the towns of Moscow, Vladimir, Suzdal', Rostov, Iur'ev-Pol'skii, Perei-aslavl'-Zalesskii, Dmitrov, Tver', Uglich, Iaroslavl', Galich, Goro-dets, Kostroma, and others. After coming within sixty miles of Novgorod, the Mongol army turned south to the more populous Russian towns along the Dnepr and Desna rivers. By the winter of 1240 the Mongols had pillaged Kozel'sk, where they met unexpectedly stiff resistance, Chernigov, Pereiaslavl', and Kiev. From Vladimir-Volynskii and vicinity they moved further into Europe, invading Poland and Hungary. Historians have generally concluded that as a result of this whirlwind, urban trade and industry became insignificant, and the towns hence became little more than military and administrative centers.

It should be noted that certain areas did not experience heavy loss of life or severe urban dislocation. The territory north of the upper Volga River, including the lands of Pskov and Novgorod, Polotsk, Beloozero, and Ustiug were spared, as were Nizhnii Novgorod and Smolensk (although Pskov and Novgorod experienced invasions from the Swedes and Teutonic Knights). The descriptions of Russia as a virtually depopulated desert that appear in the travel accounts of Plano Carpini and William of Rubruck refer to the regions of the Dnepr, Don, and southern Volga. A tithe in men, animals, and goods was imposed in Riazan', but the chronicles say nothing about whether any other towns were burdened by such a harsh tax. While northeast Russia was plundered, the brunt of the invasion fell on Riazan', Vladimir, and southern Russia. The invasion of northeast Russia lasted little more than three months, and judging from the evidence in the chronicles, a systematic effort to rebuild the destroyed towns was begun quickly.[11]

Between 1273 and 1297 the Mongols attacked northeast Russia on fifteen occasions. It is probable that the repeated attacks near Murom and Vladimir resulted in a population dispersement away from these areas toward Moscow and Tver' in the west (both of which emerge as major political and economic centers at the end of the thirteenth and beginning of the fourteenth centuries), toward Beloozero, Vologda, Ustiug, and the Sukhona River in the north, and also toward the regions of the Vyzhegda, Unzha, and Vetluga rivers.[12] Following the sack of Tver' in 1237, northeast Russia was relatively free of the Mongol sword until the 1370s and 1380s, when Mongol raids were directed first at Nizhnii Novgorod and then at the heartland of northeast Russia. Moscow was plundered in 1382 and the mid-Volga region was continually subjected to attack in the first half of the fifteenth century. The brunt of these incursions fell on the territories of Nizhnii Novgorod and Riazan'.

Certainly the Mongol period was a time of constant warfare and destruction, but one is nevertheless struck by the fact that the townsmen continued to rebuild shattered homes and maintain the urban economy. The Grand Princes of Vladimir strove to preserve the commercial ties between northeast Russia and the West, particularly through the trading mart of Novgorod, and their efforts had the general support of the Mongol khans.

Urban Commerce

There can be little doubt that Tver's remarkable expansion at the end of the thirteenth century owed much to its excellent geographic position as the link between Novgorod and northeast Russia. In 1269, Grand Prince Iaroslav Iaroslavich of Tver', after turning back a German advance into the Novgorod principality, helped conclude a trading agreement between Novgorod, Lübeck, Gotland, and Riga. The treaty of 1270 between Tver' and Novgorod noted that Novgorodian merchants were to have complete access to the lands of Vladimir-Suzdal' for trade: "And our merchants are to trade throughout all of Suzdalia according to the Tsar's charter."[13] This formula was repeated throughout the fourteenth- and fifteenth-century treaties between Novgorod and the Grand Princes of Vladimir. The key phrase is "according to the Tsar's charter." It refers to an earlier charter issued by Mangu-Temir and amply demonstrates the Mongols' deep concern to preserve an uninterrupted flow of goods from the West to Nov-

The Early Russian Town

gorod and then to northeast Russia, eventually reaching the Golden Horde through either commerce or the collection of the Mongol tribute. Mangu-Temir specifically enjoined Iaroslav of Tver' from hindering the commercial activities between Novgorod and German merchants, a practice which the Tverite prince sometimes pursued when he sought to bend Novgorod to his will.[14]

Novgorod during the Mongol period was Russia's most important mart for Western trade. Much of Novgorod's commerce in the second half of the twelfth and thirteenth centuries was channeled through Gotland and its commercial center at Visby. German merchants penetrated into Novgorod with increasing frequency from the last quarter of the twelfth century and by the early thirteenth century established two commercial districts in the town: the Foreign Quarter (*Nemetskii dvor* or *Peterhof*) and the Gotland Quarter (*Gotskii dvor*).

From the very beginning there were two distinct groups of German merchants who were permitted to remain in Novgorod no more than half a year, either in winter (*Winterfahrer*) or in summer (*Sommerfahrer*). But these restrictions were often violated. Winter was the best season to obtain furs and the German traders had to leave with the first thaw; the summer merchants arrived one or two months later, remaining until the fall. In the interval a set of keys to the Foreign Quarter was deposited with the Iur'ev monastery, but it seems that the Germans took their treasure chest with them, depositing it at Visby and distributing four keys to the aldermen of Visby, Lübeck, Soest, and Dortmund.[15]

The business of the Foreign Quarter, which by the fourteenth century overshadowed the Gotland Quarter, was conducted in the Church of St. Peter (hence the term *Peterhof*). The weights and measures were kept within the church and all commercial transactions were recorded there. Disputes between the Germans and Novgorodians were adjudicated by a merchant court composed of the chiliarch (*tysiatskii*) and two merchant elders (*starosty*); important cases included the Novgorodian mayor (*posadnik*) as well. The court sat in the Church of Ivan on the Opoki, which also held the town's weights and measures (particularly for wax, honey, and silver) and housed the most important association of Novgorod's merchants—the *Ivanskoe Sto*.

Until the second half of the thirteenth century, Smolensk attracted many Western merchants from Riga, Gotland, Lübeck, Soest, Münster, Dortmund, Groningen, and Bremen. But as towns along the Western Dvina, especially Polotsk and Vitebsk, successfully sought to prevent German traders from bypassing their markets, Smolensk became increasingly isolated from the northern trade routes of the Hansa towns. In the late fourteenth and fifteenth centuries, however, Smolensk served as an important entrepôt for Lithuanian, Tverite, and Muscovite merchants.

Novgorod imported from the Hansa towns copper, tin, lead, iron, arms, dyes, amber, glass, horses, wine, and beer. Although precise figures for the inflow of silver bars (*slitki*) into Novgorod are unavailable, it apparently was substantial, and through Novgorod silver was distributed by trade and tribute payments among the towns of northeast Russia. Those princes who held the patent (*iarlyk*) to the Grand Principality of Vladimir (generally the Tverite and Muscovite princes) were in an advantageous position because they and the merchants of their towns had the best access to the markets of Novgorod and the Golden Horde as well. Several meetings were called by the Hansa towns in Lübeck over the question of the silver outflow from the Teutonic Order to Novgorod, and it is believed that at the turn of the fifteenth century Novgorod imported at least 200 kilograms of silver yearly from the German knights.[16] To a lesser extent Novgorod also obtained gold, particularly from England and the Rhineland.

Novgorod's interest in the markets of northeast Russia lay in the acquisition of fish and grain. Owing to the plentiful supply of fish in the Russian rivers, the Hansa trade in cod and herring, while it reached Novgorod, was not of great significance. Novgorod's dependence upon grain from northeast Russia was often used by the princes of Moscow and Tver' to humble the town into accepting their lieutenants (*namestniki*), the agents of princely authority. There is no information of grain imported into Novgorod from the

The Early Russian Town

Hansa during the second half of the thirteenth and fourteenth centuries, but in the fifteenth century rye could be purchased in Reval and Narva.

Salt could be obtained from the Golden Horde, but Novgorod's needs were not met by the market at Astrakhan' and the town turned to Reval, Pernau, and Riga. However, by the late fifteenth century Novgorod was able to acquire salt from the newly established works at Sol'-Galicheskaia, Vologda, Northern Dvina, Gorodets, and Nerekhta. Flemish and then English cloth also made its way to Novgorod, much of it reaching Moscow, which exported the cloth to the Crimean Khanate in the fifteenth century.

Novgorod's major exports were furs and wax, and in these commodities the town was one of the Hansa's greatest suppliers. Through Novgorod tens of thousands of squirrel, beaver, and to a lesser degree marten, sable, and ermine pelts were shipped yearly to Reval, Derpt, and Lübeck. Novgorod became the central clearinghouse for wax exports from Russia, completely overshadowing Smolensk and Polotsk. In addition to these items Novgorod also exported leather goods, flax, and hemp, but these commodities played a minor role in the republic's commerce.

During the Mongol period the towns of northeast Russia were never completely isolated from the West or the Black Sea. Because the Hansa dominated Baltic trade and because Novgorod was its major market in Russia, it was imperative that such towns as Moscow and Tver' preserve a close political and commercial relationship with Novgorod, even if this necessitated resorting to war.

The commercial ties established between Moscow, Tver', and Lithuania in the fourteenth century continued to expand in the fifteenth century. Furs were brought from Ustiug and the Dvina lands to Moscow and Tver' and then shipped on to Vil'na and Vitebsk. In addition, Muscovite and Tverite merchants exported honey, wax, leather, fur coats, arrows, bows, and shields to Lithuania. Smaller towns such as Staritsa, Kashin, Mikulin, and Rzheva participated in this commerce and experienced rapid suburban growth after the 1360s. E. A. Rikman, who has studied the towns of the Tverite principality, is convinced that the emergence of these suburbs, populated by merchants and artisans, together with the stone construction of churches, the appearance of minted coins, and the growth of urban industry, clearly indicate that the Tverite towns enjoyed an economic and cultural renaissance in the late fourteenth and fifteenth centuries, despite the Mongol invasions.[17]

While one may not share Rikman's rose-colored assessment of the Tverite towns (he does not, for example, take into account the effects of the Black Death), it is nevertheless true that from the mid-fourteenth century there was a general if slow awakening of urban life throughout northeast Russia. In particular, towns flourished along the Volga, which had become a major artery of commerce between northeast Russia and the Golden Horde.

As Kievan Rus' fragmented in the twelfth century, particularly after the death of Mstislav Monomakh in 1132, and as the Crusades opened up new trade routes between western Europe and the East, the Dnepr River lost its former importance as the commercial link between the Baltic and the Black seas (the so-called Varangian route). Travel along the Dnepr and Don rivers had long been dangerous and the Mongol invasions did not alter this situation. But from the second quarter of the fourteenth century, when Mongol incursions into northeast Russia were greatly curtailed, Russian merchants appeared with increasing frequency in Sarai, Astrakhan' and the important markets of Tana, Surozh, and Kafa on the Black Sea.

As early as 1246 Genoese and Venetian traders travelled to Kiev, and the Genoese were encouraged by Mangu-Temir to establish a colony at Kafa, where Russian, Greek, and Armenian merchants gathered. The Mongols facilitated Russian commerce by securing the vast caravan routes stretching from China to Khiva, the Caspian Sea, Tana, Kafa, and Surozh. Genoese and Venetian traders were eager to expand their activity to the lower Volga to obtain spices, furs, fish, caviar, grain, and slaves, and to interject directly into the caravan routes. So widespread were their transactions that by 1332 Khan Uzbeg began to collect a *tamga* (custom duty) of 3 percent from all Italian merchants.[18]

The Early Russian Town

Arabic sources in the second half of the thirteenth century note that Russian boats sailing down the Volga to Sarai were a common occurrence.[19] In the beginning of the fourteenth century a Russian Colony existed in Kafa and towards the end of the 1380s a Russian settlement was maintained in Constantinople.[20] At the same time the Mongols established a quarter in Tver' at the turn of the fourteenth century and the chronicles record the presence of Muslim merchants during the uprising of 1327. In the thirteenth century Mongol pottery appeared as far north as Novgorod and it is known that throughout the Mongol period Novgorod imported such luxury items from the Golden Horde as walnuts, box-tree wood (used for making combs), glass, central Asian flagons, textiles, and glazed Arabic pottery.[21]

Much of the Volga trade was funneled into northeast Russia through Nizhnii Novgorod, which emerged in the 1350s as the political center of the Nizhnii Novgorod-Suzdal' principality and began an ambitious program of constructing stone fortifications and churches. Attracted by this commerce, Novgorodian raiders in the 1360s and 1370s embarked on a series of audacious campaigns against Nizhnii Novgorod, plundering Russian and Muslim merchants sometimes as far south as Sarai. Other raiding parties struck against the regions of the Kama and Viatka rivers, the Dvina lands, and Ustiug, Zhukotin, and Kazan'. In 1360, when one of these raids fell upon some Muslim merchants on the Kama River, the Mongols were so infuriated that they demanded that Moscow take punitive measures against these pirates and return all stolen property. Not only did Nizhnii Novgorod benefit from Russian southern commerce, but towns along the much-devastated areas of the Kliaz'ma and Oka rivers revived; thus, in 1351 the chronicles note that Murom was rebuilt and resettled.[22]

In the 1370s, however, Nizhnii Novgorod was twice pillaged by the Mongols and in 1408 Edegei sacked the town along with Pereiaslavl'-Zalesskii, Rostov, Dmitrov, Serpukhov, and Gorodets. More importantly for Russian commerce, the invasion of Timur into southern Russia completely disrupted the trade routes between Central Asia, Astrakhan', Sarai, and the Crimea, and from the 1390s Asian merchants increasingly travelled south to Syria. Timur's whirlwind destroyed the towns of Astrakhan', Sarai, Kafa, and Tana; fewer Western merchants made their way to the Crimea and Caspian seas and the Volga River was isolated from the great east-west caravan routes passing through Syria.

The Muscovite merchants who frequented Surozh in the fourteenth century (*gosti-surozhane* and *gosti-sukonniki*) were able to form corporations, which continued to function in the fifteenth century, and to dominate the fur trade to the Golden Horde and the Crimea. At the turn of the fifteenth century Kafa had superseded Surozh as the commercial center in the Crimea, but what is interesting is that the chronicles no longer note the activities of the *gosti-surozhane* and there is almost no information on the commercial relations between Russia and Kafa in the first half of the fifteenth century. The implication is obvious; Russian trade had greatly diminished.

However, during the reign of Ivan III (1462-1505), when Muscovite authority was established throughout much of northeast and northwest Russia, Russian merchants from Moscow, Tver', Kolomna, and to a lesser extent Pereiaslavl'-Zalesskii, Mozhaisk, Iaroslavl', Dmitrov, and Ustiug made their way to Kafa, usually by way of the Dnepr River and then overland through Perekop. By 1500 Russia's southern commerce had completely revived and even merchants from the northern towns of Novgorod and Pskov traveled to the Crimea, often transacting business in Kiev, Vil'na, and other Lithuanian towns along the way. The Russians brought furs, falcons, leather, arms, jewelry, and cloth shipped from England and Flanders through Novgorod. In return, they received silk, lace, taffeta, calico, saffron, musk, frankincense, walnuts, sugar, rhubarb, soap, and pearls.

The general expansion of Russian trade in the second half of the fifteenth century can also be seen in smaller towns such as Beloozero, whose market played no role in international trade but supplied many of the towns in the Muscovite, Tverite, and Novgorodian principalities with grain, animals, and foodstuffs. Huge monasteries, however, especially Troitse-Sergiev, Kirillov Belozerskii, Ferapontov, Simonov, and Spaso-Evfimev, continued to dominate much of Russia's internal trade.

Urban Handicrafts

The towns of northeast Russia never lost their character as centers of handicraft production during the Mongol period. Many historians have exaggerated the effects of the Mongol invasions, believing that the towns lost some 10 percent of their artisan population and that urban industry, virtually nonexistent in the thirteenth century, showed little sign of recovery until the mid-fourteenth and particularly the fifteenth century.[23] To be sure, the production of cloisonné enamels, characteristic of Kievan manufacture, and the niello technique disappeared, the latter until the sixteenth century. These arts were primarily centered in the city of Kiev, however, and did not appear in Vladimir-Suzdal' until the beginning of the thirteenth century. Consequently, they cannot be construed as a traditional art of northeast Russia destroyed by the Mongols. Certain old Russian arts such as filigree work, which dates from the ninth century, were not lost and reappeared in the fourteenth century, although designed on Central Asian patterns. Production of glazed polychrome ceramics declined and did not reappear until the fifteenth century.

But excluding these crafts, there is little technological difference in the manufacture of jewelry or the framing of icons and books in the Kievan and Mongol periods. Although the fine stone decorations found in the churches of Vladimir-Suzdal' and Iur'ev-Pol'skii disappeared, northeast Russia did not lack stonemasons. One need only glance at the chronicles to see continuous notations of construction of churches and walls in stone: Novgorod from the end of the thirteenth century; Moscow and Tver' from the turn of the fourteenth; Nizhnii Novgorod in the mid-fourteenth, and others.

The fundamental needs of the townsmen to clothe and arm themselves, build their dwellings and furniture, and construct their churches and walls were met by urban craftsmen, even in the thirteenth century. Within the town walls one could always find blacksmiths, potters, leather makers, carpenters, armorsmiths, weavers (also an important village industry), and so on. The towns also possessed the technology for smelting iron and copper and, from the end of the fourteenth century, both Tver' and Moscow manufactured artillery. The manufacture of religious and luxury items such as crosses, icon frames, candlesticks, church chandeliers, bracelets, and rings, cast in imported silver and copper, became widespread in the late fourteenth century, no doubt stimulated by the Black Death. Like their western counterparts, Russian townsmen were uncertain when the next plague would erupt and turned to religion or indulged in the material goods and diversions offered by life in the town.

The Absence of Russian Guilds

In spite of their economic importance, merchants and artisans played only minor roles in town administration, which lay in the hands of the prince or his deputy, usually a member of the princely or boyar class. During this period the Russian town did not acquire a distinct set of laws and privileges which juridically differentiated the townsman from the peasant. The town did not obtain the right of local self-government, free from princely interference, nor was it the beneficiary of a princely charter permitting the formation of a commune on the Western model. In northeast Russia all the important urban functions—administration, collection of taxes, supervision of the courts, military defense, foreign policy, and the minting of coins—were controlled by the prince.

In the West, the guild structure carefully regulated trade, fought to keep out foreign products which resembled those produced locally, forbade employment of foreigners when unemployment existed within the guild, and in general sought to monopolize an industry and its price structure. This type of guild system did not exist in Russia during either the Kievan or the Mongol period. Tikhomirov's and Cherepnin's attempts to view the Hundred organization (*sto*) as a guild of sorts are not convincing.[24] Rather, the *sto* should be seen as an administrative and juridical unit of urban government, headed by a "hundredman," who was usually directly under the authority of the prince. While it is possible that the brotherhoods (*bratchina*) which existed in the fourteenth and fifteenth centuries were composed of merchants and artisans, they were primarily organizations of monastic servitors and certainly did not represent separate crafts. In general, these brotherhoods were called together to celebrate major Church holidays or to settle minor disputes. The term does appear in the Pskov Law Charter, but it is evidently meant to designate a celebration of families or neighbors who were empowered to hold court over anyone who was drunk or who was making a nuisance of himself.[25]

With some exceptions, such as the *Ivanskoe sto* in Novgorod and the *gosti-surozhane* and *gosti-sukonniki* in Moscow, urban merchants and craftsmen lacked any effective form of organization. Consequently, they were completely helpless against the growth of tax-exempt monastic settlements (*dvory*) within the towns. Monastic traders and artisans prospered under the aegis of immunity charters given to the Church by the princes. The monasteries hence accumulated the greatest amounts of capital and during the second half of the fourteenth and the fifteenth century expanded their economic activities, for example resorting increasingly to hiring free labor (*naimiti*). In smaller towns like Beloozero, monasteries nearly monopolized the entire market; consequently Ivan III had to restrict somewhat their privileges in trade. Nevertheless, the monasteries controlled some of the largest salt works and served to fulfill an important economic function, the movement of foodstuffs in large bulk from one market to another.

During the Kievan and Mongol periods, the towns contained many slaves. While it is impossible to determine the precise percentage of slaves, it appears that slaves and semibondmen increased in numbers after the Black Death. Large numbers of slaves were employed as artisans in Novgorod and northeast

Russia. From the second half of the fourteenth century the term *zakladen'*, an urban dweller who commended himself (or perhaps mortgaged his property) to a prince, boyar, or the Church, appears frequently and is indicative of the growing number of bondmen. The Black Death threatened to undercut the labor supply and the tax base of the towns, and the Muscovite princes were eager to maintain administrative control over as much of the urban population as possible. Immunity charters were given to the monasteries so that they would settle the suburbs and the depopulated countryside; here the princes were willing to relax their controls over the populace. But on the other hand, they strove to prevent outside princes from purchasing townsmen. Many charters forbade landowners, either secular or ecclesiastical, to settle territories with people from the prince's own patrimony. Slave craftsmen were common on the urban estates of boyars and even the Church was a major purchaser of slaves. Though the Church may have given a slave his personal freedom, he was nevertheless bound in service. The Church purchased artisans to construct the *Uspenskii sobor* in Moscow, financing this project by levying a duty in silver upon the monasteries. The servitors (*deliui*) on the rural and urban estates of the princes were composed of both freemen and slaves. The number of urban slaves and semibondmen may have totaled 10 to 15 percent of the townsmen.

While the Black Death probably stimulated the production of religious and luxury items, it also depleted the towns of many craftsmen, and the princes were forced to resort to peasant labor for large-scale urban construction. Thus, Moscow employed peasants to build its stone fortifications in 1365, at precisely the time when the pestilence had ravaged northeast Russia. Novgorod, where the plague had exacted a huge death toll in the 1420s, also used peasants to rebuild its walls in 1430. In the second half of the fourteenth century, and in the wake of the Black Death, peasants were increasingly forced to submit to an urban corvée (*gorodovoe delo*) in order to maintain the town walls. The term appears in charters from Beloozero, Vereia, Vladimir, Galich, Kashin, Mozhaisk, Moscow, Nizhnii Novgorod, Pereiaslavl'-Zalesskii,

The Early Russian Town

Rzheva, and Iaroslavl', and was probably used in Tver'. Given these conditions of princely authority and the competition of tax-exempt monastic traders and artisans as well as the reservoir of peasant labor, it is not surprising that the towns were unable to develop guilds.

Urban Administration

Historians have often contrasted the political institutions of Novgorod with those of northeast Russia, sometimes describing Novgorod as the embodiment of the elements of democracy while northeast Russia developed the principles of monarchical government. The fact that the urban assembly (*veche*) retained its vitality in Novgorod in the fourteenth and fifteenth centuries has led so eminent a scholar as Vernadsky to liken Novgorod to the ancient Greek polis.[26] Such descriptions have oversimplified or completely distorted the political realities of the Russian town.

D'iakonov has defined the *veche* as a meeting of all free males, usually called by a prince or other townsmen, in a marketplace or other open area to discuss and vote on such matters as the invitation or expulsion of a prince, war and peace, or the issuing of mutual agreements (*riady*) between the prince and the town. Sergeevich was able to cite at least fifty examples of *veche* convocations in Kievan Rus'. Yet it must be emphasized that the *veche* in Kievan Rus' did not evolve into a permanent urban institution. The term *veche* was applied in the chronicles to meetings of the entire town, but also to smaller assemblies of boyars and urban elders, and to meetings of the lower strata of the population. Sometimes the *veche* was called to discuss military policy by princes and boyars on a campaign; at other times it designated a secret meeting of a political faction.[27] Its appearance in a town was considered to be an exceptional event, usually in a time of political or military emergency. In the Mongol period the *veche* met fairly regularly in Novgorod and Pskov, but in northeast Russia the assembly met sporadically: 1263 in Rostov, Vladimir, Suzdal', Iaroslavl', and Pereiaslavl'-Zalesskii; 1289 in Rostov; 1304 in Kostroma; 1305 in Nizhnii Novgorod; 1327 in Tver'; and 1382 in Moscow. All of these assemblies were convened during times of urban conflict, particularly during revolts against Mongol tax collectors or urban boyars, or during periods of invasion by the Mongol armies. While the *veche* in Novgorod and Pskov often acted as a court, there is no evidence of similar juridical powers in northeast Russia, nor is there any reason to believe that the *veche* in the northeast sought to establish popular courts or participate directly in the prince's administration.

In Novgorod princely rule was successfully curtailed, but Novgorod was not governed by a *veche* composed of the free urban population. The Novgorodian *veche* elected the *posadnik* from 1126, the prince after the town declared its independence from Kiev in 1136, and the archbishop from 1156, and chose the *tysiatskii* (chiliarchate) some time in the late twelfth century. However, the important studies of V. L. Ianin have convincingly demonstrated that the Novgorodian institutions and the *veche* were completely dominated by a few boyar families.[28]

In the twelfth century Novgorod represented a dual system of government between the prince and the *posadnik*, but in the course of the thirteenth century, after the town successfully prevented the efforts of Aleksandr Nevskii and Iaroslav Iaroslavich to reassert princely power, an understanding was reached with its princes over what constituted the "liberties" of Novgorod. The prince, who resided outside the fortress in the *gorodishche*, could not abrogate those charters issued by Novgorod or nullify deeds of property transactions; the prince could not administer the Novgorodian provinces without the participation of the *posadnik* and was even entirely denied administrative prerogatives in many provinces. The collection of the *dar* (a major direct tax) by the prince was permitted in the provinces but strict limitations were placed upon the hunting and fishing rights of the prince, and neither the prince, his wife, nor his boyars could own lands in the Novgorodian provinces or establish tax-exempt settlements for traders.

During the fourteenth century, princely rule was effectively replaced by a government of the *posadnik* and *tysiatskii*, with the archbishop active as titular head of the republic. But Novgorod was continually torn apart by urban factions clustered around Prusskaia street, which politically and economically dominated the Zagorodskii and Liudin boroughs, and those from the Nerevskii, Plotnitskii, and Slavenskii boroughs. All of these boroughs had their own *posadniki,* who could hold their offices for any number of years. However, the boroughs, through the *veche,* selected a mayor (*stepennyi posadnik*) to represent the entire town but whose term of office by the fifteenth century was reduced to six months. The number of borough *posadniki* in the fifteenth century reached twenty-four and to balance the *posadniki* politically, as well as to stabilize the government, the Council of Notables (*Sovet gospod*) was established, consisting of some fifty men who had generally served a term as *posadnik* and who represented the most powerful families of the town.

Archeological excavations in Novgorod have shown that the town was divided into approximately 300 to 400 urban estates which were owned principally by boyars and wealthy merchants.[29] The bulk of the Novgorodian population lived on these estates; the artisans and small tradesmen lived in houses, worked in shops, and sold their wares in stalls owned by boyars. The Hundred organization, which was controlled by the merchant class, was charged with the administration of Novgorod's streets. But within the boroughs the boyars completely dominated the *veche,* and the elections of the various urban offices rested fundamentally in the hands of some 300 to 400 great urban landlords, or boyars.

The towns of northeast Russia never looked to Novgorod as a model of urban government. In northeast Russia the *veche* did not call into question the principle of princely government, nor did it object to the princes' centralizing tendencies or control over the urban courts. In Moscow and Tver' the office of *tysiatskii* was filled by a few boyar families and represented the interests of the upper classes; it did not reflect the aspirations of the common people.[30] When the Muscovite *tysiatskii* was found murdered in the Kremlin, the urban uprising which followed vented its fury against the greater boyars, many of whom fled the town. Some years later, in 1373, Dmitrii Donskoi abolished the office entirely and there was no popular outcry. On the contrary, strong princely government was welcomed, for it served to check factional divisions within the town, provide military security, set favorable conditions for commerce, and win the blessings of the Church.

Conclusion

The history of the Russian medieval town differs fundamentally from that of the Western medieval town. Although Russian towns fully recovered from the Mongol invasions by 1500 they did not develop into communes. They lacked the feudal nexus of the medieval West, and the models of medieval urban development constructed by Pirenne and Weber are not applicable to Russia. Furthermore, since the bulk of the Russian peasantry was at this time not enserfed, the Russian town was not the island of freedom in the sea of serfdom that the town was in the West. Nevertheless, the Russian town did preserve its economic vitality. The urban market remained open, unlike the Western market where the guilds often imposed monopolistic and protectionistic policies in the fourteenth and fifteenth centuries. Although the Church and the boyars dominated the market, adventurous merchants seeking fortunes were still attracted to the towns and some were even able to enter the ranks of the boyars.

By 1500 Russian agriculture began to expand as recovery from the Mongol invasions, the Black Death, and the civil wars of the reign of Vasilii II (1425-1462) increased the demand for agricultural products. Assured of greater supplies of foodstuffs and eager to meet the needs of village industry, the towns experienced a growth in population which continued until the mid-sixteenth century. This growth was disrupted by the terror of Ivan IV (1533-1584) and by the Time of Troubles. During the terror certain towns, among them Novgorod, Kolomna, and Mozhaisk, may have lost as much as 80 to 90 percent of their population. Not until the late 1620s and 1630s did the towns again begin to recover and grow.

The complexion of the urban population remained essentially the same in both the Kievan and the Mongol period, encompassing princes, boyars, clergy, merchants, artisans, and slaves. In both periods the political and economic power of the princes predominated. While the Mongol yoke did not extinguish urban trade and manufacture, the Russian merchant remained a long-distance trader and did not become a sedentary dealer with systems of bookkeeping, credit, and bills of exchange. The Novgorodian merchants were undoubtedly more sophisticated than their counterparts in northeast Russia, who for centuries were isolated from direct commercial transactions with the Hansa towns.

The princes always considered the towns as part of their patrimony (*votchina*). The towns were areas from which service and income could be derived and passed on as part of the family inheritance. In this respect the princes during the Mongol period maintained the same attitudes toward the towns that their ancestors had displayed in Kievan Rus'. They encouraged trade and urban construction but always retained control over the political and military apparatus of the town. While the *veche* in Kievan Rus' was at times successful in replacing one prince with another, it never assailed the concept of princely rule. Novgorod and Pskov were two important exceptions, but in neither town was princely rule ever fully eliminated, nor were the commoners able to limit effectively the political and economic power of the boyars. Rather, the princes strove to subjugate the *veche* to their wills and were successful. Ivan IV did permit more control for the townsmen over the local police and over trials of criminals, collection of taxes, and general maintenance. But while Ivan prohibited further acquisition of ecclesiastical lands within the towns, the townsmen were unable to secure the right of exclusive control over urban commerce and land. In essence, as the Muscovite state was forged in the fourteenth and fifteenth centuries, the towns were incorporated into a state system which demanded services and taxes and which placed urban administration firmly within the purview of the Muscovite autocracy.

Bibliographical note: Unfortunately for the student of Russian urban history in the Kievan and Mongol periods there are no urban tax rolls or hearth counts. For the late fifteenth and early sixteenth century there are land cadastres of Novgorod which shed some light on the urban population, but the basic primary sources remain the Old Russian chronicles (*Polnoe sobranie russkikh letopisei*). Also pertinent are the princely treaties and testaments in *Dukhovnye i dogovornye gramoty velikikh i udel'nykh kniazei XIV-XVI vv.*, edited by L. V. Cherepnin and S. L. Bakhrushin; the various collections of charters and documents (*akty*) related to land purchases; grants of immunity and trade (particularly those of Novgorod and Pskov in *Gramoty Velikogo Novgoroda i Pskova*, edited by S. N. Valk *et al.*); Russian law codes, which include the charters of Novgorod, Pskov, and the Dvina territory; as well as the few travel accounts by foreigners (for example, Plano Carpini) which do exist. Soviet scholars have also done much work in medieval urban archeology and numismatics, and have begun to analyze the uncovered birchbark charters and the many seals which accompany extant documents.

1. I. I. Sreznevskii, *Materialy dlia slovaria drevnerusskogo iazyka*, 3 vols. (St. Petersburg, 1893-1903), I: 555; M. N. Tikhomirov, *Drevnerusskie goroda*, 2d ed. (Moscow, 1956), p. 232. Other terms commonly employed to designate a fortress are *detinets* and *kreml'*.

2. A. M. Sakharov, *Goroda severo-vostochnoi Rusi XIV-XV vekov* (Moscow, 1959), pp. 22-23.

3. Max Weber, *The City*, trans. D. Martindale (New York: Free Press, 1966), pp. 80-81; Henri Pirenne, *Medieval Cities*, trans. F. Halsey (New York: Doubleday Anchor, 1956), pp. 144-51; idem, *Economic and Social History of Medieval Europe*, trans. I. E. Clegg (New York: Harvest Books, 1937), pp. 51-52.

4. See the discussion in J. Mundy and P. Riesenberg, *The Medieval Town* (New York: D. Van Nostrand, 1958); and Mundy's introduction to Henri Pirenne, *Early Democracies in the Low Countries*, trans. J. V. Saunders (New York: Harper and Row, 1963).

5. Tikhomirov, p. 43.

6. P. A. Rappoport, "O tiploshi drevnerusskikh poselenii," *Kratkie soobshcheniia o dokladakh i polevykh issledovaniiakh instituta arkheologii* 110 (1967): 3-9.

7. *Novgorodskaia pervaia letopis' starshego i mladshego izvodov*, ed. A. N. Nasonov (Moscow-Leningrad, 1950), pp. 475-76; M. N. Tikhomirov, "Spisok russkikh gorodov dal'nikh i blizhnikh," *Istoricheskie zapiski* 40 (1952): 214-59.

8. Sakharov, p. 128. See also L. V. Cherepnin, *Obrazovanie russkogo tsentralizovannogo gosudarstva v XIV-XV vekov* (Moscow, 1960), pp. 330-31.

9. Vernadsky has estimated that Kiev, Novgorod, and Smolensk together numbered 400,000 and that 13 percent of the population in Kievan Rus' was urbanized, but these figures are speculative. See George Vernadsky, *Kievan Russia* (New Haven: Yale University Press, 1948), p. 105.

10. F. Rörig, *The Medieval Town* (Berkeley: University of California Press, 1969), pp. 112-13.

11. *Polnoe sobranie russkikh letopisei, izd. Arkheograficheskoiu komissiiu*, 31 vols. (St. Petersburg-Moscow, 1846-1968), 1:467; 5:186; 7:245; 10:113; 15:373. (Hereafter cited as *PSRL*.)

12. V. V. Kargalov, *Vneshnepoliticheskie faktory razvitiia feodal'noi Rusi* (Moscow, 1967), p. 201.

13. *Gramoty Velikogo Novgoroda i Pskova*, ed. S. N. Valk *et al.* (Moscow-Leningrad, 1949), 3:13.

14. Ibid., 30: 57.

15. P. Dollinger, *La Hansa XII-XVII siécles* (Paris: Éditions Montaigne, 1964), p. 43.

16. A. L. Khoroshkevich, *Torgovlia Velikogo Novgoroda v XIV-XV vekakh* (Moscow, 1963), pp. 280-83.

17. E. A. Rikman, "Goroda Tverskogo kniazhestva," *stepen'* dissertation, Institute of History, AN SSSR, Moscow, 1949, p. 178; idem, "Obsledovanie gorodov Tverskogo kniazhestva," *Kratkie soobshcheniia o dokladakh i polevykh issledovaniiakh Instituta istorii material'noi kul'tury AN SSSR* 41 (1951): 83.

18. W. Heyd, *Histoire du commerce du Levant au moyen-âge,* 2d ed., 2 vols. (Leipzig: Otto Harrassowitz, 1936), 2: 181-82, 201.

19. V. G. Tizengauzen, *Sbornik materialov otnosiashchikhsia k istorii Zolotoi Ordy,* 2 vols. (St. Petersburg-Moscow-Leningrad, 1884, 1941), 1:302.

20. V. E. Syroechkovskii, *Gosti-surozhane* (Moscow-Leningrad, 1935), pp. 15-16.

21. M. W. Thompson, ed., *Novgorod the Great* (New York: Praeger, 1967), p. 97; V. Vikhrov and B. Kolchin, "Iz istorii torgovli drevnego Novgoroda," *Sovetskaia arkheologiia* 24 (1955): 93-97.

22. *PSRL*, 15: 60; A. G. Kuz'min, *Riazanskoe letopisanie* (Moscow, 1965), p. 207.

23. Kargalov, p. 178; G. Vernadsky, *The Mongols and Russia* (New Haven: Yale University Press, 1953), pp. 338-41; B. A. Rybakov, *Remeslo drevnei Rusi* (Moscow, 1948), p. 695.

24. Tikhomirov, *Drevnerusskie goroda,* pp. 127-37; *Srednevekovaia Moskva v XIV-XV vekakh* (Moscow, 1957), pp. 104-05; L. V. Cherepnin, "O formakh ob'edinenii remeslennikov v Russkikh gorodakh," *Voprosy sotsial'no-ekonomicheskoi istorii i istochnikovedeniia perioda feodalizma v Rossii* (Moscow, 1961), pp. 20-24.

25. I. D. Martysevich, *Pskovskaia sudnaia gramota* (Moscow, 1951), article 113, pp. 117-18, 190.

26. Vernadsky, *Kievan Russia,* p. 212.

27. For a discussion of the *veche* see V. Sergeevich, *Russkie iuridicheskie drevnosti,* vol. 2, *Veche i kniaz'* (St. Petersburg, 1902); M. A. D'iakonov, *Ocherki obshchestvennogo i gosudarstvennogo stroia drevnei Rusi,* 4th ed. (St. Petersburg, 1912), pp. 117-36; *Drevnerusskoe gosudarstvo i ego mezhdunarodnoe znachenie,* ed. V. T. Pashuto et al. (Moscow, 1965), pp. 24-34.

28. V. L. Ianin, *Novgorodskie posadniki* (Moscow, 1962); "Problemy sotsial'noi organizatsii Novgorodskii respublikii," *Istoriia SSSR* 1970, no. 1: 44-54.

29. See the interesting work by P. I. Zasurtsev, *Novgorod, otkrytyi arkheologami* (Moscow, 1967).

30. Vernadsky has called the *tysiatskii* the mouthpiece of the people: *Kievan Russia,* pp. 188-89; idem, *Mongols and Russia,* p. 207.

STATE AND CITY IN
SEVENTEENTH-CENTURY MUSCOVY

David H. Miller

The seventeenth century was a time of fundamental readjustment
in the relationship of the city and the state in Russia, yet the
concept of the city remained unchanged throughout the period:
the city was primarily a source of tax revenue for the government.
This view controlled both the demands the townsmen made upon
the government and the concessions the government granted them.
The functions of the city within Muscovite society were refined
and somewhat expanded in the course of the century as the
government turned increasingly to the townsmen in its search for a
more efficient bureaucratic system to modify and control the
military command structure existing heretofore.[1] The townsmen
and the state cooperated, albeit sporadically, in the development
of the urban milieu. The townsmen's demands for an exclusive
role in urban commercial life, for the social unification of the city,
and for an end to foreign trade competition often ran ahead of the
state's economic and psychological capabilities. Conversely, the
state's demands for more tax revenue and for a larger townsman
role in local fiscal administration surged beyond the townsmen's
desires and abilities. By the time of the urban reform of 1699,
however, these two components were linked to form an effi-
cacious urban system. The cities assumed no new role in Muscovite
society, but only reinforced their previous role as the city became
a clearly identifiable legal unit of that society.

Types of Cities

To generalize about Russia's cities during the seventeenth century one must distinguish between three broad categories: 1) fortress cities; 2) agricultural-export cities; 3) commercial cities. The first category included the small, strategically located cities of the southern and western border regions populated almost entirely by military service personnel. A large number of such fortress cities were established in the late 1630s and early 1640s when the government turned its attention to border security. Agricultural-export cities were located mainly in the north, especially in the White Sea littoral. Closely linked to peasant life in both economic and administrative structure, they were significant population centers with large numbers of townsmen among their populations. The final category, commercial cities, were located primarily in central Muscovy; these are the urban settlements considered by historians as Russia's typical cities, ranging in size from 1,000 to 18,000 men, women, and children.[2] Certainly they were the largest and economically the most important cities of seventeenth-century Muscovy, the cities which set the pace and the precedents for other cities and townsmen.

The diversity of the urban population was a major area of initial contention and eventual cooperation between the city and the state. The townsmen (*posadskie liudi*) who lived and worked in the commercial sections of the city, the *posad*, constituted the majority of the inhabitants of cities of types two and three (with possible exceptions for cities which fit these categories but had an inordinate number of military men because of a strategic border location; for example, Novgorod or Pskov). The townsmen were those residents whose legal rights and obligations were defined in terms of urban residence, paying taxes, and providing services to the government as a community. Yet there were also peasants from noble and monastic estates, military personnel of the local garrison, and privileged members of Muscovite society, the "white persons" (*belomestsy*), all living and working in the city without participating in the townmen's obligations. The townsmen relied on the government to settle the conflicting privileges and obligations, to nurture the city, and to help the townsmen increase both their control over the cities and their numbers.

The massive decline in the urban population from the mid-sixteenth century to the early years of the Romanov dynasty was an important reason for the cooperation between the state and the cities. From a national total of 36,889 townsman households in the sixteenth century, the population fell to only 19,992 townsman households reported in the early 1620s.[3] Losses of over 70 percent were not uncommon as a result of the long night of economic crisis and political confusion which began during the reign of Ivan IV. Yet through the response of the government to the townsmen's demands, this trend was decisively reversed by the middle of the seventeenth century; a new period of vigor and economic expansion was clearly evident in Russia's cities when the census books of 1646 were compiled. The total number of townsman households reached 31,337 by that date, and, through government action, shortly thereafter surpassed the sixteenth-century peak. The central region was definitely the urban focus of Muscovy, for it was there that over half of all townsman households were located; two-thirds of these were east and northeast of Moscow.[4]

City and Anti-City

The revival of urban economic activity was not limited to the townsmen, however, for competing settlements filled with privileged residents who did not pay taxes thrived in and near the cities. The rigid social structure of Muscovy encouraged this competition by exempting certain groups from the tax obligations and duties paid by the townsmen.[5] Thus, the townsmen were undersold and their share of the market reduced, with a concomitant loss in their ability to meet the communal tax obligation to the government. The extraordinary levies of the early seventeenth century, such as the "Fifth Penny" and the "Tenth Penny," imposed to finance heavy expenditures on new military hardware

The Early Russian Town

and for campaigns, further weakened their position by promoting tax evasion and flight from the city to avoid increasing burdens. Taxes were levied on the townsmen as a communal group, while the apportionment of individual payments was left to the community itself. Yet since the size of the total assessment was determined through infrequent surveys of the male population, the tax burden was often inappropriately high, driving many townsmen to flee the cities to avoid taxation. It was much to a townsman's advantage to attach himself to a monastic or secular settlement and share its many privileges, including a reduction of or exemption from taxation. This in turn increased the incentive for other townsmen to follow his example, since the tax base was reduced but the assessment remained unchanged.

Despite the dominant role of the church and monasteries in providing the moral tone of Muscovite life, it was precisely the ecclesiastical establishment which presented the townsmen and the cities with their greatest challenges. The vigor of the monastic settlement, a kind of anti-city, contrasted with the struggling townsmen burdened by the state with ordinary and extraordinary tax levies and other duties. The threat of collapse for the townsmen's community increased as substantial numbers of townsmen left the cities, many to live and work on church and monastic lands nearby, shedding their townsman status through the legal subterfuge of commendation (*zakladnichestvo*) while continuing to ply their trades or pursue their crafts exactly as before. Flight from the cities to the freedom of the steppes, to estates, and occasionally to other cities added to the remaining townsmen's plight and increased their resolve to find aid from the central government.

The townsmen's problems directly affected the government because of the fiscal nexus of their relationship. As traditional restrictions on townsman movement proved inadequate, the government was bombarded with petitions calling for the return of runaway townsmen and for an end to the privileges it had once granted various members of Muscovite society. The response to such basic demands was erratic as the new government of Tsar

Mikhail Fedorovich attempted to impose effective control over a society shattered by war and foreign invasions. The state acknowledged the importance of the well-being of its cities and its townsmen, but there was a nagging inability to maintain the commitment to the townsmen, since the central administration came into conflict with the church, the monastic establishment, leading members of society, and influential governmental figures as it looked for means of settling the problems. A series of investigations to locate and return townsmen to the cities was undertaken, and decrees both reiterating previous laws against commendation and establishing new prohibitions against the sale or transfer of townsman homes and shops to tax-exempt persons appeared between 1619 and 1645; but their enforcement was sporadic at best, and the investigations had only short-term effects. Increases in the townsman population were immediately drained away by competing settlements offering all the advantages of location with far fewer burdens.

The dilemma for the state in its relationship with the townsmen was to find a way to nurture the cities and increase the income from Russia's own urban milieu while both maintaining the support of other elements of Muscovite society and continuing to encourage and to expand lucrative foreign trade between Muscovy and Europe, especially with the English and the Dutch. As a result of important trade concessions from the tsars, foreign merchants moved into Muscovy's cities during the seventeenth century, opening their own businesses, buying out townsmen, and conducting trade in their own right. This reduced the townsmen's participation in and control over the urban economy and stimulated a series of petitions to the central government for relief from such competition. Yet there was little immediate relief available, for the increased expenses of a changing foreign policy, military reforms, and the expansion of the government left the state with few alternatives, whatever its desires.

The tsar's role as the greatest merchant in Muscovy was also a cause of concern for the townsmen, for state monopolies on profitable trade items sharply reduced the opportunities for

Russia's townsmen and merchants. And as part of the development of the bureaucratic apparatus of the state, numbers of successful merchants were co-opted into the ranks of the "Guests" and the "Guest" and "Cloth Hundreds," where they became privileged agents for the state's own economic activity. This not only deprived the townsmen of their most enterprising members but also created more tax-exempt properties in the cities, for such tax exemptions were part of the privileges of these upper merchant ranks. A major element in the readjustment of the state's relationship with the city was, then, the search for a solution to the conflicting goals of increased revenue from the cities and from the state's own participation in foreign trade.

Violence and Urban Reform: 1648-1652

The early reign of Tsar Aleksis Mikhailovich (1645-1676) was an important turning point for the cities and the townsmen, for by 1649 the townsmen gained a more secure role in urban commerce, partly through a series of reforms pursued by Boris Morozov and partly as a result of violent disturbances in Moscow and a number of provincial cities. The government attempted to reallocate its financial resources, to increase its tax income by moving from direct taxation to a more painless indirect taxation, and to reform its military forces by using European models, mercenaries, and officers. As a result, however, military discontent reached a peak of intensity, when, for example, salaries for musketeers, Cossacks, and cannoneers were sharply reduced.[6] The service cavalry nobles were angry over the failure of the Morozov government to deliver on a promise made in 1645 to limit peasant movement after a census.[7] This combined anger and discontent prepared the ground for a violent outburst in Moscow in June 1648, when the townsmen petitioned against administrative abuses by a high government and city administrator, Leontii Pleshcheev.

The riot in Moscow began with townsman protests over urban problems but was soon transformed into an assault on the Morozov government by rebellious musketeers, riotous nobles, and recalcitrant boyars around the Cherkasskii princes.[8] These groups, and not the townsmen, opposed the direction of social change begun by Morozov's government. In provincial cities the response to the news of riot in Moscow was especially violent where military personnel were present, mainly in southern fortress-cities. The role of the townsmen in the provincial outbursts was limited to two northern cities, Ustiug Velikii and Sol' Vychegodsk, and there the events were much less violent. The townsmen and the state were pursuing generally compatible goals, though the road to harmony was rocky and beset with detours. The townsmen were active in 1648, continuing to press for solutions to their problems, since a new legislative initiative was possible in that summer.

The June riot in Moscow frightened the government into convoking an Assembly of the Land (*zemskii sobor*) to prepare a new code of laws for the country, granting concessions both townsmen and nobles had long sought. The Law Code of 1649 (*Sobornoe Ulozhenie*) was a landmark in the development of Muscovite society, for it established a hierarchy of society and provided the legal framework for Russian life until the early nineteenth century, when it was finally replaced. This rapidly compiled code—it was completed by January 1649—contained twenty-five chapters touching on all aspects of Muscovite life, with townsmen and peasants receiving approximately equal attention. Chapter XIX, "On the Townsmen," containing forty articles, detailed the reforms in urban life, while Chapter XI, "On the Peasants," containing thirty-four articles, presented the legislation changing peasant life. The townsmen here saw the codification of the reforms Morozov had begun, conforming to many of their previous demands.[9] The peasants lost their right of movement as serfdom was codified. These two short but important chapters of the code formed the legal basis for rural and urban life in Russia during the remainder of the century.

In the *Ulozhenie* of 1649 the state recognized its own interests in supporting the townsmen, increasing their numbers and their control over the urban economy at the expense of both magnates and the ecclesiastical establishment. A major reform contained in

The Early Russian Town

the legislation of Chapter XIX was the confiscation of lands, houses, and shops in and near the cities from tax-exempt owners, including secular magnates and the monasteries. All adjacent settlements were to be turned over to the townsmen while the trade and artisan populations of these settlements were juridically transformed into townsmen. Only townsmen were to be allowed to own and operate business establishments in the cities. An additional vital measure was the return of all former townsmen to the cities; commendation was outlawed and former townsmen who were dependents of this category were returned to the ranks of the urban taxpayers. Those in military service, in the musketeers or cannoneers, for example, or in court service were returned to the cities as well.

The city offered no escape from serfdom, however, for the codification of serfdom in Russia was reflected in the relationship of peasant and townsman. Peasants working in the cities were to be taken back to estates and monasteries and were required to supply assurances that they would not take up residence or establish businesses in the cities again. They could peddle their products in special public trade rows, but were prohibited from operating shops or stalls in the cities after 1649. The legal status of the peasant also took precedence over that of the townsman. For example, marriage to a townsman's widow or daughter did not alter the juridical status of the peasant according to the laws of 1649. The city became a compatible part of Muscovite social structure.

The urban reforms of 1649 were implemented by a Chancellery for Investigations during the years 1649-1652, with a major portion of its attention given to the commercial cities in east-central Muscovy. Of the 10,095 townsman households added by these reforms, raising the total to at least 41,432, more than 30 percent were located in this sector, while the central Moscow region accounted for nearly half of all the households added to the tax rolls. Many new townsmen were created in the fortress cities of the south and southwest, while the White Sea littoral cities accounted for a small proportion of the total.

The primary achievement of the reforms was the confiscation of lands, households, and people from the church and the monastic establishment. Fully 75 percent of the urban households confiscated in Muscovy (about which reasonably detailed information is available) came from these sources. Only about 2 percent of the townsmen's gains came at the expense of hereditary landholders, while about 5 percent of the gains were taken from service landholders.[10] The brunt of the reform fell heavily on the shoulders of the church, making clear the reasoning behind Patriarch Nikon's subsequent complaint that the Law Code of 1649 was aimed at it alone. The government's decision to allow such a magnitude of gain by the townsmen at the direct expense of the churches and the monasteries indicates an important move toward strengthening the cooperation of city and state, presaging the waning influence of the church over the government during the second half of the seventeenth century, and affirming that the cities were already considered more important than the church to the development of the state.

The Post-Ulozhenie Period

The cities did not spontaneously blossom after the reforms of 1649-1652, for the postreform years were difficult and even disastrous ones, especially in central Muscovy. Two years of widespread famine were followed by the plague of 1654-1655, which killed large numbers of urban residents and left Moscow so badly depopulated that the government was forced to encourage the movement of provincial townsmen into the capital city to fill empty homes and trade rows. Although the precise dimensions of this disaster cannot be accurately determined, mortality in Moscow was estimated at nearly 80 percent of the taxpaying population; total losses for the country may have reached 10 percent. Certainly the vitality of the cities was severely damaged just as a new peak in the townsman population had been attained.[11]

Fire, the constant threat to the wooden Russian city, restrained the development of the townsmen throughout the seventeenth century and reinforced their dependence on the central government. Moscow suffered a great fire in 1626, and during the riot of

1648 nearly half of the city's homes were burned. Provincial cities were equally devastated at all-too-frequent intervals. For example, the major provincial city of Iaroslavl' lost its entire commercial section and over half of its residences in 1658, a smaller fire damaged a portion of the city again in 1659, and another major conflagration in 1680 left half of the city in ashes. Although homes were rebuilt and shops restocked after these catastrophes, the costs in time, money, and population were high, and the effects were still noticeable long afterwards.

The effects of these disasters were exacerbated by the reappearance of the urban problems that the Law Code of 1649 had attempted to resolve. The townsmen were forced to turn back to the state to secure their gains in the urban marketplace, looking to it for enforcement of the laws guaranteeing their predominance in the cities, and for means of replenishing their sharply diminished population. The government was subject to strong crosscurrents and was therefore at times inconsistent in its policies, so the battle was constant and the gains were never secure.

The townsmen's privileged position in urban life was again challenged by the natural diversity of an urban population. Peasants, military servitors, and other social groups could not be kept entirely outside the city walls, and new settlements sprang up to compete with the cities again. Although the townsmen attempted to close the cities to other groups, they were continually frustrated in their endeavor. Peasants could engage in itinerant urban trade according to the Law Code of 1649, but they also settled permanently in the cities, living and working alongside the townsmen in violation of the law. Townsman protests about such blatant violations of the laws were immediate, if initially ineffective, and many townsmen demonstrated a rate initiative in enforcing these provisions themselves, evicting peasants from urban shops and trade stalls and occasionally even refusing to allow peasants to enter the cities. They even tried to expand the legal norms of 1649, driving away peasants who were peacefully and legally selling in the public trade rows provided for them.[12] Townsman and peasant were constant adversaries as a result of the rigid stratification of Muscovite society.

Competition from monastic settlements was not a dead issue after 1649 either, for the reforms of 1649-1652 removed a major portion of the offending populace without removing the source of the problems—monasteries still enjoyed extensive privileges from the government. The monasteries fought bitterly and with some success against the loss of lands in and near the cities, even during the reforms of the immediate post-*Ulozhenie* period. Highly skilled monastic peasants again became a source of competition for the townsmen as large numbers of monastic personnel were squeezed into the urban lots and adjacent lands left in the monasteries' possession after 1652. By 1684, the government committed itself to another series of reforms which permitted the townsmen to absorb massive numbers of monastic peasants and to incorporate new settlements into the cities, although a more permanent solution to the revival of monastic competition with the cities awaited a basic change in the position of the church and the monasteries in Russian society.[13]

The state was also the townsman's willing ally in action against illegal townsman mobility, for the inflexible structure of Muscovite society demanded that all townsman residents remain in their home cities permanently. Commendation does not appear as a major problem after the *Ulozhenie*, but the natural mobility of the townsman and merchant, who might find better opportunities for his special craft or trade in another location, revived the interest of remaining townsmen in returning such runaways to their legal residences. Petitions about such problems received a sympathetic hearing from the central government and resulted in the return of townsmen to the home cities as defined by the reforms of 1649-1652. For example, in 1665 the government ordered a new investigation for runaway townsmen, and in 1674 the cities of Iaroslavl' and Vologda successfully petitioned for the return of townsmen living in Moscow. The interests of the townsman community and the state were identical in such situations, for both wanted the tax-base in the cities kept large and productive.[14]

Yet when the townsmen came into conflict with privileged members of Muscovite society, the "white people," the government's resolve and its recognition of common interests with the townsmen faltered and failed. The purchase of townsman property by such tax-exempt persons was specifically prohibited after 1649, but it unquestionably continued during the second half of the century through direct sales, mortgages, and grants. State decrees in 1658, 1677, and in the early 1680s proclaimed an end to these abuses without noticeable effect, and by 1686 the government was willing to come to terms with the "white people," accepting the status quo and permitting the possession of urban lands held even before the reforms of 1649-1652.[15] This represented a de facto and de jure nullification of parts of the *Ulozhenie* and indicated the continued power of this privileged sector of the society.

Administrative Reform and Urban Development

Proposals for further urban economic and administrative reform during the second half of the seventeenth century also clashed with the interests of the "white people" and little was accomplished in spite of ample projects and proposals. Because of the financial crisis associated with the Thirteen Years War with Poland (1654-1667) and the continuing acute need to increase state income, the government was attracted by proposals to strengthen the townsmen, stimulate the urban economy, and provide better tax sources. The French merchant-adventurer Jan de Gron presented a project to this end after his arrival in Moscow in 1651, but though it met with official approval it was never implemented. Similar ideas expressed by the Croatian priest Iurii Krizhanich were equally unproductive, for legislation following his plans never appeared.[16] The most comprehensive plan, and one that was even put on a short-term trial, was A. L. Ordin-Nashchokin's reform in his native Pskov.

Drawing from his extensive experience with Livonian cities, Ordin-Nashchokin attempted to alleviate the difficult condition of Pskov, a city hard hit in the 1660s by its proximity to the theater of war, by the economic crisis of the state, and by a disastrous fire in 1663 which destroyed much of the city. His reform set up a city council of twelve members elected from the townsmen, and introduced restrictions on foreign participation in urban trade with the intention of improving the competitive position of the townsmen. The goal of this reform was consistent with the concept of the city, for it was intended to increase state income by nurturing the urban economy; yet it met with ferocious opposition not only from the Swedish representative, who saw the trade restrictions as a violation of the Treaty of Kardis, but also from Russians who were profiting from trade with foreigners via Pskov, and from aristocrats who played on the government's fears by recalling the Pskov revolt of 1650.[17] These combined pressures spelled the death of the Pskov experiment but not the end of projects intended to reduce foreigners' trading privileges in favor of increased townsman participation, and the increased use of urban administration as an instrument of the state bureaucracy.

The limitation of foreign merchants' trade within the country was begun by the Trade Statute of 1653, and extended by the New Trade Statute in 1667. By the terms of the latter, duty-free trade was to be abolished and increased duties imposed on imported goods. Trade by foreigners inside of Russia—a constant complaint by townsmen and merchants—was banned completely; foreign merchants were to be restricted to port trading cities. In this way the government hoped to increase its annual tax income from the cities. Yet the acute need for more income led the tsar to grant special privileges to foreign merchants; in the very year of the New Trade Statute, 1667, the Armenian Company was chartered to control trade with Persia.[18] This major concession was granted to foreigners, not Russians, in hopes of turning quick and immense profits.

The imposition of new administrative duties on the townsmen came as a result of the search for more efficient means of assessing and collecting state revenues. Fiscal and urban administration was gradually removed from the hands of military men serving as provincial governors, as the state slowly developed a bureaucratic system to secure its power. For example, in 1677 the townsmen were given complete responsibility for the audit of income ledgers for customs and tavern collections, two major sources of state income. In the tax reform of 1679, which attempted to abolish a variety of petty taxes in favor of a single levy per household, the city elder elected by the townsmen was made responsible for both collection of the household tax and its direct payment to the central administration.[19] In this way the city was increasingly woven into the fabric of absolutist government emerging at the end of the century. The administrative duties imposed on the townsmen secured the links between city and state; they did not stimulate the development of urban self-government.

The Urban Reform of 1699

The urban reform of 1699 promulgated by Peter the Great after his epochal trip to Europe combined the townsmen's wishes for greater control over the cities with the state's need for both increased urban tax revenue and a viable alternative to the military administrative structure which then controlled the cities. Peter demonstrated considerable interest in the forms of urban government operating in the European cities he visited, receiving a first-hand explanation of Amsterdam's government from the *burgomeister*, Nicholas Witsen. Soon after his return to Russia, Peter also requested further information about Magdeburg Law and about the urban government of Vienna. The fruit of his interests appeared in the decrees of January 1699, which announced new initiatives.[20]

Peter's reform attempted to coordinate both central and urban administration through the creation of a single administrative bureau to oversee urban affairs for Moscow and all provincial cities, and through the offer of self-government to the townsmen. Muscovy's townsmen were given an option to establish a town hall (*zemskaia izba*) and to elect a group of their own colleagues to control all fiscal, civil, and criminal affairs in their cities. Terminology was freely borrowed from European models, for these elected officials became known as *burmistry*, yet the election of officials by the townsmen was scarcely new, since they had long annually selected a city elder and a group of assistants to represent them. This reform gave them new titles and, more importantly, greatly expanded duties which would increase the townsmen's control over the urban milieu.

The initial reaction to the reform was cool, for the price Peter's government demanded for these privileges was extremely high: doubling the cities' previous tax levy. At first only three rather small and insignificant cities accepted the proposal, while many cities replied that faced with such an exorbitant price they could still tolerate their local governors. Even at this high price, however, the townsmen did not resist the control so long sought; by the summer of 1699, a total of sixty-four cities elected officials to handle all urban affairs as provided in the decrees, although only nine of these agreed to pay the extra taxes. There was considerable confusion between the jurisdiction of the governors and the townsmen's newly renamed officials during the period of transition, made even worse by the lack of uniform change. As a result, in October 1699 the new administrative reforms were introduced universally while the requirement of double taxation was quietly dropped.[21]

The goal of linking the cities and the state more tightly together through the urban reform of 1699 was accomplished because of the enthusiastic if initially sluggish response of the townsmen. The primary fiscal task of the reform was not as easily achieved, though, for local officials soon proved as untrustworthy as had the local governors. The urban reform of 1699 was nonetheless a major step in the administrative development and integration of the cities into the nascent absolutist state.

The total townsman population of Muscovy increased during the second half of the seventeenth century as a result of the cooperation of the cities and the state, the legislation of 1649 and subsequent years, and the rudimentary formation of a national market system. By 1678, when another enumeration of townsmen was undertaken, there was an increase of 24 percent above the 1652 figure. The number of townsman households did not increase as rapidly, however, for there were only about 7 percent more households than in 1652, indicating an increase in the density of the townsman household even before the introduction of the household as a tax unit.

The cooperation of the cities and the state was spurred by the faltering vitality of Muscovy's major urban centers during the second half of the seventeenth century, for the commercial cities of north and northeastern Russia suffered considerable population losses compared with the peaks of 1652, while the townsman population of smaller cities in Russia's western, northwestern, and southern regions was increasing. Such major commercial entrepôts as Iaroslavl', Kostroma, Vologda, and Nizhnii Novgorod along the Volga basin saw declines in their townsman populations which were generally still evident in the early eighteenth century. Fortress-cities such as Kursk and Voronezh, on the other hand, experienced significant increases in their townsman populations as compared to the pre-1649 period.[22]

The decline of the townsmen in the large cities of central Muscovy called forth the aid of the state and pushed it toward an urban reform which promised increased tax revenue. The decline in these cities increased the government's tax problems, adding to a crisis which did not end with the urban reform of 1699. The founding of St. Petersburg in 1703 and the eventual introduction of the notorious "soul tax" in 1724 were in part also responses to the problems of the commercial cities and to the state's search for a combination of efficient administration and increased tax revenue.

The changes in the relationship of city and state in the seventeenth century developed but did not alter the basic role of the city in Muscovite society: revenue provider for the state. This role was accepted by both the townsmen and the government and modified through the complementary needs of both as expressed in the *Ulozhenie* of 1649, subsequent legislative acts, trade regulations, and finally urban administrative reforms in 1699. The townsmen were vitally concerned with closing the cities' gates to competition either from Russians outside of their social group or from foreign merchants, and the *Ulozhenie* went far toward providing the necessary means. But intermittent revivals of conservative opposition within the society and even within the government itself delayed the consistent enforcement of its provisions. Simultaneously, the imperatives of the emerging bureaucratic absolutism meant that new obligations were pressed on the townsmen by the state.

The townsmen did not develop a new consciousness of their role and function in Muscovite society during the seventeenth century, but were content to seek better ways to fulfill their difficult and demanding obligations to the state. The monopoly on urban trade and commerce failed to provide the security and prosperity the townsmen sought, since it was eroded by the state's own economic demands and by the changing trade and market patterns within the country. The cities did not become the powerful economic centers the state needed, nor did they become a haven for peasants fleeing from an increasingly harsh serfdom. Instead, the narrow concept of the city shared by both state and townsmen helped make Russia's cities a subordinate sector of the society based on agriculture and serfdom which emerged from the seventeenth century.

Notes

I wish to acknowledge the financial assistance provided through the Fulbright-Hays Act and the International Research and Exchanges Board, and the cordial help extended me by the staff of the Central Archive of Ancient Acts, Moscow, the State Lenin Library, and the Public Historical Library, Moscow, during the research which made this article possible.

1. On the need to develop a bureaucracy from a "military command system" see Sir John Hicks, *A Theory of Economic History* (New York: Oxford University Press, 1969), pp. 18-19.

2. This article deals primarily with commercial cities of Muscovy. The typology is found in A. S. Lappo-Danilevskii, *Organizatsiia priamogo oblozheniia v Moskovskom gosudarstve so vremen Smuty do epokhi preobrazovanii* (St. Petersburg, 1890), pp. 112-15. See also E. Stashevskii, "Piatina 142-go goda i torgovo-promyshlennye tsentry Moskovskogo gosudarstva," *Zhurnal ministerstva narodnogo prosveshcheniia* 39, no. 5 (1912): 99-113; and P. N. Miliukov, *Spornye voprosy finansovoi istorii Moskovskogo gosudarstva* (St. Petersburg, 1892), p. 81.

3. P. P. Smirnov, *Goroda Moskovskago gosudarstva v pervoi polovine XVII veka*, 1, part 2 (Kiev, 1919): 129.

4. Smirnov, pp. 100-104, 129.

5. The following discussion of the problems of the city to 1648 is drawn from P. P. Smirnov, *Posadskie liudi i ikh klassovaia bor'ba do serediny XVII veka*, 2 vols. (Moscow-Leningrad, 1947-1948). On urban administration, see I. E. Andreevskii, *O namestnikakh, voevodakh i gubernatorakh* (St. Petersburg, 1864); and on the conflict with foreign merchants, K. V. Bazilevich, "Kollektivnye chelobit'ia torgovykh liudei i bor'ba za russkii rynok v pervoi polovine XVII veka," *Izvestiia Akademii nauk SSSR*, ser. 7, Social Sciences Section, 2 (1932): 91-123.

6. A good brief discussion of Morozov's reforms is found in P. P. Smirnov, *Pravitel'-stvo B. I. Morozova i vosstanie v Moskve 1648 g.* (Tashkent, 1929). Smirnov's *Posadskie liudi*, 2: 5-157, has a detailed analysis of these reforms.

7. An excellent recent discussion of the relations of the nobles and government is Richard Hellie, *Enserfment and Military Change in Muscovy* (Chicago: University of Chicago Press, 1971).

8. Of the extensive literature on Moscow, especially useful is S. V. Bakhrushin, *Nauchnye trudy*, 2 (Moscow, 1954): 46-91; and on provincial violence, K. V. Bazilevich, *Gorodskie vosstaniia v Moskovskom gosudarstve XVII v.* (Moscow-Leningrad, 1936). See also *The Travels of Olearius in Seventeenth-Century Russia*, trans. and ed. S. Baron (Stanford: Stanford University Press, 1967), pp. 203-14.

9. For a discussion of the articles of Chapter XIX and their sources, see Smirnov, *Posadskie liudi*, 2: 273-304. A good recent edition of the Code is found in *Sobornoe Ulozhenie 1649 goda: uchebnoe posobie dlia vyshei shkoly*, ed. M. N. Tikhomirov and P. P. Epifanov (Moscow, 1961).

10. Smirnov, *Posadskie liudi*, 2: 701-18.

11. On the plague, Alexander Brückner, *Beiträge zür Kulturgeschichte Russlands* (Leipzig: B. Elischer, 1887), is useful. For its effects on Moscow, see S. K. Bogoiavlen-skii's discussion in *Istoriia Moskovy*, vol. 1, *Period feodalizma XII-XVII vv.* (Moscow, 1952), pp. 452-53.

12. Examples of the townsmen's aggressive action against peasants are found in V. Borisov, *Starinnye akty, sluzhashchie preimushchestvenno dopolneniem k opisaniiu g. Shui* (Moscow, 1853), no. 115: 206-07, for Shuia; and for Iaroslavl' in the Central State Archive of Ancient Acts, fond 342, no. 6, pt. 6, p. 2.

13. The Savior Monastery in Iaroslavl', for example, bounced back at least twice in the course of the second half of the seventeenth century. In 1690 it was again gathering a large set of servitors and had apparently established a new settlement. V. Bochkarev, "Naselenie odnoi iz verkhne-volzhskikh monastyrshchin v iskhode XVII v.," *Iaroslavskoe estestvenno-istoricheskoe i kraevedcheskoe obshchestvo. Trudy sektsii kraevedeniia*, 3, part 2 (Iaroslavl', 1929): 113-33.

14. The decree of 1665 is in *Pamiatniki russkogo prava*, part 7 (Moscow, 1963): 296-97. See also A. G. Man'kov's discussion of townsman-peasant relations in *Razvitie krepostnogo prava vo vtoroi polovine XVII veka* (Moscow-Leningrad, 1967).

15. The decree is in *Polnoe sobranie zakonov Rossiiskoi Imperii*, 2 (St. Petersburg, 1830): no. 1157, p. 725. A study of this problem in one city is A. M. Orekhov, "Iz istorii bor'by Nizhegorodskogo posada protiv belomesttsev," *Goroda feodal'noi Rossii: sbornik statei pamiati N.V. Ustiugova* (Moscow, 1966), pp. 247-55.

16. N. I. Kostomarov, *Ocherk torgovli Moskovskago gosudarstva v XVI i XVII stoletiiakh, Sobranie sochinenii*, book 8, vol. 20 (St. Petersburg, 1906), gives a general view of developments in trade and government control of it. On monetary problems, K. V. Bazilevich's *Denezhnaia reforma Alekseia Mikhailovicha i vosstanie v Moskve v 1662 g.* (Moscow-Leningrad, 1936), is a detailed and important study. On the projects

for commercial development, Bazilevich's "Elementy merkantilizma v ekonomicheskoi politike pravitel'stva Alekseia Mikhailovicha," *Uchenye zapiski Moskovskogo universiteta*, part 41, *Istoriia*, 1 (Moscow, 1940): 3-34, provides a brief summary.

17. Pskov was a thorn in the side of the government. Novgorod and Pskov both had serious revolts in 1650; the study by M. N. Tikhomirov was recently reissued in *Klassovaia bor'ba v Rossii XVII v.* (Moscow, 1969). The most comprehensive study of the reforms in Pskov is E. V. Chistiakova, "Iz istorii klassovoi bor'by v russkom gorode XVII veka (Reforma A. L. Ordina-Nashchokina v Pskove 1665-1669 g.)," kandidat dissertation, Moscow, 1948.

18. Bazilevich, "Elementy merkantilizma," passim; see also his "Novotorgovyi ustav 1667 (k voprosu o ego istochnikakh)," *Izvestiia Akademiia nauk SSSR*, ser. 7, Social Sciences Section, 7 (1932): 589-622; and E. S. Zevakin, "Persidskii vopros v russko-evropeiskikh otnosheniiakh XVII v.," *Istoricheskie zapiski* 8 (1940): 133-56.

19. Extended discussions of these questions are found in Andreevskii, and Boris Chicherin, *Oblastnyia uchrezhdeniia Rossii v XVII-m veka* (Moscow, 1856).

20. M. M. Bogoslovskii, *Petr I: Materialy dlia biografii*, 3 (Moscow, 1946): 248-49.

21. Ibid., pp. 240, 297-332 passim.

22. P. P. Smirnov, "Dvizhenie naseleniia Moskovskogo gosudarstva," *Russkaia istoriia v ocherkakh i statiakh*, ed. M. V. Dovnar-Zapol'skii, 2 (Moscow, 1910): 62-80; Ia. E. Vodarskii, "Chislennost' i razmeshchenie posadskogo naseleniia v Rossii vo vtoroi polovine XVII v.," *Goroda feodal'noi Rossii*, pp. 271-97. Vodarskii suggests that the number of households did not increase because they became objects of taxation; thus, the density of the townsmen household increased (p. 278).

THE SERVICE CITY
IN THE EIGHTEENTH CENTURY

J. Michael Hittle

For Russia's cities, the eighteenth century was a period of slow but persistent change. While the medieval city order, solidified by events of the mid-seventeenth century, remained fundamentally intact down to the reign of Catherine II, it became ever more anachronistic, at odds both with shifting state needs and with accelerating developments in the economy and in social relations. During the last quarter of the eighteenth century, the old order finally gave way and was replaced by a new set of institutional arrangements more in keeping with altered conditions in the cities and with enhanced expectations for the city on the part of the central government.

Throughout the century the state was the dominant force on the urban scene. This is not to say that the townsmen played no role in shaping their own destiny or that other social forces were not at work in defining the urban context. But the fact remains that the central government involved itself in the most significant aspects of urban life: property relations, social structure, administrative institutions, and tax matters. At times, during mid-century for example, the state appeared to be relatively indifferent to the fate of the cities. At other times, most notably during the reigns of Peter I and Catherine II, the state aggressively addressed itself to the problems of the city. At all times, however, the Russian city can be understood only as an integral part of a polity dominated by a powerful, centralized state.

The close ties of city and state authority have deep historical roots, dating back to the rise of Muscovy. Initially the cities served as centers of defense and of princely administration but as time passed they became increasingly valued for their contributions to the royal treasury. By the mid-seventeenth century, the social composition of the cities clearly reflected these functions or services performed by the cities for the state. Each of the major social groups found in the cities—boyars, service people, contract servitors, clergy, artisans and merchants—derived its identity and its position vis-à-vis other elements of society from its particular service relationship to the state.

The actual social composition of a city varied with its size, location, and predominant function. Large cities usually contained more diverse populations than small ones; border cities tended to have a military orientation, while cities of the center were more likely to have a mercantile character. For all this diversity, it would appear that the *posadskie liudi* (hereafter townsmen), merchants, and artisans who resided on state taxable land, constituted the most important segment of the urban population of European Russia.[1] It is in the nature of the tax burden (*tiaglo*) borne by the townsmen that one finds their particular contribution to the state. Not only did *tiaglo* impose upon them heavy direct taxes, it made the townsmen administrators of the two most bountiful indirect taxes, the customs and liquor duties. Moreover, the obligation included such projects as the erection and repair of city fortifications as well as a host of lesser maintenance and public safety jobs within the city. While these services were performed by the rank and file, positions of greater responsibility in the commercial and financial administration of the state were performed by those members of the urban taxpaying community who had been selected for membership in the privileged mercantile corporations of the *gosti* and of the *gostinaia sotnia* and the *sukhonaia sotnia*.

These obligations were burdensome and led to the economic ruin of many a merchant. But from the point of view of the state the *tiaglo* relationship was necessary and desirable. It enabled the government, whose bureaucratic apparatus was as yet incomplete, to take in much-needed cash; and it gave the government direct control over the urban population who both paid and collected the taxes. Such an arrangement worked against the development of any intermediate-level institution, such as a town council, that might harbor aspirations of its own.

The social fragmentation of the Russian city left its mark on city administration as well. Residence in the city did not imply any kind of urban citizenship. Indeed, apart from the military governor, the tsar's appointed agent, there were no institutions that embraced either in their composition or in their competence the entire population of the city. Each social group was administered separately through the appropriate central government bureau (*prikaz*) or bureaus. Since the ultimate function of each of these groups was state service of one kind or another, I have chosen to use the term service city to describe the city order that emerged in medieval Muscovy and which lasted throughout much of the eighteenth century. Unquestionably, the most important services performed by the city were accomplished by the *posad* and those who had been separated from it for special state commercial and financial service. More often than not, when the state said city, it meant *posad*.

The service city persisted well into the eighteenth century. There were some alterations, to be sure, but they did not substantially affect basic institutional arrangements. The privileged corporations, for example, disappeared and many of their tasks were assumed by newly created state agencies.[2] But the *posad* society continued to perform a host of traditional service jobs. Townsmen worked as accountants, appraisers, and inspectors of manufactured items. They managed the state liquor monopolies, served at customs houses and toll-points, and collected both regular and extraordinary taxes for the government. These services might be performed in a man's own area of residence, or he might be sent a considerable distance from home. For the most part each man was held both morally and financially responsible for the fulfillment of his assignment. First guild merchants, like the *gosti* before them, occupied the most important positions.[3]

Service obligations weighed heavily on the mercantile community. In 1765 nearly one-quarter of the Archangel *posad* engaged in state service and a full 40 percent of its members performed some kind of state or local service work.[4] In Kazan, at one point, there were forty-two more positions to fill than there were eligible townsmen to fill them.[5] But the issue is more than mere numbers. Not every member of the *posad* commune was qualified for service. Indeed, a careful study of the *posad* tax rolls shows that over 40 percent of Russia's so-called merchants were hired laborers or unemployed and impoverished persons.[6] As a consequence, communes customarily elected members of the first two guilds to service posts. Even so, many businesses, poorly organized and lacking in capital, could not survive a prolonged tour of service duty by their owners.

The service relationship not only affected individual merchants but dominated the internal life of the commune as well. The commune carefully regulated its membership, elected its service people and supervised their activities, apportioned the money taxes it owed, and continually petitioned higher authorities for relief from this or that onerous burden. Much was at stake, and the *posad* gatherings witnessed some rough politicking, with factions of wealthy merchants, supported by poor but rough-and-tumble followers, vying for power. There was even an occasional take-over by the poorer elements, much to the delight of Soviet historians. In the event of disputed elections, the government granted victory to that side which seemed best able to guarantee the financial responsibility of its candidates. One must react cautiously to such government intervention; it did not constitute an arbitrary infringement on established rights of the townsmen. After all, these were not western European burghers. The Russian townsmen were servitors of a sort, and their distinguishing role in society consisted in the execution of state-determined administrative tasks. It was only fitting that the state should exercise final control over such an important means of revenue gathering.

That service was an integral part of the state order did not make it any more tolerable for those who bore its burdens. Yet, of necessity the townsmen sought to make the best of their situation. They contended that their particular contributions to the state's well-being qualified them as a privileged and deserving order of society. The most complete statement of their aspirations can be found in the reports (*nakazy*) of the city deputies to the Great Commission of Catherine II.[7] In them the merchants defended their exclusive right to urban commerce and manufacture—a right granted in 1649 but never effectively enforced—against infringements from gentry, peasants, and privileged manufacturers; and they demanded that all competition be swept from the field. Having asserted their economic rights, the merchants then entered a plea that their personal dignity be respected; too often, the argument went, they were humiliatingly referred to as *muzhiki*—no doubt because they and the peasants engaged in similar pursuits a good part of the time. To prevent such confusion in the future, the merchants sought visible signs of their worth, such as the privilege of wearing a sword or of having equipage commensurate with their social standing.

In gentry-dominated Catherinean Russia, these requests fell on less than sympathetic ears, though a few sops were eventually thrown to the merchants. What is important, however, is the fact that the townsmen, in the sixth decade of the eighteenth century, conceived of themselves as a separate estate of the realm, one that performed specialized services for the state and in return expected respect and honor similar to that accorded other servitors. Thus the service relationship had brought into being an urban taxable estate, shaped the institutions of its communal life, and helped to determine the attitudes of this estate toward other social groups in the country.

Petrine Urban Reforms

The preceding analysis has discussed in institutional terms the place of the city, and more particularly the urban taxable population, in the broader context of the whole state order. Such an approach can be misleading, however, for it implies that there was neither deviation from the norm nor change over time. In fact Russia's cities did vary and there was change during the course of the eighteenth century. But it is against the yardstick of the service city that basic alterations in the city order must ultimately be evaluated.

The vigorous actions of Peter I touched, directly or indirectly, nearly every facet of Russian life, and the cities were no exception. Well aware of their contribution to the financial health of the state, on three separate occasions Peter undertook major reforms designed to restructure urban institutional arrangements so that the cities might yield even greater revenues. Furthermore, the founding of St. Petersburg gave the tsar an opportunity to build, literally from the ground up, the city of his dreams and to provide it with an ideal set of institutions.

For all the innovations of the Petrine era, the continuities with the past were, if anything, more striking. Behind the welter of legislation and regulation lay the traditional ambiguous attitude of the government toward the city. On the one hand it spoke of the *posad* and of the city as if they were one; on the other hand it tried to establish a police apparatus that clearly had jurisdiction over all residents of a city, thus suggesting that the city was something more than its taxable commercial and artisan population. But there was no real contest between these two views. The state valued the particular services of the city more than it valued abstract principles of administration; and, since these services came primarily from the *posad*, the former view won out. An all-estate understanding of the city would have to wait its time.

Urban reform in the Petrine era, then, was not a radical revision of the relationship between city and state; it was, rather, an effort to make the city more serviceable by rationalizing its institutions, especially those which connected the *posad* commune to the state. Narrow fiscal considerations predominated in the early Petrine reform, but toward the end of Peter's reign, broader concepts of city development found expression in the tsar's urban policies.

Peter's first effort, the *burmistr* reform of 1699, conforms to this pattern. Reasoning that the townsmen suffered from rapacious military governors and that the townsmen's injuries were the state's fiscal loss, the government freed the *posad* people from the jurisdiction of the military governors in matters of justice and economic activities. The legislation turned these matters over to *burmistry*, elected by the local *posad* from its own membership. The *burmistr* institution (or *ratusha* as it came to be called) was no exercise in decentralization: the Moscow Burmistr Chamber, in addition to serving as the chief administrative organ of Moscow's townsmen, collected revenues from all local *burmistry* and then distributed them to the appropriate state agencies. The Chamber also supervised the institution on a state-wide basis. Although the *ratusha* had difficult going in its early stages, it did eventually boost the state's income from the towns by a considerable amount. In time, however, even those gains proved inadequate in the face of spiraling military expenditures, and in 1708 the *ratusha* disappeared under the provincial reform.[8]

If fiscal considerations had previously pointed toward centralization, they now led in the opposite direction. The 1708 reform made each of eight provinces responsible for the total maintenance of a fixed body of troops. The intent of the legislation was to reduce waste by eliminating an entire level of administration. The new system had no special place for the cities, just as it introduced no separate institutions for them. They were simply assimilated into the overall administrative structure of the provinces and as such fell under the jurisdiction of governors, military governors, and a variety of lesser officials with slightly Russified German titles. The townsmen continued to bear *tiaglo*, only now they returned the revenues to provincial officials instead of to the center.

The provincial reform rendered the institutional identity of the cities less precise than it had ever been. At least when the *ratusha* was in operation the state could communicate directly with its urban taxpayers, a condition that had made possible the successful execution of the 1699 reform. The new arrangements, in contrast, so buried the city in the decentralized administrative apparatus of the state that such policy-making and implementation became impossible.

Late in Peter's reign, the tsar embarked upon his most ambitious revision of municipal administration: the magistracy reform.[9] Although several key features of the reform, as outlined in the Main Magistracy Regulation of 1721, harked back to earlier practices, there was a markedly different tenor to the legislation that held great promise for the cities. Regrettably, Peter's death so soon after the initiation of the reform—a handful of magistracies appeared only in 1724—removed the driving force behind the institution. The magistracy as Peter envisioned it never saw the light of day, though in modified form it lasted out the century. Thus the importance of the reform lies as much in the intent of the legislator as in the achievements of the legislation.

In essence, the Main Magistracy Regulation continued the established practice of equating the concerns of the *posad* with those of the city. It established two categories of citizen, regular and irregular. Merchants and artisans, joined by men of special talent such as doctors, apothecaries, and skippers, and organized into two guilds, constituted the regular citizenry. The *posad* poor, referred to as base people, fell into the irregular citizenry. The magistracy, or town council, whose members were elected by and from the regular citizens, had jurisdiction over both groups. Following the centralizing principle of the *burmistr* reform, the Regulation placed the St. Petersburg Main Magistracy in charge of local offices throughout the country.

If the Regulation was institutionally conservative, its many prescriptive passages represented a new attitude toward the city. The document stressed, occasionally in disproportionate detail, the need to foster all aspects of city life, not just tax collecting. It called for police who would secure good order in matters as diverse as city economy and personal morality. It called for commodity brokers and notaries and spelled out their functions. Apparently Peter's understanding of the city had matured, for this document betrays an awareness that the ultimate means of increasing taxes lay in the creation of an ordered, physically attractive and economically prosperous city.

The early history of St. Petersburg bears the same message. Peter assembled on that inhospitable site large-scale industry, international commerce, the seats of church and state, educational institutions, and a heterogeneous population. Moreover, the accumulation of such basic building blocks of urban society was accompanied by an outpouring of legislation and regulations, some grand in objective, others petty, but all demonstrating concern for what today would be called the quality of urban life. Streets were to be paved and kept clean; building codes set both aesthetic and practical requirements; and citizens were urged to learn and to communicate through schools, a paper, and prescribed social events. Thus all the traditional functions of the city had their place in Peter's scheme of things. There was, however, no room for urban autonomy. An heir to Muscovite political tradition and a contemporary of mercantilist statesmen, Peter took the enhancement of state power as an article of faith. He could hardly be expected to build up his state by dividing authority within it.

Cities in Transition

The magistracy had some precarious moments in the years immediately after the tsar's death. Many of its competences were stripped away; the Main Magistracy was abolished and local magistracies fell under the jurisdiction of governors or military governors. Once again the townsmen found themselves at the mercy of gentry administrators. During Elizabeth's reign, though, the picture brightened. She revived the Petrine legislation on the magistracy and restored the St. Petersburg Main Magistracy. Even so, the institution never realized its potential. Hampered by bureaucratic meddling and inadequate revenues, it failed to provide the municipal leadership for which it had been created.[10]

The townsmen, of course, went on about their service duties. Indeed, it might be argued that the service city reached its apogee in the first half of the eighteenth century. Yet a number of changes in society were gradually undermining its basic features. The obsolescence of the service city had become fully apparent by the early years of the reign of Catherine II.

The most notable change was demographic. In spite of the many obstacles to mobility, people flocked to the cities in growing numbers. Most were peasants, but following the abolition of gentry service and the provincial reform of 1775, gentry and petty bureaucrats added to the influx. Some of the newcomers became permanent residents while others appeared only on a seasonal basis. Precise data are hard to come by, but recent calculations suggest that city population rose during the eighteenth century from about 3 percent of the total population to slightly more than 8 percent.[11] At the same time, however, the *posad* population remained constant relative to the entire population, somewhere around 3 percent.[12] As the non-*posad* population of the cities grew, the identification of the city and the *posad*, long the basis of governmental policy, ceased to be even an approximate reflection of the social composition of the cities. It thus constituted an anachronistic principle on which to base policy.

Significant developments occurred within the economy as well. Total output rose during the century, with the last few decades showing a noticeable quickening of the economic pulse. The cities did not always benefit from new factory starts or from freshening trade, for much of that activity had its locus in the countryside. But some cities did flourish, gaining reputations for certain manufactories or commerce, and regional commercial ties steadily strengthened.[13]

It was in the area of social relations, however, that economic change had its greatest impact. Throughout the century the townsmen lost ground in their efforts to curtail competition by peasants and privileged manufacturers. While the peasants never gained the legal right to ply a trade in the city, the practice was nearly universal. Moreover, toward mid-century peasant commercial operations received a boost from two imperial decrees. In 1745 the government permitted peasants to trade in villages and hamlets in a limited number of items of agricultural or domestic use.[14] And in 1753-1754 the elimination of internal customs removed a major obstacle to small-scale commercial transactions. The townsmen's battle for economic privilege suffered still another setback in 1775 when the government decreed that anyone could establish a manufactory without official approval.[15] This act dashed forever any hopes the merchants might have harbored that they could secure exclusive rights to the ownership of manufacturing enterprises. With serfdom strongly entrenched, Russia in 1775 was a long way from having a freely competitive market economy. Yet the day had passed—if indeed it had ever existed—when a neat, estate-based division of the economic pie could be made.

On another front, *posad* service obligations gradually lessened. The abolition of internal customs reduced the number of men called away from home as inspectors and collectors, though officials were still needed in port cities. In 1765 the government began to let contracts to private individuals for the collection of liquor taxes, a task that had previously been done by sworn men from the *posad* or by local magistracy officials. The effects of this action were striking: in some cities the total number of persons involved in service each year dropped by more than half.[16] These reductions in service were not motivated by sympathy on the part of the government for the overburdened townsmen. They simply represented the state's perennial search for more revenue.

Urban Reforms of Catherine II

When Catherine II ascended the throne nearly forty years after the issuance of the Main Magistracy Regulation, Russia's cities had fallen far short of the goals set for them in that visionary document. Physical conditions had changed little, and public services, though slightly improved, could not cope with the problems brought on by increasing population. Even more crucial, however, was the failure of the traditional service system to meet growing state needs. In the last analysis, it was the declining effectiveness of the old city order that drew the attention of the state to the problems of the cities.

From the outset, Catherine's government displayed an understanding of the nature and function of cities that corresponded more closely to reality than had the old view, which had tended to equate city and *posad*. The general survey, although initiated to straighten out rural property disputes, of necessity treated each city as a spatial whole, entirely separable from the surrounding countryside. Equally indicative of the new attitude was the election of a mayor (*golova*), representative of all inhabitants of a town, to supervise the preparation of city reports to the Great Commission. With the provincial reform of 1775, the notion that the city constituted the total population of a given territorial area and as such deserved special institutions received limited but permanent status. The law created a single position of authority over each city and town. For the capital cities this official was the *ober-politseimeister;* for cities having garrisons it was the commandant; and for smaller towns a new post was created— *gorodnichii*. Much was expected of the last. "The *gorodnichii* ought verbally to encourage the inhabitants not only to every kind of permissible industry, craft and manufacture, but even in general all people living in the cities to good morals, love of their fellow man, and orderly living."[17]

Not only did the Catherinean government view cities in new conceptual terms, it redefined the functional role of cities in the state order. In addition to being a prime source of revenues, the city was to become the focal point of a decentralized administrative apparatus, whose main goal was to preserve law and order. The consequences of this shift in emphasis were profound.

The effectiveness of the new system depended on the presence of a large number of cities, ideally spaced across the vastness of European Russia. In fact, there were not enough cities available in the right places, so it became necessary to create them. In some instances the process was feasible: the state elevated to the status of city commercially oriented suburbs, replete with merchants and artisans. In other cases, however, where such protocities were not available, the government transformed by fiat mere villages into cities. The results were predictably ludicrous. The treasurer of

The Early Russian Town

Ruposovo reported that no one had entered or left his "city" for three months.[18]

The new tasks of the cities required an overhaul of many existing urban institutions. The magistracy, for decades the embodiment of the service principle through its regulation of the townsmen's activities, emerged from the reform in drastically truncated form. Stripped of its nonjudicial competences, it was to serve chiefly as a court of law with jurisdiction limited to townsmen. A host of responsibilities—fiscal, economic, charitable, educational—formerly shared by the magistracy and by governors and military governors were transferred to newly created agencies staffed by a burgeoning bureaucracy. These agencies were carefully integrated into the bureaucratic apparatus of the state. Clearly the service city was losing its *raison d'être*.

The *posad* commune also fell victim to the reforms of 1775. Its chief functions had consisted of the regulation of service responsibilities and the apportionment of taxes among its own members. The extension of the state bureaucracy into new areas left the commune with little to regulate by way of services.[19] And even the basic work of tax apportionment changed radically in 1775 as a consequence of a revision in the tax laws.[20] The government, ever on the fiscal prowl, divided the mercantile population on the basis of wealth into two categories—merchants and *meshchane*. The merchants were to be taxed at the rate of 1 percent of their declared capital, while the *meshchane* were subject to the old tax system. Although the *meshchane* continued to apportion and collect taxes through their elders right into the nineteenth century, the reform of 1775 shattered the system of mutual responsibility which had lain at the heart of the *posad* commune. Whatever unity had existed within the ranks of the townsmen had been enforced by the need to administer services and taxes among the entire group. The disappearance of that need shattered the rationale for the old communal life.

The events of 1775 had restructured the relationship between the state and the cities; it remained for Catherine's government to address itself to the internal administration of the cities. With the magistracy limited formally to judicial functions and the *posad* commune in disarray, a basic revision of urban administration was all the more urgent. In 1785 Catherine published her Charter Granted to the Cities. In an effort to create a government that embraced all permanent residents, this document, confused and internally inconsistent, divided the urban populace into six categories, each of which was to be represented in the key organs of city administration. As it turned out in practice, the wealthy merchants retained their position of prominence.[21] (One hesitates to say power because of the built-in weaknesses of the new institutions.) There were some advances for city government, such as the right to possess real property, but by and large it had limited competences and means. The six-man council, the chief executive organ of city administration, exercised narrow authority indeed: it regulated specific aspects of the physical environment of the city. Though Catherine deserves credit for grappling with this major domestic issue, the fact remains that the Charter Granted to the Cities made only modest headway toward the creation of a city order that would be beneficial to state and townsmen alike.

On two significant points, the Catherinean reforms suffered from a conflict between legislative intent, on the one hand, and administrative and social reality, on the other. First, while the legislation sought to upgrade city and local life by drawing a larger portion of the citizenry into government affairs, a rapidly growing state bureaucracy further extended its power over the localities. Bureaucratic power tipped the scales and local initiative continued to be stifled. Second, the government sought to engage all social groups in city administration. This effort encountered strong opposition from a society riven by distinctions of estate. Indeed, there is no evidence that Catherine sought to eliminate these distinctions; rather, she wanted townsman and noble to forget their differences for the common purpose of civic advancement. It was a naive wish given the nature of Russian society.

It would appear that Catherine II, caught up in her own ideas of urban reform, understood fully neither the extent of change within the cities nor the strength of traditional social forces. As a result, her legislation displayed a greater grasp of the principles of government than of the reality to be governed. The cities entered the nineteenth century better equipped institutionally than they had been at mid-century, but they had yet to free themselves from the bonds of tradition and the heavy hand of the state.

Notes

1. Originally the *posad* was that part of an urban settlement located outside the walls of the central fortification and inhabited by artisans and traders. It was distinguished from the *gorod*, the military and administrative center, and from the *belye mesta*, the nontaxable properties of secular and clerical magnates. The inhabitants of the *posad*, bound together by state taxes, constituted the *posadskaia obshchina*, or urban commune. In this essay, the term *posad* signifies the commune, not an area of the city.

2. The disappearance of the *gosti* has been thoroughly explored by Samuel H. Baron in "The Fate of the *Gosti* in the Reign of Peter the Great," paper presented at a University of Chicago conference on Peter the Great and His Legacy, November 18-19, 1972.

3. The fullest treatment of *posad* services can be found in A. A. Kizevetter, *Posadskaia obshchina v Rossii XVIII st.* (Moscow, 1903).

4. V. N. Latkin, *Zakonodatel'nye kommissii v Rossii v XVIII st.*, 1 (St. Petersburg, 1887): 461.

5. M. M. Bogoslovskii, "Razbor sochineniia g. Kizevettera *Posadskaia obshchina v Rossii XVIII stoletiia*," in *Chteniia v Obshchestve istorii i drevnostei rossiiskikh pri Moskovskom universitete* (1906), bk. 4, sec. 5, p. 20.

6. Kizevetter, p. 141.

7. For a comprehensive review of the materials of the Great Commission see Latkin's study. Complete texts of the city *nakazy* arc in *Sbornik imperatorskogo Russkogo istoricheskogo obshchestva* (St. Petersburg, 1867-1916), vols. 93, 107, 123, 134, 147.

8. The *burmistr* reform is carefully analyzed in M. M. Bogoslovskii, "Gorodskaia reforma 1699 g.," in *Petr I: Materialy dlia biografii*, 3 (Leningrad, 1946).

9. The key documents are the Main Magistracy Regulation, *Polnoe sobranie zakonov* (hereafter cited as *PSZ*), 6, no. 3708, January 16, 1721; and the Instruction to the Magistracy, *PSZ*, 7, no. 4624, December 30, 1724.

10. For the fate of the magistracy reform see I. I. Ditiatin, *Ustroistvo i upravlenie gorodov Rossii*, 1, *Goroda Rossii v XVIII stoletii* (St. Petersburg, 1875), pp. 327-473.

11. V. K. Iatsunskii, "Nekotorye voprosy metodiki izucheniia istorii feodal'nogo goroda v Rossii," in *Goroda feodal'noi Rossii* (Moscow, 1966), p. 87.

12. F. Ia. Polianskii, *Gorodskoe remeslo i manufaktura v Rossii XVIII v.* (Moscow, 1960), p. 29.

13. See Iu. R. Klokman, *Ocherki sotsial'no-ekonomicheskoi istorii gorodov Severo-Zapada Rossii v seredine XVIII v.* (Moscow, 1960).

14. Ibid., p. 187.

15. *PSZ*, 20, no. 14,275, March 17, 1775, article 11.

16. *Ocherki istorii SSSR: Period feodalizma: Rossiia vo vtoroi polovine XVIII v.* (Moscow, 1956), p. 155.

17. *PSZ*, 20, no. 14,392, November 7, 1775, article 274.

18. Iu. R. Klokman, *Sotsial'no-ekonomicheskaia istoriia russkogo goroda: vtoraia polovina XVIII veka* (Moscow, 1967), p. 137.

19. Guild merchants were formally excused from service obligations in 1785 in the Charter Granted to the Cities. *PSZ*, 22, no. 16,188, April 21, 1785, article 101.

20. *PSZ*, 20, no. 14,275, March 17, 1775, article 47.

21. See A. A. Kizevetter, *Gil'diia moskovskago kupechestva* (Moscow, 1915).

COMPARATIVE APPROACHES TO
URBANIZATION: RUSSIA, 1750-1800

Gilbert Rozman

Russian urban history occupies a prominent place in comparative studies of cities. Eighteenth-century Russia, chosen as a representative of countries with poorly developed cities, has been repeatedly contrasted to western European countries credited with advanced institutions of urban self-government and with relatively high proportions of their populations in cities.[1] Invariably Russia is pictured as a country whose autocratic system blocked the spontaneous appearance of independent organizations representing urban commercial and craft populations and whose cities were largely artificial administrative creations with populations totaling just 3 or 4 percent of the national population. Frequently these negative impressions of Russian cities buttress even more general conclusions about the backwardness of the Russian Empire. If the assumption of retarded urban development could be proven to be substantially incorrect, then we might anticipate a reexamination of many aspects of eighteenth-century social structure in search of other evidence of Russia's relative standing.

We must avoid drawing comparisons based on differences observed in the nineteenth century and then extending them back to an earlier period. Certainly by 1850 all indices point to a rapidly widening gap between the initial countries to experience the Industrial Revolution and all other countries. However, to the extent that comparisons purporting to show urban backwardness refer to the eighteenth century, they are generally based on a variety of approaches which do not make use of the best available evidence. In particular, arguments in favor of retarded Russian urbanization are based on an unproven though widely accepted hypothesis about the salutory effects of what is termed urban self-government during this period and on inadequate knowledge of international urban statistics.

Soviet sources have identified the concept of urban self-government with what they label a legalistic approach to cities. Charging that this approach concentrates primarily on the ill-effects of official obligations upon members of various urban strata, these sources correctly point out the paucity of analysis of social indicators that demonstrate the steady advance of Russian society.[2] If one examines Soviet writings on cities carefully, however, one discovers that despite the greater attention to societal development, their emphasis actually turns out to be only a somewhat altered version of this same legalistic approach.[3] Conclusions are supported by references to the same elements of state suppression, focusing on the legal barriers which limited the full participation of urban residents in commercial activities. The argument found in Russian writings today that the state retarded the development of trade and the growth of urban population is only slightly more positive about the fate of eighteenth-century cities than are the assessments of those they attack for portraying urban growth as essentially a consequence of contacts with the West. In short, whether one thinks of the Russian city as an "artificial transplant" on unreceptive soil or as a "natural growth" that was improperly nourished, the conclusion about the frailty of the urban organism remains the same.

The various versions of the legalistic approach, which can be traced back to pre-Revolutionary Russian writers or to Karl Marx's conception of the role of the state in dealing with class antagonisms or even to Max Weber's identification of independent commercial organizations with genuine urban development, have failed to show specifically how different forms of organization permitted by law influenced the indicators of urban prosperity. If the degree of "freedom," commonly meaning self-government by certain groups of commercially prosperous urban residents, is the principal determinant of city growth, then why have modern societies with such varied patterns as Japan (both before and after World War II), the Soviet Union, and several Western nations all experienced sustained, rapid urbanization? Correspondingly, we find that prior to 1750 as many as two-fifths of the world's urban population probably lived in China and that the most rapid spurt in city development occurred in Japan during the seventeenth and early eighteenth centuries.[4] As with Russia, neither of these countries was noted for high levels of self-government by persons engaged in commercial activities. Moreover, Japan's dramatic city growth took place just after the period in its history identified with abortive attempts at urban self-government. Although it is probably the most widely applied of any comparative methodology, the legalistic approach has been unable to account for many of the major phenomena in the history of urban population.

Another approach which has been widely used for concluding that Russian cities were backward is based on the straightforward notion that the greater the percentage of a country's population in cities, the greater the level of its urban development. The merits of this approach would seem obvious, particularly since the percentage of population in cities has been universally applied as a measure (imperfect as it may be) of modernization. Nonetheless, the potential of this approach has not been realized for at least two reasons. The most obvious explanation is the scarcity and frailty of urban data. Published estimates of city populations before 1800 are often wildly at variance with one another and it is difficult to choose among them. Nevertheless, having recently examined data for China and Japan and compared them with data for Russia, I am convinced that enumerations of urban populations have been far more thorough than previously recognized. The chief problem has been that few people have carried out research in this branch of quantitative history.

The second factor operating to limit attention to comparisons of urban population is the fact that there exists an alternate approach which, in essence, challenges the usefulness of the population approach. This is the functional approach, based on the widespread view that pre-modern cities can be neatly classified according to their principal functions. Implicit in this viewpoint is the attitude that urban population statistics in a country such as Russia are deceptively high. Indeed, students of Russia have identified administrative cities, fortress cities, and agrarian cities, all of which are credited with larger populations than would have been warranted by the development of commerce and crafts alone.[5] They have shown that all but a handful of Russian settlements with more than 3,000 residents served as administrative centers, that many cities along the long and shifting borders in the west and south had originated as fortresses, and that individuals engaged in agriculture were present and even numerous in small Russian cities. Proponents of the functional approach insist that these facts are proof of the "distorted" composition of the urban population of Russia and question whether cities in which production and trade are not the principal functions should be treated as pure cities.

Underlying both the functional and the legalistic approaches is the assumption that they provide evidence of relatively stagnant craft production and urban commerce in Russia. In other words, urban organizations subject to close regulation limited the development of trade, and cities with such visible functions as administration, defense, or farming were inhospitable to thriving commerce. Ignoring the availability of more direct evidence on the patterns of trade and on the composition of the urban population, spokesmen for the functional and legalistic approaches have based their arguments on indirect evidence and imprecise measurement. In fact, had they examined more direct evidence, they would have found that internal commerce expanded rapidly in eighteenth-century Russia and that officials, soldiers, and those engaged in farming comprised a small proportion of all residents in Russian administrative centers.

Despite its many shortcomings, in one major respect the functional approach has alerted us to a problem in the presentation of population data. Although all cities regardless of origin and planning were multifunctional, systematic measurement of functions

The Early Russian Town

would disclose that small cities were decidedly more agrarian than large cities. While there is no persuasive evidence that the distribution of functions in Russian cities was markedly different from the distribution in cities of a similar size elsewhere, we should still make sure that a uniform definition of urban for all countries takes into account the lesser "urbanness" of small cities.

The first basic requirement for the population approach is accurate data. As I noted at the beginning of this essay, statistics on eighteenth-century Russian urbanization are repeatedly presented as a mark of the country's backwardness. Again we find a surprising consensus between most Soviet and non-Soviet authors. The explanation is not, as we might be tempted to assume, that data for this period have been fully published and unequivocally presented to support a single interpretation. Rather in a disappointing congruence of unimaginative historical research, writers in and out of the Soviet Union have accepted the figures of A. A. Kizevetter and, for a later date, of P. N. Miliukov as satisfactory statements of actual urban totals, despite the widely known fact that these pre-Revolutionary authors gave figures only for the proportion of the national male population who were counted in the specially designated *podat'* strata, including those legally registered as merchants and artisans but whose tax status bore no necessary relationship to actual occupational categories. The term *posad*, which ordinarily refers to a geographical unit, has also been used to signify those strata responsible for the urban *podat'* tax. Thus Kizevetter's conclusion that the percentage in the *podat'* strata remained almost constant at 3.2 or 3.1 during the years of the first three *reviziia* (enumerations properly dated in 1719, 1744, and 1762), and Miliukov's statement that the percentage had risen to 4.1 at the time of the fifth *reviziia* (in 1795) are the sources to which recent figures can be traced.[6]

Since the opportunity for quantitative research using essential archival materials has been available for Soviet scholars almost exclusively, the responsibility for inattention to the task of compiling complete urban statistics rests largely with them. Their writings generally repeat the figures assembled by the pre-Revolutionary historians based on the *podat'* population. Most recently the *Soviet Historical Encyclopedia* published in 1971 asserted that the urban population at the end of the eighteenth century was 4.1 percent.[7] An identical figure is given in the imposing collective assessment of historical knowledge on Russia, *Essays on the History of the USSR*, published in 1956.[8] During the period between these two multivolume compendiums, specialized publications devoted to cities also gave similar urban totals.[9] One of the most succinct summations of urban statistics for this period can be found in another multivolume work, *History of the USSR: From Ancient Times to Our Days*, of which the first series of six volumes appeared between 1966 and 1968. "The increase of the urban population as a whole proceeded very slowly. At the end of the century on an average only four persons out of one hundred inhabitants of the country lived in cities. During 75 years the proportion of the urban population increased by only 1%."[10]

Actually any reader who follows Soviet scholarship on the second half of the eighteenth century would be puzzled by this seeming sense of unanimity. Data on individual cities often are presented with great numbers of non-*podat'* residents included, unmistakably suggesting the need for an upward revision in the national total.[11] Even the argument that might have been used to justify concentrating only on *podat'* totals, that is, that the members of these strata were the only ones involved in the central economic tasks of the city, is effectively shattered by repeated information on the active participation of others in commerce and crafts. It is perplexing then to find that detailed study of cities during recent decades has had no impact on the repetition of the old misleading figures.

An even more obvious source of confusion is the fact that on two occasions V. K. Iatsunskii has referred to unpublished work by V. M. Kabuzan, widely known as the leading specialist on the historical population of Russia, which through "much more precise calculations" than previously have been carried out establishes that more than 8 percent of the population lived in cities during the 1780s.[12] Examination of Kabuzan's writings reveals a concern unprecedented among Soviet historians for full tabulation of archival materials, detailed accumulation of statistics, and accurate evaluation of the quality of available data. In his article "Some Materials for the Study of the Historical Geography of Russia during the 18th and the Beginning of the 19th Centuries," we find the first serious attempt to analyze materials on city populations.[13] Even though full documentation of Kabuzan's calculations as reported by Iatsunskii remains unpublished, we should try to find clarification and support for these figures and then consider the implications of the data.

The easiest and the universally accepted solution to the problem of what is meant by the urban population of Russia is to include only those who lived in administrative centers, omitting all who lived in other settlements regardless of their population and commercial significance. In fact, there were not many places with even a few thousand residents which had not become officially designated centers of government (guberniia and *uezd* centers). Furthermore, as a result of the reforms of 1775 to 1785 many of the more promising centers of commerce, generally with fewer than 2,000 inhabitants, were added to the list of *uezd* cities, replacing in some cases tiny *uezd* centers. Although after 1785 some places with only a few hundred residents remained among the ranks of *uezd* cities while other settlements with more active marketing were excluded, the equation of administrative centers and cities in Russia has considerable justification.

In spite of the unusual usefulness of an administrative definition for Russian cities, we should be aware that comparisons over time in a single country in which a reorganization of territorial divisions occurs, and moreover, comparisons between two or more societies with varying administrative levels, are complicated if we rely exclusively on administrative designations. A less restrictive definition which I have used in a study of Chinese and Japanese cities includes the population of all settlements with at least 3,000 inhabitants and marketing activities, as well as half of the population in less populous settlements which served as administrative or intermediate marketing centers. This definition permits us to categorize places as half urban, which is important if we are to resolve the problem identified by the functional approach and at the same time include in our count of cities or partial cities many settlements with small populations, for example the majority of *uezd* centers and almost all of the major nonadministrative periodic marketing centers of Russia. I have discovered that applying this definition to Russian data from 1782 results in a drop of not much more than 5 percent from the figures produced with the administrative criteria alone; the gain in population by including nonadministrative centers partially compensates for the drop in population by counting only half of those living in administrative centers with fewer than 3,000 inhabitants. Clearly the figures for Russia based on the administrative definition overstate the urban population in comparison with those based on this more universal definition, but the difference is not great.

The problems of clarification are not limited to choosing a definition for cities. Difficulties also arise in specifying the boundaries of cities and in distinguishing between permanent and temporary inhabitants. We observe in Russia a situation which existed elsewhere: legal boundaries of cities frequently excluded adjacent built-up areas not primarily settled by persons engaged in agriculture. It is important consistently to include such areas in our urban statistics if we are to improve the comparability of data in countries with different national policies toward city boundaries and in periods in which the incorporation of suburbs into cities was treated differently. Conveniently this poses no problem for eighteenth-century Russia since *reviziia* data generally subsume the suburban population in city totals. The task is more difficult for nineteenth-century Russia, however, because data generally exclude suburban residents. Since generalizations about long-run changes in urbanization are already misleading because of inaccurate dating of urban data commonly attributed to the sixth *reviziia* in 1811, we should be particularly careful to restrict our conclusions to the period from the second through the fifth *reviziia*.

Analysis of the complete archival data on the permanent registered population as well as of the few late eighteenth-century attempts to count the temporary population must be carried out before we can state with certainty the size and the composition of the full urban population. Until such analysis is available, our urban totals are certain to underestimate the population present in administrative centers by failing to count those considered temporary residents even though in numerous cases they were present for many months or even years. Nevertheless, if we exclude seasonal migrations such as the winter influx into Moscow, the number of temporary residents is not likely to have been very large, especially during the years of the *reviziia* when many people were first listed as permanent residents. Despite these shortcomings in our knowledge of the composition of the population, we are now in a position to state clearly what is meant by the population data on Russian cities.

Evidence is overwhelming in support of Kabuzan's findings that Russia in the 1780s had more than 8 percent of its population in cities, including all permanent residents of all administrative centers and their suburbs, but excluding those who were present but not permanently registered in these centers and all who were present in nonadministrative centers that might have qualified as cities by some other definition. Most convincing proof is found in the archival sources from which Kabuzan's conclusions were drawn. Providing a detailed breakdown of the urban population into categories and locations, the archival data which I saw give ample evidence that the *podat'* strata formed a minority in the cities and that most guberniia were more than 5 percent urban, while several guberniia with large cities had from 10 to 50 percent of their population in administrative centers.[14] Interestingly this information is not at variance with the results obtained by Heinrich Storch, who in 1795 had access to incomplete data from the 1782 *reviziia*. Based on these data, Storch estimated an urban total quite close to Kabuzan's findings.[15] Also, as indicated above, recent authors who have studied particular cities or guberniia have presented figures that, if carefully interpreted, correspond to a national percentage on this scale.

A second important step in applying the population approach is

Table 1

Population of Russian Administrative Cities, 1744-1795

National Population (millions)		Urban Population (millions)	Percent Urban
1744	18.2	1.4	7.4-7.8
1762	23.2	1.9	7.9-8.3
1782	28.4	2.4	8.4-8.8
1795	37.2	3.2	8.4-8.8

to delineate the changing urban percentages over decades or centuries. In lieu of full publication and analysis of archival data, I can only tentatively estimate the population in administrative centers for a period of a half century during years encompassed by the second and fifth *reviziia*. Starting with a nearly complete tabulation of the urban population in 1782 (the fourth *reviziia*) and some evidence that there was a gradual rise in the percentage of the total population in cities during this period, I have estimated in Table 1 that the urban population was between 7.5 and 8.0 percent in 1744, reached about 8.0 percent in 1762, and then rose to roughly 8.5 percent by 1795. The population in Russian administrative cities more than doubled during this half century, corresponding to and probably somewhat exceeding the rate of increase of the total population.

Does the hypothesis that Russia was more than twice as urbanized as is generally acknowledged shed new light on comparative urban development? Although international urban statistics have not yet been adequately compiled, these figures for Russia indicate a relatively high level of urbanization. Russia ranked between contemporary Japan, with its unusual 16 to 17 percent in cities, and China, with a tenacious 5 to 7 percent in cities. While Russia was behind some western European countries which had more than 10 or 15 percent of their populations in cities, the gap in many cases was still not large, certainly not as large as has been often assumed. Moreover, these figures overstate the gap in urban development, which can be calculated by trying to hold transportation conditions constant.

More detailed comparisons of population statistics have been carried out by advocates of special quantitative approaches to urban history. Probably the best known quantitative framework is the rank-size approach, according to which cities in any region or country will form a hierarchy with predictable ratios of population; the population of a city multiplied by its rank in size equals the population of the largest city. Recently this approach in a slightly modified form was applied to the history of cities in western Europe.[16] Moreover, Chauncy D. Harris has compared regions in the postwar Soviet Union in terms of the rank-size approach,[17] but it has yet to be applied to Russia in the period under consideration. In my opinion, the great population gap between the two large central cities of St. Petersburg and Moscow and the next largest cities, which counted no more than 35,000 residents in 1782, cannot be reconciled with the specifications of the rank-size approach.

The Urban Network Approach

Population data can also be analyzed by what I call the urban network approach. The first step in this approach is to identify the stages of maturation of networks of central places, including all centers of administration and of periodic or daily marketing. The progression of settlement patterns started in pre-urban societies lacking central places of any kind and moved ahead through many stages to societies with complex networks comprising many levels of central places; early urban societies in which cities existed as loosely interrelated centers matured into societies boasting simple hierarchies with two or three levels of cities and then into societies with more complex networks of up to seven levels of central places. Increasingly complex patterns of accumulation and redistribution of goods resulted in expanded networks of central places, which, in turn, contained growing percentages of the total population.

Below I have divided all central places into seven levels, using definitions which are inclusive of the definitions I used in my book, *Urban Networks in Ch'ing China and Tokugawa Japan.* Once all seven levels have been established, as they had in Russia by the early eighteenth century, a country can be said to have achieved a complete pre-modern urban network. For such countries further steps in analysis are possible, including the identification of regional variations in urbanization based on the comparison and explanation of population data.

Comparisons between regions are essential to determine the extent to which the rise in the urban population of eighteenth-century Russia was a consequence of annexations of previously urbanized areas. Using data from the fourth *reviziia*, I have estimated the level of urbanization in the following six regions: 1) North-Northwest (seven guberniia); 2) Central-Industrial (six guberniia); 3) Central-Black Earth (six guberniia); 4) Lower and Middle Volga (six guberniia); 5) Baltic-Belorussia-Ukraine-Novorossiia (ten to twelve guberniia); and 6) Urals and Siberia (five to six guberniia). Regrettably there is no opportunity here to explain the choice of regions, which is, of course, crucial to the figures obtained. Nevertheless, it can be demonstrated that neither region 5 nor any large area within this western part of the Russian Empire had a major impact in increasing the national percentage in cities. Region 5 with somewhat more than 9 percent of its population in cities probably contributed to only a slight increase in the national figure.

Previously I had found that the eighteen provinces of China and the seven regions of Japan had a similar range of urbanization with roughly twice as high a percentage in cities within the most urbanized area of each country as in the least urbanized area. This interregional distribution existed in Russia as well; the range for the six regions in Russia was between 14 and 6.5 percent, as compared with Japan's range of 24 to 12.5 percent and China's range of 9 to 4 percent. In each of these countries the least urbanized regions were major sources of goods for export to cities at levels 1 to 3 in regions with high percentages in cities.

For comparisons of national urban networks I will exclude the

The Early Russian Town

two outermost regions of Russia, regions 5 and 6 as identified above, since they were relatively autonomous areas. The remaining four core regions in 1782 consisted of 25 guberniia, 301 administrative cities (276 of which were *uezd* cities which did not serve as guberniia centers), and 18 million inhabitants, of whom more than 1.6 million lived in these 301 cities, while more than 1.5 million would be considered urban by the more universal definition given for cities in this article. Beginning with the following definitions of the seven levels of central places, it is possible to compare the distribution of central places of various sizes:

Level 1: National administrative center: more populous than any level 3 city.
Level 2: Regional center or secondary national center; also more populous than any level 3 city.
Level 3: Population: 30,000–299,999 and not classified at levels 1 or 2.
Level 4: Population: 10,000–29,999.
Level 5: Population: 3,000–9,999.
Level 6: Population: fewer than 3,000 people and an intermediate marketing center.
Level 7: Population: fewer than 3,000 people and a standard marketing center.

Some comparisons between the distribution of settlements at these seven levels in this core area of Russia and in China and Japan should provide us with initial clues about the particular conditions of Russian urbanization. In these regions of Russia during the 1780s there were approximately 1,000 central places, at all seven levels, in a total population of 18 million. By comparison, China in 1830 had 31,000 central places with a national population of 400 million people, and Japan in the 1780s had 1,700 central places with a total of 30 million people. Although Japan and Russia were more urbanized, they had proportionately fewer central places than China. Furthermore, if we group settlements into levels 1-5 and 6-7, then we find that this core area of

Russia had a ratio of roughly 1:7; of the 1,000 central places about 130 had populations numbering at least 3,000. In Japan the ratio was even higher, close to 1:4, but the corresponding ratio for China was much lower, roughly 1:20. This tells us that for every full-fledged city of 3,000 or more people there were as many as twenty smaller settlements in China which were regularly involved in the movement of goods collected from surrounding villages, but only four such settlements in Japan and an intermediate figure of seven in Russia. In this measure of efficiency in streamlining the flow of resources, Russia again ranks between Japan and China.

The comparisons between the urban networks of Japan and Russia reveal that, in general, progressively more central places at each level were used to funnel resources into cities at the next higher level in Russia. Even at level 1, where there was only one city in each country, Japan's greater mobilization of resources can be seen by the fact that Edo (Tokyo) was more than three times as populous as St. Petersburg. Russian cities were particularly rare at level 3; only Astrakhan' and Saratov could be found in these four regions. In contrast, there were twenty Japanese cities in this classification. Whereas Japan was twice as urban as Russia, it was almost three times ahead in the percentage of the national population in cities with 30,000 or more people.

Comparisons with China present a very different picture. Having only 4-5 percent as great a population as that of China in 1830, Russia in the 1780s achieved a much higher rate of urbanization at levels 1 and 2 in spite of the fact that China's ten largest cities at these levels totaled five million inhabitants. While China was far ahead at level 3, Russia partially recovered at level 4 and then established a considerable lead at level 5. As many as 37 percent of all those who lived in Russian cities could be found in cities with 3,000 to 10,000 people. And if the other two regions of the Russian Empire were included, this percentage would rise to well over 40. Russia's underrepresentation at level 3 indicates that lower level cities did not provide a great volume of resources to higher level cities, as they did in Japan. Yet Russia's overrepresentation at level 5 reveals that a considerably greater input was received from settlements at levels 6 and 7 and from the rural areas in general than was the case in China.

Of the five approaches to comparative urban studies considered here, the population approach, rank-size approach, and urban networks approach are in one basic respect complementary: all three approaches are founded on urban statistics. The population approach permits comparisons if our data are limited to rough figures showing which country was more or less urban, but of course the data must be estimated with care in order not to use this approach in a misleading manner, as has occurred in studies based on underestimations of the urban population of Russia. The rank-size approach requires more complete urban data, but it does not explain deviations from a standard pattern and therefore seems to have little applicability to eighteenth-century Russia. Only the urban network approach, which is based on the most complete data, provides a framework for examining in detail the similarities and differences between Russian urban development and the development of cities in other countries. In particular, it enables us to designate the levels of cities in which development was exceptional and then to examine related spatial divisions in social structure which corresponded to these urban patterns.

A thorough application of the urban network approach to Russia has yet to be completed, but certain conclusions are already emerging. First, with regard to the question of whether serfdom was a barrier to pre-modern urban growth, it is interesting to note that Japan like Russia had ideally closed classes and restricted geographic mobility, while in less urbanized China there were practically no legal barriers to interclass mobility and free migration. If it had any substantial impact, serfdom may well have facilitated the outflow to cities of rural production, taxes, and manpower.

Second, the legalistic and functional approaches to urban history have led us to exaggerate the importance of state policies despite the fact that the gradual growth in the urban percentage indicates that policies had no major immediate consequences. There was probably little rise in the percentage of Russians in administrative cities as a result of the extensive reforms of 1775-1785, since newly established administrative centers generally had small populations. Eighteenth-century reforms in administrative levels of cities should be conceived primarily as having speeded along the steady evolution of increasingly integrated networks of central places. The more active intervention of officials in both Japan and Russia than in China suggests that, in general, policies were more likely to promote urban growth than to retard it.

The rationale for the urban network approach resembles the proposition supported by Soviet scholars that stages and substages of societies are characterized by specific features of urban development, demonstrating what Karl Marx called "the movement of the contradiction between the city and the countryside" which summarized the economic history of every society.[18] Study of networks of cities during the second half of the eighteenth century is firmly supported by the overwhelming emphasis which Soviet scholars have recently placed on this half century as the formative period of the transition to capitalism.[19] More than for any other period, recent Soviet writings have raised the challenge of bringing clarity to the study of Russian cities between 1750 and 1800. In response to this challenge and to the confused state of comparisons involving Russian cities, I have concentrated in this essay on the essential first steps for detailed study of Russian cities, a review of the methodology of comparisons, and an initial analysis of population data. The choice of a new comparative approach based on accurate population data should prove to be a useful starting point for further study of Russian cities.

Notes

1. Sources in which this viewpoint is conveyed can be divided into three groups: 1) pre-Revolutionary Russian works, such as I. I. Ditiatin, *Ustroistvo i upravlenie gorodov Rossii* (St. Petersburg, 1875), pp. 107-09; 2) Western writings, including Jerome Blum, *Lord and Peasant in Russia* (New York: Atheneum, 1969), pp. 270, 280-81; and 3) Soviet materials, for example I. F. Rybakov, "Nekotorye voprosy genezisa kapitalisti-

The Early Russian Town

cheskogo goroda v Rossii," *Voprosy genezisa kapitalizma v Rossii* (Leningrad, 1960), pp. 229-39. In Soviet sources comparisons with western Europe are more likely to be implicit or to be qualified by remarks indicating that the same processes were present in Russia.

2. See for example P. G. Ryndziunskii, *Gorodskoe grazhdanstvo doreformennoi Rossii* (Moscow, 1958), pp. 5-12.

3. One of the clearest juxtapositions of criticism of bourgeois authors for their narrowly legalistic approach followed by presentation of an essentially Soviet legalistic position can be found in Iu. R. Klokman, *Sotsial'no-ekonomicheskaia istoriia russkogo goroda* (Moscow, 1967), pp. 53-54.

4. Gilbert Rozman, *Urban Networks in Ch'ing China and Tokugawa Japan* (Princeton: Princeton University Press, 1973).

5. A recent criticism of oversimplified urban typologies was supplied by L. N. Milov, "O tak nazyvaemykh agrarnykh gorodakh Rossii XVIII veka," *Voprosy Istorii* 6 (1968): 54-64.

6. A. A. Kizevetter, *Posadskaia obshchina v Rossii XVIII stoletiia* (Moscow, 1903), p. 113; P. N. Miliukov, *Ocherki po istorii russkoi kul'tury* 1 (St. Petersburg, 1896): 79.

7. *Sovetskaia Istoricheskaia Entsiklopediia* 13 (Moscow, 1971): 543.

8. *Ocherki istorii SSSR* 4 (Moscow, 1956): 151.

9. See for example Klokman, pp. 31, 311.

10. *Istoriia SSSR: s drevneishikh vremen do nashikh dnei* 3 (1967): 403.

11. Among the best examples are F. Ia. Polianskii, *Gorodskoe remeslo i manufaktura v Rossii XVIII veka* (Moscow, 1960), pp. 29-56; and Klokman, pp. 211-304.

12. V. K. Iatsunskii, "Nekotorye voprosy metodiki izucheniia istorii feodal'nogo goroda v Rossii," in *Goroda feodal'noi Rossii* (Moscow, 1966), p. 87; idem, "Osnovnye momenty istorii sel'skokhoziaistvennogo proizvodstva v Rossii s XVI veka do 1917 goda," *Ezhegodnik po agrarnoi istorii vostochnoi Evropy (1964)* (Kishinev, 1966), p. 58.

13. V. M. Kabuzan, "Nekotorye materialy dlia izucheniia istoricheskoi geografii Rossii XVIII—nachalo XIX vek," *Problemy istochnikovedeniia*, 11 (Moscow, 1963): 153-95.

14. Most of the materials I used are found in TSGADA, fond 248, opis' 58.

15. Heinrich Storch, *Statistische Übersicht der Statthalterschaften des Russischen Reichs* (Riga, 1795).

16. See Josiah Cox Russell, *Medieval Regions and Their Cities* (London: David and Charles, 1972).

17. Chauncy D. Harris, *Cities of the Soviet Union* (Chicago: Rand McNally, 1970).

18. Among the many sources which refer to this statement by Marx is Klokman, p. 3.

19. V.I. Shunkov *et al.*, eds., *Perekhod ot feodalizma k kapitalizmu v Rossii: Materialy vsesoiuznoi diskussii* (Moscow, 1969).

PART II
THE NINETEENTH-CENTURY CITY

The changing attitude of the state toward the city is best reflected in a series of municipal statutes implemented during the course of the nineteenth century. Walter Hanchett begins Part II by examining four statutes, the special laws of 1846 and 1862, the general statute of 1870, and the "counter-reform" of 1892.

The mid-nineteenth century represents a watershed in Russian urban history, for after the emancipation of the serfs in 1861 the pace of urban growth quickened significantly. Chauncy Harris has noted that from 1867 until 1913 the average annual growth rate was 2.3 percent, compared to an average of 1.5 percent between 1811 and 1867. Furthermore, in 1811 Russia's urban population was only one-fourteenth as large as its rural population. By 1867 it was one-sixth as large. (The urban population did not equal the rural until roughly 1960; by 1969 it surpassed the rural population by 28 percent.)[1] David Hooson has reported that in 1870, only fifteen Russian cities contained more than 50,000 inhabitants. By 1914 there existed a hundred such cities.[2] Furthermore, among the larger cities, about half doubled their population between 1883 and 1913, and another quarter trebled or more.[3]

In Part II, Richard Rowland analyzes the most important factor in this growth, urban in-migration, and points out the low correlation between in-migration and industrialization. Rowland emphasizes instead the relative importance of the attraction of job opportunities in the personal services sector. In his study of New Russia, Roger Thiede attributes a more important role to industrialization as a cause of urban growth in that region after 1860. During this century Odessa rapidly became the metropolitan center of New Russia and one of the great cities of the empire. In his case study of that city, Frederick Skinner demonstrates that Odessa's developmental progress reflected both the varying degree of state tutelage and the values of the ruling elite in the community itself.

On the eve of World War I, Moscow, with 1,800,000 residents, had a population ten times greater than it had had a hundred years earlier. Robert Gohstand examines one aspect of this growth, the spatial development of the city's trading network and the concurrent changes in the typology of commercial establishments. Particularly after 1892, however, when the municipal counter-reform stifled local initiative and restored the traditional bureaucratic domination of city affairs, rapid growth resulted in a general breakdown of urban modernization and a probable deterioration in the quality of urban life. Michael F. Hamm concludes this section with an analysis of this breakdown and contends that the neglect of urban modernization by state and city government alike has long been overlooked as a significant factor contributing to the collapse of the tsarist order.

Notes

1. Chauncy D. Harris, *Cities of the Soviet Union* (Chicago: Rand McNally, 1970), pp. 234, 239.

2. David J. M. Hooson, "The Growth of Cities in Pre-Soviet Russia," in R. P. Beckinsale and J. M. Houston, eds., *Urbanization and Its Problems—Essays in Honour of E. W. Gilbert* (Oxford: Basil Blackwell, 1970), p. 259.

3. Ibid., p. 272.

TSARIST STATUTORY REGULATION OF MUNICIPAL GOVERNMENT IN THE NINETEENTH CENTURY

Walter Hanchett

A study made by the Russian government at the beginning of the 1860s showed that only 14 of the 738 population points designated by the state as urban areas had more than 30,000 inhabitants; 568 cities and city settlements each encompassed fewer than 10,000 persons. In more than half of the 595 cities of European Russia the population was engaged almost exclusively in agricultural work. In many instances the only compelling reason for the existence of "cities" was that they were needed as administrative centers for local agencies of the central government.

St. Petersburg and Moscow were the leading exceptions to this general pattern, both in size of population and in importance as commercial and industrial centers. In these two capitals, particularly, the existing bureaucratic structure, or at times the lack of structure, of municipal administration was producing results unsatisfactory even to the tsarist authorities. Throughout the first half of the century numerous commissions and committees, often having some nongovernmental representatives as well as state officials, were created in St. Petersburg and Moscow by imperial order in an attempt to improve the administration of the two capitals, mainly in regard to fiscal matters. In at least two instances in Moscow, the newly created committees themselves gradually became the real governing force and functioned for some time as the actual administration of the city: the Committee for Equalization of Municipal Obligations, established in 1802, and the

Committee for Organization of Revenues and Expenditures, set up in 1820.[1] At other times the main responsibilities of city government were in the hands of the police and treasury agents of the central government.

The Special Municipal Statutes of 1846 and 1862

It was against this background of unsatisfactory municipal administration that a limited self-government act was issued for St. Petersburg on February 13, 1846, in an attempt to end the increasing disorder and bureaucratic stagnation in municipal affairs. Moscow's turn would come in 1862.

Similarities between the main features of the 1846 law and the essentially inoperative Charter Granted to the Cities in 1785 are many. There can be no doubt the earlier legislation was parent to the later. That the institutions established in 1846 (and in Moscow in 1862) proved more viable than those of 1785 may be ascribed to greater need for them in the mid-nineteenth century and to the somewhat increased readiness of various segments of urban society to take part in city government.

The decrees of 1785 and 1846 both attempted to regulate the structure and functioning of various urban estates, or class organizations, as well as to establish a system of general municipal administration. The latter was rather closely linked by the two laws to the system of class administration.

Both decrees provided for a very large municipal council, the general duma, that would meet only occasionally (between 1846 and 1860 the general duma of St. Petersburg assembled only seventeen times) and for a much smaller, permanently functioning executive duma (six elected members in 1785 and twelve in 1846). The general duma was to make broad policy; the executive duma was to implement those decisions and supervise the day-to-day work of city government. Presiding over both municipal bodies was the mayor, who was chosen by the tsar from the two candidates nominated by the general duma.

In 1846, as in 1785, the municipal electorate and the general

The Nineteenth-Century City

duma were divided into sections along socioeconomic lines. Furthermore, the elected members of the executive duma were chosen by the sections of the general duma. Thus, the sections, or curiae, were an important aspect of municipal government. There were some differences in these electoral and duma groupings under the two laws. Catherine's statute had created a curia entitled "actual city residents" which lumped together all owners of urban real estate whatever their social class or occupation. That statute had also given scholars, writers, sculptors, architects, and composers the right to participate in municipal government even if they owned no real estate; they were grouped together as "eminent citizens" in another curia. Nicholas I's decree called for five sections, one less than in 1785, and organized these more closely along legally defined class lines: 1) hereditary nobles possessing real estate in St. Petersburg; 2) property owners who were personal nobles, honored citizens (a special social category established by imperial decree in 1832), or declassed persons (*raznochintsy*); 3) guild merchants; 4) persons belonging to the *meshchanstvo* class organization (small entrepreneurs, clerks, and unskilled workers who were inscribed as permanent city residents); and 5) persons listed as members of the society of artisans. The increasingly large number of peasants who spent much or all of the year working in St. Petersburg but owned no property there and were not registered as members of an urban class organization had no electoral rights. This had been true also under the Charter of 1785.

Within the five curiae defined by the law of 1846 the right to participate directly in municipal elections was limited to males over twenty-one whose income equaled at least 100 silver rubles a year. Women who met the qualifications regarding age, real estate holdings, or income could not take part in elections but were allowed to give their voting rights to a male related by blood or marriage. The various limitations upon the franchise meant that the qualified electorate of St. Petersburg numbered just over 6,000 in 1846, not even 2 percent of the city's population.

The electoral assembly of each section had the right to elect at least 100 and no more than 150 representatives to the general duma. The statute provided that during deliberations in the general duma each section might function as a virtually separate assembly, interacting with the other four sections only when the matters under consideration definitely concerned municipal society in its entirety.

The rights and sphere of authority granted St. Petersburg's city government in 1846 appear to differ relatively little from those stated in the Charter of 1785 despite the growing complexity of the tasks facing municipal administration in the mid-nineteenth century. The fledgling city government was placed under the direct and close supervision of the various local and imperial representatives of tsarist authority.

Clearly, the term "conservative" is appropriate in any evaluation today of the 1846 statute. Yet the tsarist official who played a major role in drafting the legislation, N. A. Miliutin, was at that time called a "red" by some people who regarded the new municipal system as ultra-liberal.[2] Despite this interpretation of Miliutin's municipal statute, petitions came to the Ministry of Interior during the 1850s from Moscow, Odessa, and several provincial capitals requesting that a similar system of self-government be extended to them. Apparently even the very limited form of self-government received by St. Petersburg had brought sufficient improvement to stimulate public opinion in other parts of Russia. The general mood of reform that came with the accession to the throne of Alexander II was probably an even greater factor.

In Moscow in the late 1850s a call for increased public participation in city administration was voiced at an assembly of the nobles from that guberniia and was also expressed in the newspapers. October 1859 saw the central government instruct its agencies in Moscow to begin drafting a special statute for that city, using the law of 1846 as a model. Other cities in the empire had to wait for self-government until the general statute of 1870.

The local committee that prepared the initial draft of the act was headed by the liberal-minded governor-general of Moscow, P. A. Tuchkov, and included two other representatives of the state administration, while the remaining four members represented the nobility (two members), the merchants, and other owners of real estate in the city. In addition, leading Moscow public figures participated in the work of the committee on an ex officio basis. This relatively large degree of public representation and participation in compiling the original draft indicates the general movement at that time, both within certain high state circles and among educated persons, against the bureaucratic strangulation of Russian life—a movement that deservedly earned for the 1860s the title "the epoch of the great reforms." The reform spirit also led to a system of self-government for Moscow more liberal in certain ways than that granted St. Petersburg in 1846. A number of corresponding changes were introduced into St. Petersburg local government during the early 1860s.

The Moscow committee's draft of a self-government act was completed in March 1860 and was then sent to St. Petersburg for revision and confirmation by the central bureaucracy and the tsar. This took two more years and more than a year went by after confirmation before the institutions created by the act came into operation. They continued to function until they were replaced early in 1873 by those brought into being by the general municipal statute of 1870.

The close links between urban class organizations and municipal government were continued in the statute of March 20, 1862. Franchise qualifications and governmental structure changed little. The general duma was cut down to a more workable size: 175 councilors. It now met as a common body rather than assembling in separate sections. Elections to the general duma were in two stages: each of the five sections of qualified voters chose an electoral assembly of 100 members who then elected 35 councilors to the general duma. Sections were now represented equally in the 10-member executive duma, whereas under the 1846 law the artisans and *meshchanstvo* had been underrepresented. Also in contrast to the system established earlier for St. Petersburg, the Moscow executive duma did not hold the power of absolute veto over decisions of the general duma, nor was a "representative of the throne" automatically a participant in general duma sessions.

Modernization of Russia's antiquated governmental, social, and economic systems began in earnest under the impact of the empire's defeat in the Crimean War. Emancipation of the serfs in 1861, though it would take years to be implemented fully, meant the existing flow of peasant laborers to urban areas would soon increase sharply for most cities in the empire. Before many more years municipal administrations would have to cope with a growing variety and complexity of urgent social and economic problems resulting from, or intensified by, urbanization. Reorganization of the general system of city government was essential.

On April 26, 1862, Minister of Interior P. A. Valuev, in a circular to guberniia governors throughout the empire, called for the formation of local citizens' committees to advise his ministry on what the public wanted in a general statute on municipal government. Valuev said it was necessary that "society itself take a more thoughtful part in its own affairs because the government cannot permanently carry the burden of care in regard to the needs of the cities, which themselves ought to be taking care of their interests and needs."[3] The minister's statement suggests that an important motive behind the tsarist government's decision to establish municipal self-government for Russia as a whole was the desire to minimize pressure on the state budget. Some Russian students of city self-government asserted this was the sole motive.[4] Certainly many policies adopted by the tsarist authorities toward Russian cities in the years following proclamation of the 1870 statute had as their overriding and declared purpose reducing or avoiding the outflow of state funds for urban needs.

The process of working out the new municipal statute dragged on for more than eight years. Under the auspices of the Ministry of Interior, material was collected during 1863-1864 on the history of Russian city administration and on the municipal institutions of the leading western European states. Two volumes of statistics were compiled on economic conditions in the cities of European Russia. The citizens' committees, created in the cities of

European Russia as a result of Valuev's directive, enumerated the characteristics the public wanted to see in municipal government. Reports were forwarded, without bureaucratic editing, to the Ministry of Interior. In the main, these local committees called for an end to interference by the state bureaucracy in purely local matters. The committees felt that cities should have a definite degree of independence in their management of the municipal economy and that central governmental authorities should not have the right of permanent interference in municipal affairs. The committee reports were consulted by the Economic Department of the Ministry of Interior when it began to draft the 1870 act.

A "final" draft emerged from the bureaucratic mill in 1866 and was sent for consideration to the highest tsarist legislative organ, the State Council. Before the draft could be officially approved by the council, Valuev was replaced as Minister of Interior by A. E. Timashev. The State Council now returned the draft to Timashev for further review by his ministry. A revised draft sent to the State Council was again returned to the Ministry of Interior because the reworking of the project had been done almost entirely without the participation of persons having practical experience in municipal affairs. Another preliminary draft was then drawn up and submitted for consideration to a committee of experts—one duma councilor each from Moscow and St. Petersburg and eight municipal mayors. This committee held fourteen sessions and helped work up the final draft of the statute which, after a brief discussion in the State Council and the introduction there of several changes, was finally confirmed by Tsar Alexander II on June 16, 1870.

The successive revisions of the proposed statute during its more than eight years of preparation not only testify to the labyrinthine nature of the tsarist legislative process; they also reflect the decline in the reform movement following the first terrorist attempts on the life of the tsar. Nevertheless, there is general agreement among students of Russian government that the 1870 act, despite its numerous undemocratic features, brought improvement in municipal administration and gave greater rights to the cities than its successor, the empire-wide municipal act of 1892. In many ways, the 1870 law marked the apex of statutory freedom for municipal self-rule in the history of the Russian empire.

The law of 1870 is also noteworthy as the first municipal statute in Russian history that was concerned almost entirely with legislating for the self-government of the city as a whole. The municipal statutes of 1785, 1846, and 1862 had given considerable attention to regulating the structure and functions of urban estates. Urban class organizations did, of course, continue to exist, but no longer were they tied so closely to the system of municipal government.

The 1870 municipal statute was initially applied in 423 cities, mainly in European Russia. In general, with the exception of the three Baltic guberniias (Livland, Estland, and Kurland), where the tsarist municipal statute was applied with modifications in 1877, the ethnically non-Russian borderlands and Siberia remained outside the act's provisions. Even where applied in European Russia, it was not put into effect in all cities. The determination of which cities were to receive the statute often seems to have been arbitrary. More than half of the 423 cities in which the statute was operative had populations of 5,000 or less. Regulations for the structure and functioning of municipal administration in most of the cities in which the 1870 act was not applied were based heavily on Catherine's Charter of 1785 and its later revisions.[5] Very probably, many of these provisions continued to be inoperative, as in earlier decades.

The public reaction to the new municipal statute seems generally to have been favorable. M. P. Shchepkin, who was both an active participant in and a student of Moscow city government from the 1850s to 1908, explained the initially positive response in his city by saying, "Moscow had never before this time seen anything better, anything with broader public rights, and it is not surprising that she received this 'species' [of municipal government] with satisfaction and gratitude, for she was not yet aware with much exactness or certainty of what constituted the essence of the self-government to which she was entitled." Despite his general dislike of this statute, as well as of other tsarist municipal acts, because of their undemocratic features and their restrictions on the full freedom of municipal government, Shchepkin noted that the friendly public reception given the 1870 law and the new governmental structure it established had some basis in fact: "Here was the first plan in which general rules provided relative limitations on the interference of the central government and its local authorities in the internal economic affairs of the cities."[6]

The Structure of City Government
under the 1870 Statute

As under earlier statutes, there were two major organs of municipal government: a large policy-making assembly, now called simply the duma, and a considerably smaller administrative board, known as the *uprava*. The latter was elected by the duma as was the mayor, who presided over both bodies. The duma was free to go outside its own membership to fill these posts. Size of the duma was fixed at 250 councilors for St. Petersburg, 180 for Moscow, and smaller numbers for other cities. The duma was to meet as a single assembly, not fragmented into sections. In contrast to the situation under earlier municipal statutes, determination of the size of the *uprava* was left to the duma and could be changed without authorization from the state. The regular term of office for duma councilors, *uprava* members, and the mayor was four years. This, too, was a change; previously mayors had served longer terms than the councilors who elected them. Terms of *uprava* members were staggered to give continuity to that executive-administrative organ.

Earlier tsarist legislation had limited the general duma to one or two meetings a year. Under the statute on rural self-government (the *zemstvo* act of January 1, 1864), rural assemblies were permitted only one session annually. These restrictions significantly limited the possibility of councilors' discussing most local problems in any detail. The 1870 statute, however, allowed convocation of a city duma as often each year as the mayor or a specified proportion of duma councilors felt necessary; no regular interval or frequency of meeting was prescribed by law. Many of the larger cities, and perhaps some of the smaller ones also, made frequent use of this new right. During the 1880s and early 1890s in Moscow, for example, the duma usually met at least twice a month and in certain years almost weekly.

In general, the rights and duties of the mayor were defined in the statute in such a way as to create an executive officer with sufficient powers to restrain development within the duma of opposition to the central authorities. For example, no proposal could be discussed in the duma unless the mayor had been notified about it at least three days prior to the session and no councilor could speak in the assembly unless he had informed the mayor of his intention before the meeting opened. The duma itself had no right to override its presiding officer if he denied a councilor the chance to speak. If a mayor or the presiding officer failed to exercise these controls he himself was subject to state punishment.[7]

Though the curial system of elections to the municipal assembly was retained from the preceding statutes, significant changes occurred in defining the franchise and the composition of what was now three curiae. No longer was a person's class affiliation a direct factor. Any male, even a peasant, who during the two years preceding an election owned real estate subject to municipal taxes or who had paid any other city taxes or fees, including those amounting to as little as a ruble or two for a license to set up a stall in a street market, gained the right to vote directly for duma councilors. Minimal voting age was raised to twenty-five. Women meeting these qualifications continued to have the right to designate a related male to exercise their franchise. Even institutions which paid municipal taxes or fees could vote by proxy.

This delineation of the franchise was similar to that used in Prussian city elections, but in Russia, with a less developed commercial and industrial economy, it resulted in a markedly smaller electorate. Interestingly, the proportion of Russian urban population left outside the franchise was lowest in the smaller cities because there many people owned homes; in the larger cities renting of rooms or apartments was more common.

During the preparatory work on the 1870 statute many of the citizens' advisory committees had suggested a broader suffrage. The explanation given in Russia for limiting the municipal franchise in the way just outlined was that only those persons and institutions who paid the cost of maintaining city government should have the right to elect the duma which levied the taxes and fees and spent the city's funds. However, the resulting small and relatively narrow electorate was also in harmony with the increasing reemphasis on the traditional tsarist policy of greatly limiting public participation in governmental affairs.

Division of the qualified electorate into three curiae was done solely on the basis of the fiscal dues the persons and institutions had paid the city. The names of all potential voters were placed on a list in the order of the total amount of monies paid into the municipal treasury during the preceding two years. The payments made by all these persons and institutions were then added together and the sum obtained was divided into three equal parts. The qualified electors at or near the top of the list who had jointly paid the highest third of total taxes and fees composed the first curia. Those lower on the list who as a group had paid the second one-third of the total sum constituted the second curia. The remaining persons and institutions on the list, those who had paid the lowest amounts of city taxes and fees, a relatively large group, made up the third curia. In Moscow in 1884, for example, this system resulted in the first curia having 222 qualified electors, the second, 1,360, while the third had 18,310. Since the statute of 1870 provided that each curia would elect one-third of the total number of duma councilors the system clearly gave predominance to the wealthier parts of the population. The electoral system in rural self-government worked toward a similar end. However, in municipal elections the poorer voters at least cast their ballots directly for councilor candidates of their choice; in rural elections peasants could only choose the electors, who then carried out the actual balloting for *zemstvo* councilors.

The City Government's Sphere of Authority
under the 1870 Law

Article 1 of the 1870 statute declared that management of the municipal economy and of the city's external well-being constituted the sphere of activity of municipal government. The act then went on to enumerate the specific functions of municipal government: determining the city's administrative structure within the general system established by the act; managing the economic affairs of city government (for example, levying and collecting taxes, controlling municipal governmental funds, floating loans, issuing contracts and franchises to commercial firms for municipal services) in accordance with the provisions of the statute; organizing the city in accordance with a city plan confirmed by the state authorities (zoning, laying out of streets); managing, on the basis of regulations in the statute, the building and maintenance of streets, squares, sidewalks, bridges, canals, and other public throughways, public parks, water supply and sewage systems, and municipal lighting; ensuring the supply of foodstuffs for the public; establishing markets and bazaars; protecting public health within the limits set forth in the statute and in other tsarist legislation; taking preventive measures, again within the limits outlined in the statute and in other tsarist legislation, against fire and other calamities, and providing for insurance against losses caused by them; aiding in the protection and development of local trade and industry, of stock exchanges, and of credit institutions on the basis of the rules in the April 26, 1883, statute on municipal public banks; establishing, at the expense of the city, charitable institutions and hospitals and managing them on the basis laid down for management of similar institutions under the control of rural self-government; participating, again on the same basis as rural self-government, in the field of public education; establishing theaters, libraries, museums, and similar institutions; presenting to the central government data and petitions on local needs; publishing materials under municipal imprint; and "other obligations laid by law on public government."

An almost universal complaint of writers on tsarist Russian city government was that the 1870 statute restricted the municipalities to an exceedingly small sphere of activity by stating in the opening article that the authority of city government encompassed only the municipal economy and the city's external well-being. Many writers, ignoring the exact wording of the article, went one step further and asserted that it attempted to limit city government solely to responsibility for the municipal economy.

Actually the range of functions permitted a municipal government extended, as can be seen from the enumeration above, beyond the purely economic field. Perhaps even too many responsibilities were placed upon the newly created and largely inexperienced city governments. It was, in fact, the independence of action allowed municipal government that was far too limited. The various qualifying clauses "on the basis of the regulations of the statute," "within the limits set forth in the statute and other tsarist legislation." ("on the same basis as granted rural self-government") usually refer to stultifying restrictions placed on the operational freedom of self-government in regard to matters nominally within its sphere of activity. In practice, tsarist officials frequently did attempt to use these restrictions to limit municipal government to a largely economic role.

But when viewed in the context of the historical development of Russian city government, the statute of 1870 is outstanding, for it clearly stated for the first time that municipal government had some right to operate without the interference of the central government:

> The municipal public government, within the limits of authority granted to it, functions independently [*samostoiatel'no*]. The instances and procedures in which the actions and decisions of this government are subject to the confirmation and supervision of the state authorities are indicated below in [specified] articles . . . .

A Russian journal on municipal affairs later termed these "the golden words" of the 1870 act because they clearly specified the instances of state interference, however numerous, and granted independence in the remaining, even if narrow, sphere.[8]

Within the areas subject to state supervision under the statute of

1870, it was the criterion of legality that the leading provincial representative of the central government, usually the guberniia governor, was to use in judging the permissibility of the actions of a city government. There was only one possible exception to this principle (discussed below), and in no instance could a governor unilaterally invalidate a municipal decree. Establishment of legality as the predominant criterion to be used by the tsarist authorities in evaluating municipal actions was at least as important as "the golden words" in granting city self-government a degree of independence under the 1870 act.

The *zemstvos* found themselves in quite a different situation. The *zemstvo* statute of 1864 provided that a guberniia governor had "the right to stop the carrying out of any decree of zemstvo institutions that is contrary to the laws *or to the general well-being of the state*" (italics mine). Furthermore, suspension of a *zemstvo* decree by a governor could amount practically to nullification of it, for the only appeal was to the First Department of the Senate (the empire's supreme court) in St. Petersburg. This body often took years to resolve cases submitted to it.

Under the municipal statute of 1870 the power of the state could still impinge on the actions and decisions of a city government at many points and in a complex fashion. This can be seen firstly in the structure and role of the guberniia boards on municipal affairs. The 1870 act created such a board for each guberniia and placed it under the chairmanship of the guberniia governor. The board served as a court of first instance in disputes arising between a city government and the state authorities. It also handled controversies between a municipal government on the one hand and rural self-government or class organizations on the other if the guberniia governor had not succeeded in mediating these on his own. Finally, these boards heard cases involving disputes between private parties and a city government and, in certain instances, between the city *uprava* and the mayor or between the *uprava* and the duma.

Since many cases to be decided by this board involved disputes to which the governor himself or other state authorities and agencies were parties, his presiding position on this board gave him great leverage in defending his own and the state's interests in general whenever they conflicted with the rights of local self-government. The composition of these boards varied from place to place in the empire and also depended on the case being heard, but in all instances the state members constituted a majority and the public representatives were a minority. This meant that the central government's representatives on the board, if they voted as a bloc, could ensure decisions favorable to the state. It did not always work out that way, however. For instance, in 1886 fifteen cases came before the board in Moscow guberniia concerning actions of the Moscow city duma; the city's position was upheld in nine cases, including one of the two cases brought against the municipality by the governor himself.[9]

If any of the parties to a case before the guberniia board on municipal affairs was dissatisfied with the board's decision, he could within a six-week period appeal it to the First Department of the Governing Senate for final resolution.

Another avenue of state control over municipal government lay in the requirement that only the governor could place duma decrees into effect. Copies of all municipal decrees had to be forwarded to him by the mayor "without delay." If the governor found no violation of law in the duma decree, he was required by the statute to transmit it to the guberniia's official bulletin for publication, thereby bringing the duma decision into force. After a duma decree had appeared in the guberniia bulletin, it could then be published by the city government in its own journals. On the other hand, if the governor felt that a duma decision was illegal, he turned it over to the guberniia board on municipal affairs for a ruling. In this connection, the statute granted the governor a temporary suspensive veto, for he could hold up, but for no longer than one month, the execution of any duma decision he was transmitting for consideration to the guberniia board on municipal affairs.

In regard to compulsory ordinances, a special category of municipal legislation regulating the behavior of all city residents in matters of health, sanitation, and public order, the governor had only to assert that he found an "obstacle" to the publication of a certain ordinance and he could then transfer the matter to the guberniia board on municipal affairs for its action. This is the one instance under the 1870 act in which the governor apparently could apply a broader and looser criterion than legality in his judgment of a municipal government action. Even here, as just noted, he could not unilaterally abrogate municipal legislation.

Russian municipal governments lacked one power that can be highly useful to local self-governments—the power not to act. In cases in which a municipal government failed to carry out a task whose execution was made obligatory by the 1870 statute and other laws of the empire, the governor reminded the city government that it was remiss. If the municipality nevertheless persisted in its failure to act, the governor could ask the guberniia board on municipal affairs for authorization to carry out the city's obligation at the expense of the municipal treasury.

Another important element in state-city relations was the police. Local police had long been directly under state control in Russia. Nevertheless, not all the citizens' committees which had sent in reports during the preparatory work on the 1870 act were convinced that what is customary is also right. Several of the committees expressed the desire that city self-government have as its enforcing arm not centrally-controlled but public, that is, truly municipal, police. In some instances the committees even called for the police to be elected so that the urban population would be safeguarded from arbitrary rule. Not surprisingly these requests went unanswered. The municipal statute of 1870 left the so-called city police under state control. Municipal governments were required to appropriate substantial sums each year for the financial support of the city police. Yet a municipality could not really rely upon the police to serve as the enforcement arm of city government. This frustrating situation existed similarly for rural self-government. It did much to weaken the authority and decrease the significance of local self-government in tsarist Russia.

A final example of state tutelage over municipal government

under the 1870 act concerns the provision granting municipal governments the right to maintain a certain supervision over the carrying on of trade in the city. In the case of St. Petersburg, Moscow, and Odessa, any instructions from the city duma to the *uprava*, the administrative board, on the way this supervision was to be effected had to be confirmed by no less a state authority than the Minister of Interior in agreement with the Minister of Finance. In other cities, such confirmation had to be obtained from the guberniia governor in agreement with the top state treasury official of the guberniia.

Perhaps the most balanced evaluation of the historical role played by the 1870 form of city government in the development of Russian municipal life through the early 1890s was offered early in the twentieth century by G. I. Shreider:

> The municipal public government organized by the municipal statute of 1870—despite the fact that it was persecuted, restricted, and limited—just the same was *self*-government. And this is the reason why, despite all the unfavorable external and internal conditions, in the final analysis it did more than a little, even quite a lot, for the improvement of the conditions of the rapidly developing urban life, for the satisfaction of varied needs and interests.[10]

Turning Back: The Municipal Statute of 1892

By the latter part of the 1870s dissatisfaction with the recently established system of municipal government was being expressed in the cities themselves and by state authorities, though for different reasons. Municipal spokesmen were complaining about the burden of obligatory expenditures the state imposed upon city government and about the numerous statutory limitations on the powers granted the municipalities. Some elements in the central bureaucracy were, on the other hand, becoming alarmed about what they regarded as chaotic conditions in city elections, especially in the third curia, and about the lack of full state control over municipal administration.

There were also persons in the central government who were

sympathetic to strengthening public self-government. Early in the 1880s certain members of a tsarist commission, headed by State-Secretary M. S. Kakhanov, who had served in 1880-1881 as an assistant minister of interior in the reform-minded government of Loris-Melikov, proposed that municipal suffrage be extended to apartment dwellers paying more than a certain rent. The curia system was to be reorganized, with the first curia being composed of property owners, the second of merchants, and the third of apartment renters. Presumably these changes would also have had one detrimental effect: disenfranchisement of former voters who had qualified only on the basis of paying minimal municipal fees. More clearly positive were the recommendations that the state free the cities of some obligatory expenditures and grant municipal governments the right to have their own police forces. Finally these spokesmen for improved local government urged that tutelage of the central authorities over the municipalities be lessened. All of this was to be part of a general reorganization and continuing reform of local administration, beginning with the peasant village and reaching into administration at the guberniia level.[11]

These proposals failed to become law. The Kakhanov Commission was disbanded in May 1885 with its work still incomplete. Tsarist policy was being pushed determinedly along an ultraconservative, paternalistic path by men such as D. A. Tolstoi, who became Minister of Interior in 1883, K. P. Pobedonostsev, tutor of Alexander III and since 1880 secretary of the Synod of the Russian Orthodox Church, and M. N. Katkov, editor of the newspaper *Moskovskiia vedomosti*. All three men held strong views against public self-government. Counterreforms enacted in 1889 and 1890 introduced state-appointed agents, the so-called land captains, into the countryside to supervise the peasants, abolished the elected office of rural justice of the peace, and weakened the representation and electoral participation of peasants in the selection of councilors for the *zemstvo* assemblies.

In 1892 city government's turn came to experience this Russian "counterreformation." The new tsarist municipal statute of that year, replacing the one of 1870, had been in preparation under the direction of the Ministry of Interior for about two years. The only public participation allowed consisted of solicitation of views about the draft statute from certain mayors, who were not permitted to inform even their closest colleagues in municipal administration about the nature of the proposed law. To a greater degree than in 1870 the new statute of June 11, 1892, treated municipal government as a heavily subordinate, integral component of a unified system of state administration rather than as a slightly separate and parallel governmental unit, in part responsive to local sentiment.

The 1892 municipal statute was applied much more broadly throughout the empire than its predecessor. Altogether, 758 cities came under the provisions of the 1892 law. In general, only the cities of the Polish provinces and the Duchy of Finland were excluded (the former continued to lack self-government and the latter had long been permitted its own system of local self-government). Special provisions were included in the act for cities in the Baltic provinces.

Except for elimination of the *uprava* in 270 smaller cities and transfer of its functions to the mayor, no change was made in the basic municipal structure. However, maximum duma membership in St. Petersburg and Moscow was reduced to 160 councilors; for Odessa and provincial capitals with populations over 100,000 the figure was set at 80. In other cities the size of the duma was even smaller. This was in harmony with the general belief that larger assemblies had proved unwieldy. The new statute also tried to correct another weakness of self-government under the 1870 law: the frequent absences of duma councilors from assembly sessions. A duma member absent without sufficient cause was now, on the first occasion, to be publicly rebuked by the mayor. A second absence was to result in a fine; on the third occasion he was threatened with possible expulsion as well as a fine. Furthermore, if despite these measures a duma failed to achieve a quorum twice in a row when it was to consider reports from the *uprava*, these reports were to be sent on to the guberniia governor for his action just as if they had been approved by the duma. On the other hand the law reveals a certain fear on the part of those who drafted the statute that duma sessions might get too lively; included was a provision stipulating imposition of a fine or incarceration up to a week for violating order during duma meetings. Similar regulations were decreed for *zemstvo* assemblies.

In the 1892 act the number of persons to be elected to the municipal administrative board, the *uprava*, was related specifically to the size of a city's population. Until then it had been left entirely to each duma to determine. And now elections of board members required confirmation by state authorities. If a duma failed in two consecutive elections for the same *uprava* post to choose someone satisfactory to the designated officials, the state administration gained the right to fill the position by appointment. Even board members who came to office through election were considered as being in state service. The same held true for mayors, assistant mayors, and municipal secretaries. Only the latter post had been attached to the state bureaucracy by the preceding law and then only in major cities and provincial capitals.

In 1892 city government lost part of its freedom to decide how often the duma needed to meet. Under the new law the municipal assembly had to hold at least four and no more than twenty-four sessions a year. Also, in contrast to the earlier statute, no provision was made for a group of councilors to petition that the duma be convoked.

The functions allotted city government remained practically the same as before except that no specific statement appeared in the statute about the right to present petitions to the central government concerning local needs. Added to the statutory provisions were lengthy enumerations of specific municipal actions requiring confirmation by the guberniia governor or the Minister of Interior. These articles, along with others spelling out in greater detail than in 1870 the tutelage of the central authorities over the municipalities, contributed to the 1892 statute being half-again as long as its predecessor.

The two most important changes introduced in 1892, and to Russian proponents of self-government the two most unwelcome ones, concerned the franchise and the basis on which the state authorities could abrogate enactments of a municipal government.

Jews were completely barred from participating in elections, nor could they be voted into any municipal office. In "areas of permanent Jewish settlement" (the euphemism for the Pale), Jews might be appointed as duma councilors by the successor to the guberniia board on municipal affairs (reorganized in 1890 as the guberniia board on zemstvo and municipal affairs) but even there they could not exceed 10 percent of duma membership.

The fiscal basis for suffrage was raised substantially. No longer would just any piece of real estate subject to city taxes bestow upon its owner the right to vote. Now it had to be property of relatively high value; in St. Petersburg and Moscow the minimum was set at 3,000 rubles. Similarly, payment of a ruble or two in city license fees no longer conveyed electoral privileges; now only license fees levied upon large commercial and industrial enterprises sufficed. The imposition of these increased fiscal requirements led to a precipitous drop in the number of qualified voters, especially in large and middle-sized cities. Even a reduction in the residency requirement to one year did little to offset the impact of the new standards. In 1893 there were only about 6,000 persons and institutions in Moscow who met the electoral qualifications, a decline of almost 75 percent from the figure just before implementation of the 1892 statute, this in a city of approximately 900,000 inhabitants.

The statute brought an end to the curia system.[12] All voters were to cast their ballots in a single electoral assembly. If a city had too many potential voters for them to assemble conveniently in one place, however, then separate territorial districts might be set up, with the voters in each district assembly choosing a number of councilors proportionate to the district's share of the total electorate.

Those who drafted the 1892 law apparently anticipated, and correctly so, that complex procedures stipulated for voting in councilor elections would often make it difficult to fill all duma seats by ballot. The legislators stipulated that when it proved impossible to elect at least two-thirds the number of councilors allotted a duma the Minister of Interior was to bring the number of occupied seats up to that proportion by appointing as councilors persons who had served as elected members of the preceding duma.

Modification of the formula defining the right of state authorities to intervene in municipal affairs takes less space to describe than the electoral changes just noted but its significance was even more detrimental for urban self-rule.[13] The "golden words" of 1870 are not to be found in the 1892 statute and no longer was concern over the legality of a municipal action almost the sole criterion for intervention by the state. In various of its articles the new law gave the guberniia governor and other designated authorities the right to delay implementation and ultimately to nullify municipal decisions and enactments "which do not correspond to the general well-being and needs of the state or [which] clearly violate the interests of the local population." The governor was granted "supervision over the *correctness* and legality of the actions of municipal public administration" (italics mine). Possibilities for state intervention in municipal affairs had been enormously broadened by the addition of a few words and the absence of several others. Only the continuing requirements that any act of interdiction by the governor had to be brought within a certain time before the guberniia board on *zemstvo* and municipal affairs for further consideration kept the gate from being wide open.

To Russian cities which had experienced even the limited self-government established by the 1870 statute, the law of 1892 gave nothing and took away much. The electorate permitted by the 1892 statute was less representative of the total urban population than under any tsarist legislation going all the way back beyond Catherine's Charter Granted to the Cities in 1785. The freedom of decision and action allowed city governments was noticeably more restricted than in 1870. In some ways the 1892 act can be regarded as the crest of the wave of "reaction by decree" that followed the "epoch of great reforms." No subsequent legislation would attempt so blatantly to counter the growing movement in

Russia for public involvement in government at all levels, although Nicholas II might still speak of such aspirations in 1895 as "senseless dreams."

Despite its growing incongruity with the general political development of Russia, especially after the turn of the century, the 1892 statute proved surprisingly long-lived. Even the broad revolutionary upsurge in 1905, which served as catalyst to so many other changes, was insufficient to alter the general statutory framework of municipal government. Numerous proposals for reform were put forward then and during the following years by persons and organizations outside the government and even within the state bureaucracy, especially after the outbreak of World War I. Unfortunately, with the exception of the city of St. Petersburg, which had come under a special statute in 1903, Russian municipalities continued to function under the stifling regulations of the 1892 statute until the February 1917 Revolution brought an end to tsarist rule.

Notes

The basic sources are the municipal statutes themselves. These can be found in the chronologically organized volumes of the complete collection of tsarist Russian laws, *Polnoe sobranie zakonov Rossiiskoi imperii*.

1. G. Iaroslavskii, "Gorodskoe samoupravlenie Moskvy," in *Moskva v eia proshlom i nastoiashchem*, 12 vols. (Moscow, 1910-1912), 12: 21-24.

2. G. A. Dzhanshiev, *Epokha velikh reform*, 10th ed. (St. Petersburg, 1907), p. 541.

3. Quoted by G. I. Shreider, "Gorod i gorodskoe polozhenie 1870 goda," in *Istoriia Rossii v XIX veke*, 9 vols. (St. Petersburg, 1907-1911), 4: 18.

4. Shreider, for example, held this view. See his "Gorodskaia kontr'-reforma 11 iunia 1892 goda," in *Istoriia Rossii v XIX veke*, 5: 184. So did M. P. Shchepkin; see his *Obshchestvennoe samoupravlenie v Moskve: Proekt gorodovogo polozheniia* (Moscow, 1906), pp. xvi-xvii.

5. *Svod zakonov Rossiiskoi imperii* (1876), 2, part 1: 457-64.

6. Shchepkin, p. xvii.

7. *Svod zakonov Rossiiskoi imperii* (1876), 2, part 1: 579.

8. *Gorodskoe delo*, 1909, 16: 834.

9. *Izvestiia Moskovskoi gorodskoi dumy*, 1887, no. 3, part 2: cols. 182-85.

10. Shreider, in "Gorod i gorodskoe polozhenie 1870 goda," p. 26.

11. Shreider, "Gorodskaia kontr'-reforma," pp. 187-88; *Entsiklopedicheskii slovar'*, 43 vols. in 86 parts (St. Petersburg and Leipzig, 1890-1907), 14A (28): 403-04.

12. The curia system was partially reestablished in St. Petersburg in 1903 when a special tsarist statute granted electoral rights to those apartment dwellers in that city who paid a relatively high rent. Two curiae were created along fiscal lines somewhat similar to those of 1870. This special act also extended the number of municipal officeholders whose election or appointment had to be approved by the central government.

13. Shchepkin, p. xx.

URBAN IN-MIGRATION IN
LATE NINETEENTH-CENTURY RUSSIA

Richard H. Rowland

During the nineteenth century, an appreciable amount of migration to urban centers was occurring in Russia. Unfortunately, there are too few data with which to study this crucial factor in urbanization, urban growth, and social change throughout most of nineteenth-century Russia. In 1897, however, the first and only census of the Russian Empire was taken.[1] This census provides place-of-birth data for hundreds of Russian cities and therefore the basis for a fairly detailed study of urban in-migration. Until recently no major study of urban in-migration in late nineteenth-century Russia had been undertaken on the basis of this census.[2] I have recently completed such a study, however, which is presented in summary form in this essay.[3]

My general purpose here is to describe and analyze this urban in-migration.[4] The descriptive section is particularly concerned with the impact of in-migration on urbanization and urban growth, and the characteristics of the urban in-migrants. The analytical section is primarily concerned with the relative attractiveness of various types of urban job opportunities. The major emphasis is on a comparison of the patterns of urban in-migration in late nineteenth-century Russia with generalizations derived elsewhere. In addition, the role of the Russian state in urban in-migration is evaluated.

The major source of data for this study is the 1897 census of the Russian Empire. Although the 1897 census has deficiencies (which is not unusual for the first census taken by an underdeveloped country), it has many favorable attributes and is probably the best source of data on Russian society in the late nineteenth century.[5] Among such attributes is the presentation of a fairly wide range of socioeconomic characteristics; especially crucial for this study is the presentation of a wide array of place-of-birth and work force data.

Particular terms which, for the purposes of this study, require definition include: 1) urban center; 2) urban in-migrant; 3) characteristics of urban in-migrants; and 4) work force categories. Reasons for including the first three terms are obvious. Work force data for urban centers are used to discover the major types of jobs which were attracting migrants to cities. Unfortunately such work force data are not available for migrants per se and no unemployment data are available.

Because detailed definitions of the major terms have been discussed adequately elsewhere,[6] only summary definitions are presented here: 1) Urban center: Any one of the 223 settlements in 1897 Russia that both had a de facto population of 15,000 and over and was defined as an urban center in the census. 2) Urban in-migrant: A resident of a given urban center in 1897 Russia who was born outside the urban center in question but within the boundaries of the empire, including Finland. 3) Characteristics of urban in-migrants: Those that can be obtained for all 223 cities from the 1897 census include: a) sex; b) social class (peasants, nobles, and the petty bourgeoisie); and c) distance of migration, both short and long.[7] Those that can be obtained from a variety of other sources for only a few cities include work force status and age. 4) Work force sectors: These include all self-dependents in agriculture, manufacturing, construction, transportation, trade and credit, institutions and free professions, personal services, nonactive occupations, and the armed forces.

Impact of Urban In-Migration on Urban Growth and Urbanization

Russia had a low level of urbanization at the end of the nineteenth century. In 1897, for example, only 9.9 percent of the population resided in centers defined here as urban. Nevertheless, this level was roughly the same as the world average, and the rate of urbanization and urban growth was somewhat higher than the world average at this time.[8]

Based upon the general experience of other European countries in the nineteenth century and earlier, we may hypothesize that urban in-migration was the dominant factor in this substantial process of urban growth and urbanization. This is because the two other chief mechanisms of urban growth were not substantial. As Kingsley Davis notes, reclassification of settlements from rural to urban status has never been significant, and urban natural increase was very low or even nonexistent in the past, largely because of high urban mortality rates.[9] Urban mortality was also apparently high in late nineteenth-century Russia.[10]

Testing of the above hypothesis through the use of the vital statistics or residual method lends support to its validity. This was done through an investigation of seventy-four centers which comprised 59.0 percent of the 1897 urban population. Data reveal that between 1885 and 1897 absolute net in-migration accounted for nearly four-fifths (78.7 percent) of the growth of these centers.[11] Thus, in-migration was apparently the dominant factor in the substantial urban growth and urbanization in late nineteenth-century Russia. The importance of in-migration to the urbanization process is further corroborated by the 1897 census itself. It reveals that more than half (52.5 percent) of the urban population were in-migrants.

Characteristics of the Urban In-Migrants

Given those characteristics of the urban in-migrants for which data are available, the following hypotheses may be put forth. First, because the vast bulk of the imperial population was comprised of a peasantry which was experiencing considerable poverty, we might expect such a group to dominate the movement to urban centers. Second, because studies elsewhere for a roughly comparable time suggest that the majority of urban in-migrants were females,[12] we might also expect this sex to dominate the movement to cities in Russia. Third, since most migrations occur over short distances,[13] we might also expect that the bulk of the urban in-migrants in Russia were short-distance migrants. Fourth, because most migrations are economically motivated,[14] we might also hypothesize that the majority of the urban in-migrants were in the work force. Finally, because it has been very well documented elsewhere that young adults dominate most migrations,[15] we might again expect such a group to dominate urban in-migration in late nineteenth-century Russia. In short, with respect to available data, I would hypothesize that the majority of the urban in-migrants were peasants, females, short-distance migrants, work force members, and young adults. My investigation supports four of these five hypotheses.

First, as expected, the bulk (57.2 percent) of the migrants to the 223 urban centers were peasants. This suggests that the movement to urban centers was primarily rural-to-urban in nature. This proportion might have been even greater had there not been legal restrictions placed upon peasant migration from the communes. If a peasant wanted to leave a commune permanently he had to fulfill a number of obligations beforehand. As Geroid Robinson points out, such fulfillment was often quite difficult.[16]

The second hypothesis, however, was not supported, although females comprised over 40 percent of the migrants. The sex ratio of the urban in-migrants was 139.6 males per 100 females. A major reason for the rejection of the hypothesis appears to be the fact that males comprised a higher percentage of the total population in Russia than they did in the other European nations upon whose experience the hypothesis was based. For example, according to Adna Weber, in England and Wales in 1891 there were 1,064 females for every 1,000 males.[17] In Russia, the corresponding figure was 1,011 females per 1,000 males. Therefore, it might be assumed that females would potentially comprise a higher share of the urban in-migrants in these other countries than in Russia, partly because males comprised a lower share of their total population. Another reason for males playing a lesser role in urban in-migration in other European countries at this time was the fact that probably a relatively high percentage of them were going to the Americas and not to nearby cities.

The relatively minor role played by females in urban in-migration in Russia was not confined to total urban in-migration. Even among short-distance migrants there were 115.7 males for every 100 females. This tends to refute one of E. G. Ravenstein's "laws of migration," which states that "females appear to predominate among short-journey migrants."[18]

As for short-distance migrants in general, they did, as hypothesized, comprise the bulk (61.4 percent) of the migrants to cities in Russia.

The hypotheses concerning work force status and age were also supported. To test such hypotheses, data other than general census data had to be used because such characteristics were not available in the census for the 223 urban centers. In general, it appears that a substantial majority of the in-migrants were in the work force and that roughly half were young adults, here defined as those in the 20-39 year age cohort.[19]

In summary, data indicate that migration to urban centers in late nineteenth-century Russia generally consisted of young male workers of the peasantry who arrived from nearby rural areas, a pattern which conforms generally to those observed elsewhere.

Analysis

In general, it can be stated that urban in-migration was not the direct product of some governmental policy specifically aimed at stimulating migration to urban centers. Therefore other factors must be sought. To help analyze urban in-migration in late nineteenth-century Russia, I have used the push-pull model.[20] Because, as indicated above, most migrations are economically motivated, we may hypothesize that urban in-migration in late nineteenth-century Russia was due to the push of the lack of job opportunities in rural areas and the pull of the presence of job opportunities in urban areas.

It does appear that such factors were very important in Russia. First, in spite of the emancipation of serfs in 1861, rural Russia was characterized by acute impoverishment and overpopulation in the late nineteenth century.[21] Because the majority of the urban in-migrants were peasants, it seems reasonable to conclude that the movement to urban centers was greatly stimulated by harsh rural conditions. The pull of job opportunities in urban areas was also of considerable importance.[22] Such opportunities occurred in association with the rapid expansion of the Russian economy in the late nineteenth century.

But, as mentioned at the outset, this essay is especially concerned with the relative attractiveness of various types of urban job opportunities. Based on the experience of many countries in the early stages of development, we may hypothesize that urban in-migration in late nineteenth-century Russia would be especially closely related to the personal services sector, which includes domestic service and day labor.[23] Such a relationship is understandable, particularly in light of the fact that the bulk of these jobs require low levels of skill and the bulk of the in-migrants were relatively unskilled peasants. In order to test this hypothesis, individual rank correlations based upon the 223 centers were run between the level of urban in-migration (that is, the percent of an urban center's population comprised by in-migrants) and the percent of an urban center's population comprised by each of the work force sectors listed above. The results revealed that the highest individual relationship was, in fact, between urban in-migration and personal services (.671). In short, from the evidence available it can be inferred that job opportunities in the personal services sector were the prime attractors of migrants to urban centers in late nineteenth-century Russia.

Not unexpectedly, a major part of this relationship involved females migrating towards opportunities in domestic service. In fact, a rank correlation coefficient of .726 existed between the personal services sector and the percentage of an urban center's population comprised by female in-migrants. This strong relationship further buttresses one of the most well-established relationships in migration studies; indeed, Weber suggests that domestic service was, along with marriage, the major attractor of females to cities in the nineteenth century.[24] As for male in-migrants, their strong relationship (.578) with personal services undoubtedly involved day-labor (that is, casual labor or the performance of menial jobs). The urban in-migrant's role as a day laborer is also not unusual for underdeveloped countries; Gerald Breese suggests, in fact, that the migrant is little qualified to do much else.[25]

Because jobs in the personal services sector are low in status, it may be questionable that the migrants were actually attracted by such jobs. It seems likely that many of these migrants moved from rural areas to cities out of desperation and took jobs in the personal services sector simply because they were not qualified to do much else or could not find other work. On the other hand, it is also probable that many of these low-skilled migrants perceived jobs in the personal services as preferable to life in the rural areas.

Regardless of the actual motive, the high relationship between personal services and urban in-migration suggests that urban in-migration in late nineteenth-century Russia was not making considerable progress toward solving the empire's problem of substantial underemployment, because domestic service and day-labor involve considerable underemployment (either sitting idly around the house or drifting around the city performing menial jobs here and there). Once again, the Russian situation is quite similar to that observed elsewhere.[26]

It is interesting to note that a comparatively weak relationship (.104) existed between the level of urban in-migration and the percent of an urban center's population which was in the manufacturing work force. In short, it can be inferred that the urban in-migrants were apparently not strongly attracted by urban manufacturing jobs, despite the fact that Russia was experiencing appreciable industrialization during the 1890s.[27]

Why was there not a stronger relationship between urban in-migration and industrialization? One answer involves definitional problems, in that the manufacturing category included the relatively unattractive and declining handicraft sector.[28] I therefore attempted to eliminate handicraft occupations as much as possible.[29] This could be accomplished to a certain extent for 142 urban centers. Subsequently, I ran a rank correlation on the basis of these centers between the level of in-migration and the percent of an urban center's population in the "factory" work force (the manufacturing work force minus the handicrafts work force). A higher relationship resulted (.311). Accordingly, because industrialization was greatly promoted by the tsarist regime, it can also be concluded that the government had an indirect impact on urban in-migration.[30]

Nevertheless, this higher relationship between urban in-migration and manufacturing is still not particularly strong, especially as compared to the relationship involving personal services. Other factors reducing the attractiveness of urban manufacturing apparently included: 1) the long working hours and low wages in manufacturing jobs and the absence of social legislation;[31] 2) the difference in the nature of manufacturing work as compared to farm work and the necessity of making adjustments to this difference;[32] 3) the possibility that jobs for the peasants were not available in sufficient quantity because underemployed urbanites could more quickly take the new factory jobs and because of the considerable capital intensiveness of Russian industry;[33] and 4) the fact that more than half of Russian industry was located in rural areas,[34] which undoubtedly diverted many potential migrants from going towards *urban* factories. Some of these factors are, of course, characteristic of underdeveloped countries in general.

The low relationship between urban in-migration and industrialization reflects the fact that there was a low relationship between urbanization and industrialization in late nineteenth-century Russia (a point which is discussed in a later chapter of this book). The existence of such a low relationship has been questioned by Professor Roger Thiede, and Robert A. Lewis and I have accordingly written a rebuttal to his assertion that a significant relationship existed between urbanization and industrialization in late nineteenth-century Russia.[35] In particular, we believe that his conclusions are based upon questionable data, and that our conclusions are reasonable in light of the data from the 1897 census and the experience of many other countries in the early stages of modernization.

Notes

I would like to thank Dr. Robert A. Lewis, Department of Geography, Columbia University, for his help in the preparation of this essay.

1. Russian Empire, Tsent'ralnyi Statisticheskii Komitet Ministerstva Vnutrennikh Del, *Pervaia vseobshchaia perepis' naseleniia Rossiiskoi Imperii, 1897 g.*, 89 volumes (St. Petersburg, 1899-1904).

2. Urban in-migration based upon the 1897 census has been only briefly touched upon in works devoted to population and/or migration in general. Such works include: J. William Leasure and Robert A. Lewis, "Internal Migration in Russia in the Late Nineteenth Century," *Slavic Review* 27 (September 1968): 375-94; J. William Leasure and Robert A. Lewis, "Internal Migration in the USSR: 1897-1926," *Demography* 4, no. 2 (1967): 479-86; A. G. Rashin, *Naselenie Rossii za 100 Let* (Moscow, 1956), pp. 129-48.

3. Richard H. Rowland, "Urban In-Migration in Late Nineteenth Century Russia," Ph.D. dissertation, Department of Geography, Columbia University, 1971.

4. Unless otherwise indicated, "Russia" or the "Russian Empire" in this study refers to the eighty-nine gubernii of late nineteenth-century Russia; Finland and the vassal states of Khiva and Bukhara are not included. A guberniia was the major first-order political unit in the Russian Empire. Some of the eighty-nine units were called *oblasti*, but because they were few in number the term guberniia is used here for the sake of convenience. Gubernii were in turn subdivided into units generally called *uezdy*. Thus, guberniia and *uezd* are somewhat analogous to state and county in the United States.

5. Rowland, pp. 48-52.

6. Ibid., pp. 59-110.

7. Short- and long-distance migration here correspond to distance category 1 in Rowland, pp. 88-90.

8. For a detailed discussion of these comparisons, see Rowland, pp. 111-15.

9. Kingsley Davis, "The Urbanization of the Human Population," *Scientific American* 213 (September 1965) 44-45.

10. Rashin, pp. 232-56.

11. For a detailed discussion of the derivation of this estimate, see Rowland, pp. 116-17.

12. For example, see William F. Petersen, *Population,* 2d ed. (London: Macmillan, 1969), p. 263; Adna F. Weber, *The Growth of Cities in the Nineteenth Century* (New York: Macmillan, 1899), p. 276.

13. Donald J. Bogue, *Principles of Demography* (New York: John Wiley and Sons, 1969), pp. 755-56.

14. E. G. Ravenstein, "The Laws of Migration," *Journal of the Royal Statistical Society* 52 (June 1889): 286; United Nations, Department of Social Affairs, Population

Division, *The Determinants and Consequences of Population Trends* (New York, 1953), p. 132.

15. Weber, pp. 280-81; Petersen, p. 262.

16. Geroid T. Robinson, *Rural Russia under the Old Régime* (New York: Macmillan, 1932), pp. 73, 76, 91-93.

17. Weber, p. 287.

18. Ravenstein, p. 288.

19. For a detailed discussion of the derivation of these estimates, see Rowland, pp. 140-45.

20. For a good discussion of this model, see Bogue, pp. 753-56; Everett S. Lee, "A Theory of Migration," *Demography* 3, no. 1 (1966): 47-57.

21. For an excellent discussion of such conditions in rural Russia, see Robinson, especially chapter 6.

22. See Rowland, pp. 151-57.

23. For example, see Weber, pp. 390-91.

24. Weber, pp. 278, 284.

25. Gerald Breese, *Urbanization in Newly Developing Countries* (Englewood Cliffs, N. J.: Prentice-Hall, 1966), pp. 77-78.

26. For example, see International Labour Office, *Action against Underemployment* (Geneva, 1959), pp. 132-34.

27. Alexander Gerschenkron, "The Rate of Industrial Growth in Russia since 1885," *Journal of Economic History*, Supplement 6 (1947): 146-47.

28. For a discussion of such traits of the handicraft sector, see Peter I. Liashchenko, *History of the National Economy of Russia* (New York: Macmillan, 1949), p. 552; M. Tugan-Baranovskii, *Russkaia fabrika v proshlom i nastoiashchem*, 3d ed., 1 (St. Petersburg, 1907): 496-97, 505.

29. For a detailed discussion of the procedures involved, see Rowland, pp. 185-95.

30. Gerschenkron, pp. 145-50.

31. Ibid., p. 150.

32. Alexander Gerschenkron, "Agrarian Policies and Industrialization, Russia, 1861-1917," in *The Industrial Revolutions and After: Incomes, Population, and Technological Change*, vol. 6, part 2 of *The Cambridge Economic History of Europe*, ed. H. J. Habakkuk and M. Postan (Cambridge, Eng.: Cambridge University Press, 1965), p. 755.

33. A. J. Jaffe, *People, Jobs, and Economic Development* (Glencoe, Ill.: Free Press, 1959), p. 15; Alexander Gerschenkron, "Problems and Patterns of Russian Economic Development," in *The Transformation of Russian Society*, ed. Cyril E. Black (Cambridge, Mass.: Harvard University Press, 1969), pp. 48-49.

34. For example, census data reveal that 60.9 percent of the total manufacturing work force of the empire was in rural areas, that is, areas outside the 223 urban centers under investigation.

35. Robert A. Lewis and Richard H. Rowland, "A Further Investigation of Urbanization and Industrialization in Pre-Revolutionary Russia," *Professional Geographer* 26 (May 1974): 177-82.

INDUSTRY AND URBANIZATION
IN NEW RUSSIA FROM 1860 TO 1910

Roger L. Thiede

The growth of cities is universally associated with industrialization. As T. S. Ashton noted, it is during the period of industrial growth that "there is a conversion of rural into urban communities and a rise of new social classes."[1] In a like manner, E. E. Lampard observed that "the coincident growth of cities, population and non-agricultural employment seems to have been a characteristic feature of all economically advancing societies."[2] Toward the end of the nineteenth century, the Russian Empire entered the "take-off" stage of industrialization. This essay is concerned with the question of how this rapid economic change was manifested in city growth during the last years of the tsarist regime. Specifically, it provides a partial understanding of this complex problem by examining the changes in the growth of cities of New Russia, the southern steppe of European Russia herein defined, from west to east, as the provinces of Kherson, Tavrida, Ekaterinoslav, and the five westernmost districts of the Don Oblast (see Map 1). This region provides an excellent case study, for here occurred not only the most remarkable rates of industrial development, led by the coal, iron, and steel industries, but intensive railroad construction, as well as notable progress in the creation of a productive commercial agricultural economy.

A basic, workable definition of the city is a necessary first step. The official city (*gorod*) of pre-Revolutionary Russia was essentially an administrative settlement with weak rights of self-management, and did not necessarily have basic nonagricultural economic functions. Along with the *gorod* the Russians included among the lists of urban settlements (*gorodskie poseleniia*) places designated as *posady, mestechky, prigoroda* and *slobody*. These terms were not based on any economic criteria; furthermcre, the fact that the numbers and types of these "urban" places varied greatly from year to year and from list to list underscores the arbitrary and imprecise criteria used to designate these settlements as nonagricultural.[3] The inadequacy of the terms city and urban in reflecting nonagricultural economic functions and showing a realistic distinction between city and village was recognized and documented many times by both officials of government agencies and independent scholars. One such example is found in the report of a commission of the Ministry of Interior: "Obviously only the smallest number of them [the urban settlements] possessed to a greater or lesser degree, the necessary conditions of urban life. Another more significant part has a mixed character partially approximating rural settlements. Finally the very largest number of urban settlements have either an exclusively agricultural character or an indefinite character since their inhabitants are limited in their means of subsistence locally and seek it principally elsewhere."[4]

On the other hand, there were many officially designated villages which as early as the middle of the nineteenth century had developed nonagricultural economic functions. With the coming of the railroad, the development of a national market, and the birth of industrialization, the number of this type of settlement increased. Few of these became official cities, partially because St. Petersburg looked unfavorably on such requests (it opposed all forms of self-management no matter how limited), and partially because to the entrepreneurs existence in a legal city meant supplementary taxes with a paucity of added privileges. In the words of one authority. "Thus occurred those well known curiosities of the lack of convergence of the administrative centers with the actual important points of commercial and industrial activities."[5]

Although numerous suggestions were made to modify the mean-

The Nineteenth-Century City

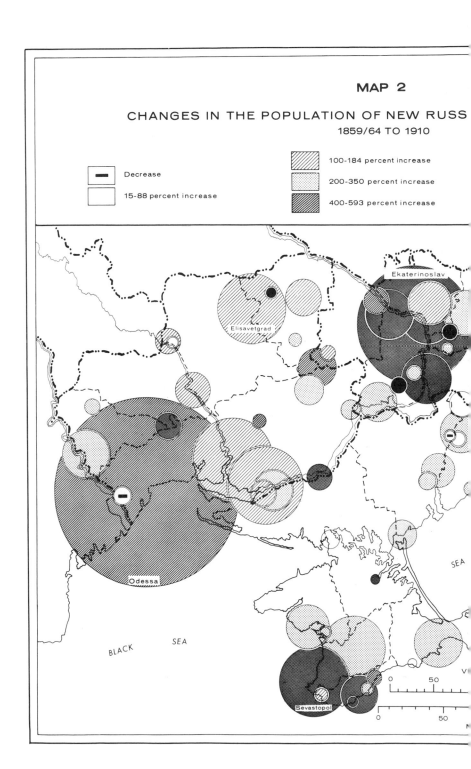

MAP 2

CHANGES IN THE POPULATION OF NEW RUSS

1859/64 TO 1910

Decrease

15-88 percent increase

100-184 percent increase

200-350 percent increase

400-593 percent increase

Ekaterinoslav

Elisavetgrad

Odessa

BLACK   SEA

SEA

Sevastopol

0   50

0   50

V

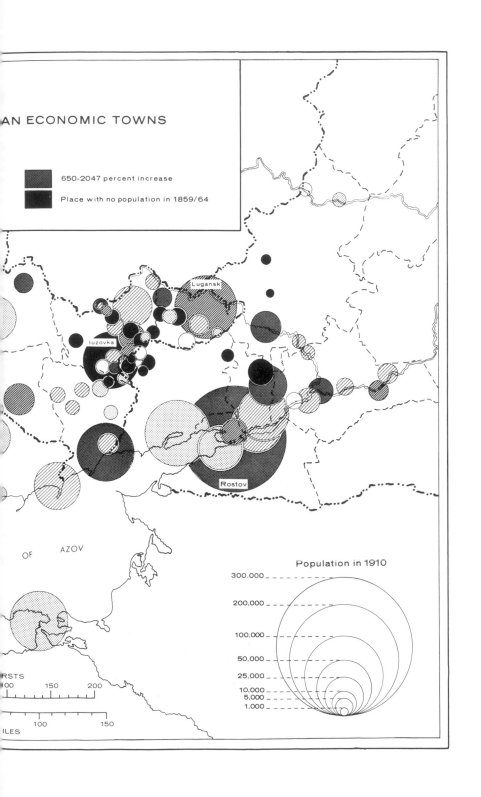

AN ECONOMIC TOWNS

650-2047 percent increase

Place with no population in 1859/64

Lugansk

Iuzovka

Rostov

OF   AZOV

Population in 1910

300,000

200,000

100,000

50,000

25,000

10,000
5,000
1,000

RSTS
100   150   200

100   150
ILES

ings of the terms city and urban, only one study attempted to divide the Russian settlements on the basis of their economic function. This was the work done by V. P. Semenov-Tian-Shanskii and published by the Imperial Geographical Society.[6] Semenov-Tian-Shanskii coined the expression "economic city" to refer to a settlement of at least 1,000 people that had, as of 1900, a per capita commercial and industrial turnover (the sum of the value of all commercial transactions and mining and manufacturing activities divided by the population) of at least 100 rubles. This value represented to him the minimum annual income necessary for the subsistence of the lowest economic classes (domestic servants and day laborers) of a city. Although these criteria are subject to criticism as to the reliability of the data and, more severely, the fact that the per capita index is not a true reflection of per capita income, they seem to me a more realistic reflection of a city's function than any other criteria, including the legal definition. This essay focuses on the growth of these economic cities in New Russia from the late 1850s and early 1860s, a time well before the inception of the industrial revolution, to the early twentieth century.

Classification and Distribution of New Russian Cities

In the first decade of the twentieth century there were 122 populated places that met the requirements of the term economic city. In order to deal more effectively with these cities in terms of function, location, and growth, I have classified them into four categories dependent on the proportion of their total turnover accounted for by trade and industry, on the basis of the data presented by the Ministry of Trade and Industries.[7]

Category I includes those cities where trade comprised all or an overwhelmingly high share (82 to 100 percent) of the economic turnover, with industry, therefore, accounting for only 0 to 18 percent of the turnover. Those settlements in which trade made up between 63 and 80 percent of the total turnover—still predominantly trade centers, but ones with a significant percentage (20 to

37) of the value of the turnover accounted for by industry—were placed in category II. Cities where the value of industrial production exceeded 39 percent (or greater than the mean of 38 percent for all towns of the region) were considered to be industrial settlements. These cities, in turn, were clearly divisible into two groups: category III, industrial/trade cities, in which industry accounted for 39 to 58 percent of the value of the total turnover, and the nearly exclusively industrial cities (category IV) in which the value of industrial production comprised between 67 and 99 percent of the total value of the industrial and commercial activities.

In order to analyze the functional characteristics of the trade cities (categories I and II) and the industrial cities (categories III and IV) within their spatial arrangement more thoroughly and meaningfully, the classification scheme was further subdivided as follows: the trade cities were distributed into five groups according to the means of transportation that, at the turn of the century, gave them access to the broadest hinterland. These five subclasses are: a) seaports: the commercial cities which were engaged in exporting abroad the products of southern Russian agriculture; b) railroad cities: nonseaports within a half day's journey (11 versts or approximately 7.5 miles) of a railroad station; c) cities along the seacoast which did not carry on export trade and were not within a half day's journey of a railroad station but which engaged actively in lighter trade and/or were developing reputations as resort centers along the southern shore of the Crimea; d) river ports: trade cities not fitting any of the three classes above but oriented toward a navigable river with a commercial pier; and e) other trade settlements oriented exclusively to overland, nonrail transport.

The New Russian industrial cities are grouped according to the type of industry which was most evident in each of the settlements. Of the seven categories of industry used by the Ministry of Trade and Industries, two dominated in New Russian cities. These were: a) mining, and industries working the mineral wealth of the region, and b) the processing of the vegetable products of agriculture. Those cities where the majority of the industrial turnover was accounted for by the former category, which in New Russia consisted largely of the mining of coal, iron ore, manganese, limestone, mercury, and salt, the basic ferrous metallurgical industry, the reworking of metals, and the manufacture of agricultural equipment and assorted metal products, are classed as mining and metallurgical cities. These settlements are in turn broken down according to their specific type of mining or metal processing and their location within the region, *viz:* 1) Donbass industrial towns, either predominantly a) metallurgical, or b) coal mining; 2) metallurgical cities of the Dnepr Bend; 3) iron ore mining settlements of Krivoi Rog; 4) metallurgy cities of the Azov coast; and 5) other, which includes settlements of a) salt mining, b) manganese mining, and c) the manufacture of agricultural equipment.

The cities whose industrial structure was predominantly that of processing the agricultural products of New Russia are designated as food processing towns. Two remaining settlements where neither of these two classes comprised a majority of the industrial turnover but where both together were prominent are classed as mixed industrial cities.

Using this classification system for New Russia, the remainder of this study undertakes an analysis of the economic functions of the cities, their spatial distribution, and the growth of their populations according to their functional classification from the middle of the nineteenth century to the early twentieth century.

According to the above classification scheme, sixty-nine (57 percent) of the economic cities of New Russia may be classified as trade towns, leaving fifty-three cities (43 percent) in the industrial category. The largest number of trade settlements, twenty-five, were railroad cities. These were widely distributed throughout New Russia, from Tiraspol in western Kherson Province to Malchevskaia in the Don Oblast; from Simferopol in the Crimea to Lozovaia in northern Ekaterinoslav Province.

Thirteen of the sixteen river ports were located on the Don and Dnepr rivers, while the active seaports of the region consisted of the seven Black Sea cities, led by Odessa, and five ports on the Sea of Azov. With the exception of Azov, the coastal/resort settlements were concentrated on the southern shore of the Crimean peninsula. The nine remaining trade settlements, those oriented to nonrail, overland trade, were widely scattered from western Kherson to eastern Ekaterinoslav Province.

The majority of the industrial cities of New Russia—forty-two—met the qualifications of mining and metallurgical settlements, with the greatest number, thirty, or almost three-quarters, concentrated within the Donets coal basin, forming here with a few trading cities the largest agglomeration of cities in the region. The remaining mining and metallurgical cities were located principally on the northern bend of the Dnepr, in the Krivoi Rog district and near the northern shore of the Sea of Azov.

The eleven remaining industrial settlements (nine food processing and two mixed settlements) were scattered from Nakhichevan in the Don Oblast to Migeia in northwestern Kherson Province and from northern Tavrida (Galbshtadt) to Pavlograd in northern Ekaterinoslav Province.

The Growth of New Russian Cities

The cities of New Russia accounted altogether for 85.8 percent of the value of all trade and industrial activities of the region. More than two-thirds of the total value of this city turnover occurred in the trade towns: 57 percent of the cities by number accounted for 68 percent of the commercial and industrial activities. Looking at the commercial turnover alone, of the 617.2 million rubles of trade transactions (86 percent of the trade turnover for the entire region) almost 85 percent, or 522.4 million rubles, took place in the trade cities, whereas only 94.8 million rubles (15 percent) occurred in the fifty-three industrial cities. On the other hand, the trade cities accounted for a sizable 40.1 percent of the total industrial turnover of the cities. Taking into consideration these two major groups, trade and industrial cities, it appears reasonable to conclude that the former assumed a large proportion of the industrial life of the region, whereas the industrial settlements

Table 1

The Distribution and Growth of the Urban Population of
New Russia, 1859/64 to 1910

	Population (in thousands)			Percent of Total Urban Population			Percent of Increase in Urban Population		
	1859/64	1897	1910	1859/64	1897	1910	1859/64 to 1897	1897 to 1910	1859/64 to 1910
I. Trade cities	475.7	1,346.9	1,842.7	76.8	72.7	68.7	183	37	287
a. Seaports	302.9	920.3	1,283.7	48.9	49.7	47.9	204	39	324
b. Railroad cities	86.8	239.0	279.5	14.0	12.9	10.4	175	17	222
c. River ports	48.9	108.5	152.9	7.9	5.9	5.7	122	41	213
d. Coastal and resort cities	11.9	36.9	62.1	1.9	2.0	2.3	210	41	422
e. Other	25.2	42.2	64.5	4.1	2.3	2.4	67	53	156
II. Industrial cities	143.4	505.9	838.1	23.2	27.3	31.3	253	66	484
a. Mining and metallurgy	80.1	359.8	619.9	12.9	19.4	23.1	349	72	674
b. Food processing	44.5	98.9	136.6	7.2	5.3	5.1	122	36	207
c. Mixed	18.8	47.2	81.6	3.0	2.5	3.0	151	73	334
All cities	619.1	1,852.8	2,680.8	100.0	100.0	100.0	199	45	333

Sources: See note 8.

Table 2

*Distribution of Growth of the Urban Population
by Percent of Turnover Accounted for by Industry*

Category	% Turnover by Industry	No. Cities	Population (in thousands)			Percent Increase		
			1859/64	1897	1910	1859/64-1897	1897-1910	1859/64-1910
I	0-18	47*	137.7	426.6	599.6	209.8	40.5	335.4
II	20-37	23	338.0	920.3	1,243.2	172.2	35.1	267.8
III	39-58	13	91.1	286.0	470.6	213.9	64.5	416.6
IV	67-99	39	54.3	219.9	367.5	320.5	67.1	602.7
Totals		122	619.1	1,852.8	2,680.8	199.3	44.7	333.0

*The number of cities in existence in 1859/64 for which population data are available for each of these four groupings: I - 42, II - 22, III - 12, and IV - 27, for a total of 103 cities.

Sources: see note 8.

were of little significance overall in the commercial activities of New Russia.

Table 1 indicates for the functional classes of the New Russian cities the sum of the population of the individual cities for the years 1859, 1864, 1897, and ca. 1910,[8] the share of each class in the total urban population, and the growth of the urban population by class for the periods 1859/64 to 1897, 1897 to 1910, and 1859/64 to 1910. Map 2 indicates the size of the individual cities for 1910 and indicates the relative growth of the population for each city during the period 1859/64 to 1910.

The urban population even more than the turnover of the commercial and industrial enterprises was concentrated in the trade cities; here in 1897 resided almost 73 percent (1.3 million people) of the urban population compared to the 27.3 percent in the industrial cities. In contrast to the 1859/64 count, however, these proportions represented a decline in the share of the population of the trade cities (from 76.8 percent) and concomitantly an increase (from 23.2 percent) in the percentage of the total population in the industrial cities. In other words the population of the trade cities increased 183 percent during the period from about 1860 to 1897, or at a rate slightly lower than the increase of 199 percent for all the cities, while the number of inhabitants of the industrial cities was 253 percent larger in 1897 than in the early 1860s.

By the end of the first decade of the twentieth century the proportion of the urban population living in trade cities had declined further, to 68.7 percent of the total urban population. That of the industrial cities was approaching a proportion of one-third of the population—31.3 percent. Between 1897 and 1910 the rise of population of the industrial cities continued to increase at an accelerated rate over the growth of the trade cities, with the population of the former in 1910 being 66 percent greater than in 1897, and that of the latter settlements being 37 percent greater, compared to an average increase of 45 percent for all the settlements.

During the last half century of tsarism, New Russian industrial cities grew at a faster rate than the more exclusively trade cities. Table 2 divides the urban population into the four-way classification scheme based on the share of the turnover accounted for by industry. As one can see, for the entire period from 1859/64 to 1910 the population of the cities where industry accounted for 67 percent or more of the commercial/industrial turnover grew at a rate twice the average for the trade cities. Those of category III (percentage of industry 39-58) surpassed the average growth of the trade settlements by nearly half again as much. The population of the first category of trade cities, however, exceeded the growth of that of the second slightly, a condition explained in part by the establishment of railroad station towns and the very rapid growth of such seaports as Sevastopol and Mariupol, whose populations grew approximately tenfold during this period.

Undoubtedly the differential in the growth of the population in these categories is to some degree affected by the fact that categories I and IV contained respectively five and twelve cities in 1897 and 1910 that did not exist in 1859/64. This does not, however, explain the difference in the rates of growth between categories II and III, each of which had only one less settlement in 1859/64 than in 1897 and 1910. Moreover, the variation in the growth of the trade cities and the industrial cities for the period from 1897 to 1910 when the number of towns is held constant and when the rate of growth of the cities of both categories III and IV was almost twice (1.8 times) that of the two categories of trade cities (whose growth rates were almost equal), lends further justification to the conclusion that industrial cities grew faster than trade cities. In New Russia at least, in the fifty years, and particularly the last twelve to thirteen years, prior to World War I, industry played a greater role than trade in the urbanization process. This is most evident in spite of the fact that the method used here actually understates the impact of industrialization on the growth of New Russian cities for it assumes that a city classed as industrial in 1900 could also be so classed in 1860, which is often untrue. One need only be reminded of the low level of industrial activity in New Russia in 1860 to see the weakness of this assumption. Of the seventeen cities with large-scale metallurgical establishments classified as mining and metallurgical cities, only Lugansk (whose government metallurgical works were frequently inoperative) could have been so classified in the 1860s.

Within the two major categories of trade and industrial settlements there was, however, considerable variation not only in the growth rates of individual settlements but also in the size, productive capacity, and types of commerce and industry, as well as in spatial factors promoting the viability of the settlement.

Conclusions

Robert A. Lewis and Richard H. Rowland in their article, "Urbanization in Russia and the U.S.S.R., 1897-1966," arrive at the conclusion that by 1897 the effect of industrialization on urbanization "as a whole was negligible," and industrialization became a significant factor in city growth only toward the end of the period 1897 to 1926.[9] This certainly does not appear to be the case for New Russia, where the industrial economic cities as a group demonstrated a population growth rate considerably higher than that of the trade cities. These findings, of course, do not negate the conclusions of Lewis and Rowland. They do, however, in conjunction with an article by this author which demonstrated for the eleven major economic regions of European Russia a definite positive correlation between the increase in numbers of industrial workers and the growth of economic cities from about 1860 to 1910,[10] suggest that industrialization had a greater impact on city growth than Lewis and Rowland would allow during the latter years of the empire. A more accurate understanding of the relationship between industrial growth and city growth for the entire empire can best be derived through a close examination of the economic cities, province by province, as in the above investigation of New Russia.

1. T. S. Ashton, *The Industrial Revolution, 1760-1839* (London: Oxford University Press, 1962), p. 142.

2. Eric E. Lampard, "The History of Cities in the Economically Advanced Areas," *Economic Development and Cultural Change* 3, part 2 (January 1955): 81.

3. For a more detailed discussion of urban definitions in pre-Revolutionary Russia, see R. L. Thiede, "Town and Function in Tsarist Russia: A Geographical Analysis of Trade and Industry in the Towns of New Russia, 1860-1910," Ph.D. dissertation, Dept. of Geography, University of Washington, 1970, pp. 15-57, 204-32.

4. Russia, Ministerstvo vnutrennykh del, *Materialy otnosiashchesiia do novago obshchestvennago ustroistva v gorodakh imperii* (St. Petersburg, 1877), 1: 188.

5. V. V. Sviatlovskii, *Zhilishchnyi vopros*, 4 (St. Petersburg, 1902): 22.

6. V. P. Semenov-Tian-Shanskii, "Gorod i derevnia v Evropeiskoi Rossii," *Zapiski Imperatorskago Russkago geograficheskago obshchestva po otdeleniiu statistiki* 10, issue 2 (1910).

7. Russia, Ministerstvo torgovli i promyshlennosti, *Torgovlia i promyshlennost' Evropeiskoi Rossii po raionam* (St. Petersburg, n. d.), 8, sect. 2: 2-126; 9, sect. 2: 1-86; 10, sect. 2: 26, 109, 124.

8. Russia, Ministerstvo vnutrennykh del, Tsentral'nyi statisticheskii komitet, *Spisok naselennykh mest po svedeniiam 1859 godu* (St. Petersburg, 1863-1868), 12: 1-64; 13: 1-127; 41 (*1864 godu*): 1-102; 47: 1-154; idem, *Pervaia vseobshchaia perepis' naseleniia rossiiskoi imperii 1897, Gorod i poseleniia v uezdakh imeiushchie 2,000 i bolee zhitelei* (St. Petersburg, 1905), pp. 21-82; idem, *Naseleniia gorodov po perepis' 28-go ianvaria 1897 g.* (St. Petersburg, 1897), pp. 9, 19, 22; idem, *Goroda Rossii v 1910 godu* (St. Petersburg, 1914), pp. 530-33; Semenov-Tian-Shanski, pp. 150-76. The last source was used for the 1897 population of settlements under 2,000 and the 1910 estimated figure for places with fewer than 10,000 persons. The economic cities for which 1910 estimated figures were used represented only 9.3 percent of the total urban figure in 1910 and 11.0 percent in 1897. The effect of using estimated figures on the aggregate differential growth rates of trade and industrial settlements from 1897 to 1910 was negligible since the growth rates of those trade settlements and industrial settlements with estimated 1910 figures were virtually identical: a 23.2 percent increase for trade settlements and a 22.6 percent increase for industrial settlements.

9. Robert A. Lewis and Richard H. Rowland, "Urbanization in Russia and the U.S.S.R.: 1897-1966," *Annals of the Association of American Geographers* 49, no. 4 (December 1969): 791.

10. R. L. Thiede, "Urbanization and Industrialization in Pre-Revolutionary Russia," *Professional Geographer* 25, no. 1 (February 1973): 16-21. In this article I correlate the growth of aggregate regional employment in manufacturing from 1854 to 1908 with the growth of the total population of economic cities by region from ca. 1860 to 1910. This simple linear correlation yielded a correlation coefficient of .79 with r significant at the .01 level.

TRENDS IN PLANNING PRACTICES:
THE BUILDING OF ODESSA, 1794-1917

Frederick W. Skinner

The emergence in the nineteenth century of the great port city of Odessa represents one of the most striking features of Russian urbanization during the late imperial period. Founded by Catherine II in 1794 to promote the development of commerce on the Black Sea, Odessa exhibited one of the fastest growth rates of any Russian city and became within a matter of decades the metropolitan center of the south and one of the great cities of the empire.

In 1800 there were some 7,500 persons residing in the city; by mid-century the figure had increased to more than 100,000, by the end of the century to more than 400,000, and by 1915 to 656,000.[1] Only St. Petersburg, Moscow, and Warsaw contained more people than Odessa by the late nineteenth century. Furthermore, as the major outlet for the produce of a vast and wealthy hinterland, Odessa experienced rapid economic growth in conjunction with the development of agriculture in southern Russia and the rising demand for Russian grain in the markets of western Europe. In 1801-1805 the value of all exports and imports clearing the city's harbor averaged four million silver rubles annually; by 1856-1860 the figure had risen to 35 million, by 1896-1900 to 93 million, and by 1911-1913 to 103 million.[2] Practically all of the wheat and more than half of the other grains Russia exported were funneled through Odessa; only St. Petersburg's harbor cleared a larger volume of goods each year.

The cultural life of the city developed rapidly as well. If only the most rudimentary outlines of culture were in evidence at the beginning of the nineteenth century, by the middle of the century Odessa's schools, libraries, theaters, and museums enabled it to vie easily with Kiev as the leading center of culture and learning in the south. The Richelieu Lyceum, transformed into Novorossiisk University in 1865, and the famed Italian Theater brought special renown to the city. Nor was the city's physical development any less impressive. In 1800, Odessa consisted of little more than the remnants of the Tatar village on which it was sited; forty years later, it had been transformed into a planned city built almost entirely of stone and possessing some of the finest examples of Russian neoclassic architecture outside the capital city itself. The beauty of its buildings, the regularity of its streets and squares, and the magnificence of the site itself prompted admirers to dub the city the "Palmyra of the South" and Russia's "southern beauty." In every major respect, Odessa displayed a vitality in its developmental patterns that renders it a strikingly visible example of the quickening pace of Russian urbanization in the nineteenth century.

Other essays in this collection examine such important aspects of late imperial urban life as municipal government, administration, commerce, industry, population, and political activity. The immediate setting for these and a host of other matters was of course the city itself, existing not as an abstract concept but as a sensible world of streets, houses, parks, trams, sewers, and the multitude of other physical objects and systems that make up what we know as the urban environment. The intention of the present essay is to examine this structural dimension of the Russian city by focusing on the main characteristics of the building of Odessa during the pre-Revolutionary phase of its urban development. While Odessa's development exceeded the level achieved in the majority of Russian cities, it typifies the manner in which the larger urban centers of the empire evolved physically in association with the modernization of Russian society during the last century of tsarist rule.

The State and City Planning

Unlike their counterparts in western Europe and even more so in America, Russian cities developed not through the interaction of socioeconomic and political forces at the local level but according to strictly defined procedures set down by the central government. The body of laws contained in the Building Statute (the earliest entry of which is dated January 27, 1649), the relevant sections of the *Complete Collection of Laws,* and separate town charters represented a digest of official thinking toward urban development and a master blueprint for putting those ideas into practice. No city plan could be altered to the slightest extent without the approval of the tsar and no building could be erected that did not conform in its outward appearance to prescribed features of design and scale. The state's conception of the nature and purpose of city planning was therefore of enormous importance in the shaping of Russia's cities.

Two historically distinct views of city planning prevailed in the period under review. In the eighteenth and early nineteenth centuries, the main goal of the state was to reconstruct the existing cities of Russia and build new ones (primarily in those areas recently absorbed into the empire) in accordance with the rationalistic town planning concepts associated with the Age of Enlightenment. While some attention was devoted to such matters as fire protection, sanitation, and water supply, emphasis was placed almost exclusively on the spatial organization of the major physical components of the city, especially the city center and the main streets leading into it. This concern with external form predominated from the time of Peter I (1682-1725), Russia's first city planner of the modern age, through the reign of Nicholas I (1825-1855).

As the pace of urbanization quickened during the middle decades of the nineteenth century, the goal of city planning shifted from an emphasis on the outward appearance of cities to the more fundamental problem of the condition of life within the community. For the first time, the concept of *blagoustroistvo* (organization of public services and amenities) found its way into planning practices. Interest continued to be shown in the external development of the city but much more attention was now directed toward the modernization of the structure itself through the improvement of water supply, sanitation, street lighting and paving, municipal transportation, and the other systems and services that are essential for the maintenance and indeed the very survival of modern urban life. This shift in emphasis, which formed a part of the post-Crimean War reform of Russian society, characterized the major focus of city planning from the reign of Alexander II (1855-1881) through the remainder of the imperial era.

These two approaches represented different conceptions as to what the city should be and corresponded to different stages in the art of city building. Initially, the city was seen as an object of beauty representing man's ability to organize space according to preconceived notions of design and scale. Concern was therefore shown for the aesthetic quality of the city, the special domain of the architect, sculptor, and landscape gardener. In time, however, it came to be understood that the city made no sense merely as a work of art; if it was to serve secular interests and sustain the human component that gave it life, it needed to function as well. What was required was the development of a supporting infrastructure of public services, and for this to be accomplished it was necessary to draw upon the altogether different talents of the technician. The engineer therefore became the new city planner and through his work ensured a permanent place for the city in the life of the nation.

The history of Odessa's development corresponds very closely to the evolution of planning practices outlined above and illustrates the extent to which the state was largely responsible, either directly or indirectly, for the amount of progress achieved in any given period. The city passed through four distinct stages of development, each marking a major turning point in the relations between state and city. The first two periods corresponded to what may be called the structural approach to city planning, the latter two to the systems approach. In terms of progress, the first and third periods registered the greatest gains because of a generally constructive relationship between state and city, while the second and fourth proved least successful for exactly the opposite reason.

The Establishment of Odessa

During the Russo-Turkish war of 1787-1791, Russian forces scored a minor victory the night of September 13, 1789, when they captured the Turkish fortress of Khadzhibei, located on the Black Sea coast twenty-seven miles northeast of the Dniester River. Five years later, on May 27, 1794, Empress Catherine II issued the following proclamation: "Desiring to extend Russian trade on the Black Sea and recognizing the advantageous position of Khadzhibei and its many attendant uses, we have found it desirable to establish there a naval harbor together with a port for commercial vessels."[3] On the same day, the empress approved the plan for the new city and port that had been drawn up by Franz de Voland, a Dutch engineer who subsequently developed the plans for many of the other new cities in southern Russia. The plan conformed to eighteenth-century town planning concepts by calling for a gridiron pattern of streets and squares, wide boulevards, and open vistas onto the sea, the obvious focal point of the city. Construction was formally begun on August 22, 1794, and in the following year the site was given the new name of Odessa in the belief that the ancient Greek town of Odessos had been located at this spot.

Progress proved slow and uneven during the remaining two years of Catherine's reign and practically ceased during the rule of her successor, Paul I (1796-1801), who displayed an open hostility toward the entire project. With the ascendancy to the throne of Alexander I (1801-1825), however, any uncertainties as to Odessa's future were dispelled once and for all. Alexander took an immediate interest in the city by promulgating a series of decrees in 1801-1802 that granted the city various financial concessions and other privileges. But the measure of greatest importance came in 1803 when the Duc de Richelieu, a lateral descendant of the famous Cardinal de Richelieu of France and a personal friend of the tsar, was appointed governor of the city and region. Richelieu administered Odessa from 1803 to 1814 and in that short space of time achieved truly remarkable results. Upon his arrival, he lamented to Alexander that Odessa was "nothing but a poor village" that could offer him at best only a "ghastly exile."[4] By the time of his departure for France eleven years later, he was able to report that the population of the city and its environs had grown from some 7,500 persons to more than 35,000; the number of houses had increased from 400 to 2,600; schools, churches, a theater, a hospital, and other public buildings had been constructed; street lighting and paving had made their appearance; the port facilities had been greatly improved, and the value of commerce, which totaled one and one-half million paper rubles in 1796 for all of the Black Sea and Sea of Azov ports, had risen to twenty-five million for Odessa alone.[5]

Richelieu rightfully earned Alexander's praises, transmitted following a tour of the southern provinces in 1818: "Odessa has principally attracted my attention. The sight of this beautiful city, whose flourishing state bears witness to an administration so honest, enlightened, and energetic, has increased still further the sentiments of esteem that your lofty career inspires in me."[6]

Fortunately, this progress continued during the governorship of Count Alexander de Langeron, Richelieu's fellow countryman and close friend, whose administration lasted from 1815 to 1822 and brought to a close the first period in Odessa's development. The designation of Odessa as a free port in 1819, a dispensation that remained in force until 1857 with an inestimable effect on the growth of the city, represented the high-water mark of Langeron's administration and the final act that was required to establish this new city firmly on the shores of the Black Sea. In a little less than thirty years, an insignificant Tatar village had been transformed into a major commercial center of the empire. All signs pointed toward a future of great promise and success.

The main problem facing the state during this initial period was to establish the various foundations, physical and otherwise, upon which Odessa could develop, for commerce could advance only to the extent that the city could provide auxiliary support. To create a city *ex nihilo* and endow it with all the attributes of organized community life represented a prodigious undertaking, but the task did not prove impossible in light of the willingness of the state to provide the necessary financial support, matériel, and manpower and the fortunate combination during most of these years of capable leadership at both the national and the local level. The positive role of the state, manifested above all by the special concern shown for the city by Alexander I, ensured a successful outcome to the venture.

The Outward Expansion of the City

On the surface, continued rapid progress seemed very much in evidence during the second period of development, extending from 1823 to 1863 during the governorships of Prince Michael Vorontsov and Count Alexander Stroganov. Odessa's population more than tripled, rising to 119,000 by 1863.[7] The value of commerce increased from an annual average of 6.8 million silver rubles in 1823-1827 to 41.6 million in 1858-1862.[8] Newspapers and periodicals began appearing on a regular basis, new schools and libraries were opened, theaters and churches were constructed, scholarly and professional societies were established. The city more than doubled in size through the incorporation within its limits of several suburbs to the north, west, and south, hundreds of new buildings were constructed, and the port area was improved. Perhaps the most notable and certainly the most visible achievement was the development of Odessa's major architectural landmark, Primorskii Boulevard, laid out in 1826-1841 along the edge of the city overlooking the sea. With its majestic row of buildings designed in the manner of the Italian Renaissance by the architects Boffo, Toricelli, and Mel'nikov and its juncture with the port at the center by a monumental staircase descending to the sea in a cascade of steps and landings, the boulevard represents in its entirety one of the finest examples outside St. Petersburg itself of the type of neoclassic ensemble design that was so masterfully executed during the Nicholaevan era.

But these outward signs of progress, as important as they were in testifying to the continued success of the city, masked a serious imbalance in developmental patterns. The grandiose buildings and public spaces that were constructed during these years were beautiful to behold but they proved of only marginal value in promoting the welfare of the majority of residents or advancing the commercial capabilities of the city. Appearances aside, the development of the supportive infrastructure of public services and amenities proceeded at a very slow pace and in certain respects not at all.

The condition of Odessa's streets, for example, remained deplorable during this entire period. An English traveler wrote in 1849: "The state of the streets, which are not paved, may be imagined by the following caricature, which we once saw when residing in this city: a Frenchman, just arrived from Marseilles, is represented sticking up to his knees in the mud, and exclaiming '*Je me fixe ici*,' and under this was written, 'How to establish oneself at Odessa.' "[9] Despite attempts to pave the streets with local building materials, all efforts failed until the early 1860s when the reformed municipal government took over the matter.

The state of street lighting represented another deficiency. Lighting had been introduced as early as 1811 but continually lagged behind the needs of the community. Most of the lamps that had been installed were concentrated in the central quarters of the city where the wealthy lived and worked; on a street such as Uspenskaia, which extended through a poorer neighborhood to the south of the city center, there was only one lamp for every quarter mile of roadway, while in the suburbs there were practically none at all.

The supply of fresh water to the city posed yet another serious problem that went unattended throughout these years. Until the early 1870s, when a piped water-supply system was finally completed connecting the city with the Dniester River, Odessites were forced to rely upon cisterns for the collection of rainwater, which contributed more to the spread of infectious diseases than to the supply of potable water, and on wells, which were largely in the hands of private speculators who sold the water by the barrel at inflated prices; because of Odessa's free-port status, Pushkin joked that it was cheaper to drink wine than water in the city. As long as Odessa lacked an adequate water-supply system there could of course be no mention of proper sanitation facilities, and as long as the latter were lacking the city's death rate remained abnormally high, in comparison not only to the cities of western Europe but to the other major cities of European Russia.[10] Finally, the condition of Odessa's port, the city's main source of income and the sole reason for its existence, deteriorated steadily during this period due to inadequate governmental funding of developmental projects; by mid-century its dilapidated facilities, shallow waters, and unpaved and unlighted approaches called into question the very survival of commerce in the city.

Clearly, behind the facade of rationally planned streets, stately buildings, and the classical line of Primorskii Boulevard lay a disfunctioning urban environment more reminiscent of the Asiatic village from which Odessa had sprung than the city of European comfort so glowingly described in the guidebooks of the day. The disequilibrium between the traditional values of official society and the manifold needs of the community at large was no more apparent than in the uneven development of Odessa's physical structure during this second period of building in the city.

These disproportions in planning practices stemmed in the first place from the inability or unwillingness of the state to devise new means of dealing with cities undergoing a very rapid rate of expansion. An emphasis on structures rather than on systems was no longer adequate to the task at hand. But beyond this general explanation, the problem of statism associated with the reign of Nicholas I must be cited as a major cause for the difficulties of these years. The emperor's penchant for organization and bureaucratic control affected urban development as much as any other aspect of Russian life; the smallest improvement, whether it concerned the erection of a metal fence around the city park or the extension of a public building by a few yards, consumed an unbelievable amount of paper, talent, and time that, given the pressing needs facing the community, could have been put to much better use.[11] Nicholas's failure to reform the city's municipal government and financial statutes served only to complicate the problem; even if the administrative process had been more flexible, the community still would have lacked the means of resolving problems of development on its own initiative.

None of this is to suggest that Odessa did not progress at all during the Nicholaevan era. But it is to say that, given the restrictive nature of the political system operative at the time, change could only occur within narrowly defined limits and by firmly established procedures, and that progress under such conditions simply was not sufficient to resolve outstanding problems of development in the city. While the ascendancy of Alexander II to the throne in 1855 marked the transition to a new and much more promising period of development, old patterns persisted until the reforms of the 1860s.

The Internal Development of the City

The third period of development, extending from 1863 to 1892 during the tenure of reformed municipal government, registered by far the greatest successes of the pre-Revolutionary era since it was during these years that the state provided the means whereby Odessa could resolve at last the range of problems that had blocked the modernization of its physical structure and jeopardized its commercial position. The reorientation of planning goals discussed at the outset of this essay, the reform of municipal government, and the improvement of municipal finances all contributed to the remarkable achievements of this period.

On the very eve of the reform of municipal government, the governor of Odessa transmitted a dispatch to the Minister of Interior requesting permission to allocate 20,500 rubles from city funds for improvement of roads and bridges in urgent need of repair. The minister authorized the necessary expenditures in his answer of August 31, 1862, but concluded his message on the following note of censure: "Bearing in mind that the afore-mentioned roads and bridges could not suddenly have fallen into disrepair and that the municipal government, which is required by law to look after everything that is to the good of the community, had ample opportunity to learn of the unsatisfactory condition of the aforementioned structures and to take necessary measures to correct them, I consider it my duty to report about this to you and to request that you bring it to the attention of the municipal government."[12] As insignificant as this matter is in and of itself, it points up the liabilities inherent in a system of municipal govern-ment that had remained unchanged for the empire as a whole since Catherine II issued her Charter Granted to the Cities in 1785. Representative of only a fraction of the urban population and lacking any independent authority of their own, the local govern-ing bodies possessed neither the incentive nor the power to carry out the tasks legally set before them.

This situation changed dramatically for the better with the municipal government reform of 1863, introduced in Odessa on the model of the 1846 St. Petersburg statute, and the more liberal Russian-wide reform of 1870. For the first time, all tax-paying residents of the city were brought directly into the governing process, either as electors or as elected officials, and granted primary responsibility for the conduct of community affairs, in-cluding urban development. The effect of the reforms became apparent immediately. Whereas the Odessa municipal council had rarely met prior to 1863, and then only to rubber-stamp directives sent down by higher officials, the newly constituted duma held a total of 178 meetings in the first three years alone and debated proposals covering the entire range of problems facing the city.[13] Nor was this debate simply empty talk, for municipal income rose in direct proportion to the new powers and responsibilities of municipal government. In 1863 city receipts totaled 414,891 rubles; by 1872 they had increased to 993,568, by 1874 to

1,263,560, and by 1893 to 3,373,651.[14] While much of this income flowed out on the expenditure side of the ledger to finance such non-community-related programs as the quartering of government troops, the support of state institutions located in the city, and the maintenance of police forces, over half of all expenditures found their way into the funding of urban development projects and other programs directly related to the welfare of the community. Moreover, the central government invested millions of rubles of its own money in the construction of public buildings and in the development of the port facilities. Altogether, the combination of greater jurisdictional authority at the local level and increased financial resources enabled the city to carry out the most far-reaching urban development program of the pre-Revolutionary era.

These years were marked in the first place by a spate of construction activity in both the private and the public sector that reflected the rising wealth and confidence of the entrepreneurial classes, on the one hand, and the new assertiveness of the municipal government on the other. New residences, banks, credit buildings, trading houses, hotels, stores, grain elevators, flour mills, and the like sprouted like mushrooms all over Odessa, although the finer establishments and those of a nonindustrial nature tended to be concentrated in the central quarters of the city. Of the scores of building projects funded by the city, the most impressive by far was the new opera house, constructed in 1883-1887 at a cost of 1.3 million rubles; designed in the Baroque style by the Viennese architects Fellner and Hellmer, it remains the pride of all Odessites to this day.

Secondly, the city and state joined hands in a massive public works project designed to modernize Odessa's antiquated port facilities. In the early 1860s, the port presented the sad spectacle of silted harbors, rotting wharves, primitive means for loading and unloading cargo, and a complete absence of slips, dockyards, workshops, or even a suitable admiralty. The government had spent a total of some four million rubles on the construction and maintenance of the port during the period 1794-1864, but this

The Nineteenth-Century City

sum clearly had been insufficient to ensure the degree of development required by the continuing growth of commerce in the city. The last construction work had been carried out in 1850 when a third pier was added to one of the two harbors, yet between 1850 and 1861 the number of ships clearing the port increased from 717 to 1,343 while the value of commerce rose from 21 million rubles to over 48 million.[15] Recognizing the need for massive and immediate aid, Alexander II allotted 4.7 million rubles of state money in 1865 for construction and dredging operations, and these monies were augmented by 7 million additional rubles in the 1870s and 1880s. By spending almost three times as much in thirty years as it had during the previous seven decades of Odessa's existence, the government provided the kind of support that was required to ensure the preeminence of its most important port in the south.

Finally and by far of greatest significance, the city at last faced up to the problem of developing the services and amenities upon which its ability to function as a modern municipality and commercial center ultimately depended. Contracts concluded in 1862 with the British firm of Furness and Company and in 1864 with a Russian firm finally rendered Odessa's streets passable in all seasons of the year through the laying of granite-block paving. Within less than twenty years, all of the streets and squares in the central quarters of the city were paved, as were half to three-quarters of those in the suburbs. Street lighting was greatly improved through the negotiation of a contract with a German firm in 1864; by the early 1890s over 2,000 gas lamps had been installed along the streets, and electric lighting had made its appearance in the theater and other public buildings. A contract concluded in 1870 with the Moscow merchant William Schwaben and the British financier John Moore resulted within just three years in the introduction of piped water to the city from the Dniester River, twenty-seven miles to the southwest; by the length of its line, the Odessa Waterworks represented the most extensive water-supply system serving any city in Russia. The availability of a steady and reliable source of water enabled the city to improve its sanitation facilities, and as the latter were developed, Odessa's annual death rate dropped from an average of thirty-three per thousand in the 1870s to twenty per thousand in the 1890s.[16] Finally, municipal transportation was revolutionized with the introduction of the horse-drawn tram in the 1870s and steam- and electric-tram service in the 1890s and later. The extension of tram lines to outlying areas along the coast had the double effect of enabling the city to develop its potential as a resort and health center into a major money-making venture and of promoting significant changes in residential patterns by making it possible for *dacha* owners to reside permanently in the countryside and commute to work by rail. As in most of the cities of Russia, the tram was developed by Belgian concessionaires.

The building program of this period was not without its faults, most notably in the failure of the municipal government to pursue the development of public services and amenities as fully in the suburbs as in the central quarters of the city, its apparent lack of interest in improving the standards of housing available to persons of lower socioeconomic standing, and its practice of extending franchises to foreign entrepreneurs, who often ignored public needs to the satisfaction of their own private interests. Yet in the former two instances the fault was not peculiar to Russia alone, while in the latter case the municipal government had little choice but to turn to foreign expertise in light of the relative technological backwardness of its own country. All in all, the amount of progress achieved in these thirty years was most remarkable when one considers the magnitude of the problems facing the city in practically all aspects of municipal life in the early 1860s. The record provides visible proof of the results that could be obtained when the state granted primary responsibility for urban development to those most directly concerned.

The Relative Decline of the City

Unfortunately, the progress registered during the reform years did not endure during the fourth and final period of development, extending from the "counter-reform" of municipal government in 1892 to the collapse of the tsarist regime in 1917. The changes in state policy initiated late in the reign of Alexander III (1881-1894) and pursued by Nicholas II (1894-1917), coupled with financial stress, rising social discontent, and war, vitally affected the conditions under which Odessa had prospered in the past. This was particularly true in terms of the more or less conciliatory relationship between state and city that had proved so beneficial during the previous period. As a result, urban development slowed down considerably at the same time that new and ever more pressing problems made their presence felt. It was on this note of relative decline in the midst of a growing political crisis in the country at large that the pre-Revolutionary phase of Odessa's development came abruptly to an end in 1917.

The root cause of the difficulties associated with these final years was the promulgation of the new municipal government statute of 1892, which deprived the municipal government of some of its best talent as well as much of its morale by restricting both the franchise and the extent of authority available to local governing bodies. All of the old evils reappeared in Odessa politics—apathy on the part of the community, absenteeism on the part of the elected representatives, and interference in municipal affairs by higher administrative officials. These problems were compounded in 1907-1912 when General Ivan Tolmachev, a member of the reactionary Union of the Russian People and an avowed anti-Semite, ruled the city with an iron grip that all but ruled out any legal opposition to official policies. An observer wrote in 1913, "Nowhere as much as in Odessa can one see so clearly, as if in a prism, all of the rotten fruit produced by governmental disdain for cities, ineffectual municipal government, and administrative arbitrariness."[17] Efforts by responsible persons both in and out of government to reform this system proved of no avail in the few remaining years of tsarist rule.

In addition, municipal finances deteriorated steadily due to a combination of factors at the national and local levels. On the one hand, the new municipal government statute restricted the amount of revenue that cities could obtain from local taxation while it increased the number of "obligatory expenditures" cities were required to make to the state; moreover, credit from state banks became tighter and the central government reduced the amount of its investment in local developmental projects as more pressing national problems began to be felt. On the other hand, Odessa's customs receipts failed to rise as rapidly as in the past due to a slowdown in trade at the port, revenue from property taxes decreased as merchants and industrialists quit the city in the face of economic stagnation and mounting social disorder, and other tax revenues failed to reach the city treasury through the permissive attitude of the municipal government regarding the collection of arrears. In the face of this loss of income, the city found itself forced to increase its expenditures in the social field as the population increased by yet another 150,000 persons, many of whom were unemployed laborers in serious need of food, shelter, and medical care. The inevitable result of these various factors was to produce large deficits in the annual budget, the first to appear in such magnitude in the history of municipal finance in Odessa. During the period 1897-1913, deficits were registered in every year but one, and reached the staggering total of 8,284,240 rubles; they averaged over half a million rubles annually.[18] The regular appearance of such large discrepancies between income and expenditures indicated a financial crisis that only deepened during the following four years of war and revolution.

As in the Nicholaevan era, Odessa once again found itself lacking both the authority and the resources to carry out an adequate urban development program. Progress of course did not cease altogether, but by the early twentieth century the momentum of the reform period clearly had been broken. Practically all of the major construction of new buildings (private, municipal, and state) occurred during the decade 1894-1904, that is, prior to the years of revolutionary upheaval. In terms of municipal construction, the most ambitious project was the new city hospital, built in 1900-1902 at a cost to the city of some two million rubles. Improvements were also carried out on the tramway system through the construction of several new lines and the conversion of a larger part of the system to electrical service, and the waterworks were municipalized and developed further. But even during these years decline was in evidence. In the private sector, new building starts dropped by 61 percent in the period 1901-1905 alone.[19] In the public sector, the inadequate pace of development was confirmed by the Odessa governor in his annual report of 1904: "Although much has been done during the previous year in improving the city, it is unfortunately without question that Odessa still is in need of a great deal for the complete development of its services and amenities and that, at present, this is quite beyond the reach of the municipal government due to insufficient funds."[20]

In the post-1905 period, private construction ceased altogether in certain years as the wealthy merchants and others who previously had invested so heavily in urban development projects continued to flee the city.[21] The municipal government allowed the financially lucrative resorts and health spas on the outskirts of the city to fall into terrible disrepair, it failed to maintain the upkeep of public services and to extend them to the poorer suburbs, and it continued to ignore the need of ameliorating the wretched housing conditions that daily affected the well-being of thousands of persons in the city. Finally, the port facilities were again allowed to deteriorate at the same time that new, more modernized ports, such as Nikolaev, Kherson, and Rostov-on-the-Don, were beginning to draw trade away from the "Russian Marseilles." Local officials repeatedly petitioned the central government for a new developmental program that would provide for the construction of new piers and the modernization of loading and unloading devices, but the necessary funds, variously set at from seventeen to thirty million rubles, were not forthcoming. The outbreak of war in 1914 foreclosed the possibility of rectifying this or any similar problem prior to the collapse of the tsarist regime in 1917.

In the end, this crisis in urban development was overshadowed by the far more serious political crisis besetting the country as a whole. Yet the one could not be divorced from the other. Both stemmed from the same impasse in the relations between state and society that emerged during these final years of the imperial era. Neither could be resolved until those relations were restored to some degree of harmony.

Concluding Remarks

This sketch of Odessa's development in the pre-Revolutionary era, while necessarily brief, lends itself to at least the following observations by way of summary and conclusion.

In the first place, given the dominant position of the state in Russian society, it is clear that the central government played a decisive role in shaping the course of Odessa's development. As a general rule, the level of development possible at any given time depended upon the relations existing between state and city, with the key to success lying in the extent to which the interests of the central government coincided with the needs of the community. The discussion has indicated that a generally positive relationship characterized the first and third periods of development since it was during these years that the state, eager to promote commerce in Odessa, pursued a coordinated program designed to develop not only the port and related facilities but the structural and functional components of the city itself, the assumption being that the success of commerce ultimately depended upon the health of the supporting urban environment; accordingly Odessa enjoyed its greatest success in urban development during these years. The second and fourth periods, on the other hand, were marked by a noticeable deterioration in relations as the state, whether through loss of nerve or lack of imagination, failed to develop new approaches toward urban development that could resolve the range of problems faced by a city undergoing an extremely rapid rate of expansion; consequently the pace of development enjoyed in the previous periods was severely disrupted, to the harm not only of the welfare of the community but of the economic position of Odessa in the empire as a whole. On balance, while Odessa could not have been established without the massive assistance of the state, it would appear that the domineering role of the central government proved more a hindrance than a help in the subsequent development of the city. It was only during the three decades when municipal government had real meaning that the city managed to carry out a rapid modernization program.

Secondly, the main features of Odessa's development can be seen as a function not only of the role of the state but of the values of the ruling elite in the community itself. The aristocracy formed the leading social group in Odessa politics from 1794 to 1863 and its view of the city as a kind of elegant drawing room setting for the acting out of its own importance found eloquent expression in the imposing buildings and planned spaces that were constructed during this period. Enjoying the comforts and conveniences that were the special domain of the privileged classes, the aristocracy failed to devote sufficient attention to the condition of life as it affected most residents of the city. This imbalance in developmental patterns was corrected to a large extent during the era of reformed municipal government, which began in 1863 and saw the bourgeoisie succeed the aristocracy as the dominant element in official society. Taking a special pride in their city and recognizing that what mattered in the end was not static symbols of nobiliary grace but the degree to which the system could work, these practical-minded merchants, businessmen, and professionals set about developing the essential services and amenities that would allow Odessa to function as a modern municipality. As important as this change of attitude was for the further progress of the city, however, the bourgeoisie betrayed its own class origins by concentrating its efforts on the improvement of the central quarters of the city, where it lived and worked, rather than the poorer and more populous suburbs. Only since the Revolution has yet another elite, drawn from various class elements and basing its actions on new social doctrines, attempted to equalize development in all sections of the city. This latest phase of planning in Odessa has produced notable results but has not yet led to the complete eradication of the discrepancies in urban development inherited from the imperial age.

Finally, the record of Odessa's development indicates that substantial progress was made, especially in the second half of the nineteenth century, in modernizing Russia's major urban centers. Although this study has dealt with only one city, the example of Odessa can be applied in all essential respects to the pattern of development in St. Petersburg, Moscow, Kiev, and the other principal cities of the empire. It is true that a number of factors in society at large disrupted the pace of development during the final years of the imperial regime, but the fact remains that by the early twentieth century all of the physical components of the major cities of the empire had been firmly emplaced, so that it was only necessary for succeeding generations to build upon them. Moreover, these cities, Odessa included, were beginning to serve as models for the lesser cities to follow as they pursued their own developmental programs. It was only a matter of time, therefore, before Russia could be expected to place its cities on a general footing with those in the West. To the extent that this has occurred, much of the credit must go to the city planners and builders of the pre-Revolutionary era. Their work forms the core of the Russian city as we know it today.

Notes

1. *Novyi entsiklopedicheskii slovar'*, 29 (Petrograd, 1916): 271, 273.

2. M. L. Harvey, "The Development of Russian Commerce on the Black Sea and Its Significance," Ph.D. dissertation, University of California, 1938, pp. 76, 159.

3. *Pol'noe sobranie zakonov Rossiiskoi imperii, sobranie pervoe* (St. Petersburg, 1830), 23: 514.

4. Duc de Richelieu, "Mémoire sur Odessa, 1813," *Sbornik imperatorskogo Russkogo istoricheskogo obshchestva*, 54 (St. Petersburg, 1886): 334.

5. Ibid., pp. 369-70.

6. Alexander to Richelieu, June 1, 1818, ibid., p. 516.

7. *Novyi entsiklopedicheskii slovar'*, 29: 273.

8. Data for 1823-1827 from Odesskoe gorodskoe obshchestvennoe upravlenie, *Odessa, 1794-1894* (Odessa, 1894), p. 792; for 1858-1862 from A. Skal'kovskii, "Torgovlia, zavodskaia, fabrichnaia i remeslennaia promyshlennost' v Odesse," *Trudy Odesskogo statisticheskogo komiteta*, 1 (Odessa, 1865): 260.

9. J. Murray, *Handbook for Northern Europe, Finland, and Russia*, 2 (London, 1849): 609.

10. In the decade 1851-1860, for example, an average of one out of every twenty-three persons died annually in Odessa in comparison to averages of one out of forty-five for Stuttgart (1850-1859), one out of forty-one for London (1850-1859), one out of thirty-two for Paris (1846-1850), one out of thirty-one for Brussels (1850-1856), and one out of thirty for both St. Petersburg and Moscow (1870s). M. I. Finkel', "Issledovanie o smertnosti v Odesse," *Trudy*, 1: 158; *Entsiklopedicheskii slovar'*, 28 (St. Petersburg, 1900): 314.

11. Tsentral'nyi gosudarstvennyi istoricheskii arkhiv SSSR (hereafter cited as TsGIA-SSSR), f. 1287, op. 29, d. 281 (1844-1845); f. 1287, op. 29, d. 402 (1845). As other examples, local officials in Odessa argued for over a year with bureaucrats in the Ministry of Interior and engineers in the Ministry of Communications and Public Buildings over the simple matter of constructing a cistern to collect rainwater; they argued with the same officials for over ten years concerning the best means of developing a piped water-supply system, and in the end the project was dropped as being impractical. TsGIA-SSSR, f. 1287, op. 29, d. 980 (1849-1850); f. 1287, op. 29, d. 19 (1837-1848).

12. TsGIA-SSSR, f. 1287, op. 29, d. 1288 (1862).

13. *Odessa, 1794-1894*, p. 93.

14. Ibid., pp. 124, 132-33. The revenue increase resulted from the natural rise of customs receipts as trade continued to expand, from increased property tax revenue as property rose in value, and from a variety of new taxes that the city received authorization to levy. A number of large state loans granted specifically for the promotion of urban development programs augmented the figures cited above.

15. P. Beliavskii, "Odesskii port," *Trudy*, 1: 266; Skal'kovskii, pp. 259-60.

16. *Gorodskoe delo*, 1909, no. 12: 610.

17. L. A. Velikhov, "Odesskie vpechatleniia," *Gorodskoe delo*, 1913, no. 1: 161.

18. Data taken from annual budgetary figures in *Obzor Odesskogo gradonachal'stva* for the years 1897-1913 (Odessa, 1898-1914).

19. The number of building permits granted by the municipal government dropped from 566 in 1901 to 346 in 1905. *Zodchii*, 1902, no. 4, p. 48; 1906, no. 9, p. 82.

20. TsGIA-SSSR, f. 1284, op. 194, d. 69 (1904), p. 5.

21. No new buildings were constructed in 1907 and only two were built in 1908. The number of merchants registered in the first two guilds dropped from 956 in 1906 to 639 in 1909. L. A. Velikhov, "Moia poezdka v Odessu," *Gorodskoe delo*, 1910, no. 6: 375-76.

THE SHAPING OF MOSCOW
BY NINETEENTH-CENTURY TRADE

Robert Gohstand

The second half of the nineteenth century, especially after 1861, was a period of rapid growth for Moscow. Between 1846 and 1897 the city's population approximately tripled (to about one million), overwhelmingly through in-migration, while manufacturing and crafts activities similarly expanded. Employment in large-scale industry, already significant at mid-century, rose from about 46,000 in 1853 to nearly 77,000 in 1890. The value of production of large-scale industry increased nearly five-fold.[1] These developments were accompanied by a dramatic expansion of urbanized territory, especially in the industrializing outer districts (Maps 2 and 3).[2] Changing technology also affected the city's appearance, with replacement of wooden structures by buildings of brick or stone, the construction of railroads (especially in the 1860s), and the improvement of public services, such as lighting, paving, and local transport. The period was one of greatly increased personal and social mobility, quickened economic development, and modernization. It is against this background that we must assess the changing geography of trade within the city.

This essay presents a summary picture of the spatial development of Moscow's trading network, of the changing typology of commercial establishments, and of the numbers and character of the trading population in the period from the middle of the nineteenth century to World War I.

The process of change in the geography of trade in Moscow in the late nineteenth century was linked with changes in population distribution, in the morphology of trading establishments, and in the customs and habits of both buyers and sellers. Therefore, before proceeding to the ultimate question of the changes in the distribution of trade and the phases into which this process can be divided, it is proper to survey briefly both the changing typology of trading establishments and some of the changes in the trading population.

Establishments. During the last half of the nineteenth century new types of trading establishments appeared in Moscow, certain traditional ones underwent modernization, while yet others persisted in time-honored forms. The oldest forms of trading establishments still in existence were the related phenomena of the street vendor and the open-air market. Of great antiquity, they survived in viable form into the early twentieth century. At mid-nineteenth century, as shown by Map 4, Moscow had approximately forty-one open-air markets of varying size, with total annual sales of nearly eight million rubles,[3] a sum variously estimated at between 16 and 25 percent of all internal trade. The regular markets, typically held on Sunday, Wednesday, and Friday, were supplemented by occasional fairs, such as the *Gribnoi* (mushroom) and *Verbnyi* (pussy willow) fairs held in the vicinity of the Kremlin. The open-air markets exercised both retail and wholesale functions, and included generalized service markets and those with quite restricted specializations. There was even a "thieves' market" (*Tolkuchii*), dealing mainly in cast-off clothing, in the central Kitai Gorod (see Maps 1, 11). As the century advanced, the markets displayed surprising viability and persistence, fading from the downtown area but flourishing in the outlying districts, with their poorer populations of recent peasant origin.

Street vendors similarly maintained their appeal. They were regulated by municipal licensing, which became stricter after 1889

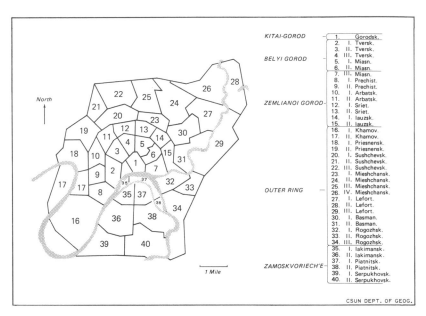

MAP 1   DISTRICTS OF MOSCOW

and tended to keep their number fairly constant at about five thousand in the 1880s and 1890s.[4] This official count was probably low, however, and there were many vendors who operated without license. Street vending was a time-honored method of entry into the ranks of the trading community with minimum investment and red tape. The vendors were popular with the common people and have survived in Russia to this day. In the nineteenth century they sold a wide variety of merchandise, such as fruit, children's toys, fish and meat, cooked food of all kinds, drinks, tobacco, books, sewing notions, ready-to-wear clothing, and services such as shoe polishing and repair and knife-sharpening.

In medieval times the most important open-air market was the one within the Kremlin, located at the focus of land and water transportation routes and under the eye of a state authority which itself engaged in commerce. Evicted from the Kremlin by Ivan the Terrible, the market was relocated on the other side of Red

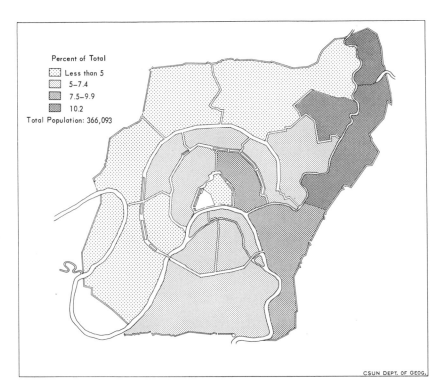

MAP 2   POPULATION, 1846

Square, in Kitai Gorod, the location in which it remained. It rapidly assumed a permanent and durable form, with stalls being converted into enclosed shops, and thus evolved into another characteristic Russian commercial form, one with oriental overtones, the Trade Rows, in which individual passageways concentrated on particular specialties. The rows were divided into three major sections, Upper, Middle, and Lower (the latter being the closest to the Moskva River; see Maps 5 and 11). The Upper Rows increasingly assumed retailing functions, while the others tended to wholesaling specializations. By the beginning of the nineteenth century the passageways between the rows had been roofed over, producing a primitive arcade. This labyrinth in 1846 contained no less than 1,960 establishments[5] and, because of locational advantages and conservative tradition, exerted a powerful influence on

The Shaping of Moscow by Trade   *163*

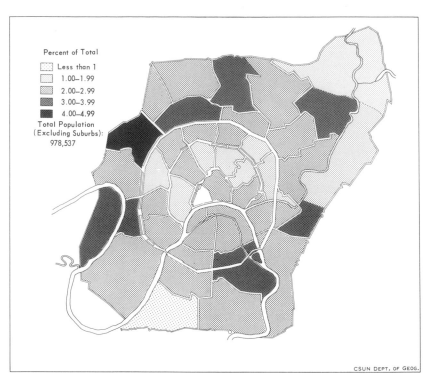

MAP 3   POPULATION, 1897

Moscow's trade, causing the lion's share to be concentrated in the Kitai Gorod until late in the century (Map 5).[6]

The constituent units of the Trade Rows—smallish, unheated, dim shops, open at the front during business hours and shuttered at night—were known as *lavki*. The *lavka* within or outside the Trade Rows, the open-air market, and the street vendor made up the three basic traditional forms of retail trade establishments in Moscow at mid-nineteenth century.

The process of physical modernization of the traditional *lavka* and row forms centered around the development of a newer form of shop, the *magazin*, and the recombination of *magaziny* into a new type of arcade, the *passazh*. It seems clear from contemporary accounts that the *magazin* was a foreign introduction (the word itself, of course, is French), and its appearance is associated with the formation of a new and specialized fashionable shopping district in the western segment of the Belyi Gorod (Map 1), away from Moscow's traditional commercial center in the Kitai. This shopping district had already formed by the late eighteenth century, but received particular impetus after the war of 1812. The *magazin*, which embodied fully enclosed premises, vitrines, heating, and elegant atmosphere, really began to blossom only in the 1840s (although in that decade *lavki* were still eighteen times as numerous) or even somewhat later. In the latter decades of the century the *magazin* increasingly supplanted the traditional *lavka*.

On the most fashionable streets, such as the celebrated Kuznetskii Most, a shortage of display frontage led in turn to a clustering of *magaziny* into *passazhy* or arcades. Superficially, this pattern of evolution is much like the combination of *lavki* into trade rows, but the style of execution and the resulting product were quite different. Where the trade row was cramped, cold, and shabby, the *passazh* was spacious, heated, and elegant. The ultimate victory of *passazh* over trade row was won in the late 1880s, when the by then moldering Upper Trade Rows on Red Square were, at government insistence and against apirited resistance by their occupants, torn down and rebuilt as a *passazh*.[7] The *passazh* may date from as early as the 1840s, but did not appear in any numbers till the late 1860s and the 1870s.

Finally, after the turn of the twentieth century, the department store made its appearance, distinguishable from the *passazh* by its single ownership and arrangement of wares in a unified space rather than through the system of individually leased *magaziny* which made up the *passazh*.

In the last part of the nineteenth century, therefore, the principal building blocks of retailing in Moscow included the traditional *lavka*, the trade row, the open-air market, the street vendor, and the newer *magazin* or *passazh*.[8]

The process of modernization of Moscow's trading establishments and practices was a slow one and would have been slower had it not been for foreign influences, particularly the French and German. This gradualism can be attributed in part to the city's close links with countryside and provincial town, and also in part to the conservative attitudes of its merchants (at least until the late 1880s).

The significance of trade. The role of trade in Moscow's life is difficult to assess in financial terms, due to the scarcity and unreliability of financial data. We must therefore rely primarily on information expressed in terms of population share and proportion of buildings occupied. Even this type of information is spotty and of doubtful reliability for the period before the 1880s.

Based upon available data on the numbers of *kuptsy* (merchants), *meshchanie* (urban bourgeoisie), shop assistants, and establishments of various types, I estimate that in 1846 perhaps 37,000 persons (including dependents) engaged in trade, or roughly 10 to 11 percent of the population.[9] By 1882, for which much more reliable data are available, there were 97,098 persons (including dependents) engaged in trade occupations other than the provision of lodging and prepared food and drink, and another 26,013 in the latter group.[10] Thus the two categories together comprised approximately 16 percent of the population. The percentage showed a slight increase by 1897 but may be considered representative of the relative importance of the trade occupations in the 1880s and 1890s. It is apparent, therefore, that in the late nineteenth century, as compared with the pre-Emancipation era, trade played a more important role (both relatively and absolutely) in the composition of the Moscow work force.

The number of *magaziny* and *lavki* also increased, from about 7,800 in 1846 to 12,650 in 1890,[11] the establishments in the latter year being larger on the average and enjoying considerably higher turnover. Yet the increase in the numbers of establishments did not keep pace with the growth of population. Between 1846 and 1890 the number of *magaziny* and *lavki* increased by some 60 to 65 percent while the population increased by about 145 percent. While some of this lag is explicable by increase in the average size of establishment, the lag also reflects a certain failure on the part of the mercantile community to take commercial advantage

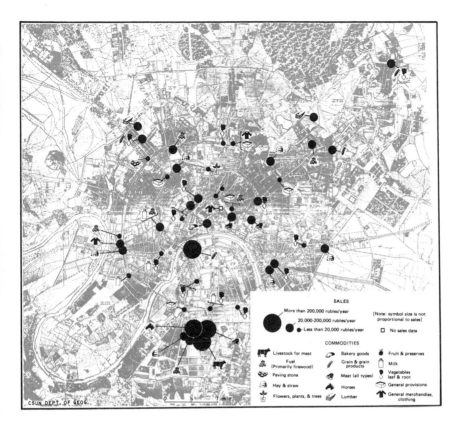

MAP 4   OPEN AIR MARKETS, 1846

of the burgeoning populations of the outer districts, leaving the field to open-air markets and street vendors.

The causes of the increase in the role of trade in the city's economy were multiple, and included the availability of a larger urban market after the Emancipation, as well as much improved systems of transportation and communication. These developments acted to enhance greatly Moscow's importance as a national commercial center.

The relative importance of various branches of trade can be estimated on a variety of bases; for example, upon numbers of establishments, or numbers of people engaged, or financial turnover. The available financial data are so spotty and of such

The Shaping of Moscow by Trade   167

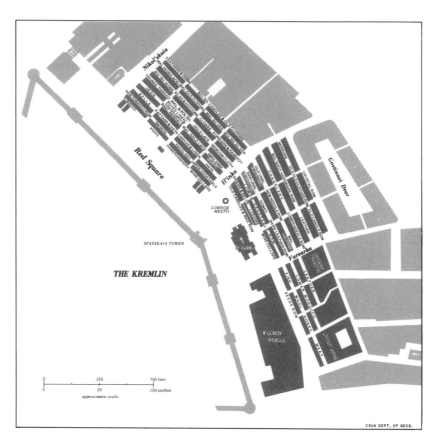

MAP 5   THE MOSCOW TRADE ROWS, 1846

doubtful validity as to be usable only in limited contexts. Our information on numbers of establishments and population engaged is better.

With respect to the specializations of establishments, the data for 1890 are the most readily available. Of Moscow's 12,650 establishments in trade specializations other than the provision of lodging and prepared food and drink, 32.8 percent dealt in various food products and another 6.8 percent sold wine, beer, and spirits. The next largest group was that dealing in textiles and apparel (with a roughly equal division between the two), amounting to 30.1 percent of the total and reflecting Moscow's manufacturing and commercial importance in this field. Other fairly significant categories of trade were: sale of building materials and fuel (4.6 percent); metals and hardware (2.7 percent); crockery, furniture, and housewares (3.0 percent); and trade in used items (3.2 percent). In addition, Moscow boasted 586 establishments providing lodging, and 1,517 offering prepared food and drink.[12]

To summarize the relative importance of branches of trade, using the numbers of persons engaged, I selected the census year 1897. The total self-supporting population of Moscow, including the suburbs, was 718,170. Of these, 100,511, or 14.0 percent, were engaged in some form of trade. Of this group, 20.7 percent were occupied in trade in food products, with another 3.5 percent trading in beverages. Sale of textiles and clothing occupied another 11.8 percent. The provision of lodging and prepared food and drink engaged 20.8 percent. Other important categories were the provision of services relating to bodily cleanliness and hygiene (12.7 percent), roving trade (4.6 percent), general mixed trade (8.2 percent), and trade intermediaries (5.1 percent).[13]

Overall, Moscow's commercial structure, in terms of numbers of establishments and numbers of people engaged, stood upon three legs: trade in food; trade in textiles and clothing; and the broad field of personal services.

The Commercial Pattern

Importance of the center. The central commercial zone, consisting initially of the Kitai Gorod (Gorodskaia district) and later (from the early nineteenth century) of the Kitai business district with the subsidiary fashionable shopping of the Belyi Gorod business district, almost completely dominated the city's trade until after the closing of the old Upper Trade Rows in 1886; even after 1890, Moscow had a commercially powerful downtown. Only a few statistics are necessary to make this clear. A rough estimate for the early 1880s gave the Kitai 45.6 percent of the city's total financial turnover in trade, with the Belyi Gorod claiming another 32 percent. The enormous territory of the Outer Ring (outside the

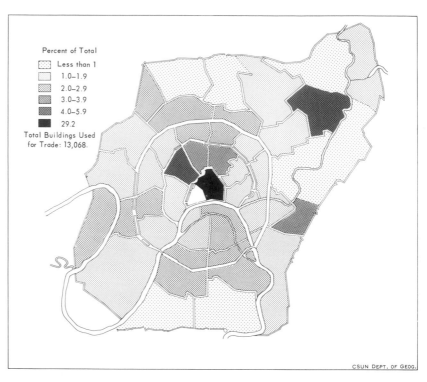

MAP 6   BUILDINGS DEVOTED TO TRADE, 1882

Within the map legend:

Percent of Total
Less than 1
1.0–1.9
2.0–2.9
3.0–3.9
4.0–5.9
29.2
Total Buildings Used
for Trade: 13,068.

outer ring of boulevards and north of the Moskva River), in contrast, had less than 9 percent, and the area south of the river, less than 5 percent.[14] In 1882, 27 percent of the Kitai's population was engaged in trade (excluding the provision of lodging, prepared food and drink, in which the district also played a leading role), as against a city-wide average of 12.9 percent.[15] In 1885, the Kitai alone employed 43.7 percent of all the city's *prikashchiki* (shop assistants and clerks) working in the fields of trade, transportation, and insurance,[16] while in 1882 more than 29 percent of the city's commercial buildings were in the Kitai (Map 6). Again, no less than 67 percent of the district's buildings served a trading purpose (Map 7), a much higher proportion than in any other district.

In categories of trade, the Kitai was particularly strong in the

Percent of Total
Less than 5
5.0–9.9
10.0–14.9
15.0–29.9
67.1

Average for Moscow:
14.6 percent.

CSUN DEPT. OF GEOG.

MAP 7   BUILDINGS DEVOTED TO TRADE, 1882
Percentage of the buildings in each sub-district
devoted to trading purposes

branches of textiles and clothing. The Kitai had 72 percent of the city's dealers in dry goods and 40 percent of those selling clothing (Map 8). When the establishments of the Belyi Gorod's fashion district are included, the strong position of the downtown becomes even more evident. The same dominance is observable in many other categories of trade, especially in luxury goods of all kinds (for an example, see Map 9) and financial operations. Even in that item of universal need—food—the downtown had proportionately more outlets than its share of population (Map 10).

Further evidence of the center's relative importance is found in land values (Map 11). The Kitai and the neighboring fashionable shopping zone of the Belyi Gorod boasted by far the highest land

The Shaping of Moscow by Trade   *171*

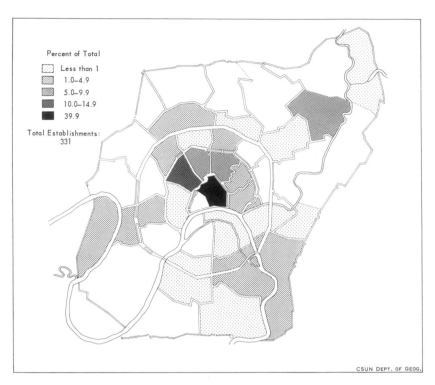

Percent of Total

Less than 1
1.0–4.9
5.0–9.9
10.0–14.9
39.9

Total Establishments:
331

CSUN DEPT. OF GEOG.

MAP 8   ESTABLISHMENTS DEALING IN CLOTHING, 1890
Ready-to-wear, shirts, caps and hats, furs

values. The maxima were in the Kitai and the peak fell along the Il'inka street, the prime financial center.[17]

As the trading network was extended and strengthened in the outer zones, the domination of the downtown began to decline somewhat after 1890, but the center retained its preeminent position.

The maintenance of such a highly centralized structure may be attributed to a number of causes: a solidarity of outlook on the part of the more conservative merchants; an outer city which in many ways resembled a collection of industrializing villages and was populated by people with low buying power; the long-standing convergence of transport routes towards the city center; and taxation practices which discouraged modernization or relocation

The Nineteenth-Century City

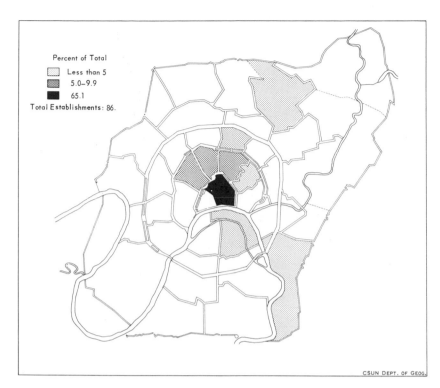

Percent of Total

Less than 5
5.0–9.9
65.1

Total Establishments: 86.

CSUN DEPT. OF GEOG.

**MAP 9   ESTABLISHMENTS DEALING IN GOLD, SILVER,
AND PRECIOUS OBJECTS, 1890**

of establishments (for example, a special tax on heated premises).[18] All these and other factors helped perpetuate a dominant
downtown on the one hand and open-air markets and street
vendors elsewhere in the city. On balance, the growing peripheral
zone remained inadequately served by trade.

The development of the central business district. It is an interesting peculiarity in the geographical development of the Moscow
central business district that it did not develop solely through the
classical method of extension. Instead, twin central business districts with individual characteristics developed in the Kitai Gorod
and the Belyi Gorod. These two nodes did not coalesce into a
single unit until quite late in the nineteenth century, and even

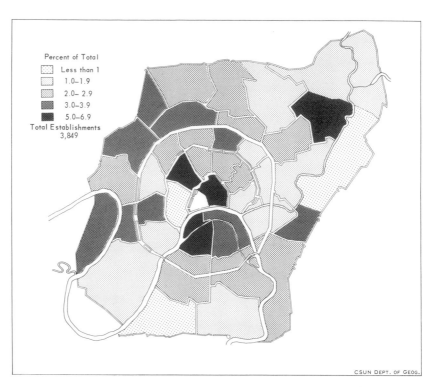

Percent of Total
- Less than 1
- 1.0–1.9
- 2.0–2.9
- 3.0–3.9
- 5.0–6.9

Total Establishments
3,849

CSUN DEPT. OF GEOG.

MAP 10   ESTABLISHMENTS DEALING IN FOOD PRODUCTS, 1890
Excludes grain and livestock in unprocessed form

then, as seen in Map 11, they maintained themselves as the distinct functional subregions commonly seen in most cities' central business districts.

The daytime inhabitants of the Kitai Gorod fostered the trading tradition of this original and most important commercial zone. Their long-standing traditions contributed to a certain reluctance to change the medieval mode or locale of their businesses. That insularity was further strengthened by the wall surrounding them.

Since the early eighteenth century (or somewhat earlier), the upper classes had been moving westward out of the Kitai to estates in Belyi Gorod. By the mid-eighteenth century, foreigners had opened stylish shops in Belyi Gorod to serve this specialized luxury market. The resulting node of fashionable shops formed the Belyi Gorod central business district, whose merchants led the way to such innovations as the *magazin*, the *passazh*, and eventually the department store. By the nineteenth century the zone was more than just another local shopping district; it had taken on the attributes of a rival central business district. Thereafter, in spite of some Kitai tenants' satisfaction with things as they were, a rivalry between the Kitai and the Belyi eventually led to the adoption of the foreign merchandising innovations. (Recall that in 1886 the old Upper Trade Rows were at long last closed and were eventually converted into a *passazh*.) The Kitai managed to retain its overall preeminence, but by the beginning of the twentieth century, when the two central business districts could finally be said to have merged, its functions were tending to greater specialization in finance, offices, and wholesaling, while the most thriving and fashionable retailing was carried on in the Belyi Gorod. This sequence of events bears out the theory that a central business district tends to grow or advance in the direction of upper-class residences while simultaneously abandoning territory elsewhere. The direction of advance in Moscow was westward, towards the estates and cultural and administrative institutions of the Belyi Gorod, while the zone of discard was the old crafts quarter on the southern edge of the Kitai (Map 11).

Evolution of the pattern. We may now proceed to some generalizations concerning the spatial evolution of Moscow's trading network.

It is possible to detect a system in the growth of the network in which, as population increases, its initial centers come to be supported and surrounded by subsidiary centers, the process continuing until a classical market threshold and range hierarchy (consisting of first-, second-, and third-order centers, and so on) is achieved. In the early nineteenth century the Kitai Gorod with its Trade Rows dominated the spatial structure of trading, surrounded by a subordinate system of open-air markets and occasional *lavki* which provided limited local shopping or, in some cases, important specialist markets in such commodities as grain, live-

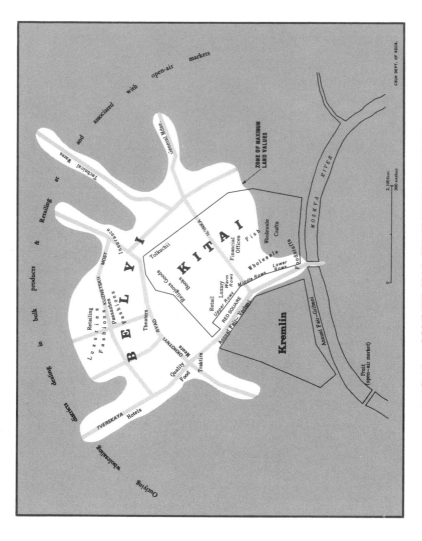

MAP 11   COMMERCIAL SPECIALIZATIONS IN
CENTRAL MOSCOW, 1880s and 1890s

stock, or meat and game. By 1846 it is possible to discern a system of three or four tiers. The Kitai remains the apex. As Map 4 illustrates, the surrounding open-air markets, quite regularly arranged around the system's center, can be classified into three levels of importance: large and middle-sized markets of city-wide or regional significance, which frequently specialized in particular commodities, and the smaller, neighborhood-service markets (much akin to village markets), generally having annual sales of less than 20,000 rubles.

In the second half of the nineteenth century, social and economic changes of national scope had an impact on the geography of Moscow's trade. The emancipation of the serfs triggered a surge in urban population and provided labor for developing industries. Another great change was the introduction of railroads, which entered the city in numbers in the 1860s.[19]

In these circumstances, the process of formation of a more complex commercial hierarchy advanced further, but at a relatively slow pace until the 1880s. By then, the signs of change in the morphology and location of trade were many and unmistakable, but in most parts of the city traditional commercial practices were still observed. The Trade Rows on Red Square were the staunch repository of this tradition, but by the 1880s their deterioration was obvious and their demolition in 1886 had the effect of a sudden reinforcement of existing modernizing tendencies.

From the late 1880s, traditional habits of trade, such as bargaining, sharp practice, enormous markups on small inventory, and so on, declined, surviving principally in the open-air markets, which continued to enjoy a fair degree of prosperity in areas removed from the city center. There was increased application of modern methods of credit and accounting in both mercantile and banking operations. The horse-car network of the period also had at least a limited role in the stimulation of downtown trade.

The Kitai commercial center and the special-purpose fashionable shopping center in the Belyi Gorod, which had evolved in parallel fashion, merged into a modern multifunctional central business district. As the central area modernized, open-air markets receded from downtown but retained considerable significance elsewhere in the city, particularly in districts where the population was made up largely of recent migrants from the countryside. The open-air markets served as locational foci for permanent shops, and there resulted a fairly even distribution of local shopping districts consisting of open-air market cores and surrounding shops. Furthermore, in the years between 1886 and World War I the outer districts acquired more trading establishments. Thus, with increased sophistication of the commercial hierarchy, the influence of the center was somewhat reduced and balanced by the system of neighborhood shopping districts. At the turn of the century, internal circulation was further improved by the long-delayed arrival of an electric tram system, which both eased and widened the range of choice in the journey-to-shop. In the field of wholesaling, the marketing of bulk products, such as grain and lumber, shifted to locations near railroad main lines and stations.

In the center, the importance of arcade shopping increased (the Trading Rows reopened in 1893 as a fashionable arcade), and the old-fashioned *lavka* virtually disappeared in favor of the *magazin*. By 1900, downtown Moscow came to resemble downtowns in other major European or North American cities. The Kitai Gorod displayed increasing emphasis on its financial, office, and wholesaling operations (the former Middle and Lower Rows had been rebuilt as wholesaling and office centers), and decreasing emphasis on retailing, which gradually shifted to the Belyi Gorod and represented an extension of the central business district in the direction of better-class residences, principally to the west and northwest.

To sum up, I have developed a picture in which an initial high-order center (the Kitai), surrounded by country villages, becomes ringed, as population grows, by a subsidiary hierarchy of lesser commercial nodes. These lesser centers are at first the open-air markets, themselves divisible into at least two levels of threshold and range. In the last half of the nineteenth century the original center evolves into a modern central business district, and the subsidiary centers, in many cases maintaining their open-air market components, into local shopping centers.

Implications for Contemporary Moscow

After 1917, a very potent force in the shaping of the downtown— the influence and tastes of people of fashion—was eliminated. Not until recently has there been important reshaping of the relic morphology and locational pattern of trade of the pre-Revolutionary era. State planning decisions have modified the old patterns, but Moscow's retail trade today displays a considerable degree of continuity in locational terms with its nineteenth-century antecedents. A significant alteration of the capitalist location pattern was produced by the government's decision to remove trade from the Kitai (except for the Upper Trade Rows, which in 1953 were restored to retailing as the G.U.M. department store) and to convert the buildings to offices (at least perpetuating the old office functions). The Belyi Gorod central business district, which represented the wave of the future in the nineteenth century, has become *the* central business district. There, retailing continues on the fashionable streets of yesteryear, sometimes housing the same nineteenth-century specializations in the original buildings. Even the magnificent new development of the Kalinin *prospekt*, with large apartment complexes and shops below, represents but a reasonable extension of the nineteenth-century central business district in the same generally westward direction it was pursuing in 1914.

In the outer districts which already existed in the last century, the shopping is still commonly based on the commercial districts of that era and may occupy the same quarters. Elsewhere, retail establishments are typically located in the ground floors of apartment buildings, all too often producing a diffuse retail pattern demanding journeys-to-shop of tedious length.

Maintaining or reverting to what seems to have been a common situation in the last century, peripheral Moscow districts are as yet inadequately served by retail trade, although efforts are being made to correct the deficiency. This situation stems from the rapid pace and high priority of building of living space, repeating the pattern of the post-Emancipation period, when trade did not keep pace with the influx of migrants from the countryside.

Thus, it is clear that explorations of the structure of existing Russian cities should begin with an examination of preexisting patterns, including the commercial patterns of the nineteenth century, the era when the groundwork of the contemporary urban structure was laid.

Notes

1. *Istoriia Moskvy,* vol. 4, B. P. Koz'min and V. K. Iatsunskii, eds. (Moscow, 1954), p. 73.

2. Sources for maps illustrating this essay are as follows:

Base: Figs. 1, 11: Author. Figs. 2, 3, 6-10: Moskovskaia gorodskaia uprava, Statisticheskii otdel, *Statisticheskii atlas goroda Moskvy* (Moscow, 1887, 1890). (Hereafter cited as *Stat. atlas.*) Fig. 4: G. L. Shubert, *Plan stolichnago goroda Moskvy* (St. Petersburg, 1841). Fig. 5: M. Rudol'f, *Ukazatel' mestnosti v Kremle i Kitae Gorode stolichnago goroda Moskvy* (Moscow, 1846).

Data: Figs. 2 and 4: *Otchet Moskovskago Ober-politseimeistera za 1846 god* (Moscow, 1847), p. 69, Table 16. (Hereafter cited as *Otchet.*) Fig. 3: Ministerstvo vnutrennikh del, tsentral'nyi statisticheskii komitet, *Pervaia vseobshchaia perepis' naseleniia Rossiiskoi imperii, 1897 g.,* part 24: *Gorod Moskva* (St. Petersburg, 1901, 1904), computed from Tetrad' 1 (1901), Table 3. (Hereafter cited as *Perepis', 1897.*) Fig. 5: Rudol'f, *Ukazatel',* and K. Nistrem, *Spetsial'noe obozrenie Moskvy,* (Moscow, 1846). Fig. 6: *Stat. atlas,* 1890, Table 4. Fig. 7: Ibid., Plate 12. Figs. 8-10: Moskovskaia gorodskaia uprava, statisticheskoe otdelenie, *Torgovo-promyshlennyia zavedeniia goroda Moskvy v 1885-1890 gg.* (Moscow, 1892), computed from Table 1. (Hereafter cited as *Torgovo-promysh. zavedeniia.*) Fig. 11: Author.

3. *Otchet,* Table 16.

4. Moskovskaia Gorodskaia Duma, *Perepis' Moskvy 1882 goda,* vol. 2: *Naselenie i zaniatiia* (Moscow, 1885), Suppl. Table 18, pp. 309-12 (hereafter cited as *Perepis', 1882*); and *Perepis', 1897,* Tetrad' 2 (1904), Table 20, pp. 162-69.

5. *Otchet,* Table 21. The 1,960 *lavki* in the rows constituted about 27 percent of the city's total.

6. The row names depicted on Map 5 do not invariably reflect the true specialties of 1846, since the names were very durable features. The Gostinnoi Dvor was a traditional wholesaling center.

7. Walter S. Hanchett, "Moscow in the Late Nineteenth Century: A Study in Municipal Self-Government," Ph.D. dissertation, Department of History, University of Chicago, 1964, pp. 310-19; A. S. Razmadze, *Torgovye riady na Krasnoi ploshchadi v Moskve* (Kiev, 1893); I. A. Slonov, *Iz zhizni torgovoi Moskvy (Polveka nazad)* (Moscow, 1914), pp. 120-22.

8. Lack of space unfortunately prevents a discussion of the typology of Moscow's service and specifically wholesale establishments. The wholesaling function was exercised in part by open-air markets and trade rows.

9. Statistics from the mid-nineteenth century are sketchy and unreliable, and this estimate must be treated with caution.

10. *Perepis', 1882*, Suppl. Table 18, pp. 313-16, 337-38.

11. *Otchet*, compiled from pp. 87-98, Tables 15, 20-23, 25; *Torgovo-promysh. zavedeniia*, Table 1.

12. *Torgovo-promysh. zavedeniia*, Table 1.

13. *Perepis', 1897*, Tetrad' 2 (1904), compiled from Table 20, pp. 162-69.

14. *Torgovo-promysh. zavedeniia*, p. 52.

15. *Stat. atlas*, 1887, Plate 21. This statistic does not take into account the substantial numbers of tradesmen who daily entered the district from their residences elsewhere. Were such data available, the Kitai's importance would be even more obvious.

16. *Torgovo-promysh. zavedeniia*, computed from Table 7, pp. 52-57.

17. A more precise delimitation of the central business district is attempted in the author's unpublished Ph.D. dissertation: R. Gohstand, "The Internal Geography of Trade in Moscow from the Mid-nineteenth Century to the First World War," Department of Geography, University of California, Berkeley, 1973.

18. A. Kra--vskii, *Mozhno li v Moskve torgovat' chestno?* (Moscow, 1886).

19. The first railroad into Moscow was the one from St. Petersburg, opened in 1851, but the busiest decades in the development of Moscow's rail connections were the 1860s and 1870s. Iu. G. Saushkin, *Moskva: Geograficheskaia kharakteristika* (Moscow, 1964), pp. 96-98.

THE BREAKDOWN OF URBAN MODERNIZATION: A PRELUDE TO THE REVOLUTIONS OF 1917

Michael F. Hamm

Scholars who have analyzed the collapse of the tsarist order generally have emphasized several contributing factors. Among them are political reaction and the growing demand for fundamental political and social change; rural overpopulation and underproductivity; industrial backwardness and the resulting implications for Russia's military posture in Europe and the Far East; and the aggravation of the nationalities question, particularly in response to the policies of Russification. I believe that an additional problem, the general breakdown of urban modernization, merits equal attention as a factor contributing to the demise of the imperial regime.

Signs indicating the emergence of an "urban question" appeared well before the end of the century. During the reign of Nicholas I, investigators reported crowded conditions in housing. Reginald Zelnik has noted that in the 1860s, disease-ridden St. Petersburg was "the most deadly of all major European cities" and that the decade "saw a general trend in the direction of crowded living conditions, poor sanitation, ill health and disease, petty crime, and depravity among the lower classes of the capital."[1] From the 1860s, cities began to grow rapidly as rural misery, industrialization, and the attraction of job opportunities in the personal services sector elicited substantial in-migration. While the "golden words" of the Municipal Statute of 1870 allowed city leaders to tackle many of the tasks of modernization, the counter-reform of 1892 returned city affairs to the more traditional milieu of strict state tutelage and bureaucratic domination. In general, after 1892 both state and city government neglected the weighty tasks of urban modernization. The quality of life in urban Russia consequently deteriorated. Indifference to the problems of urbanization at a time when cities were beginning to grow rapidly engendered an "urban question," which by the eve of World War I assumed crisis proportions in the view of many city leaders.

The Inadequacies of Municipal Finance

The growth of the urban question can be traced above all to the paucity of funds earmarked for city modernization. At the turn of the century, historian G. I. Shreider described city government as the "bookkeeper and cashier" of the local economy, which was managed by the state.[2] While this assessment is somewhat oversimplified, the state did impose onerous restrictions on the city's ability to raise revenue. For example, the local tax base was limited by the exemption of state property, including railway and church property, from local assessment. In St. Petersburg the value of untaxed property exceeded that of taxable property.

Both state and city government had the right to assess real estate for tax purposes. Assessment was supposed to be made every ten years, but it was often postponed because of opposition from the wealthy property owners who controlled municipal governments. Consequently, while land prices in the central city rose by as much as 500 times their 1905 value during the ensuing decade, anachronistic assessment rates meant that city government did not always benefit fully from this rapid rise in value. Hence on the eve of World War I, city and *zemstvo* expenditures came to only 15 percent of the imperial budget. In contrast, in such highly developed countries as England and Belgium, the sum of local expenditures exceeded that of the national budgets.[3]

The importance of direct taxes, particularly on real estate, declined somewhat during and after the 1890s, while income from city-owned enterprises increased in importance. The fact that the *zemstvo* could tax city real estate and use the revenue to defray expenses that were strictly rural in scope further convinced city governments that higher assessments were unwise. On the other hand, city enterprises could generate income and expedite modernization as well. These enterprises included slaughterhouses, streetcars, pawnshops, bakeries, and printing shops as well as gas, electricity, water, and sewerage. Extension of critical utilities such as water and sewerage remained slow, however, for neither state nor city government showed much zeal in requiring property owners to hook into these systems. Nevertheless, by 1900 the capitals and the cities of southern Russia (led by Odessa) and the Caucasus were expending the greatest energy in developing municipal enterprises, while the crowded cities of the western provinces, where per capita municipal income was the lowest in the empire, lagged well behind in this endeavor.[4]

The Municipal Statute of 1892 compelled city governments to help defray the cost of quartering imperial troops and to subsidize other services for the state. In many cities these obligations consumed a third or more of the city budget, at times absorbing nearly the entire budget. For example, Brest-Litovsk, with a budget of 233,428 rubles in 1911, spent 107,256 rubles for state police salaries and on subsidies for the housing of imperial troops. Dvinsk spent 118,000 rubles for the quartering of troops and only 4,290 rubles for hygiene and sanitation.

In addition, the state failed to provide an adequate supply of cheap, readily available credit, so necessary for urban developmental projects. Large cities were therefore forced to rely on foreign money markets, where borrowing was often costly, while smaller cities were sometimes unable to borrow at all. Between 1908 and 1912, Russia's cities borrowed 261,000,000 rubles, of which 196,000,000 came from foreign markets.[5] While the actual and per capita debt of Russia's larger cities remained low in comparison with major European cities, Moscow city leader N. Astrov estimated that prior to the war, "the average debt of a Russian town amounted to almost twice as much as its annual budget."[6]

The Nineteenth-Century City

In many cases, direct grants from the state did increase in importance as a source of revenue after the turn of the century. However, they remained at a level well below need. In fact, city officials at times had difficulty collecting funds that already had been authorized. For example, according to the statute of December 5, 1912, the state was to assume responsibility for paying part of the cost of caring for the mentally ill and half of local police salaries. But the Minister of Finance protested on the grounds that the law was intended only to benefit the *zemstva*. The matter then went before the Senate, which ruled in favor of the cities. Nevertheless, at the end of 1916, St. Petersburg—and presumably other cities—still was not receiving any revenue because government officials could not agree on the size of the various subsidies. Even more illustrative is the fact that in 1916 the state had still not paid St. Petersburg more than one million rubles it owed as a result of a land expropriation made necessary by construction of the Nikolaevsky railroad in 1863.[7]

Overall, only the cities of Russian Finland escaped these fiscal burdens, many of which were created or maintained by the Municipal Statute of 1892. Finnish cities had their own governing statute which permitted them to receive a portion of the revenue derived from the Finnish income tax. Russian leaders pressed for a similar benefit when the State Duma and the State Council passed a progressive income tax bill in 1916. By then, however, the whole tsarist order was on the verge of collapse.

While city budgets grew significantly during the period 1892-1917, they did not grow quickly enough to cope with the needs of a rapidly growing urban population. And in comparative terms even the capitals—which enjoyed more advantages than other Russian cities—fared poorly. A study that appeared on the eve of World War I in the journal *Gorodskoe delo* (*Urban Affairs*) indicated that Germany spent five times more per capita than Russia on urban amenities and services in cities under 100,000 and about four times more per capita in all her cities combined.[8] During the war the St. Petersburg city duma heard a report which stated that while Vienna's city government was spending fifty rubles per head, Berlin's seventy, and Paris's sixty, the St. Petersburg duma was spending only thirty-two rubles per head. And according to Kadet leader Shingarev, the budgets of Paris, New York, and London *each* exceeded the *total* budget of all Russian cities combined on the eve of the war.[9]

These fiscal realities were an important cause of the deterioration of the urban environment that characterized the period 1892-1917. To illustrate, at the beginning of the twentieth century Vitebsk, a large city by contemporary standards, had no elementary school. Simferopol' had no city hospital, while in Moscow's crowded hospitals the sick were sometimes placed in closets. Few city governments were making serious attempts to confront pressing problems in housing and sanitation. According to 1904 data, of 1,084 cities with populations of more than 10,000, 892 had no established water supply and only 38 were "drained." Only 55 had streetcar lines and only 105 had gas or electric lighting. Of the 1,084 cities, 320 had no paved roads at all.[10] In an article entitled "Financial Help for the Cities," which was published during the war, the author observed that even in Moscow, the wealthiest of Russia's cities, sewerage facilities were maintained for only one-third of the city's area. According to his figures, of 1,063 cities with populations between 10,000 and 100,000, only 204 (or 19.1 percent) had water lines (and many of these did not purify the water) and only 16 (or roughly 1 percent) had sewerage facilities.[11] The statistics on water and sewerage, incidentally, help explain why the largest single expenditure of city governments was often in the area of public health, although local per capita expenditure on health was roughly twelve times greater in England, and approximately six times greater in France and Germany in 1905-1906, according to Shingarev.[12]

"Slowly and Lazily Revolves Our Municipal Machine"

The Municipal Statute of 1892 excluded nearly all urban residents from the franchise. In the provinces that comprised the Pale, as many as 90 percent of the voters who had been eligible under the

1870 statute were disenfranchised in 1892. In general, the new statute eliminated the small property owner (formerly the entire third curia and part of the second) from the electorate. After 1892 the number of eligible voters seldom exceeded 1 percent of the urban population.

While the statute restricted participation in municipal affairs to a wealthy and conservative elite, it also broadened the ability of the state to intervene in local affairs by allowing the governor to veto a municipal action on the grounds of both legality and "expediency," or whether the law corresponded to what was politically acceptable to the state. Furthermore, traditional bureaucratic inefficiency took its toll, since at times long periods would pass before state officials approved a city action, which by then might be obsolete. Dozens of petty matters appeared on city government agendas, often forcing issues of substance to be deferred for long periods of time. Consequently, attendance at city duma meetings was often poor, despite the punitive measures that were included in the statute for the purpose of enforcing attendance. Russian progressives began to voice concern about the tendency of the intelligentsia to shun participation in city affairs because of the futility of working under existing conditions.

Apathy and indolence therefore came to characterize municipal government and constituted another facet of the urban question. In light of the restrictions on the ability of city government to act independently and to make and implement policy, it is not surprising that the new electoral elite quickly manifested its disinterest in city elections. During the first elections held under the new statute (1893 and 1897) only 17 percent of Moscow's eligible electorate voted. In Odessa one-third voted, but only one-seventh of the tiny electorate turned out for a supplementary election.[13] According to Walter Hanchett, during the eighteenth and early nineteenth centuries the nobility had traditionally abstained from participating in municipal affairs. "This tradition had generally been abandoned by the Moscow nobility in the 1860s and 1870s under the impact of the public spirit prevalent during the reform era. In the 1880s the older pattern apparently was beginning to reassert itself."[14] This older pattern was reinforced by the 1892 statute.

Frederick Skinner has already noted the impact of the statute on one city, Odessa, in this regard, and the resultant stagnation in urban development. As for Moscow, one correspondent for the progressive newspaper *Utro Rossii* singled out the issue of the long-tabled plans for a new river port to illustrate his contention that the indolence of the city *uprava* was responsible for the failure of the city to accomplish developmental objectives. "Slowly and lazily revolves our municipal machine," he concluded.[15] Even during the war, despite the effort of the Union of Towns, *Gorodskoe delo* found it necessary to advocate the formation of more groups of citizens to expedite city work. And, while noting some improvement, the journal criticized Russia's newspapers, capital and provincial, for relegating urban issues and city government activities to the back pages.

The Impact of World War I

World War I came at a particularly inopportune time for Russia's cities. After two decades during which the state had done little to alleviate the burdens on the cities or to expedite urban development, on the eve of the war it began to show signs of responsiveness to the problem. A December 21, 1913, enactment allowed 1 percent of state property tax revenue to be returned to the cities. In addition, a modest expansion of credit was provided, with the goal of reducing dependency on foreign money markets. But the onset of the war turned attention away from reform just as it exacerbated conditions in most Russian cities.

In the face of serious breakdowns in the railway supply network and in the absence of effective leadership and organization within the imperial government, city officials took on a sizable share of the burden of securing enough food and fuel for survival, of meeting the needs of thousands of refugees, and of combating the epidemics and hygienic problems that they brought. However, limited by the restrictions of the 1892 statute, city officials were so handicapped that these efforts were often ineffective.

Particularly critical was the inability to secure adequate amounts of food and fuel for the urban populace, a problem which ultimately resulted in the February Revolution of 1917. Due largely to breakdowns in the railway network, of 659 cities responding to an October 1915 questionnaire, 500 reported food shortages, mainly in grain. The magnitude of the supply shortage rendered ineffective attempts by city governments to buy provisions for the populace and sell them at lower prices. In November 1915 the Special Council on Provisioning recommended that cities stop trying to make independent purchases. Soviet historian V. S. Diakin believes that the absence of coordination among city governments was an important factor in creating an environment even more favorable for speculation and higher prices.[16] In addition various governors noted in May 1916 that the most malicious speculators were frequently members of city government.[17]

The war brought new financial woe to most city administrations. Larger cities attempted to finance wartime exigencies by securing new loans. This became difficult because the war dried several foreign money markets. Moscow failed in its attempt to borrow 37 million rubles at the traditional 4.5 percent and was forced to resort to shorter term, higher interest notes. While borrowing under wartime conditions was costly, city governments generally found the alternatives in conflict with the vested interests of the narrow elite which dominated municipal life. In St. Petersburg the city duma rejected conversion to the state's rates of real estate assessment, which were significantly higher than those of the city. Conversion would have earned an additional annual income of three million rubles for the city.[18] Hence St. Petersburg relied heavily on income derived from municipally owned enterprises. The streetcar was the most important of these; but since it was used mainly by the poorer inhabitants, raises in the fare were deemed discriminatory and evoked public protest.

Moscow's budget grew from 47.6 million rubles in 1913 to more than 70 million rubles in 1916. Expenditures in education, sanitation, and "public services" grew by about 40 percent during this period. But income also grew steadily, aided by a small upward adjustment in the assessment rates in 1914. However, more than half of Moscow's income came from revenue generated from city-owned utilities and enterprises, including water and sewerage, the streetcar, and a network of pawnshops. The problem here was that much of the revenue was consumed by physical plant expansion and modernization, maintenance costs, and debt repayment; profit did not increase enough to compensate for higher costs elsewhere.[19]

During the war Moscow did receive substantial aid in the form of grants from the state totaling 8.4 million rubles in 1916, compared to just under 3 million rubles in 1913. But these statistics tell only part of the story, for rampant inflation erased much of the gain in municipal income and became a critical problem for city government and resident alike, even in cities far removed from the fighting. Wages were increased frequently during the war for most workers, but seldom in accordance with the rate of inflation.

One result was the renewal of strikes and other forms of labor unrest which had abated during the first year of the war. In Moscow the most dramatic economic strikes, or strikes resulting from economic grievances such as inadequate wages, occurred during September-October 1915 (fifty-six strikes involving 29,000 workers) and May 1916 (sixty-seven strikes, 26,000 workers).[20] For St. Petersburg Table 1 indicates the magnitude of the wartime strike movement.

While the strikers reflected dissatisfaction with rampant inflation, scarcities of necessary commodities, low wages, and poor working conditions, as well as a growing political militancy, there seems little doubt that the inadequacies of the urban environment also contributed to the growing discontent. Sparse, poor-quality housing and soaring rents were among the most critical of these inadequacies. In May 1916 St. Petersburg city authorities exempted landlords from mandatory maintenance of their properties except in cases where the roof was collapsing. The rationale behind this was that exemption would compensate the landlord for rising fuel costs. On May 11, 1916, *Rech'* proclaimed that for

Table 1

The Wartime Strike Movement in St. Petersburg[21]

Period	Politically Motivated Strikes			Economically Motivated Strikes		
	Strikes	Strikers	Workdays Lost	Strikes	Strikers	Workdays Lost
19 July 1914-July 1915	59	36,144	53,651	88	40,218	127,213
Aug. 1915-Aug. 1916	260	313,268	854,305	373	228,590	741,734
Sept. 1916-Feb. 22, 1917	406	477,181	744,490	124	112,170	279,406

many St. Petersburg families the housing shortage and rental increases created more anxiety than the massive breakdowns in the provisioning of food and fuel. The Kadet fraction in the State Duma proposed a form of rent control but the government prorogued the Duma and enacted its own measures by the traditional means of Article 87 of the Fundamental Laws. These measures did not apply to the poorest quarters, however, those without heat and those that were leased below a certain rent. Furthermore, most leases were renewed in May and June; since the controls went into effect after that time, landlords were allowed increases that were good for another year. This problem typified the frustration of the average urban resident, who had virtually no representation in either the State Duma or the city government.

In Moscow, wartime financial retrenchment caused several major projects to be delayed or postponed indefinitely. Plans to build a new port were again interrupted, even though the imperial government regarded the project as an important means of relieving pressure on the congested and inadequate railway network. The war also postponed construction of the Metropolitena, an electric subway system that had been planned and pursued with unusual energy prior to 1914. Moscow's streetcar network had been finished in 1912, but it did not extend to the area surrounding the city that contained some 600 "suburban" settlements.

The war had little impact on some areas of Moscow's budget, most notably on education and public welfare. City funds helped finance subsidies to 100,000 families whose heads had been called into military service. Moscow also built a community for refugees, Kalitnikovsky. In 1916 this settlement had an estimated population of 4,500, while roughly 8,000 additional refugees remained in the city. Expenses for the care of refugees grew to 500,000 rubles per month for the city, and in 1916 it was reported that the city government was continuing to "solicit and hope" for reimbursement from the state.[22] The city duma also helped underwrite Red Cross information and assistance centers in Moscow, Copenhagen, and The Hague for the purpose of aiding Russians who were prisoners of war. Oddly, Moscow conducted its own foreign aid program. In October 1914 the city duma dispatched 100,000 rubles to ravaged communities in Poland, another 100,000 to Belgium, 100,000 to the "heroic Serbs," and 25,000 to Montenegro. In 1916 Serbian leader Pašić attended a city duma meeting where a resolution was passed awarding Serbia another 100,000 rubles.

But if World War I had only a limited impact on city life in Moscow, the city's experience was not typical and can be explained by two factors. First, Moscow was the wealthiest of Russia's cities. As Mayor N. Astrov was later to explain, the city had at least three times the 320 million rubles worth of assets officially listed in 1915.[23] Second, the budgets of Moscow and St. Petersburg amounted to roughly one-third of the entire budget of all Russian cities together. For most cities, the war strained resources that were generally inadequate before 1914. Indeed, a survey taken by the Kievan duma of seventy selected cities, excluding the largest urban centers, indicated that by 1915 spending in categories such as education and public welfare had been significantly curtailed in order to meet problems created by the war.[24]

The Urban Question: Local Response

Increasing frustration over the statutory and bureaucratic impediments which continued to prevent developmental progress produced some positive responses, most notably signs of revitalized public initiative at the local level. For example, the period 1904-1917 witnessed a series of attempts to create empire-wide city associations which could hold congresses where mutual problems and possible solutions could be discussed. The first efforts were actually made by the mayor of Ufa in 1891 although the statute of the following year squelched the movement until the political "spring" of 1904. During that year, thanks largely to the efforts of Kharkov Mayor A. Pogorelko, the idea was revived and city leaders met on several occasions during the turbulent year 1905. One meeting in June attracted 120 delegates from 89 cities. Debate on the general political issues that surfaced as a result of the Revolution consumed most of the time and effort; however city leaders did speak strongly on behalf of the urgency of independence for local government, of the need to broaden the franchise extensively, and of the need to hold future congresses at regular intervals.

Political reaction terminated the movement until 1910, when representatives of twenty-four cities met in Odessa, where they were coolly received by the conservative city government. In fact Odessa sent no delegate; neither did Moscow, Warsaw, Kharkov, or Saratov, prompting one conferee to state, "This is one of those tragicomic misfortunes that can occur only in Russia."[25] St. Petersburg hosted a meeting in 1912 but much more significant was the Kievan municipal congress of September 1913, where some 200 delegates approved a series of resolutions reflecting the paramount concern of the times, mitigation of the financial strangulation of the city by means of thorough fiscal reform. Moscow city leaders formed the All-Russian Union of Towns in 1914 to assist the floundering government in alleviating the grave logistical problems caused by the war. The Union owed some of its organizational precedence to the congress movement, and its leaders shared the belief of the pre-war movement that fundamental political and fiscal reforms were a critical prerequisite to the achievement of social stability in urban Russia.

A second indication of the revitalization of municipal leadership can be seen in the creation of several new urban journals and in the efforts of many established journals to alter their formats. New journals catering to analysis of pertinent city problems and possible solutions, rather than to mere publication of budgetary estimates, appeared in Samara and Kishinev in 1910-1911. *Gorodskoe delo*, a national urban organ, began publication in 1909, while the *Penzenskii gorodskoi vestnik*, which was first published in 1911, gained an especially high reputation for quality and relevance for a provincial journal. Simferopol, Irkutsk, Tashkent, Archangel, and Kiev also adopted the new approach in their city journals, thus providing a new forum for problem-solving and for infusing new life into local government.[26]

Unfortunately this had a very limited impact on the tsarist government. And while the moderate and progressive political parties all made reform of the 1892 statute an important political goal, only the new sense of urgency brought about by World War I spurred these groups to act. During the February-June 1916 legislative session of the Fourth Duma the leaders of the Progressive Bloc worked out a reform bill containing more than 200 articles, including compulsory professional training for city officials, expansion of revenue sources, curtailment of bureaucratic interference in city affairs, and an end to the ability of state officials to reject city duma regulations on the basis of "inexpediency," or failure to conform to the prevailing politics of the state. Even so the bill never appeared on the Duma floor because of unresolved controversy over the purely political issue of franchise reform. The Octobrists supported a small extension of the franchise but only with the employment of a curial system of voting that would maintain the power of the city's economic elite. The Kadets demanded both franchise extension and the absence of curiae.

The political spring of 1904-1905 produced a highly vocal reformist movement of municipal leaders who came to believe that the urban question was rapidly becoming an urban crisis. The respected organ of the Moscow city duma reported in 1911 that a new "municipal consciousness" was characteristic of the times and was replacing some of the "mold" that covered city affairs.[27] Significantly, demands for change were not confined to radical or even progressive political elements. Kievan official Demchenko, a large landowner and leader of the city duma's rightist majority, told the Kievan municipal congress in 1913 that financial conditions would not improve and Russia would not progress until the 1892 statute was replaced. The government frowned on such public attacks on the statute and city leaders were told to confine their remarks and proposals to the "practical" and "nonpolitical" sphere. In reality the two spheres could not be separated. Nevertheless, the activism of city leaders, however constructive, failed to convince the imperial government that urban Russia required urgent and pervasive reform.

Controversial and emotional issues involving rights for national minorities further complicated the question of municipal reform and divided the progressive movement. Many liberals feared genuine decentralization of power because friction between nationalities could so easily paralyze local government.[28] The Jewish question was the most volatile national issue and helped poison the debate on municipal reform within the Progressive Bloc. During this debate most liberals advocated a return to the principles of 1870 whereby up to one-third of city duma representatives in the Pale could be Jews and up to one-fifth in cities outside the Pale. The Octobrists and other conservatives sought to exclude Jews completely from city affairs by establishing a separate Jewish curia which would not even take part in general city elections.[29]

Conclusion

The Municipal Statute of 1892 clearly revealed the myopic perspective of the tsarist government toward the whole complex of problems related to urbanization. Ironically the statute disallowed deficits in city spending. This compelled local dumas to employ fictitious figures and other evasive devices in their bookkeeping. In 1907, one source noted with despair that in the Crimea, Sebastopol and Kerch "cannot even conceal [their] deficits by manipulation."[30] In a budget of 300,000 rubles, Kerch officials projected a deficit of at least 111,000, down from 200,000 a year earlier.

Reduction of the deficit had been achieved by closing some fifty schools, one example of the high cost of the government's myopia in terms of social and economic progress.

While neglect was eroding the quality of city life, city growth continued at a rapid pace. Housing became a major problem as the rate of urban growth surpassed the pace of new housing construction. In 1910 one study noted that even a room in someone else's apartment was considered a luxury, and that wages were lower and rents higher than anywhere in western Europe.[31] In St. Petersburg this helped contribute to what another study called the "astonishing openness and scope of child prostitution."[32]

Actually, many of the crowded working class districts were technically settlements outside the city where residents lacked self-government institutions and enjoyed almost no amenities or services. Efficient and inexpensive transportation systems linking these settlements to the city did not exist. Baku had thirty primary schools; its large "suburb" Chernii had one. Sanitary conditions in Chernii were "beyond description." At one point, 20,000 of its residents "literally besieged" the Baku city duma, but with no results.[33] The existence of these suburban slums continued well into the twentieth century. Although in recent times they have been reduced or eliminated, the unskilled suburban dweller and "worker-peasant" still remain at a disadvantage. They pay the cost of commuting but are denied the economic, educational, and cultural advantages of the large eastern European city.

Within the cities themselves, growth brought severe crowding. By 1900 St. Petersburg already had nearly 50,000 one- or two-room apartments with an average of four inhabitants per room. Overall, rent for housing qualified the city as the most expensive major city in Europe, surpassing even Berlin, although rent for one-room apartments was even higher in Moscow.[34] The private sector remained largely responsible for housing, and some new projects, such as V. N. Semënov's Prozorovka, a garden city community near Moscow sponsored by the Moscow-Kazan Railway for its workers, began to take shape. But city-built housing units, increasingly common in Europe partly because they were often self-supporting, were rare in Russia, largely because of insufficient capital. According to rough but illustrative data compiled in 1904, the average city apartment throughout the empire sheltered eleven souls; in 10 percent of the cities the average apartment housed at least twenty inhabitants.[35] Provincial cities with large non-Russian populations often fared the worst, for their residents endured the twin burdens of urban stagnation and minority discrimination. In the Jewish ghettoes of the Pale, with their crowded, unpaved streets, a daytime workshop might serve at night as sleeping quarters for as many as twenty-five individuals. In Vil'na nearly 38 percent of the city's large Jewish population lived by means of private charity, while 25 to 30 percent of the population of cities such as Dvinsk, Zhitomir, Nikolaev, and Poltava was comprised of Jewish beggars.[36]

The problem of crowding showed no signs of abating as World War I approached. Housing inspection continued to be erratic and inadequate; comprehensive city planning remained rare. Between January 1910 and July 1914 the industrial labor force grew by more than 30 percent,[37] further compounding the problems. These dismal conditions very likely aggravated what Reginald Zelnik has already noted in the 1870s as an increasingly intractable social situation and a "new era of urban class conflict."[38] Leopold Haimson, in his analysis of social stability in urban Russia on the eve of World War I, has perceived among the workers, especially in St. Petersburg, a "growing spirit of *buntarstvo*—of violent if still diffuse opposition to all authority—and an instinctive sense of class solidarity, as they encountered the repressive measures of state power and what appeared to them the indifference of privileged society."[39] As much as any other facet of Russian life, conditions in the cities blatantly manifested this indifference, especially after 1892.

For the sake of perspective, it should be stated that Russia's urban experience was by no means unusual. Throughout Europe in the nineteenth century, local needs were left to the discretion of the central governments. As for developing regions in general, "in

areas undergoing rapid change from traditionalism to modernization the city is usually unprepared both physically and organiza-
tionally to deal with the great burdens thrust upon it."[40] The
slow development of appropriate urban institutions can be blamed
in part on the "naivete of the newcomers to urban life. They had
no knowledge of how to live in the new context, nor any of the
civil discipline that would be required of them."[41]

But the breakdown of urban modernization should be viewed as
yet another factor that accelerated the demise of the imperial
order. As L. A. Velikhov, the leading spokesman for municipal
reform in the State Duma, warned prophetically on the eve of
World War I, the "backwardness of our material culture and public
hygiene is staggering. Millions of lives are poisoned by the wild
disorder of our populated places, by epidemics, fires, and the
horrors of alcoholism and poverty. Local governments have strug-
gled in vain to find the means to fight this physical degeneration.
Capital is concentrated in the state treasury and income sources
are exhausted. Under such conditions the spiritual strengths of the
Russian people are being wasted and are growing scarce."[42]

Notes

I wish to thank the American Philosophical Society, Penrose Fund, and Centre
College for their support in 1972 and 1973 of the research for this essay.

1. Reginald E. Zelnik, *Labor and Society in Tsarist Russia: The Factory Workers of
St. Petersburg, 1855-1870* (Stanford: Stanford University Press, 1971), pp. 241-42, 251.

2. G. I. Shreider, "Gorodskaia kontr'-reforma 11 iiunia 1892 goda," *Istoriia Rossii v
XIX v.* 9 vols. (St. Petersburg, n.d.), 5: 199. See also V. Ostrovskii in *Izvestiia soiuz
gorodov* (Moscow), no. 39, December 1916.

3. A. I. Shingarev, "The Reform of Local Finance in Russia," *Russian Review*
(London), 1, no. 1 (1912): 42.

4. See A. Mikhailovskii, "Biudzhety russkikh gorodov," *Izvestiia Moskovskoi gorodskoi dumy* (Moscow), October 1905, pp. 1-46, for a region-by-region study of city
financing at the turn of the century. Hereafter cited as *IMGD.*

5. "Gorodskie finansy v perezhivaemuiu epokhu," *Gorodskoe delo* 1915, no. 2: 67.
Hereafter cited as *G.D.*

6. Nicholas J. Astrov, "The Municipal Government and the All-Russian Union of
Towns," in Paul P. Gronsky and Nicholas J. Astrov, *The War and the Russian Government* (New Haven: Yale University Press, 1929), p. 150.

7. "K voprosu ob uluchshenii gorodskikh finansov," *G.D.*, 1916, no. 23: 1114.

8. "Munitsipalnoe obozrenie," *G.D.*, 1913, nos. 13-14: 945. Figures are from 1909.

9. Shingarev, p. 46.

10. H. Lerche, "State Credit for Town and County Councils," *Russian Review* 1, no. 3 (1912): 45-46.

11. V. Almazov in *Rech'* (Petrograd), March 10, 1916.

12. Shingarev, p. 43.

13. Shreider, p. 202. After 1903 St. Petersburg was given its own unique statute which gave the franchise to well-to-do apartment renters. The statute did not result in significant progress for the city.

14. Walter Hanchett, "Moscow in the Late Nineteenth Century: A Study in Municipal Self-Government," Ph.D. dissertation, University of Chicago, 1964, p. 210.

15. *Utro Rossii* (Moscow), February 21, 1916, p. 4. Plans for the port were first discussed in 1903 but in essence were tabled from 1904 until 1912. Only when the Minister of Ways of Communication threatened to take over the project did the city *uprava* again devote attention to the plan.

16. V. S. Diakin, *Russkaia burzhuaziia i tsarizm v gody pervoi mirovoi voiny, 1914-1917* (Leningrad, 1967), especially pp. 132-33, 213. See also *Izvestiia Osobago Soveshchaniia po prodovol'stvennomu delu*, no. 22 (1916): 1-14.

17. "Soveshchanie gubernatorov v 1916 godu," *Krasnyi arkhiv* 33 (Moscow, 1929): 163.

18. "K voprosu," p. 1116.

19. A. Mikhailovskii, "Deiatel'nost Moskovskago gorodskoi upravleniia v' 1913-1916 gg.," *IMGD*, September 1916, pp. 3-4.

20. G. G. Kasarov, "Stachechnoe dvizhenie v Moskve v gody pervoi mirovoi voiny (19 iiulia 1914-25 fevralia 1917 g.)," *Vestnik Moshovskugo universiteta*, no. 6 (1970): 42.

21. I. P. Leiberov, "O revoliutsionnykh vystupleniakh petrogradskogo proletariata v gody pervoi mirovoi voiny i fevral'skoi revoliutsii," *Voprosy istorii*, no. 2 (1964): 65.

22. Mikhailovskii, "Deiatel'nost," pp. 59-64.

23. N. Astrov, "Moskva i vserossiiskii soiuz gorodov," Panina Collection, Russian and East European Archive of History and Culture, Columbia University, p. 2.

24. See "Vliianie voiny na finansy gorodov," *Izvestiia Kievskoi gorodskoi dumy*, no. 11, November 1914, pp. 111-14. See also *G.D.*, 1915, no. 21.

25. *G.D.*, 1910, no. 19: 1347. The congress was organized by the Odessa branch of the Technical Society of Imperial Russia.

26. See B. Veselovskii, "Munitsipal'naia pressa v Rossii," *Izvestiia Petrogradskoi gorodskoi dumy*, October 1916, *Prilozhenie k' dokladu 833*, no. 1. Also see *IMGD*, May 1911; and *Izvestiia Kievskoi gorodskoi dumy*, September 1914, pp. 3-5.

27. *IMGD*, February 1911, pp. 41-42.

28. For example see A. K. Pogorelko, *Doklad Kharkovskogo gorodskogo golovy o rezul'tatakh soveshchanii zemskikh i gorodskikh deiateli . . .* (Kharkov, 1905), especially pp. 92-107.

29. *Evreiskaia zhizn'* (Moscow), May 15, 1916.

30. *Samoupravlenie* (Moscow), no. 25 (June 3, 1907): 16.

31. See the article by K. Pazhitov in *G.D.*, 1910, no. 19, especially pp. 1313-14.

32. *IMGD*, September 1910, carried a lengthy article on efforts to combat prostitution. See especially p. 108.

33. *G.D.*, 1909, no. 19: 995. To make matters worse, Baku received some 200,000 rubles a year in taxes from residents of Chernii. Incidentally, nearly 600 such settlements ringed Moscow by 1913.

34. See K. Pazhitov in *G.D.*, 1910, no. 20: 1372-83; and Pazhitov in *IMGD*, October 1914, pp. 29-53.

35. These statistics were cited in a report given to the Odessa municipal congress and published in *G.D.*, 1910, no. 20, especially p. 1392.

36. See *Evrei v Rossii* (Moscow, 1906); and M. Ancharova, *Evreiskoe bezpravie i ego plody* (Moscow, 1917), p. 16.

37. Leopold Haimson, "The Problem of Social Stability in Urban Russia, 1905-1917," *Slavic Review* 23 (December 1964): 635.

38. Zelnik, p. 385.

39. Haimson, p. 629.

40. Amos H. Hawley, *Urban Society: An Ecological Approach* (New York: Ronald Press, 1971), p. 306.

41. Ibid., p. 117.

42. *G.D.*, 1913, no. 23: 1556-58.

PART III
THE TWENTIETH CENTURY:
AN ERA OF GROWTH
AND PLANNING

Although the urban population of the Soviet Union declined during the chaos of the civil war, between December 1926 and January 1939 Soviet cities grew by an average annual rate of 6.5 percent.[1] The dynamic urban growth of this period, the result of Stalin's forced industrialization and collectivization schemes, "was unequalled in either the earlier history of Russia or the later periods in the Soviet Union or in the history of other countries before World War II."[2] While the urban population comprised only 18 percent of the Soviet population in 1926, it equalled the rural population by the end of 1960 and exceeded it by 28 percent by January 1, 1969. Robert Lewis and Richard Rowland begin Part III by examining the major national and regional trends in this era of rapid urban growth.

The central theme of this section, however, is the impact of another twentieth-century phenomenon, central planning, on the Soviet city. S. Frederick Starr, in examining two models of urban form, the "classical" and the garden city, observes, "It was the task of the October Revolution not to destroy these tendencies but to take them over and adapt them to the particular objectives of Bolshevism." Milka Bliznakov discusses the early planning theories of the "urbanists" and "deurbanists." David T. Cattell, in his essay on the Soviet city and consumer welfare planning, concludes that "for all its experience in planning, the Soviet system has not developed adequate techniques for comprehensive planning at the local level." Moscow has been a model of Soviet urban development and B. M. Frolic analyzes the new plan for the development of that city. Frolic believes that the goals of this plan are relatively modest and realistic in light of previous planning endeavors and notes that "planning goals are more realizable if they involve physical rather than social restructuring."

Notes

1. Chauncey D. Harris, *Cities of the Soviet Union* (Chicago: Rand McNally, 1970, p. 234, Table 25.
2. Ibid., p. 299.

URBANIZATION IN RUSSIA AND
THE USSR, 1897-1970

Robert A. Lewis & Richard H. Rowland

The purpose of this essay is to describe and analyze the major patterns of urbanization which have occurred in Russia and the USSR during the past century. Other studies have investigated urbanization during parts of the 1897-1970 period,[1] but none has done so for the entire period on the basis of a comparable definition of the term urban and a comparable set of territorial units. This study, consequently, attempts to investigate urbanization in Russia and the USSR generally on such a basis. In particular, it is concerned with major national and regional trends in urbanization. The role of the Russian and Soviet governments in such trends is also evaluated.

Sources and Definitions

The major sources of data for this study are the Russian and Soviet censuses of 1897, 1926, 1939, 1959, and 1970.[2] In addition, because data were gathered for territory within the present-day boundaries of the USSR, censuses from eastern Europe were also used.[3] Because the territorial units and urban definitions in the various Russian and Soviet censuses have frequently changed, regional comparisons over time have been hindered. Recent studies with which we have been associated, however, have done much to overcome this problem. First of all, we have selected one set of territorial units, the nineteen Soviet economic regions of 1961, and have ordered a wide range of population data from each census year into these regions.[4]

In addition, we have adopted a definition of the term urban which is comparable from one census to another. Any settlement with a population of 15,000 and over is regarded as an urban center in this study,[5] except where otherwise indicated.

Finally, a distinction should be made between the terms urbanization and urban growth. Urbanization is intimately related to social change and refers to the process of population concentration which involves the percentage of a region's population residing in urban centers (the level of urbanization) and an increase in that percentage. Urban growth, on the other hand, simply refers to the increase in the urban population per se, without any reference to the total population.[6]

National Patterns of Urbanization

By any indicator, the Russian Empire was not highly urbanized during the nineteenth century. In 1820, only 2.4 percent of its population resided in settlements of 20,000 or more inhabitants.[7] By 1885, the level of urbanization based upon the same size criterion had increased to 7.4 percent, and by 1897 a level of 9.4 percent had been attained.[8]

Although these nineteenth-century levels were quite low, a comparison with world data compiled by Kingsley Davis and Hilda Hertz reveals that Russia's position was not as low as these data might suggest.[9] According to Davis and Hertz, in 1900, 9.2 percent of the world's population resided in settlements with a population of 20,000 or more. But, as we have seen, the Russian level in 1897 was slightly above this percentage. Therefore, although Russia was not highly urbanized in the late nineteenth century, it was not substantially below the world norm.

More important perhaps is the increase in the level of urbanization during the latter part of the nineteenth century. As mentioned above, the percent of the empire's population residing in centers of 20,000 and over increased from 7.4 percent to 9.4 percent between 1885 and 1897. This means that the level of urbanization increased by .17 percentage points per year and by 2.0 percent per year. In comparison, the corresponding world figures for the 1850-1900 period were only .10 and 1.5, respectively. Therefore, in the last decades of the nineteenth century, the pace of urbanization in Russia was, like the level of urbanization, apparently higher than world standards and was certainly not substantially below such standards.

In order to assess urbanization from 1897 to the present, we used the present-day territory of the USSR and the 15,000 and over criterion. Levels of urbanization based upon such criteria were 9.9 for 1897, 13.3 for 1926, 25.3 for 1939, 38.2 for 1959, and 45.7 for 1970. Thus between 1897 and 1970 the level of urbanization increased more than four and one-half times, and by 1970 nearly half of the total population resided in such urban centers.

The rapidity of the urbanization process in Russia and the USSR is again best dramatized by a comparison with the world-wide process. For example, between 1897 and 1970 the level of urbanization in the USSR based on the 100,000 and over criterion increased from 4.1 percent to 31.7 percent, a percentage point increase of 27.6 and a percentage increase of 673.2.[10] During a virtually identical period (1900-1970), the world level increased from 5.5 percent to 23.2 percent, a percentage point increase of only 17.7 and a percentage increase of only 321.8.[11] Thus, since the turn of the century, the pace of urbanization in Russia and the USSR has been much higher than that of the world.

Data from the United Nations further attest to the rapidity of the process of urbanization in the USSR from other perspectives. First, they suggest not only that the rate of urbanization in the USSR has been well above the world average, but that between 1920 and 1970 it also was the most rapid of any of the eight major world regions which they distinguish.[12] In addition, they suggest that in one ten-year period (1930-1940) the rate of urbanization in the USSR was by far the highest ten-year rate achieved by any region between 1920 and 1970; in fact, it was perhaps the highest rate ever experienced in human history. The outstanding nature of this interwar period is reflected on the basis of the 15,000 and over definition. Computations based upon figures presented earlier in this essay reveal that the 1926-1939 period was in fact the period of the most rapid urbanization. Of course, the beginning of the five-year plans in the USSR with their emphasis on rapid industrialization accounts for the astonishing rate of urbanization in the 1930s.

Thus, in summary, the pace of urbanization in Russia and the USSR during the last century and a half either has been close to world standards, especially in the nineteenth century, or has been outstanding as compared to world standards, especially in the twentieth century.

Analysis of National Patterns

The most immediate and obvious explanation for the increased level of urbanization in Russia and the USSR is the fact that the rate of growth of the urban population has exceeded that of the total population and, since a dichotomous classification of settlements is being used, that of the rural population. Between 1897 and 1970 the urban population based on the 15,000 and over definition increased by almost nine times (795.7 percent, or 3.0 percent a year); in contrast the total population increased only about two times (93.3 percent, or 0.9 percent a year) and the rural population increased only slightly (16.5 percent, or 0.2 percent a year). Theoretically, urbanization can occur without urban growth; namely, where the rate of decline of the urban population is not as great as the rate of decline of the total and rural populations. Such a case, however, is rare. Thus for urbanization to occur urban growth usually must occur. Consequently, although urban growth and urbanization are not synonymous, the former is usually a necessary factor in the latter. The USSR is no exception, especially since the total and rural populations also increased between 1897 and 1970. In short, urbanization in the

The Twentieth-Century City

USSR could not have occurred without urban growth in the overall 1897-1970 period.

To delve deeper into reasons for Russian and Soviet urbanization it is necessary to examine the immediate factors which contribute to urban growth and especially to urban growth exceeding the growth of the total and rural populations. Kingsley Davis has presented a useful model which includes such factors.[13] He suggests that urban growth and urbanization are related to three elements: urban natural increase, migration to urban centers, and reclassification of settlements from rural to urban. Some combinations of these three elements are the most immediate factors in urban growth. These three elements can also be used directly to interpret urbanization. Namely, urbanization is enhanced by 1) urban natural increase exceeding rural natural increase, 2) net rural-to-urban migration, and 3) reclassification. Each of these situations enhances urban growth more than it does rural growth and thus enhances urbanization. Net rural-to-urban migration and reclassification in fact have a double-barreled effect on urbanization in that they not only add to the urban population but simultaneously deplete the rural population. Throughout human history migration has probably been the most influential of the three elements; urban natural increase has rarely if ever exceeded rural natural increase, and reclassification has been insignificant.[14]

Therefore, we might hypothesize that rural-to-urban migration was of prime importance in Russia and the USSR. Unfortunately, not all aspects of the model can be investigated due to the lack of data. Nevertheless, those data which are available do support the hypothesis. First, one of the authors has elsewhere estimated that net rural-to-urban migration accounted for approximately four-fifths of the urban growth between 1885 and 1897.[15] Other sources allow an investigation for the period 1926-1970. They indicate that of the total increase of the urban population during this period (105 million), 56.3 percent was due to net rural-to-urban migration, 26.8 percent was due to natural increase, and 17.0 percent was due to reclassification.[16] Thus, it may be con-

cluded that net rural-to-urban migration has been the major immediate factor in Russian and Soviet urban growth and urbanization.

It should be pointed out, however, that the role of migration is
apparently decreasing in importance. Whereas net rural-to-urban
migration accounted for 62.1 percent of the urban growth between 1926 and 1959, its share dropped to 44.9 percent between
1959 and 1970. A decrease was also registered by reclassification
(18.4 to 14.0 percent). Therefore, only natural increase increased
its share (19.5 to 41.0 percent).[17] Such a development is not
unusual in the evolution of urbanization. Migration was frequently
more important in the past than in more recent years because high
urban mortality rates prevented any substantial natural increase in
cities. Net rural-to-urban migration was thus about the only way
cities could grow. In more recent times, however, improved living
standards have generally reduced urban mortality rates, allowing
for a higher degree of urban natural increase. In addition, in the
later stages of urbanization the size of the rural population becomes relatively smaller, therefore reducing the pool of potential
rural-to-urban migrants. Ultimately, when the theoretical situation
of 100 percent urbanization is reached, rural-to-urban migration,
of course, cannot occur. Therefore, the Russian and Soviet trend
with respect to the relative importance of the three major immediate factors of urban growth is quite reasonable. Furthermore,
given the situations of collectivization and World War II in the
1926-1959 period and relative peace in the 1959-1970 period, it is
even easier to understand the increased importance of urban
natural increase. Protracted periods of chaos and turmoil in the
earlier period, of course, reduced the importance of urban natural
increase at that time.

But to understand more completely the remarkable Russian and
Soviet urbanization which has occurred, we must seek out underlying factors. In keeping with the theme of this book, the role of
the state should first be examined. In general, it can be safely said
that Russian and Soviet urbanization has not been the direct
product of some major governmental policy. However, it should
also be mentioned that the state has not been totally unconcerned

The Twentieth-Century City

with urbanization. For example, the Soviet government has indicated that it would like to limit the growth of large cities,[18] although such a policy has not been implemented to any great extent. Thus, governmental policies have generally not had much direct influence on the urbanization process in Russia and the USSR.

It is indisputable, however, that the state has had a tremendous indirect impact on the urbanization process through its promotion of industrialization. The authors have elsewhere demonstrated statistically the significant impact of industrialization on urbanization between 1897 and 1959-1961. In particular, based upon the nineteen economic regions, they found a rank correlation coefficient (r_s) of .803 between 1) the percentage point change in the level of urbanization between 1897 and 1959 and 2) the percentage point change in the percent of a region's total population comprised by industrial workers between 1897 and 1959-1961.[19]

Based upon more recent data it is now possible to investigate similarly the role of industrialization during the periods 1897-1970 and 1959-1970. Unfortunately, the desired data for 1970 per se are not available, so other steps had to be undertaken to estimate the number of industrial workers by economic region for 1970.[20] Subsequently, one rank correlation was run on the basis of the nineteen economic regions for each of the two periods. Both correlations were between the percentage point change in the level of urbanization and the percentage point change in the percent of a region's population comprised by industrial workers. Respective rank correlation coefficients were .854 and .678. Thus, it appears that industrialization also had a great impact on Russian and Soviet urbanization in both the 1897-1970 and 1959-1970 periods.

However, as the authors discovered in their earlier study, the impact of industrialization was not uniform throughout the entire period beginning in 1897. In particular, industrialization did not appear to have a strong impact on urbanization between 1897 and 1926 (r_s=.361) although it did have such an impact between 1926 and 1959-1961 (r_s=.794).[21] In our earlier study, we suggested a number of reasons for the low relationship. Since then, we have hypothesized that definitional problems also may have accounted for the low relationship in the earlier period; namely, the fact that the 1897 and 1926 manufacturing categories included handicrafts may have upset the relationship. Implicit in the hypothesized urbanization-industrialization relationship is the fact that industrialization generally involved only modern factory industrialization. Since the handicraft sector was stagnating it could not be regarded as a great stimulus to urbanization.

Therefore, we have attempted to delete handicraft workers from the industrial category and to examine the relationship between the residual category, "factory industry," and urbanization. Such procedures involve a number of difficulties. First, no handicraft data are available from censuses in areas which were outside Russia and the USSR in 1897 and 1926 but are within the USSR today; that is, handicraft data could not be gathered for 100 percent of every region. Second, the 1897 and 1926 definitions of handicrafts are not identical. Also, the 1897 handicraft category was more difficult to extract. Whereas the 1926 census contains an explicit handicraft category, the 1897 census does not, necessitating more arbitrary measures to derive a handicraft sector for 1897.[22] Ultimately the derived number of handicraft workers was subtracted from the total number of industrial workers in 1897 and 1926, leading to a category which may be operationally defined as "factory workers." A rank correlation was then run on the basis of the nineteen regions between the percentage point change in the level of urbanization from 1897 to 1926 and the percentage point change in the percent of a region's total population comprised by "factory" workers.[23] The result was a higher relationship (r_s=.469). The relationship still was not very strong, however, especially since the relationship for other periods was much higher. Thus between 1897 and 1926 urbanization was still not highly related to industrialization.

The low relationship between urbanization and industrialization in this earlier period was also evident when correlations were run within the individual years themselves; namely, regional variations

The Twentieth-Century City

in the level of urbanization were correlated with variations in the percent of the total population comprised by industrial workers. Rank correlation coefficients were .416 for 1897, .705 for 1926, .828 for 1959-1961, and .836 for 1970. Thus, 1897 was the only year when a high relationship did not occur; in fact, even when the handicraft sector was eliminated and the correlation involved only factory industry, the relationship was still not high (r_s=.307). Thus, it appears that in the late nineteenth century urbanization was not yet highly related to industrialization.

Some insights into the low relationship in 1897 can be gained by examining the most deviant regions, those which had greatly different ranks with respect to the indices of urbanization and industrialization. Outstanding regions were the Volgo-Viatsk (the region around Nizhnii Novgorod or Gor'kii), the Transcaucasus, the Urals, Moldavia, and the South (the Southern Ukraine, including Odessa and the Crimea). The large deviations experienced by the Volgo-Viatsk and the Urals were apparently due to the fact that a very high percent (roughly 80) of their industrial work force was in rural areas.[24] Thus, although they had a relatively high degree of industrialization, it did not result in a high level of urbanization. This situation was not unique to these regions. Roughly 60 percent of the entire industrial work force of the empire was found in rural areas.[25] Thus, although industrialization was occurring it did not necessarily enhance urbanization. One reason appears to have been the fact that because of restrictions on peasant out-migration from rural areas, many industrialists apparently responded by building their factories in rural areas in order to be closer to the supply of labor. As Lenin put it, "the muzhik [peasant] is not allowed to go to the factory, so the factory goes to the muzhik."[26]

The other three regions offer different insights. Each had a relatively high percent of the industrial work force in urban areas and each ranked much higher with respect to urbanization than to industrialization. Thus it appears that their relatively high levels of urbanization were due to other factors. The South, which was the most urbanized of all the nineteen regions in 1897, provides the most clear-cut answer. This region contained some of the major grain exporting ports in Russia, especially Odessa and Nikolaev. This suggests that tertiary activities (trade, transportation, governmental activities, and others) were still of great importance in Russian urbanization at this time. This is borne out by a rank correlation based on the nineteen regions in 1897 between the level of urbanization and the percent of a region's population comprised by the tertiary work force.[27] The emergent r_S of .738 suggests that the service sector was a more important factor in urbanization at this early period than was industrialization. It also suggests that urbanization in Russia in the late nineteenth century was still in its preindustrial phase. In addition, it is interesting to note that the expansion of the tertiary sector was also a major factor in urbanization between 1897 and 1959; namely, based upon the nineteen regions, there was an r_S of .793 between the percentage point change in the level of urbanization and the percentage point change in the percent of a region's population comprised by the tertiary work force.

In summary, urbanization in Russia and the USSR has been especially related to net rural-to-urban migration, industrialization, and the expansion of the service sector. Some changes have occurred, however, in the degree of relationship. Most notably, net rural-to-urban migration has declined in relative importance and industrialization has generally increased in importance.

Regional Patterns of Urbanization

Notable changes have also occurred in the regional patterns of urbanization. Between 1897 and 1970 the pace of urbanization was higher in the eastern regions than in the west.[28] During this period the east's level of urbanization increased by 37.8 percentage points and 600.0 percent; corresponding figures for the west were only 35.7 and 336.4, respectively. As we suggested in a previous study, these regional patterns existed also between 1897 and 1959.[29] During the latter period, the east's level increased by 33.6 percentage points and 533.3 percent; in contrast, the west's figures were but 26.8 and 250.5, respectively. The higher rate of urbanization in the east, of course, reflects the planned shift of industry to this mineral-rich area and the fact that it did not experience the tremendous wartime devastation that the western regions fell victim to.

Since 1959, however, this regional pattern has been dramatically reversed. Between 1959 and 1970 the level of urbanization in the west increased by 8.9 percentage points and 23.7 percent; in the east the level increased by only 4.2 percentage points and 10.5 percent. In particular, the five highest regional gains with respect to percentage point change were registered by Belorussia, the West, the Volgo-Viatsk, the Central Chernozem (the agricultural area between Moscow and the Ukraine), and the Volga. With respect to percentage change the leaders were Belorussia, the Central Chernozem, Moldavia, the Southwest (the western Ukraine), and the Volgo-Viatsk. All of these regions are in the west.

This reversal in the regional pattern of urbanization reflects especially the reversal of the "Great Siberian Migration"; Siberia, which has been a major area of in-migration during the last century, is now a major area of net out-migration. Between 1959 and 1970 there was a net out-migration of almost 800,000 people from West Siberia, 60,000 from East Siberia, and more than 900,000 from the Urals.[30] On the basis of the urban population these regions apparently still have net in-migration, but their corresponding rates are among the very lowest in the country.[31] Such migrational patterns appear to be related to the fact that living standards here are relatively low, especially in terms of real wages and climate.[32] These factors, consequently, seem applicable to the relatively low pace of urbanization now occurring. Thus, in spite of a labor shortage in the east and in spite of the fact that the government gives wage incentives to attract people there, a high degree of out-migration is occurring, with a slackened pace of urbanization being one consequence. The eastern regions are not unique in that the USSR has other regions not experiencing expected patterns of migration given their labor supply conditions (for example, the North Caucasus has a labor surplus but net in-migration).[33] Such disparities between regional migration patterns and regional patterns of labor supply and demand present a major problem to the Soviet government.

As for the revitalization of the urban process in the west, a number of factors seem outstanding. One is the fact that these regions have not experienced the devastation which they confronted in the earlier intercensus periods. Another is that the shift of industry away from the west has apparently almost stopped. In 1959-1961 and 1970, the percent of the total industrial workers located in the west was roughly the same (72.7 and 72.4, respectively). In addition, the high correlation between urbanization and industrialization between 1959 and 1970 also implies that many of the rapidly urbanizing western regions were generally industrializing relatively rapidly. This rejuvenated industrialization in the west is in turn apparently due to: 1) the increased investment in the west, which evidently has many small and medium-sized towns with a labor surplus; 2) improvements in transportation facilities, which now make it easier to transport raw materials to the west, thus reducing the need to move industries east; 3) the switch in the energy balance from coal to oil and natural gas, which are relatively more plentiful in the west than is coal and are easier to transport; 4) the expansion of Soviet trade with the United States and Europe; 5) the nuclear age, which makes it less crucial to move to the east for military purposes; and 6) the above-mentioned difficulties of stimulating a greater eastward migration.[34]

Summary and Conclusions

The purpose of this essay has been to describe and analyze broadly major national and regional patterns of urbanization in Russia and the USSR during the last century, generally under a comparable definition of the term urban and one set of territorial units.

Investigation of major national trends revealed that the pace of urbanization in Russia and the USSR has generally been either close to or well above the world average. In fact, during the last half century the USSR has experienced the most rapid urbanization of any of the major world regions. In addition, during the 1930s its rate of urbanization was perhaps the most rapid ever experienced in human history.

Analysis revealed that of the immediate factors in urbanization and urban growth, net rural-to-urban migration has apparently been the principal factor, a pattern roughly similar to the world-wide situation throughout history. The relative influence of rural-to-urban migration has been declining, however, especially at the expense of urban natural increase. The increasing influence of the latter is largely due to elimination of high urban mortality, the general lack of chaos and turmoil in the last two decades, and the fact that rural-to-urban migration generally declines in the later stages of urbanization with the relative reduction of the rural population.

More intense investigation revealed that the urbanization process was strongly related to the rapid industrialization which has occurred in Russia and the USSR during the past century. This relationship has been especially strong in more recent decades. In the late nineteenth century it appears that the industrialization was not a highly potent influence on urbanization, especially because of the rural orientation of manufacturing. Instead, urbanization at this time appeared to be more strongly related to service activities. This situation was particularly exemplified by the relatively highly urbanized Southern region, which was dominated by grain-trading centers.

Changes have also occurred in the regional patterns of urbanization. The eastern regions were generally urbanizing at a more rapid rate than the western regions between 1897 and 1970. In the last decade of this period, however, this pattern has changed in that the pace of urbanization is now greater in the west. A major reason for this change has been the emergence of net out-migration from the east, traditionally an area of high in-migration, due to the relatively low living standards there. In addition, the shift of industry to the east has greatly diminished and many western

regions are experiencing appreciable rates of industrialization.
The role of the Russian and Soviet governments in these developments has been both indirect and substantial. None of the patterns discussed has been the direct result of governmental policies to bring about their realization. Nevertheless, governmental policies have had a dramatic indirect influence on the patterns. Outstanding, of course, has been the governmental plan to emphasize industrialization. It is inconceivable that the rapid pace of Soviet urbanization could have occurred in the absence of a governmental policy which has given top priority to rapid industrialization. In addition, the relatively rapid urbanization in the east during the overall period has been partly the result of governmental plans to industrialize this mineral-rich area; in fact, the government has given wage incentives to attract people to these areas, although they have not been sufficient to prevent substantial out-migration in more recent years.

Notes

This research was supported by Grant No. 3 RO1 HD 05585 of the Center for Population Research of the National Institute of Child Health and Human Development and the International Institute for the Study of Human Reproduction, Columbia University.

1. For example see: Robert A. Lewis and Richard H. Rowland, "Urbanization in Russia and the USSR: 1897-1966," *Annals of the Association of American Geographers*, 59 (December 1969): 776-96; Chauncy D. Harris, *Cities of the Soviet Union* (Chicago: Rand McNally, 1970); Chauncy D. Harris, "Urbanization and Population Growth in the Soviet Union, 1959-1970," *Geographical Review* 61 (January 1971): 102-24; D. I. Valentei, V. V. Pokshishevskii, and B. S. Khorev, *Problemy urbanizatsii v SSSR* (Moscow, 1971).

2. Citations for the first four censuses can be found in Lewis and Rowland, pp. 776-77. The data for 1970 come from: 1) *Izvestiia*, April 19, 1970, p. 1; 2) Prezidium Verkhovnogo Soveta Soiuza Sovetskikh Sotsialisticheskikh Respublik, *SSSR: Administrativno-Territorial'noe delenie Soiuznykh Respublik na 1 Iiulia 1971 goda* (Moscow), pp. 17-502, 620-33; 3) Tsentral'noe Statisticheskoe Upravlenie pri Sovete Ministrov SSSR, *Narodnoe khaziaistvo SSSR v 1970 g.* (Moscow, 1971), p. 12.

3. For a listing of these censuses, see Lewis and Rowland, p. 777. Whenever possible, the total and urban populations of these areas were applied to the years of the Russian and Soviet censuses by means of interpolation or extrapolation.

4. For a map and list of these regions, see Lewis and Rowland, pp. 778, 782. For a detailed discussion of the procedures involved for 1897-1959, see J. William Leasure and

Robert A. Lewis, *Population Changes in Russia and the USSR: A Set of Comparable Territorial Units* (San Diego: San Diego State College Press, 1966). For 1970, other adjustments had to be made because the 1970 economic regions are not all the same as those for 1961. Since the differences generally involve the transfer of an entire political-administrative unit from one region to another, the adjustments were relatively simple: shifting data from a transferred unit back to its appropriate 1961 region. As far as we can tell, the boundaries of all units were virtually the same for 1961 and 1970, with two exceptions: roughly 40,000 square kilometers were shifted from Kazakhstan to Uzbekistan. Although part of this territory was subsequently shifted back to Kazakhstan, 1970 data now available are still presented in the larger Uzbek and, consequently, smaller Kazakh units. We have adjusted the published 1970 populations of the two republics so that they roughly conform to the 1961 regions.

5. For a detailed discussion of the reasons for such a definition, see Lewis and Rowland, p. 778.

6. For a more detailed discussion of these terms, see Lewis and Rowland, p. 779.

7. Adna F. Weber, *The Growth of Cities in the Nineteenth Century* (New York: Macmillan, 1899), p. 145. This figure is based on the imperial boundaries of 1820.

8. The 1885 figure is based on data from Russian Empire, Tsentral'nyi Statisticheskii Komitet Ministerstva Vnutrennikh Del, *Statistika Rossiiskoi Imperii,* vol. 1: *Sbornik svedenii po Rossii za 1884-1885 gg.* (St. Petersburg, 1887), pp. 1-27. For a more detailed discussion of the derivation of these percentages, see Richard H. Rowland, "Urban In-Migration in Late Nineteenth Century Russia," Ph.D. dissertation, Department of Geography, Columbia University, 1971, pp. 111-15. Both figures are for the Russian Empire excluding Finland.

9. Kingsley Davis and Hilda Hertz, "Patterns of World Urbanization for 1800-1950," in United Nations, Bureau of Social Affairs, *Report on the World Social Situation including Studies of Urbanization in Underdeveloped Areas* (New York, 1957), p. 114.

10. The 1970 figure is based on the summation of the population in all urban centers of 100,000 and over (76,506,000) including urban settlements subordinated to the *gorsovety* of Moscow, Leningrad, Baku, and Minsk. This figure therefore exceeds the published Soviet totals (for example, *Izvestiia,* April 19, 1970, p. 1) of 75,600,000, partly because it includes the subordinated centers. The difference is of little consequence since the levels of urbanization are almost identical (31.7 percent vs. 31.3 percent, respectively).

11. The 1900 figure is from Davis and Hertz, p. 114. The 1970 figure has been derived from Davis's projected 1970 populations. Kingsley Davis, *World Urbanization 1950-1970,* vol. 1: *Basic Data for Cities, Countries, and Regions* (Berkeley: University of California, Institute of International Studies, 1969), pp. 57-82. The validity of Davis's estimates for 1970 is substantiated at least in the case of the USSR. His estimated total population is 244,125,000 and his estimated 100,000 and over population is 74,982,000. Such figures are only 1 percent higher and 2 percent lower, respectively, than the actual Soviet census figures for 1970.

12. United Nations, Department of Economic and Social Affairs, *Growth of the World's Urban and Rural Population, 1920-2000* (New York, 1969), pp. 31, 58. The 1970 figures are projections. The validity of these estimates is also substantiated, at least in the case of the USSR; the level of urbanization based upon the 20,000 and over criterion here is 43 percent as compared to the actual level of 44 percent.

13. Kingsley Davis, "The Urbanization of the Human Population," *Scientific American* 213 (September 1965): 44.

14. Ibid.

15. Rowland, pp. 115-17.

16. B. Ts. Urlanis, *Rost naseleniia v SSSR* (Moscow, 1966), p. 34; *Izvestiia*, April 19, 1970, p. 1. These data are based upon the various census definitions of urban.

17. Urlanis, p. 34; *Izvestiia*, April 19, 1970, p. 1.

18. For example, see Holland Hunter, *Soviet Transportation Experience* (Washington, D.C.: Brookings Institution, 1968), pp. 118-22.

19. Lewis and Rowland, p. 791. The term 1959-1961 denotes the fact that the percentage involves the total population of 1959 and the number of industrial workers for 1961; the number of industrial workers in the nineteen economic regions cannot be obtained for 1959. The 1961 data come from Tsentral'noe Statisticheskoe Upravlenie, *Narodnoe khoziaistvo SSSR v 1961 g.* (Moscow, 1962), pp. 132-33, 462. For a more complete discussion of the industrial categories used for all years, see Leasure and Lewis, pp. 38-39, footnote 1.

20. The only industrial data for economic regions in 1970 available at the time of writing are those showing the percentage increase in gross industrial production between 1950 and select subsequent years, including 1960 and 1970 but not 1959 or 1961. They can be found in Tsentral'noe Statisticheskoe Upravlenie, *Narodnoe khoziaistvo SSSR v 1970 g.* (Moscow, 1971), p. 139. These data have two deficiencies: like all Soviet industrial production data, they include double-counting, and they are based upon the current nineteen economic regions and not the 1961 regions used for all of our studies of Russian and Soviet urbanization; the current regions do not differ substantially from the 1961 regions, however. Due to the lack of other data we have used these production data. From them, it is possible to calculate average annual rates of the growth of industrial production between 1960 and 1970. Because we were ultimately concerned with industrial workers and not production, however, we decided to apply these regional production data to regional data on industrial workers. To do this we assumed that regional variations in industrial production increase would be roughly similar to variations in the increase in the number of industrial workers. Because the average annual rate of increase in the number of industrial workers for the entire USSR between 1960 and 1970 was only 37.8 percent of the average annual increase in the rate of production (see *Narodnoe khoziaistvo SSSR v 1970 g.*, pp. 139, 158), we multiplied the regional average annual rates of production by .378. This gave a rough estimate of the average annual percentage increase in the number of industrial workers between 1960 and 1970. These annual rates for workers were then used to project the number of industrial workers in 1961 to 1970 based upon the economic regions of 1961.

21. Lewis and Rowland, p. 791.

22. For a detailed discussion of the 1897 procedures, see Rowland, pp. 185-95.

23. The total population used here is that for areas for which data were available and not necessarily the entire population of the region. Also, because for 1926 no data were available for the West region (the Baltic states), it was necessary to estimate its percent by other means. Because in 1897 its percent was 1.091 times the national average, we decided to multiply the 1926 national average (1.9 percent) by 1.091 to estimate this region's percent in 1926.

24. Data concerning the urban-rural distribution of the industrial work force are based upon census definitions of urban and rural. These figures were used because they were relatively easily available and would not differ substantially from those based upon the urban definition used in this study.

25. These data are for the boundaries of the Russian Empire in 1897.

26. V. I. Lenin, *The Development of Capitalism in Russia* (Moscow: Foreign Languages Publishing House, 1956), p. 574.

27. The tertiary work force is a fairly crude category in that it is simply a residual of the total work force minus the agricultural and industrial work forces as defined in Leasure and Lewis, pp. 38-40. Although it includes "construction," it still is largely dominated by service activities.

28. The "eastern regions" here consist of the Urals, West Siberia, East Siberia, the Far East, Kazahkstan, and Central Asia. The "western regions" are the remaining thirteen.

29. Lewis and Rowland, pp. 783-89.

30. These figures were computed by means of the residual method. For each region we subtracted the absolute natural increase between 1959 and 1970 from the total population increase. Since no data are available which list the entire absolute natural increase between 1959 and 1970, we had to estimate such a figure. We based our estimates on the July 1964 regional natural increase rates, since this date lies at the mid-point of the 1959-1970 period, and because rates could not be obtained for all years. These rates can be found in *Vestnik statistiki*, no. 12 (1966): 83-85. These rates were multiplied by the July 1964 population of each region, resulting in absolute natural increase for each region in 1964. The July 1964 population was estimated by summing the January 1964 and January 1965 populations and dividing the sum by two. Estimates for these populations can be found in Tsentral'noe Statisticheskoe Upravlenie, *Narodnoe khoziaistvo SSSR v 1963 g.* (Moscow, 1965), pp. 12-17; and Tsentral'noe Statisticheskoe Upravlenie, *Narodnoe khoziaistvo SSSR v 1964 g.* (Moscow, 1965), pp. 12-17. Because the set of economic regions for which the rates and populations were given again did not correspond exactly to our set of regions, we had to make adjustments. Estimates of absolute natural increase for our set of regions in 1964 were then multiplied by 11 to give an estimate of absolute natural increase between 1959 and 1970. One final refinement was to multiply these 11 year totals by a correction factor of 1.03. This factor represents the ratio between 1) the 1959-1970 absolute national population increase, which was assumed to be entirely due to natural increase since there was hardly any immigration to or emigration from the USSR during this period, and 2) the estimated absolute natural increase for the USSR based on the summation of the above regional estimates.

31. *Vestnik statistiki*, no. 10 (1968): 89.

32. V. I. Perevedentsev, "Sovremennaia migratsiia naseleniia v SSSR," in *Narodonaselenie i ekonomika* (Moscow, 1967), pp. 99-118; N. P. Kalinovskii, "Mezhraionnoe vyravnivanie real'noi zarabotnoi platy kak faktor privlecheniia kadrov," in ibid., pp. 145-56.

33. Perevedentsev, p. 104.

34. For a discussion of some of these developments, see Theodore Shabad, "Changing Resource Policies of the U.S.S.R.," *Focus* 19 (February 1969): 7-8.

THE REVIVAL AND SCHISM OF URBAN
PLANNING IN TWENTIETH-CENTURY RUSSIA

S. Frederick Starr

When does the story of modern city planning in Russia begin? It has long been customary to start with the year 1917. Early Soviet planners themselves posited such a chronology and defended it with all the force of revolutionary conviction. Most subsequent specialists on the subject have accepted their arguments and built their own analyses around them. A sharply different perspective, however, is at least implied by recent studies on Russia's heritage of city building from the time of Peter I through the early nineteenth century. According to this view, the Russian Revolution continued and broadened an earlier tradition of state-sponsored planning, updating it, of course, to meet the requirements of an emerging industrial society.[1]

These rival claims have yet to be adjudicated, or even to be set forth with any real thoroughness. When this does take place the overly schematic and even simplistic character of both will very likely become apparent. For, on the one hand, to insist on the importance of discontinuities in urban planning caused by the Revolution is to deny or at least to play down the many instances of both plans and personnel being carried over from the old order to the new. And on the other hand, to stress the continuity of a single state-centered tradition in Russia is to assert the existence of a neat thread uniting schools of planning which were in fact separated by a gap of three-quarters of a century.

A third perspective, which this essay will defend, holds that however great the impact of the October Revolution on Russian urban planning, most of the "revolutionary" currents in the field were profoundly indebted to an earlier movement, one which had been founded only around the turn of the century but which by 1917 had succeeded in posing, but by no means deciding between, at least two radically differing programs for urban development. The emergence of these programs marks both the beginning of modern city planning in Russia and the reincorporation into that new movement of much that had characterized Russia's earlier planning heritage. Discussions during the period 1900-1917 certainly did not define all the parameters of debate in the early Soviet period, but, due to both the intensity with which they were pursued on the very eve of 1917 and their formative impact on specific individuals active after the revolutions, they left their clear imprint on Soviet discussion of city planning up to mid-century.

The two programs or models of urban form which were developed and refined during the late imperial period were, first, what for the sake of convenience I will term the "classical" but which was in reality a blend of baroque and neoclassical concepts,[2] and second, that of the garden city.[3] Neither was Russian in origin, the former having been earlier imported from the France of the *ancien régime*, the latter making its appearance on the heels of the founding of the International Garden City Movement in England. But as they became domesticated, each came to meet genuine needs of the moment and to stand as a vital and evocative symbol of future hopes. It was the task of the October Revolution not to destroy these tendencies but to take them over and adapt them to the particular objectives of Bolshevism.

The Revival of Classical Planning

The origin of modern city planning in Russia is cloaked in paradox. Though looking to the future, it was brought into being by people preoccupied with the past; though revolutionary in aim, it sought first of all to preserve the architectural legacy of the monarchy in its most resplendent phase, the eighteenth century. The explanation for this peculiar genesis is to be found in the dramatic changes taking place in one city, St. Petersburg, and in the response to them of certain leaders of *fin de siècle* aesthetic life in Russia.

The Russian capital at the time of this turn of events typified the situation in many cities whose greatness was founded before the industrial era and which were forced to accommodate themselves to the changed circumstances imposed by a factory economy. The population had nearly trebled in half a century, with most of the new immigrants being peasant-workers drawn from the countryside. Much of the new building, whether industrial, administrative, or domestic, was undertaken by private concerns. State agencies charged with the regulation only of public building found themselves at a loss to control this new construction, especially since development was occurring at such rapid-fire pace. The city directorate created in the Reform of 1870 proved equally inadequate to the task, and the Technical Building Committee established by the Ministry of Internal Affairs in 1885 to monitor all city planning and architectural activity in the empire quickly restricted its concern to defining technical standards for engineering work, ignoring broader questions of urban development. At the same time, those other state agencies whose city-planning activities under Catherine II had once made Russia the European leader in deliberately conceived town construction had atrophied even before large-scale industrialization began.

The results were chaotic in the extreme. In St. Petersburg, where Peter I had once enforced a ban on wooden construction, 65 percent of all new building in 1890 was wood.[4] Whole districts to the south, southwest, and northeast were log-built tinderboxes, subject to the ancient menace of fire. The relative weakness of the public sector caused much-needed sewerage facilities increasingly to lag behind building. Even the boldest strokes of imperial planning, those ensembles of streets, squares, and monumental edifices that are the glory of the Northern Palmyra, were being encroached upon by hastily conceived business and apartment blocks. The Neva bank of the Admiralty had been built up in the 1880s, the Rossi outbuildings to the Mikhailovskii Palace were ripped down, the Winter Palace was painted a deep barn red, the lower end of Nevskii Prospekt was built over with banking houses, and even a mammoth hall was projected for an artificial island in the Little Neva, which would have destroyed the ensemble dominated by the neoclassical Stock Exchange. Capitalism showed little respect for the statist conception underlying Peter's city, and the Great Russian nationalism rampant at the time belittled the baroque geometry of foreign planners and francified Russians. Nobody, it seemed, spoke for the city of St. Petersburg. "Patriotisme du clocher" was dead.

Founders of the new urbanism may all have been aware of these developments but they responded most keenly to the erosion of the classical city. Those who led the movement came precisely from those segments of educated society most closely linked with the old city and least engaged with the new industrialism: certain Westernized gentry and especially families of that older middle class which owed its privileged position to imperial patronage. The remarkable Benois family and its circle epitomized both groups.

Descended from humble antirevolutionary emigrés from France, the Benois family, as architects, had benefited over two generations from royal favor. Leontii (b. 1859), leader of the St. Petersburg revival in planning, continued this tradition, following his father as rector of the Academy of Arts and architect to the court. But by the twentieth century the Academy had renounced its planning role and the position of court architect had been reduced to the construction of sylvan dachas for a tsar who loathed the capital.

In his memoirs, Alexandre Benois, painter and cofounder of the World of Art circle, provides valuable insights on his own and his elder brother Leontii's efforts to reclaim the St. Petersburg of their forebears. In his boyhood the family had summered near Okhta on the northeastern edge of St. Petersburg, where they rented an Empire style guest house in the decaying garden of the former Bezborodko estate. The dilapidated main villa now billeted an army of foreign workers who worked at a paper factory built on a corner of the grounds of the estate. The "belching chimney and perpetual noise" of the factory, the disarray of the workers' quarters, all contrasted unfavorably to the vanishing orderliness of the gardens. And was not the estate of Kushelevka a miniature version of the city itself? "All evoked in me a vague feeling of sadness," recalled Benois, "a sort of anxious foreboding of more destruction to come."[5]

Such thoughts were readily translated into art. Both Alexandre and his brother Leontii turned with morbid fascination to the fashionable symbolist works of the French painters Sue, Chudant and especially Charles Guerin, soon painting their own russified versions of the court of Louis XIV strolling in the park at Versailles.[6] With the founding of the *World of Art* journal, the revival of imperial and aristocratic St. Petersburg was in full swing. Konstantin Somov, Anna Ostroumova-Lebedeva, Grigorii Lukomskii, and the brothers Benois all discovered in the city a mine of visual images, a spectacular theatrical set which met both their aesthetic and social inclinations.

It would be tempting to dismiss this movement as the creation of a rather precious group of snobs, Wagnerian aesthetes infatuated with what Alexandre Benois confessed to be the "disintegration of a glorious era" and content to survey the wreckage from behind lace curtains, quietly singing, as did Benois, "Petersburg über alles."[7]

True, the revivalists did pander to the social ambitions of a considerable number of merchant princes, equipping them with mansions in the style of Russian classicism which proclaimed their equality with the old nobility.[8] But they did more. For the first time in Russian art, they made the physical city itself an object of aesthetic scrutiny; not merely its individual monuments, as was the concern of the Schinkel revival occurring simultaneously in Berlin, but its ensembles of buildings in the Empire style, its squares, its baroque prospects and classical gardens. Impelled by a vision of aesthetic and cultural unity, these artists and architects set about imposing their vision on a reality bent at every turn upon destroying it. Through a series of public exhibitions held in the decade after the collapse of the Revolution of 1905 they brought from obscurity the architects and planners who had created that unity in the first place; they excoriated the worst desecrations of the architectural heritage of their city, and they founded journals such as *Starye Gody* (The Old Years) to convey their message to a sympathetic public elsewhere in Russia. Thanks to the efforts of Leontii Benois, strict laws on historic preservation were passed and enforced,[9] and the Academy of Arts resumed an active role in defending the aesthetic integrity of Russian cities against the assaults of philistinism.

Nor did the revivalists confine themselves to rearguard actions against the present; during the last decade before World War I they sallied forth to wrest the process of city development from the hands of chance and submit it once more to rational planning. On one flank the attack focused on the planning of separate ensembles and districts. The leading champion of this effort was the young Ivan Fomin, fresh from Moscow and from a brief but ultimately disenchanting flirtation with the German *Jugendstil* currents.[10] Once in St. Petersburg he apprenticed to Leontii Benois and built a number of villas which established him as a master of what Rayner Banham in another context termed the "stripped classical style."[11] It was at this time that he drafted plans for a series of new regions and ensembles. Fomin's scheme for a "New Petersburg" provides a representative sample of revivalist work in this genre.[12] Planned for the mosquito-ridden Golodai Island in the northern estuary of the Neva, it consisted of a large apartment complex laid out along three main thoroughfares radiating from a central semi-circular plaza. Against the background of earlier classical ensembles in Russia there was little that was distinctive about Fomin's New Petersburg—but therein lay its true merit. For in the context of the rambling districts of squalid and randomly conceived wooden and brick structures which had sprung up in the late nineteenth century, New Petersburg was a model of rationality, conceived in a single style that was both monumental and functional, and on a scale which no single St. Petersburg entrepreneur could have underwritten.

On another flank the revivalists forged beyond the confines of the historic models which they idolized. Leontii Benois opened this wider campaign in 1908 when he convinced the Academy of Arts that it should lead in the formulation for the capital of "a general plan, carefully considered and worked out, covering all the rebuilding that is required."[13] After an initial rebuff from the city duma, Benois set to work with the architects N. Lansere and M. Peretiatkovich and an engineer from the Ministry of Communications, F. Enakiev, to draft the plan independently. By 1910 the initial maps were completed. Their project bears a superficial resemblance to Möring and Eberstadt's 1909 plan for a "Greater Berlin," by which the two Russian planners were inspired. Moreover, it was in preparation at precisely the same time as Otto Wagner's classicizing plan for the further development of Vienna and Daniel Burnham's more modest and less fully elaborated proposal for rationalizing the street plan of Chicago. Very much part of a broader movement, the Benois-Enakiev proposal for St. Petersburg remains of particular importance for Russia, for it constituted the most ambitious pre-Revolutionary effort to regularize and replan any city in the empire.

Enakiev meanwhile had published a book entitled *Tasks for the Reform of St. Petersburg* in which he demonstrated the need not merely to expand eighteenth-century schema nor even to make "safe" the chaotic newer districts through the means Baron Haussmann had applied in Paris, but rather to develop a single, comprehensive approach which would take into account the movement of motorized traffic, needs of hygiene, and the general social and economic welfare of an industrial metropolis.[14]

Enakiev's book broadened the rapidly emerging urbanist movement beyond its earlier preoccupation with preserving the past. His utter practicality and cool mastery of detail were precisely those qualities most needed to balance the Benois' more narrowly historical and aesthetic concerns; he could blandly note, for instance, that the mayors of Cleveland and St. Louis understood better than Russian civic leaders that beautiful cities might also be prosperous ones. When in 1916 Benois again appeared before the duma, this time armed with Enakiev's position paper, he carried the day.[15] The duma hailed his presentation "On the Question of the Planned Development of the Construction of Petrograd and Its Surroundings," and took particular note of the fact that what had begun as a program to save the city center had now evolved into a plan for the development of an entire metropolitan region. Benois was commissioned forthwith to draft new statutes "On the Planning and Construction of Petrograd" and at the same time a competition was proclaimed as a means of enlisting the best minds available for the planning effort.

These resolutions bear witness to the fact that one aspect of the modern movement in Russian city planning had come of age. That movement owed much to the heritage of earlier planning in Russia, but each aspect of its indebtedness came to be oriented as much to the future as to the past. First, it sought to retain in the modern city that grandeur which the baroque and Romantic Classical planners had first created as a backdrop for public ceremonies and formal processions. The years between the Revolution of 1905 and World War I were scarcely ideal ones for the staging of such spectacles, preoccupied as the state was with broadening the basis of its support through practical legislation. Yet the new urbanists reminded Russia that cities and buildings, too, could serve to publicize the ideals of the society. Second, the movement prized the unity and even uniformity of style which the earlier St. Petersburg architects had done so much to achieve. Fomin, Benois, and their colleagues conceived picturesque diversity and organic evolution as being virtually synonymous with disorder, whereas they esteemed rationality in planning and building as the very qualities which had originally brought St. Petersburg from the Finnish swamps. Third, the revivalists had a Petrine addiction to planning and architectural productions on a scale so large that in Russia the state alone was capable of funding and executing them. At a time when Count Witte and his successors held that private industries and voluntary associations should be groomed to assume responsibility for much of the development of Russia, the urbanists called in the government once more, settling for the elective city administration when necessary but preferring to deal directly with the central state apparatus. Fourth, like the great planners of early St. Petersburg, they had little involvement with or overriding concern for private property. In contrast to public agencies of the immediately preceding decades, they gladly subordinated private and individual interest to the demands of their general plan, and waited eagerly for the day when the state would resume its former willingness to alienate private land in its own interest.[16]

In short, the revivalists pioneered in the formulation of many notions central to twentieth-century planning in Russia and elsewhere. Having done so, they then worked to make it a respectable academic discipline, campaigning successfully for the introduction in Russia of courses in *Städtebau* like those offered in Vienna, and for the establishment of the first chair in city planning at the Academy of Arts.[17] These achievements together transcend in importance the movement's more limited practical accomplishments in bricks and mortar.

The Garden City Ideal in Russia

The second great school of urbanism to grow up in early twentieth-century Russia has the same relation to the first as two gears to one another: closely meshed and impelled by the same force, they nonetheless moved in opposite directions. Both were oppressed by the grim condition of Russian cities, by what Benois termed the "absence of ideals and poetry"[18] of contemporary urban life, and both envisaged solutions which would not merely ameliorate but eradicate the evils they deplored. But from this point they took different courses. It would be too facile to assert that the revivalists looked from the middle classes upward in society, while the garden city school looked from the same vantage point downward. After all, the revivalists, too, had concerned themselves with problems of public sanitation and parks and had even led in the founding of recreational and cultural facilities for workers which strikingly anticipate the workers' clubs of the

1920s.[19] Yet the claim would not entirely miss the mark, for the garden city movement not merely took an interest in these issues but was preoccupied with them, and more particularly with meeting the mammoth need for low-income housing, of which the revivalists showed no special awareness at all.

If the ideal of the classical revivalists was defined in concrete visual images, that of the more speculative garden city movement was embodied best in verbal expressions. These were not drawn from Russian literature, for besides the Decembrist Ulybishev's *Dream* of 1818[20] and a few other minor attempts, the urge towards utopia in Russia had been spent largely on idealizations of the peasant village community. Rather, Russian urbanists derived the image of the garden city and even its name from Ebenezer Howard's book, *Tomorrow: A Peaceful Path to Real Reform*, published in London in 1898.[21] With detail worthy of Fourier and evangelical verve in the spirit of Owen, Howard called for the establishment of small and economically autonomous settlements of 30,000 to be built amid zones of fields and forest. Such towns would ring the great metropolises and gradually replace them. With the death of the super-city would die the social problems which industrialization had engendered.

Vindicated by the successful garden city established at Letchworth in England, Howard's ideal spread rapidly across northern Europe, reaching Russia via Germany in reviews published as early as 1902. The garden city was bound to be attractive to Russians of a reformist stripe, for Howard himself had acknowledged his indebtedness to the writings of Kropotkin, just as the Belgian Emile Vandervelde had drawn heavily on the writings of other Russian writers in his equally popular book, *L'exode rural et le retour aux champs*.[22] In the period 1905-1912 nearly every major journal in Russia reviewed Howard's and Vandervelde's tracts and a series of Russian specialists printed their own detailed analyses of garden cities built in western Europe.[23]

Two factors of a more practical nature further disposed Russians towards the garden city idea. On the one hand, the construction of the first interurban rail lines was already stimulating the building of commuter suburbs around Moscow, St. Petersburg, Riga, and other large cities. Most of these bore the marks of extreme haste and lack of planning and those which did not were reserved for the wealthy, but their mere existence made the garden city appear far more practicable than might otherwise have been the case. On the other hand, most Russian towns and villages were already garden cities in the sense of their being far less densely populated than the old cities of western Europe. When the city fathers of Vernyi (Alma-Ata) in Central Asia simply declared their town to be a garden city they may have been demonstrating their misunderstanding of Howard's full program, but not to the extent that a similar claim would have appeared in Germany or even England.[24] Those garden cities actually built in Russia almost all allotted more open space to each building lot than Howard had anticipated for western Europe.

The formal organization of a Russian branch of the International Garden City Society dates to the autumn of 1913, at which time a charter for the Society of Garden Cities was approved in St. Petersburg.[25] All the founders were from St. Petersburg, many having met one another while participating in a 1909 tour of English new towns sponsored by the German branch of the movement. Their backgrounds tell much about the leaders, for whereas the founders of the classical revival were all associated with the Academy of Arts, officers of the Society of Garden Cities included two doctors and two lawyers, with but one architect among them. Several hundred prominent persons in the two capitals paid their five rubles to join, but more significant is the fact that the movement attracted a third of its adherents from elsewhere in the Russian empire, with those from the rapidly expanding Ukrainian cities predominating.

This diffusion of interest to less developed regions of Russia was entirely to be expected, given the strongly populist orientation of the garden city program. In the first place, it insisted that all town land be publicly owned and that its disposition through leasehold be controlled by a democratic assembly of the community itself rather than by more centralized governmental agencies.[26] In the

The Twentieth-Century City

second place, the movement accepted industrialization as a fact and approved its further expansion, but only on the condition that industry be decentralized to the maximum extent possible. In the third place, garden city spokesmen considered the only building material sufficiently inexpensive to solve the housing problem to be wood. The return to Russia's traditional building material was not merely a technical decision, for no ready alternative yet existed, but one of principle. Wooden structures could be built by the owners themselves or by peasant hewers (*desiatniki*), whereas stone or brick construction entailed capital investment and in Russia had generally involved the state. In opting for wood they also committed themselves to one- or two-family cottages, as opposed to the barracks-type apartment favored by those with a more urban orientation. A book on *Das Englische Haus* by Hermann Muthesius, founder of the Deutscher Werkbund, was cited to justify this position, but the position itself was taken as part of a generally positive attitude towards the culture of the Russian peasant.

Such attitudes, of course, were readily transferable to politics. The charter of the Society required it to stand "outside parties" but in fact the alignment of many garden city enthusiasts with left-wing liberal groups and especially with the right wing of the Socialist Revolutionaries could scarcely be disguised. A 1913 tract entitled *Socialism without Politics: Garden Cities of the Future and Present*, forthrightly proclaimed this stance.[27] The author, V. Dadonov, declared flatly that a Marxist-type revolution was both "impossible and pointless," and that a better path to socialism lay through municipal initiative and the cooperative movement, aided when possible by those capitalists sympathetic to the cause of social equity.

D. D. Protopopov, a St. Petersburg lawyer who became the principal spokesman for the group, translated these statements into practical terms. From 1909 he helped edit the journal *Gorodskoe delo*, doing much to transform it into a mouthpiece for the movement. In 1910 at the Odessa All Russian Congress of Activists and Specialists in City Building, and again at the Fourth

Congress of Russian Architects held in 1914, he crusaded for cities to take control of as much land as possible and for citizens of towns and cities to involve themselves more actively in local self-government lest initiative in urban planning slip into bureaucratic hands.[28] In the summer of 1914 he represented Russia at the International Congress of Garden Cities in Liverpool and succeeded in introducing three of the six resolutions taken by the congress. As war erupted, he returned to Russia to participate in the newly organized Union of Cities and later to support the Progressive Bloc in the Fourth Duma.

All the while Protopopov and his colleagues aided and publicized the many efforts to build garden cities underway in Russia before 1917. The first evidence of direct influence of Howard's ideas on a community within the Russian empire was the Kaiserwald suburb of Riga, planned in 1905-1908 and built in 1911.[29] Embodying garden city notions on density, building regulations, and parks, and replacing the "corridor street" with gently curving avenues, this village was at the same time lacking in both the social facilities and the productive function which lay at the heart of Howard's scheme.

Other suburbs embodying at least some features of Howard's plan were emerging from the drawing boards at about the same time. Some, such as Alexander Vesnin's Nikolskoe near Moscow (1908) merit note because their planners went on to important careers in the movement, but one particularly carried the hopes of the Society of Garden Cities.[30] That one was Prozorovka, designed by Vladimir Semënov, a civil engineer who was to become the leading city planner of Soviet Russia until his death in 1960. Semënov, an arch-Anglophile, had met Howard during a prolonged stay in England and had only recently published a major volume on garden cities and city planning in general, *Blagoustroistvo gorodov*.[31]

Prozorovka appears even today as a page out of Howard's notebook. Its civic centers, walkways, radial plan, parks, and green belt all conform closely to the British model. Even the housing— one- and two-story cottages for one to eight families—recalls more closely the British model than the more fully individuated housing favored by other Russian planners. Its only shortcoming derived from the fact that it was intended by its sponsors, the directors of the Moscow-Kazan railway, as a bedroom community for workers posted along the line and hence had no economic base of its own. Criticized severely for this, Semënov's town was nonetheless a huge success and exercised a catalytic influence over potential sponsors of other new towns. Soon the Moscow duma was debating proposals for garden cities for workers to be built on public lands, and the prestigious Moscow Architectural Society was sponsoring a competition for another garden city to be built near Ostankino.[32] Several others were projected for the environs of Petrograd, Kiev, Kharkov, Odessa, Ekaterinburg, Tula, and even Barnaul in Siberia,[33] while in the Crimea the resort towns of Laspi, Komperiia-Sarych, and Lirana were all conceived under the direct influence of the garden city model.[34] Bearing in mind that the first American garden city was built only in 1928 and was in many respects no more advanced a scheme than Prozorovka, the achievement of the pre-Revolutionary movement in Russia is the more impressive.

The New Urban and Anti-Urban
Ideals after 1917

By 1917, then, there existed two well developed programs for the further development of Russian cities: the application of modified classical principles to the larger industrial and administrative centers, and the garden city for satellite towns and smaller rural communities. On a practical level, each was quite compatible with the other. They did not compete for the same funds, and a decision in favor of one did not signify one's opposition to the other. Hence, Ivan Fomin could build the garden city resort of Laspi and continue his neoclassical plans for Petrograd. But on another level their essential incompatibility could not be doubted. For however much they might advocate parks and green spaces, the revivalists were in love with large cities and all the dignity and culture they possessed, while proponents of the garden city, for all their talk of eliminating the dichotomy of city and countryside, affirmed the more intimate virtues of the small town and village. The revolution of urban workers and rural peasants ended by bringing these two ideals into open conflict.

Few segments of educated society greeted both the February and October revolutions as positively as did city planners. Some welcomed the collapse in February of bureaucratic agencies that had heretofore impeded their efforts, while others focused their enthusiasm on the Soviet decree of August 20, 1918, abolishing the private ownership of land. Dmitrii Protopopov joined Kerensky's government as vice-president of the Local Government Board, while a battery of others at once assumed positions of responsibility after Lenin's coup. Leontii Benois was imprisoned by the Bolsheviks and endured several exceedingly difficult years after 1917, but before a half decade had passed even he was reinstated as president of the Leningrad Society of Architects and in his old professorship. Nearly all the others—Semënov, the Vesnin brothers, Fomin—soon reemerged as leaders in the field. It is to be doubted whether any learned profession suffered such a low rate of emigration after the Russian revolution as city planning. This fact alone assured a certain continuity of discourse, notwithstanding the important new possibilities and directions opened by the Revolution.

This continuity was vividly demonstrated in projects of the 1920s. The Garden City Society lapsed in 1918, only to be refounded in Moscow under governmental patronage in 1922.[35] At the same time, its program was reborn in the efforts by the Moscow soviet to transform the capital into a garden city,[36] and in the several "Red Garden Cities" which were built by state agencies such as the Commissariat of Public Health and by industry in the NEP period. Some of these, such as K. Karasev's village for the Istomin Cotton Factory in Smolensk province, followed closely Semënov's pre-Revolutionary Prozorovka, while several others, notably A. Ol's Red October village near Petrograd and V. Maiat's Krasnyi Bogatyr near Moscow, bear evidence of their authors' having had their copy of Howard close by the drawing board. Of these many efforts, however, only a few factory towns and old cities such as Iaroslavl' which were raised from ruin after the Civil War[37] possessed the independent productive base which the founder had insisted upon.

The weakened economy contributed to the prestige of wood and hence to the overwhelming popularity of rural-type cottage construction during the 1920s. Even as the industrially oriented Soviet regime was accepting the practical necessity of making its peace with the peasantry, some of the greatest modern architects in Russia sang paeons to the traditional peasant cottage as the best solution to the housing crisis and even came to idealize the peasant stove, focal point of the rural family.[38] But this was too much for those who, following Engels, believed that a communist society must smash the idiocy of rural life and destroy the individuation of the traditional family. Few communal apartments were actually constructed, but the attack leveled against the cottage in the name of collective housing threw an important element of the garden city program into disrepute as a bourgeois holdover. A further blow was struck by technocratic advocates of concrete and steel who held, with Iurii Larin, that "wood is barbaric."[39] And the voices of classical urbanists were particularly shrill as they polemicized against the anarchistic and sentimental pretenses of the deurbanists and declared their intention to create Soviet cities which would exceed in size and monumentality even the greatest achievements of the tsarist era. Finally, Stalin's war on the peasantry brought political discredit to the movement by branding the garden city ideal to be the epitome of "kulak democracy."[40]

Meanwhile, readers of the architectural press in the 1920s were led to believe that revivalists and other advocates of the large city had been put completely to rout by partisans of the small town. Proponents of the Red Garden City singled out the revivalists' emphasis on symmetry and size as the greatest dangers to their own movement, and the extreme deurbanists at the Constructivists' journal *SA* simply pronounced the principles of classical planning to be dead.[41] Far from it! One planner, for example, defending his star-shaped layout for a town to be called Zvezda, argued in words straight from Quarenghi that "correct forms and straight streets always beautify a town."[42] Many monumental parks commemorating the Revolution were purely classical in concept, most public buildings were built in a style employing classical techniques, and even the projects Bolshaia Moskva and Bolshoi Peterburg, which were the greatest efforts of the era to convert large centers into garden cities, called for a generous infusion of dramatic prospects, formal squares, and even buildings in a modernized Empire style.

Consequently, when a new cult of the state emerged in the 1930s and the Communist Party called for an appreciation of the architectural heritage and of classicism in particular,[43] no fresh revival was needed. Principles of classical city planning were alive and well, having been preserved by a group of architects whose names read like a *Who's Who* of the younger revivalists of 1914: Fomin was there, as were Zholtovskii, Tamanian, Shchuko, and others. After World War II it fell to these men and their students to rebuild the major cities of European Russia. With unabashed enthusiasm for the past, Ivan Fialko constructed axial walks and Roman temples in Stalingrad, while Lenin Prospekt in Minsk and Gorkii Street in Moscow were rebuilt to serve as settings for processions, and parks of victory were established in Leningrad and scores of other cities according to canons of planning tracing directly to turn-of-the-century studies of the parks at Versailles.

One may wonder how the two patterns of city planning considered here could exert an influence so strong as to transcend the political and social watershed marked by the October Revolution. Surely, it will be observed, the October Revolution produced solutions more radical than these to the problems of city design and housing.

Of course, it did. Nikolai Miliutin's "linear city," Moisei Ginsburg's ingenious portable towns, the supercollectivized phalansteries proposed by Leonard Sabsovich—all these surpass in boldness practically anything occurring elsewhere during the interwar years and all must be traced directly to efforts by their authors to

238   The Twentieth-Century City

translate Marxist precepts into actual urban forms.[44] Yet even these efforts were deeply indebted to the rival ideals of the garden village and the classical city; throughout the most utopian discussions of small "agrocities" or of Corbusier's rigidly geometric metropolis, this indebtedness proclaims itself. The pre-1917 currents could be continued even during Stalin's Cultural Revolution because the utopians for the most part had been trained before the Revolution when the majority of older architects and civic leaders still considered the "new" classical planning and garden cities to be daring innovations and by no means simply the excrescences of late Imperial society. Hence, for decades thereafter one could turn to these currents with relative impunity, the more readily since foreign experience seemed also to confirm their relevance.

This is not to deny that the vogue of classical planning and the garden city did not eventually subside. But unlike the more utopian schemes of the 1920s which also faded, the two movements under consideration retained a certain influence even on those who were not themselves participants in them. A postwar generation of younger architects and planners had been trained to respect their ideals, and even when they felt compelled to alter them drastically in order to adapt them to changed circumstances, the two currents continued to provide important bearing points in discussions on town planning. Efforts to limit the size of cities, opposition to dense habitation and to streets built like corridors, preservation of open land through green belts, and the provision of social amenities along with new housing—all these principles of Soviet planning had their genesis in the garden city idea.[45] Similarly, the classical revival was to exercise a powerful influence on the planning and architecture of Soviet cities, a bombastic version of Romantic Classicism dominating the scene until the post-Stalin generation led a return to Corbusier's formula of skyscraper apartments surrounded by parks. Even thereafter, the desire for theatrical settings for state ceremonies, the urge towards formal and geometric order, and the emphasis on ensembles created in harmonious styles have frequently been met with solutions which belie their origins in neoclassicism.

Nor has the old schism between the two currents ever been fully resolved. Stately avenues of apartment blocs are still being built in open countryside, even as economic journals call for cottage construction;[46] grandiose avenues so immense as to make strong men feel like Gogol's Akakii Akakevich are being laid out in new urban districts just as efforts are being made to submit the ever-growing cities to a more human measure.

This tension between city and countryside, of course, is by no means unique to Russia, and has been felt in all industrial societies at some point during the course of their development. But in Russia its most critical phase coincided with a period in which the city more clearly than ever represented the aspirations of the state, while the urge towards the small town represented a step away from these aspirations, a move towards the self-administered village commune where traditionally most inhabitants of Great Russia lived. It is the peculiar fate of Russian city planning in the first half of the twentieth century that each of these tendencies was early given clear expression in schemes for the planning of cities and villages. Each was permitted to develop to the limit of its potential, but the conflict inherent between them remained, for no single urban form could have satisfied a population and government moving rapidly but unsurely from a rural to an urban orientation.

Notes

1. As early as 1953 A. M. Tverskoi, on the basis of his study of the seventeenth century, called for a reassessment of the planning tradition throughout Russian history, in *Russkoe gradostroitel'stvo do kontsa xvii veka* (Moscow, 1953), pp. 200-201; for a review of recent writings on twentieth-century Russian architecture and planning see S. F. Starr, "Writings from the 1960s on the Modern Movement in Russia," *Journal of the Society of Architectural Historians* 30, no. 2 (May 1971): 170-78.

2. E. A. Borisova's excellent review of this movement deals mainly with its architectural aspects: "Neoklassitsism," in E. A. Borisova and T. P. Kazhdan, *Russkaia arkhitektura kontsa xix-nachala xx veka* (Moscow, 1971), pp. 167-219.

3. On the garden city movement see V. L. Ruzhzhe, "Goroda-sady: maloizvestnye proekty russkikh zodchikh," *Stroitelstvo i arkhitektura Leningrada*, 1961, no. 2; and idem, "Arkhitekturnye-planirovochnye idei goroda-sada v Rossii v kontse xix-nachale xx vv.," *Izvestiia vysshikh uchebnykh zavedenii Min. vysshego i srednego obrazovaniia, ser.*

Stroitelstvo i arkhitektura (Novosibirsk, 1961), no. 5, pp. 180-88; Eric L. Richard, "The Garden City in Russian Urbanism, 1904-1933," senior thesis, Princeton University, 1972. The major published sources on the movement are articles appearing in *Gorodskoe delo* and *Garden Cities and Town Planning*.

4. "Razvitie stroitelnogo dela v Peterburge, 1883-1897," *Stroitel; vestnik arkhitektury, domovladeniia i sanitarnoi konstruktsii*, 1899, nos. 7-8: 265.

5. Alexandre Benois, *Memoirs*, M. Budberg, trans., 2 vols. (London, 1960), 1: 220.

6. See works selected from the Paris Salon of 1903, in *Mir iskusstva*, 10 (1903): 101-05.

7. Benois, 1: 17.

8. I. V. Zholtovskii's house for the Armenian merchant Tarasov in Moscow is typical of these. Certain aristocrats continued to patronize this style as well, as Fomin's estate for Prince Gagarin and palace for Polovtsov indicate. M. Minkus, N. Pekareva, *I. A. Fomin* (Moscow, 1953), chapter 1.

9. V. L. Ruzhzhe, "Razvitie tvorcheskikh vozzrenii v russkoi arkhitekture v kontse xix-nachale xx vv," *Izvestiia vysshego i srednego spetsialnogo obrazovaniia SSSR, ser. Stroitelstvo i arkhitektura*, 1960, no. 5: 146-53.

10. For Fomin's work in this genre see *Mir iskusstva* 9 (1902): 97-113. For his reversion to classicism see his essay "Moskovskii klassitsizm," *Mir iskusstva* 7 (1904): 149-98.

11. Rayner Banham, *Theory and Design in the First Machine Age*, 2d ed. (New York, 1960), pp. 53, 95-97.

12. G. Lukomskii, "O postroike Novogo Peterburga," *Zodchii*, 1912, no. 52: 519-21; T. P. Kazhdan, "Gradostroitelstvo," in Borisova and Kazhdan, *Russkaia arkhitektura*, pp. 62-65.

13. *Zodchii*, 1909, no. 17:175-77.

14. F. E. Enakiev, *Zadachi preobrazovaniia S. Peterburga* (St. Petersburg, 1912), pp. 19-22.

15. V. L. Ruzhzhe, "Gradostroitelnye vzgliady arkhitektora L. N. Benua," *Arkhitekturnoe nasledstvo*, part 7 (Moscow, 1955): 72-74.

16. One commentator, praising the 1909 law which broadened the power of the London County Council to alienate private land, termed it "purely Petrine in its radicalism." *Gorodskoe delo*, 1914, no. 5:274.

17. First proposed by K. G. Skolimovskii in 1904, *Stroitel*, 1904, nos. 3-4: 112-13; repeated (successfully) by M. Peretiatkovich and G. Lukomskii in 1910, *Zodchii*, 1910, no. 35: 355.

18. Cited by Ruzhzhe, "Arkhitekturnye-planirovochnye idei," p. 184.

19. Proposed as early as 1903 (*Zodchii*, 1903, no. 30: 366), these were established in 1915 by the Moscow duma. *Izvestiia moskovskoi gorodskoi dumy* 41, no. 2 (February 1917): 41-60.

20. V. L. Modzalevskii, "K istorii 'zelenoi lampy,' " in *Dekabristy i ikh vremia*, 2 vols. (Moscow, 1927) 1: 53-57.

21. Later issued as *Garden Cities of Tomorrow;* Russian translation by A. Blokh with introduction by Ebenezer Howard, *Goroda budushchego* (Moscow, 1904).

22. Paris, 1903. Vandervelde, a socialist, became widely known in Russia for his writings on sociology and after the October Revolution spoke out in defense of the harsh treatment accorded other socialist parties by the Bolsheviks. See his introduction to S. O. Zagorskii, *L'evolution actuelle du bolshevisme russe* (Paris, 1921).

23. Among the major spokesmen of the movement in Russia were M. G. Dikanskii, *Postroika gorodov: ikh plany i krasota* (Petrograd, 1915); A. K. Ensh, *Goroda sady (gorod budushchego)* (St. Petersburg, 1913); Z. G. Frenkel, "Zadachi pravilnoi zastroiki

poselennykh mest . . . ," *Obshchestvennyi vrach*, 1912, no. 1: 46-49; and particularly P. G. Mizhuev, *Sady-goroda i zhilishchnyi vopros v Anglii* (Petrograd, 1916).

24. On Paul Gourdet's claims for Vernyi see Richard, pp. 41-43.

25. "Ustav obshchestva gorodov-sadov," *Gorodskoe delo*, 1914, no. 2: 122-25.

26. See for example A. Petrov, "Zemelnoe khoziaistvo g. Barnaula," *Izvestiia moskovskoi gorodskoi dumy* 41, no. 1 (1917):97-99; as well as D. Protopopov, "Po povodu proekta sanitarnogo zhilishchnogo zakona," *Gorodskoe delo*, 1911, nos. 15-16: 140-41.

27. V. Dadonov, *Sotsializm bez politiki; goroda-sady budushchego v nastaiashchem* (Moscow, 1913), p. 12.

28. Protopopov's major statements on behalf of the garden city movement are to be found in *Gorodskoe delo*, 1909-1911, as well as in his essay (with A. Bloch), "The Housing Question and the Garden City Movement in Russia," *Garden City and Town Planning*, 4, no. 17 (1914): 107-09.

29. A. Ensh, "Pervyi gorod-sad v Rossii," *Gorodskoe delo*, 1911, no. 22: 1571-75; I. W. Irshick, "A Forest Settlement at Riga," *Garden City and Town Planning* 12, no. 8 (1922): 146.

30. Kazhdan, "Gradostroitelstvo," p. 73.

31. Moscow, 1912; on Prozorovskaia see "Pervyi gorod-sad v Rossii," *Gorodskoe delo*, 1912, no. 22: 1398-1403.

32. Ruzhzhe, "Arkhitekturnye planirovochnye idei," p. 184.

33. See A. Petrov, "Zemelnoe khoziaistvo g. Barnaula"; Protopopov, "Po povodu proekta"; and A. I. Petrov, "Mr. Howard's Ideals in Siberia," *Garden City and Town Planning* 15, no. 4 (1925): 94.

34. Kazhdan, "Gradostroitel'stvo," pp. 75-78; V. L. Ruzhzhe, "Generalnyi plan kurorta Laspi," *Sovetskaia arkhitektura*, 1963, no. 15: 152-57; see also the contemporary statement by I. Fomin, "Rol arkhitektora v dele ustroistva russkikh kurortov," *Ezhenedelnik obshchestva arkhitektorov-khudozhnikov*, 1915, no. 41: 378-80.

35. Akademiia nauk SSSR, Institut istorii iskusstv, *Iz istorii sovetskoi arkhitektury, 1917-1925*, K. N. Afanasiev, ed. (Moscow, 1963), pp. 119-20.

36. Ibid., pp. 32-66; V. E. Khazanova, *Sovetskaia arkhitektura pervykh let Oktiabria, 1917-1925* (Moscow, 1970), pp. 83-85; on analogous efforts in Petrograd see Afanasiev, pp. 67-100.

37. Afanasiev, pp. 101-09; Khazanova, *Sovetskaia arkhitektura* pp. 93-96.

38. G. B. Barkhin, *Rabochii dom i rabochii poselek-sad* (Moscow, 1922); idem, *Sovremennye rabochie zhilishcha* (Moscow, 1925), p. 13. In 1926, 68 percent of all new housing was built of wood; Iu. Larin and B. Belousov, *Za novoe zhilishche* (Moscow, 1930), pp. 108-10.

39. Iu. Larin, *Zhilishche i byt* (Moscow, 1931), p. 5.

40. A. Mikhailov, *Grupirovka sovetskoi arkhitektury* (Moscow-Leningrad, 1932), p. 15.

41. *Sovremennaia arkhitektura*, 1926, no. 4: 91-92; nos. 5-6: 125-27.

42. Cited by Khazanova, *Sovetskaia arkhitektura*, p. 53.

43. Central Committee resolution of April 23, 1932.

44. These are reviewed in Anatole Kopp, *Ville et rèvolution* (Paris, 1967), and presented in greater detail in Akademiia nauk SSSR, Institut istorii iskusstv, *Iz istorii sovetskoi arkhitektury, 1926-1932 gg.*, K. N. Afanasiev, ed. (Moscow, 1970), and in the forthcoming sequel volume.

45. For Khrushchev's explicit praise for the British heirs of Howard, and for the reception of these planners in Russia, see *Town and Country Planning* 26, no. 10 (1958): 385.

46. *Voprosy ekonomiki*, 1970, no. 11: 94-96.

URBAN PLANNING IN THE USSR:
INTEGRATIVE THEORIES

Milka Bliznakov

The Period of Planning Extravagance

The years immediately following the Bolshevik Revolution were a fluid period which provided opportunities for new approaches in areas that had not yet received official direction. Urban planning, an area in which the Bolshevik Party had no predetermined model, was one example. Consequently, the 1920s became a period rich in original urban designs and in imaginative theoretical solutions to urban problems. The leaders of the new planning movements came from the so-called Left Front. If not involved politically, they were at least intellectually committed to changes leading to a socialist state and to new architectural and urban forms ideologically appropriate to socialism. Among the leading urban designers were the Vesnin brothers—Leonid (1880-1933), Victor (1882-1950), and Alexander (1883-1959)—the founders of Russian Constructivism in architecture; Moisei Ginsburg (1892-1946), the principal theoretician of Constructivism; and Nokolai Ladovsky, the initiator of ASNOVA, the first organization designed to develop and promote modern architecture.

The 1920s witnessed theoretical debates on the form of the future socialist city and the ardent formulation of urban planning principles. Two basic movements emerged before the end of this period: the first stood for urbanization of rural areas through the concentration of the agricultural population in medium-sized towns and through the development of new industrial centers all over the country; the second movement was committed to deurbanization, to the dispersion of cities by the creation of new continuous communities distributed alongside major transportation and power arteries. Both movements stimulated a substantial number of designs and planning schemes. Although the theory of deurbanization was rejected and the theory of urbanization was severely criticized, several aspects of both movements were incorporated into subsequent planning, among them limitations on population growth in metropolitan areas, parallel zoning of industry and housing, and the superblock as the basic residential unit. While hundreds of extensively planned new towns were founded during the following forty years, none of them fully implemented the ideas of either movement. Hence, conclusions about the merits of the theories are rather tenuous.

World War I, the revolutions, and the ensuing Civil War interrupted all building and planning activities. Nevertheless, two municipal projects, Ivan Fomin's New Petersburg and V. N. Semënov's Prozorovka, both from 1912, exemplify planning trends in this period. The New Petersburg project was an attempt to develop St. Petersburg's Golodai Island along the planning and design traditions of classicism. It never advanced beyond the design stage. Prozorovka, a settlement near Moscow, was planned for the workers of the Moscow-Kazan railroad and was strongly influenced by garden city theories. It was partially constructed, highly publicized, and widely discussed. Semënov's reputation as a city planner was further enhanced by the publication in 1912 of his *Good Urban Planning* (*Blagoustroistvo gorodov*),[1] which is still read in the Soviet Union.

The Soviet government, committed to Marxist ideology and its practical translation into all aspects of public and private life, played a decisive role in the shaping of Soviet urban planning theories and in the institutionalization of the architectural and planning professions. The ideology of the government was also the main source of inspiration and guidance for Soviet planners and architects. From Friedrich Engels's *Anti-Dühring* they inferred that in a socialist state the contradictions between the city and the village must be eliminated. Karl Marx in *Das Kapital* elaborated on the process of urbanization and explained the conflict between town and village as the result of the presence of antagonistic classes created by the capitalist system. The idea that architects must devise buildings which would encourage the dissolution of the family as a private economic entity (the household) and replace it with the collective domestic economy (public housing, communal preparation and distribution of food) also stemmed from *Das Kapital*. Directions for future economic, social, and cultural development were outlined by Bolshevik leaders in public speeches and were legalized by party decrees. The "Decree on the Nationalization of the Land" (February 1918) and the "Decree on Abolition of Private Property in Cities" (October 1918) gave impetus to unorthodox planning theories. The decrees were interpreted by urban planners as lifting the restrictions on existing land use, on the existing labor divisions within the urban population, and on the existing economic basis of the cities.

In keeping with the recommendations of Lenin, the Eighth Party Congress accepted in 1920 a general program for the planned industrial development of the state. It stipulated the creation of new industrial centers and provided standards for the quality of urban life, including the areas of education, culture, recreation, and health. From 1918 onward, the Soviet government became the only client for urban planners and architects. All planning projects for large cities and for the more important smaller towns were to be approved by the Council of People's Commissars (Sovnarkom). The remaining projects were to be approved by local governmental organs. In general, building and planning activities were to revolve around the Committee for State Construction of the High Council of the National Economy, which was empowered to review construction plans and specifications. The People's Commissariat for Internal Affairs also influenced the development of Soviet planning by issuing in the early 1920s its "Rules for the Planning and Building of Towns." This publication provided specific requirements, for example, that 10 percent of the residential area must be left for public parks and recreation (with no housing unit to be farther than 2,000 feet from a park) and that each industrial zone must be separated from the rest of the town by a green belt with a minimum width of 300 feet.[2]

The early planning efforts of the Soviet government contained considerable amounts of social utopianism, romantic understatement, and oversimplification of planning and budgetary problems. This situation was reflected in the urban theories and schemes for the ideal socialist city. In addition to these sociopolitical pressures and to indigenous practices in planning, Western planning ideas exerted a strong influence on the formation of Soviet urban theories, not only the ideas of the late nineteenth century, but to an even greater extent the works of Ludwig Hilbersmeier, Le Corbusier, Bruno Taut, and Frank Lloyd Wright. The Soviet urbanists were profoundly affected by Hilbersmeier and Le Corbusier, while the Soviet deurbanists were stimulated by Taut and Wright.

The most prominent and outspoken theoretician of the urbanists was L. Sabsovich, who in 1929 believed that the full collectivization of agriculture would be completed within two to three years, that the country would be covered with a modern network of transportation and communication within three to four years, and that in ten years' time the Soviet Union would surpass the United States in national industrial production. He assumed that all existing towns and villages could be rebuilt as new socialist towns within fifteen to twenty years. The economic basis and the *raison d' être* of any industrial socialist town would be its industrial complex, while in an agricultural town, repair and service shops and storage of agricultural machinery and equipment would play an equivalent role. Thus, Sabsovich envisioned the entire population living in medium-sized cities. He argued that the concentration of the population in compact towns would increase the free land area for agricultural production, while simultaneously every inhabitant would benefit from the cultural, educational, health, and other public services of the urban environment.

The optimum socialist town would be, according to Sabsovich, a mixed agro-industrial economic unit with a maximum population of fifty to sixty thousand inhabitants. The mixed economy would enable every town to be self-contained and would be a natural outcome of the town's development. In this context Sabsovich argued that if initially the town was intended to contain an agricultural population, it subsequently would require some industry for the processing of agricultural production, such as fruit and vegetable canning. If, on the other hand, the town was initially intended to be an industrial community, it would need an agricultural contingent to provide it with fresh foods. Hence chicken and dairy farms, vegetable gardens, and fruit orchards were to border the city. These farms could also employ elderly citizens, use child labor for educational purposes, and serve factory workers as a therapeutic outdoor working-place.

The urbanists believed that the house-commune was the most appropriate residence for the socialist town. According to their calculations, the adult population (over seventeen years of age) would number about 40,000 to 42,000 in a town of 60,000 inhabitants. If 2,000 to 3,000 people lived in each house-commune of approximately twenty stories, the housing needs of the town could be satisfied with fifteen to twenty house-communes. Children were not to live with their parents. Nurseries and kindergartens for small children were to be constructed close to the house-communes, thus allowing parents to visit them easily. School-age children were to be separated completely from their parents and live in dormitories on special educational campuses. The educational campus was located at the edge of the town, either close to the farms, where children could enjoy outdoor living and at the same time could help with the farm work, or close to the industrial complex, where they could prepare for future participation in the industrial labor force.

Sabsovich recommended that the industrial, residential, and agricultural zones be developed in parallel ribbons, with the residential zone in the middle but divided from the industrial zone by a narrow densely wooded strip. This design was intended to allow workers to walk to work (with the maximum walking time set as fifteen to twenty minutes) and to the open agricultural fields. Streets and blocks as known in the capitalist town (a block built mainly around its periphery and divided from the surrounding blocks by streets) were to be eliminated in the socialist town. All buildings, including administrative and public buildings, were to be constructed in parks connected with the main traffic arteries by secondary roads. Administrative and public buildings would be located in a park in the center of the residential area.[3]

Sabsovich's theory was the basis of many urban planning and design proposals. The most notable were the Vesnin brothers' projects for the regions of Stalingrad and Zaporozh'e. Of all the new towns begun in the late 1920s which incorporated the planning ideals of the urbanists, none was completed according to the original urban plan. The urbanist idea most often applied was that of the house-commune, or the residential combine, as Sabsovich often called it. Not surprisingly, it was this dimension that was most often criticized, both by party officials and by the workers who lived in the communes.

The house-commune was not designed for family living. The objective of the designers was to readjust the inhabitants to a communal way of life and thus to speed up the dissolution of the family. In principle, a house-commune consisted of small individual rooms for sleep and repose. (Sabsovich recommended 55 square feet to a maximum of 100 square feet per room.) All other activities were to take place in common spaces, either in the same building or in a separate structure, and consisted usually of rooms for dining, reading, lectures and meetings, games and hobbies, and eventually a gymnasium. While most of the house-communes, with their long corridors and repetitive rooms, resembled hotels or dormitories, a few architects developed highly imaginative but quite impractical prototypes. The design of Ivan Leonidov for Dom Promyshlennosti (residence for industrial workers) is considered the ultimate in the development of the house-commune. It was a high-rise structure with the ground floor and the roof terrace allocated to sport and recreation and with an intermediate floor for common dining. All other floors were identical glass-enclosed spaces without any interior partitions. About two-thirds of each floor was divided by planting boxes and by carpeting into 120 equal squares of 55 square feet each. Every worker was alloted one such square with only a bed in it for sleeping. The remaining third of the floor area was common space for relaxation, reading, games, and exercises. Even a running track and a swimming pool were provided within the same open floor space.

The project provoked an uproar of criticism. The arguments against the house-communes derived from two basic premises: first, the Russian worker was not about to accept the communal way of life as superior to the private, to the family. Most of the inhabitants, even the bachelors, did not eat in the community dining room but preferred to take their food from the communal kitchen to their own cubicles. Almost everybody enjoyed reading or studying in the privacy of his room more than in the common spaces. The other dissatisfaction was related to the architectural appearance of the buildings. Occupants complained about the impersonality, the lack of identifying motifs or distinguishing features to which they could relate their own dwelling place within the housing complex. They resented being transformed into mere ciphers; they resented being depersonalized. The discontent and resentment produced by the house-commune was refelcted in a decree of July 14, 1932, entitled "The Type of Housing," which made it imperative that all future housing contain separate apartments for individual families, and that each apartment building have a unique architectural appearance.[4]

On the other hand, the deurbanists believed that urbanization with its centralized, crowded, and congested cities was the natural consequence of the capitalist economic system. In their opinion the objective of Soviet urban planning was not the development of socialist towns that were different from capitalist towns, but the redistribution of the Soviet population in accordance with new principles which would serve to disperse rather than concentrate the population. The most eloquent spokesman for the deurbanization movement was Moisei Okhitovich. Moisei Ginsburg was their most talented architect, while an impressive group of economists, sociologists, and medical doctors served as consultants. The deurbanists offered a theoretical solution called "the socialist population resettlement," which promoted neither urban nor rural life but which sought the uniform dispersion of the urban and rural population over the entire territory, thereby creating a townless, fully decentralized, and evenly populated country. It was believed that the process of dispersion resulted from a natural human desire which had already been manifested in Russia and abroad with the development of suburban and satellite cities. The Soviet state had only to accelerate and regulate this natural trend by decentralizing the administrative and public services, industry, and the educational and research institutions.

The deurbanists argued that to replace big cities with smaller towns, as the urbanists proposed, was only to exchange a larger problem for a smaller one. They advocated instead that all sources of employment, such as industry and public services, should be dispersed and connected by a good system of roads, which would become the arteries for new residential developments. The deurbanists counted mainly on the automobile for fast, flexible, and individually adjustable transportation. Advanced technological and industrial development, a good communication network, and a highly developed system of transportation and power supply all were prerequisites to the implementation of the schemes of the deurbanizers.

Ginsburg and his collaborators envisioned the construction of separate dwelling units, one for each adult, arranged alongside traffic arteries in a continuous park. Each dwelling would consist of a covered parking space below and a single room above. The room, seldom over 150 square feet, would serve as a living room during the day and as a bedroom at night. As in the house-commune, all activities except sleeping and repose were to be carried on in communal spaces. But in contrast to the urbanists, the deurbanists arranged the communal dining rooms, the recreational and cultural centers, and the educational and public facilities periodically alongside the traffic arteries. The driving time to and from work was set at thirty to forty minutes maximum. Industrial complexes and other major places of employment had to be erected at about one hour's driving distance from each other and had to be linked with the continuous strip of residential and community facilities. Ginsburg asserted that the individual cottage-like dwellings, surrounded by trees, would provide the closest possible contact with open outdoor space and fresh air, and would offer simultaneously maximum privacy and optimum conditions for the occupant's rest and recuperation of creative energy.[5] The urban schemes inspired by the theory of deurbanization, such as the one described above, were known as ribbon city or green city designs.

An original and very functional urban scheme, the so-called linear city, which could satisfy urbanist and deurbanist alike, was proposed by Nikolai Miliutin, who in the later 1920s was the chairman of the State Commission for the Construction of New Cities. Miliutin's linear city advocated population resettlement and the creation of industrial and residential zones in parallel bands, separated by a continuous green strip of about 500 to 600 yards. This green buffer was expected to protect the housing from industrial pollution and from traffic noise from the artery, which in turn was located between the green strip and the industrial zone. The residential zone bordered on the other side with farming area, thus conveniently serving the industrial as well as the farm workers. The parallel development of industry and housing in Miliutin's scheme corresponded to the urbanists' thinking, while its potential for unlimited linear extension reflected also the ideals of the deurbanists. However, the linear city was not perforce continuous, as was the ribbon city, since at any horizontal stretch it contained all the necessary functional elements of an urban environment—housing, educational facilities, and recreation, all located in the green buffer zone, as well as industry as a place of employment.

The opinions of the urbanists, the deurbanists, and Miliutin converged on one important point, that the big cities inherited from the capitalist period must be discarded as useless in a socialist state. They recommended that the government immediately curb the growth of cities and begin dispersing the population by transferring major industries, administrative services, and educational and research facilities to areas miles away from the city limits. Only then could the old cities be replanned and rebuilt as socialist cities. But at a time when the Soviet government was faced with serious economic problems, including a housing shortage and industrial inadequacy, views that discredited the value of existing cities were completely unacceptable. The official position of the state was expressed by Lazar Kaganovich in his report to the June 1931 plenary session of the Central Committee of the Bolshevik Party. Kaganovich pointed out that the cities, towns, and all settlements of the Soviet Union became automatically socialist as the result of the Bolshevik Revolution, nationalization, and the abolition of private ownership. Anyone who denied the socialist character of the cities was labeled a saboteur.[6] The most consequential decision for Soviet urban planning made at this plenary session was the resolution to suspend new industrial development in major cities such as Moscow and Leningrad at the beginning of 1932 and to extend the construction of new industrial centers in rural areas.

The Organization of Planning Activities

Only one formal organization for urban planning existed in the USSR, the Union of Architects-Urbanists (ARU), founded in 1928 by Nikolai Ladovsky and a group of architects, engineers, medical doctors, and economists. The goal of the organization was to arouse wide public interest in the problems connected with city planning and to formulate a scientific approach to these problems through research and analysis. "ARU considers urbanism a scientific discipline aiming to discover the general governing laws of the organization of human settlements . . . and by defining these laws to be able to foresee the process of their formation . . . thus bring this process onto the path of socialist planning."[7] The research of ARU led by Ladovsky was directed mainly towards the psychological influence of urban architecture on the inhabitants and towards the qualification of architecture as a formative force shaping the ideology of people. Ladovsky's interest in this particular aspect of architecture dates back to the beginning of the 1920s. The materials he collected during a decade of research were unfortunately never published. The change of government policy at the beginning of the 1930s interrupted his research. ARU was abolished in 1932 along with all other architectural and artistic organizations and its architect members were required to join the Union of Soviet Architects, the only formal architectural organization in the Soviet Union since then.

The first state urban planning agency, Giprogor (State Institute for Urban Planning) was formed as late as 1930. It had a large staff and in its three years of operation produced urban plans for over a hundred small and large towns. Giprogor did not have an official urban planning policy and among its staff were urbanists (who incorporated their ideas in such projects as Stalingrad, Viatka, and Novosibirsk), deurbanists headed by Ginsburg, and a large group that was influenced by the design of the foreign architects and planners working in the State Planning Agency. The foreign "specialists" (who numbered about 150, mostly Germans but also Americans, Swiss, and others) worked as a separate group until 1932, when they became a part of the newly founded State Planning Agency, Standardgorproekt. As the number of planning and design agencies increased, party control over them became more complicated. This problem was overcome by the resolution of the Moscow City Committee of the Bolshevik Party of September 23, 1933, whereby planning and design procedures were completely reorganized. All urban planning projects were to be undertaken by one agency Gorstroiproekt, and all projects for industrial development by Promstroiproekt (both agencies being subordinated to the Commissariat of Heavy Industry). Architectural design was to be practiced only in state design studios subordinated to local governments. At this time, Arplan, a controlling organ, was established under the direction of Lazar Kaganovich. Its function was to review and approve each master plan and each design before its acceptance for construction, not only from a functional but also from an aesthetic viewpoint. The planning and aesthetic canons of the state were thus easily enforced and the results are generally reflected in the Soviet architecture of the following three decades.

The Period of Compromise Implementation

Soviet national economic development after 1927 was outlined and directed by consecutive five-year plans. These plans never contained a fully comprehensive urban theory. After Kaganovich had defined the socialist city as any settlement on the territory of the Soviet Union, urban planners were no longer impelled to search for new urban elements, but rather could reuse those of the preceding century. Furthermore, the separation of urban planning from economic, industrial, and transportation planning in 1933 enforced a definite limitation; urban designers were to solve mainly the problems of housing, the aesthetic unity of the urban environment, and the appropriate form of the administrative urban center. Smaller towns were designed with a single center of civic and administrative buildings, which surrounded a large town square, and with a main street of public buildings leading towards it. Larger towns had several similar centers (or subcenters) interconnected by wide avenues. The town center acted as the visual focus, political heart, and pride of the urban composition. The buildings had to express the "greatness of the epoch of socialism" and inevitably were overdesigned and exaggerated in a pompous and often ostentatious manner. The main square was generally oversized in order to serve for mass meetings, parades, and demonstrations. The main avenue was designed as part of the urban complex and the buildings bordering it were of uniform height and of similar appearance, thus modelling the street with their facades.

The residential zone was designed as a homogeneous repetition of superblocks, the most favored residential unit in the 1930s. It consisted of low-rise apartment buildings (up to four or five floors because these did not require elevators) placed generally around the perimeter of the block, thus leaving the center free for playgrounds, kindergartens, and sometimes schools or a grocery store. The size of the superblock was determined by the optimum use of social services and recreational facilities. (For example, a block with housing for 200 to 250 inhabitants would make optimum use of one cafeteria.) A more casual layout of the housing within the superblock was criticized as destroying the integrity of the street and imparing its harmonious architectural congruity.

This attitude changed after World War II when many of the planning concepts were reexamined and revised in connection with the reconstruction of the many destroyed or damaged towns. The superblock was found to be economically wasteful because of its low density and to be architecturally monotonous because of its uniform height and repetitiousness. Many towns had already expanded beyond their originally planned boundaries and thus had lost their initial integrity. Postwar urban planning emphasized the importance of compact and economical land use while simultaneously providing large areas for future growth. The superblock was replaced by the larger neighborhood unit, the *microrayon*, which was designed for 6,000 to 8,000 inhabitants. Higher population density and greater spatial variety were achieved by freely arranging low- and high-rise apartments, varying from four to nine stories, with adequate green spaces between them. Park and recreation areas tended to be interconnected in a continuous greenbelt, while schools and kindergartens became separate entities with their own grounds. Food stores, cleaners, and cafeterias formed a small public center. Ordinarily, five or six microrayon neighborhoods were grouped together to form a residential zone with a larger public center consisting of shopping and commercial buildings, a cultural center, library, and similar public structures.

Soviet urban planners claim that 900 new towns were erected between 1926 and 1966, two-thirds of which incorporated older and smaller settlements. These towns were founded according to a general plan which took into consideration the optimum distribution of the working force, maximum industrial efficiency, and rational use of energy resources. Many of these towns were established in the eastern and northern regions of the Soviet Union, while those founded in the more densely populated areas of the Ukraine, White Russia, and the Baltic states provided an outlet for the excessive population growth of the larger cities. Although the planners have not implemented the tenets of the 1920s in any systematic way, a revival of Miliutin's linear city idea in conjunction with the urbanists' proposal for an administrative and cultural center in the middle of the town can be discerned in the most recent plans. One may hope that this modest beginning will lead to the development of pertinent, contemporary urban planning theories.

Notes

1. Fomin's and Semënov's projects are published in A. V. Bunin, *Istoriia gradostroitel'nogo iskusstva* (Moscow, 1953), pp. 480, 481.

2. V. E. Khazanova, *Sovetskaia arkhitektura pervykh let oktiabria, 1917-1925* (Moscow, 1970), p. 59.

3. The most complete single source on Sabsovich's theory is the booklet he published in 1930, *Sotsialisticheskie goroda* (Moscow, 1930).

4. The decree is published in *Stroitel'stvo Moskvy* 8/9 (1932), opposite p. 1.

5. The periodical *S. A. Sovremennaia Arkhitektura*, of which Ginsburg was one of the editors, published during 1929 and 1930 many articles and projects by the deurbanists. Some of the polemics of both groups are collected in B. Lunin, *Goroda Sotsializma i Sotsialisticheskaia rekonstruktsiia byta* (Moscow, 1930).

6. Some of Kaganovich's views on urban planning have been published as *Socialist Reconstruction of Moscow and Other Cities in the USSR*, (New York: International Publishers, 1930). For his report to the June 1931 plenum, see L. M. Kaganovich, *L'Urbanisme soviétque* (Paris, 1931).

7. "Deklaratsiia Sectora ARU," *Sovetskaia Arkhitektura* 1/2 (1931): 19.

SOVIET CITIES AND
CONSUMER WELFARE PLANNING

David T. Cattell

For the Soviet urban workers, the 1920s were a decade of communist dreams and harsh realities. Between 1917 and 1921 rents were abolished, city transport became free, housing became abundant, and Soviet architects and planners looked to the construction of new communal cities. But these "steps" toward communism were a facade covering an existence of increasing hardship.

Inflation was the force that made rents and all forms of money payment useless. Urban housing in the early 1920s became abundant because of the casualties of war and because the lack of food and jobs sent workers back to their ancestral villages. The population of Leningrad declined by two-thirds and that of most other cities declined by one-third or more.[1] Even though local governments took over private housing and public services for the equal benefit of all workers, without resources from rents, fares, or taxes they could not maintain the housing or services for long. Housing seriously deteriorated and communal services gradually came to a halt. Most cities stopped producing gas, urban transport was reduced to a few tram cars, and restaurants, public baths, and other consumer services became few and scattered.[2] Even with the gradual restoration of the economy and the restoration of rents and fares after 1921, the cities continued to decline.[3] The regime purposely held the income of cities to minimal levels in favor of industrial priorities.[4] Before long, local authorities were hard pressed to find housing and provide services for the workers returning to the factories.

In an effort to improve housing conditions, rent cooperatives were organized to collect, maintain, and manage public housing. Worker building cooperatives and private individual construction were encouraged to provide new housing. The urban housing shortage became so desperate that after 1925 the regime was forced to allocate about 22 percent of its small capital budget to this sector. This increase did not really improve urban life, however. In fact, with the influx of the population into the cities, the average housing space per person declined from seven square meters in 1917 to six square meters in 1928 and the quality of the new housing as well as that of the old remained inferior. Furthermore, local governments were slow in restoring and expanding other services, such as public transportation, gas, sewage disposal, and paved roads.[5] Nevertheless, throughout the 1920s the architects and ideologists continued to buoy the hopes of the workers with plans for future proletarian cities of abundance. But except for a few model apartments these dreams remained on paper.

Stalin and Consumer Welfare

The 1930s and 1940s were decades of even more harsh realities for urban dwellers. Stalin's industrialization drive reduced mass welfare to a new low priority, and World War II brought mass destruction to most of the cities of European Russia.[6] The exceptions were those services which contributed directly to industrialization, such as education and health. These were subsidized and brought under central control. Despite insufficient resources, municipal governments were responsible for the daily welfare of the citizenry. They took over manufacture of most of the consumer goods needed for local consumption, established food distribution systems, provided retail outlets of all types, and maintained systems of public transport. And for both the consumer and industry they supplied water, sewage disposal, gas, electricity, and paved roads. But urban governments were not equal to the tasks and especially in new cities could not manage the rapid influx of new workers. The regime therefore turned to industry to supplement the insufficient resources of local government. As a means of providing greater labor incentives, industrial enterprises were encouraged from their profits and surpluses to supply housing and consumer services to their own workers. As a result, in the newer cities industries came to own and control as much as 90 percent of the housing and a good part of all consumer services.[7] But even with the help of industry the overall conditions of life in the cities continued to decline. By 1952, for example, the average housing space per person had dropped to about five square meters from six square meters in 1928. Furthermore, the widespread corruption and individual incentive system under Stalin resulted in sharp inequalities. The new middle and upper managerial and professional class had individual apartments and country dachas while the masses lived, on the average, three persons to a room, often with only two or three square meters per person. Even dreams about communist cities of abundance ceased and the idealists were liquidated by Stalin in the mid-1930s. The few architectural monuments built were dedicated to the glory of Stalin and the nation, rather than to the masses, as represented by the underground palaces of the Moscow subway and the Stalinesque skyscrapers built at the end of the 1940s.

The Schemes of Khrushchev

Beginning with the "new course" of Malenkov in 1953 the Soviet leaders began shifting priorities more in favor of consumer welfare. In this regard their first concern was to improve the quality of life in Soviet cities. It was assumed that the Soviet system was more than equal to the task. The record of industrialization and rapid recovery after World War II, the growing resources of the economy, twenty years of experience with central planning, the Party's ability to mobilize the population, and scientific socialism would make short work of the problem. But from Stalin they had inherited a disordered urban system far more confused than it appeared on the surface. A jumble of local governments and their agencies, various central and republic ministries, and numerous industrial enterprises supplied services to parts of the urban population. The confusion was compounded because the distribution of responsibility varied from city to city. While theoretically the central government was supposed to be coordinating the activities through the central planning system and by frequent decrees, in fact each administering authority had acted without regard for other urban units, effectively ignoring most central directives. This was particularly true of industrial enterprises.

The first major assault on the chaos of urban administration was taken in regard to new housing construction. It was immediately evident that the housing shortage would not be solved by merely allocating more capital. The first step was to reorganize the housing construction industry to make it compatible with central planning and control, that is, to remove the hundreds of small and large construction units attached to enterprises, ministries, and local governments, and to consolidate them into large territorial construction managements (*glavki*) patterned after heavy industry.[8] The reorganization augured well for improved housing because construction, particularly the new type of prefabricated housing, lent itself to the Soviet pattern of heavy industry.

The housing reorganization, however, was interrupted in 1957 by Khrushchev's *sovnarkhoz* scheme. The reform divided the Soviet Union into 105 economic regions and drastically reshuffled the administrative and planning apparatus to fit these new regions. The scheme was offered as a panacea not only to improve party and central controls but to better coordinate major industries, reduce administrative overhead, increase industrial autonomy, and integrate and improve local consumer services. According to Khrushchev, urban communities working with regional economic councils would be able to coordinate and expand services. Khrushchev and his lieutenants did not bother to work out the details of the program, however. Even more important, they failed to win over the bureaucracy, which sabotaged the scheme from the beginning. In the resulting confusion and struggle for power the major victims were city governments. In spite of promises to the contrary, the authority of local governments over housing, public services, and consumer industry declined.[9] Heavy industrial enterprises dominated the *sovnarkhoz* and local planning for their own interests. Only as a result of the general increase of capital investment in housing and other services did urban communities derive some benefits. These, however, were primarily confined to the large cities such as Kharkov and Magnitogorsk where major enterprises had large resources, or to cities such as Moscow, Leningrad, and Kiev where the city administrations had special status. Smaller cities barely felt the impact of the housing boom and all the decrees directing new industry to be built in these cities and commanding *sovnarkhoz* authorities to help develop small cities came to nothing.[10]

With the miscarriage of the *sovnarkhoz* reform Khrushchev was forced to return to centralization, and one of the first moves in this direction in 1961 was to bring construction and building materials increasingly under Moscow's direct control. All construction including housing was made a part of a state construction plan.[11] With the consolidation and centralization of construction and building materials it became possible to maximize the use of prefabricated panels and modular units, which significantly reduced costs, accelerated construction, and improved quality.[12] Once again, however, only the larger cities with their considerable capacity were able to benefit from the new prefabricated construction.[13]

The *sovnarkhoz* reform was only one of the sources of confusion which stood in the way of improving urban life. While physically cities expanded rapidly as a result of new housing projects, few developed any scheme to rationalize and control development. Even in the case of the few large cities which had plans, they were out of date, based on the wrong assumptions, and unenforceable. But along with the absence of long-range schemes, coordinated short-range planning also was nonexistent. The necessary ties between construction of new housing and supplying of services were not provided. New communities frequently had to wait two and three years for vital services.[14]

The absence of comprehensive planning was not the only problem. Cities often were not allocated sufficient capital resources to supply new services. The traditional Soviet answer of centralizing in order to expand and coordinate could not provide the immediate solution. To include in the housing construction plan the expansion of all the numerous services was beyond the capacity of the central planners. Furthermore, the problems of constructing and maintaining water systems, sewerage systems, transport, retail trade, and housing varied from city to city, and these areas were operated by many and various agencies. The ministries of communal economy of the republics charged with the task of coordination were reduced to issuing numerous decrees trying to control and standardize procedures, but in practice these directives meant little. Thus the *ad hoc* and confused nature of supplying urban services which had grown up under Stalin continued under Khrushchev. In fact the *sovnarkhoz* reforms of 1957 had created additional chaos and new rivalries.[15]

Long-Range Urban Planning

Even though Khrushchev sought quick solutions through assault tactics, Soviet architects and city administrators decided that the fundamental solution to the urban problem would be in long-range development plans for each city. For controlled and coordinated expansion, long-term developmental plans were offered as the panacea. Like Khrushchev, city officials and architects were convinced that scientific socialism and three decades of Soviet industrial planning would provide the answers. The idea of urban developmental planning was not new. Several cities had initiated such plans in the 1920s and even Stalin, who had not been willing to expend large sums on urban development, had promoted a long-term plan for Moscow in the 1930s and for Leningrad and other cities after World War II.

The campaign to expand city planning in the 1950s and 1960s proved not to be a panacea and ran into serious difficulties. Under the best of conditions it took the better part of a decade to draft and approve a plan; in the meantime millions of square meters of

The Twentieth-Century City

new housing were sprouting around cities at the whim of directors of enterprises and city officials. Furthermore, for most cities there were not enough architect-planners even to initiate the task, and those available were concentrated in Moscow and Leningrad, remote from the cities whose future they were drafting.[16] Thousands of new architect-engineers were needed for both long- and short-range planning but no major steps were taken to train more until the mid-1960s. Even among the planners there were no reliable long-range estimates on which to base a plan. For individual cities there was no information on what new industries could be expected, or what consumer output the regime would promote, such as private automobiles for which extensive road networks and facilities would be needed. Good population growth estimates for cities did not even exist.

Still other difficulties resulted from the application of scientific socialism. For example, as the primary unit of urban planning the geographers and architect-engineers had created the microrayon. Each microrayon, with a radius of 400-700 meters, was to be organized into an integrated community with its own services, including retail trade, nursery schools, housing bureaus, and recreational facilities. Old as well as new sections of cities were forced into this pattern. But experience and investigations by sociologists who were being brought into planning toward the end of the 1960s showed that the urban dwellers were not accepting the microrayon. The patterns of their lives in respect to working, shopping, recreation, and friendships had little to do with the microrayon.[17] Finally and most important, long-range plans were meaningless unless they were enforced and unless coordinated yearly plans implemented the objectives. But as indicated above, no coordinated plans were drawn up during the Khrushchev years. Furthermore, in certain sectors other than housing, for example retail goods, the *sovnarkhoz* reform had left local planning in an even weaker position than it had been under Stalin. Hence, neither the *sovnarkhoz* reform, the amalgamation of the civil construction industry, nor long-range planning was able to coordinate new housing construction successfully. Improved cooperation between the central ministries and the local governments took on new significance.

Central Planning and Local Coordination

Not all the services supplied by local government had been caught in the web of restricted resources and confused management and responsibility. Those that escaped included education, health, gas, electricity, and militia, and in general can be characterized in two ways. First, they were important either to the output of basic industries or to the maintenance of totalitarian control. Second, central authorities maintained direct control over their expansion and administration and used local government merely to house central administrative agencies. Although the chief administrators were members of the local government and usually served on the executive committee of the local soviet, they were appointed by and were responsible directly and primarily to union-republic authorities. For example, gas supplies were important to many industries as well as to householders and since most cities in the 1920s were without enough resources to renew production, the central government provided the necessary capital. As demand increased, Moscow and the republics planned and constructed new facilities, and with the opening of natural gas fields, constructed a grid of pipelines to the urban areas. Increasingly the cities had little to do with the manufacture of gas and became only the distributors and sales agents to the householders and industrial consumers. Furthermore, the central government strictly controlled the price of the gas, keeping it almost at cost and allowing local governments only a minimum profit. Thus for all these services control resided primarily at the republic level, with overall supervision at the all-union level. In each city the republic had an agent attached to local government to manage the service, and in this way integrated central direction with local administration. Thus it is not surprising that the regime should look to this prefect system of reconciling central direction with local peculiarities to solve questions of mass welfare.[18] Although the problem of housing construction was more complicated in that it involved the need to integrate central direction with not just a narrow sector of local concern but the whole gamut of local services, a similar solution was possible.

From the experience of the 1950s it was increasingly evident that it would be impossible for central planners to integrate new construction with efficient land use and the supplying of the numerous services needed by new housing. Basic planning and administration must of necessity remain primarily a local concern. Some means of coordinating at the local level was essential, but without losing central direction. The chosen instrument became the chief architect of each city as the agent of Gosstroi, the State Construction Committee. He assumed the responsibility to provide a comprehensive plan of urban development and to supervise its administration. The chief architect was given wide power to review, veto, and in general control all phases of local housing construction. He also assumed the authority to initiate the long-range plan and to work closely with its development, although the actual drafting might be contracted out to architect-engineering institutes specializing in such work. In short, together with the local executive committee, the construction *glavki*, and those industries desiring new housing, the chief architect worked out the yearly plan for new civil construction. His assent as well as that of the local executive committee is now necessary before the projected plan can be sent to higher levels for approval and inclusion in the overall state plan. In developing the plan, it is his responsibility to resolve with local authorities the problems of supplying new housing developments with water, sewerage systems, gas, electricity, telephones, day nurseries, retail outlets, recreational facilities, and all other such requirements. Once the plan is approved, his office receives and reviews the individual plans for each civil construction project and issues a building permit. During the period of construction his office has extensive supervisory power and must certify the quality of the completed structure. Thus the veto and supervisory powers of the chief architect are almost absolute. His authority over industrial construction, however, is limited primarily to its location and to matters relating to the architectural facade.

The fulfillment of the civil construction plan does not depend only on the authority of the chief architect, however. It depends equally on his ability to work with both central authorities and local officials. From the center he needs the allocation of sufficient basic resources and from the local executive committee he needs cooperation in providing the communal services required for new construction. Since 1963 cities have appointed committees on construction, composed of representatives from the Party, local building organizations, the State Construction Bank, trade unions, the union of architects, fire and sanitary officials, and others, to help coordinate these functions. In addition to coordinating planning among the interested parties, this committee is also responsible for mobilizing local notables to lobby on behalf of the plan in higher organizational echelons. A successful housing program therefore depends on the chief architect, the chairman of the city's executive committee, and the secretary of the local Party organization working together within or outside the coordinating committee, and on their ability to secure capital and materials from Gosplan and Gosstroi. This system has experienced difficulties, however, because of the shortage of suitably trained architect-engineers to fill the key position of chief architect in the thousands of Soviet cities.[19] Individuals holding this position must be both trained professionals and capable administrator-politicians. This problem has diminished in recent years with the expansion of training facilities and the growing prestige of the position. In time there should be enough qualified chief architects and staff to meet the needs of even the smaller cities.

The Expanding Urban Slums

Khrushchev had planned that by 1970 the urban population would finally achieve the sanitary norm established in 1922 of 9 square meters of housing space (exclusive of service areas) per person, and 14 square meters by 1980. At the time of his removal in 1964-1965, the average had reached only 6.8 square meters, with the goal of 9 meters not likely to be achieved even in another decade without tremendous additional efforts. Furthermore, the entire consumer economy had begun to feel the pressures of the attempts to attain the housing goal. Brezhnev and Kosygin therefore decided to postpone Khrushchev's housing goals more or less indefinitely and to level off the production of new state-supported urban housing at between 50 to 60 million square meters of general housing space per year.[20] Thus, while not changing the overall thrust of Khrushchev's consumer welfare goals and reforms, his successors sought a more balanced program and adopted a more cautious attitude toward reform.

To balance Khrushchev's initiative in the area of new urban housing, Brezhnev and Kosygin in 1967 began a program to raise the quality of new housing in rural areas,[21] and in the cities they shifted priorities to urban renewal and maintenance. Vast new urban centers were not only absorbing large amounts of capital, they were using up valuable agricultural and even industrial areas and forcing the extension of services over a wide area at a high cost. In the meantime, the central sectors of cities continued to decline, with much of the old housing deteriorating almost beyond repair. Instead of continuing to expand the area of the city, it became increasingly more economical to replace old structures with multistoried apartments.

The whole sector of housing maintenance, which had not kept pace with new construction, has been in even more serious need of attention. Here costs have been high and quality low. The major difficulties include the excessively low rents collected from both new and old housing, which do not generate enough income for either maintenance or repair, the low wages of maintenance personnel, the shortage of mechanized equipment, and the low quality of new housing, which requires immediate and continuous repairs as soon as it is completed.[22] The cost of repairs is doubling about every five years and will soon be more than the capital outlay for new housing. In the case of the RSFSR, expenditures by repair construction organizations went from 338 million rubles in 1960 to 904 million in 1968 and are expected to reach 2 to 2.5 billion rubles in 1975.[23] In the same eight years capital investment in new housing increased only slightly. As serious as the problem is becoming the regime has been slow to respond. The administration of maintenance has been reorganized into large units to reduce overhead and there is increased emphasis on urban renewal. Since analyses have shown that the cost of capital repair on old buildings is often equal to or more than new construction, the regime has permitted local governments to abolish more and more of its old housing to cut costs.[24] But the basic problem still exists and there has been no comprehensive "assault" on the problem. The Ninth Five Year Plan, 1971-1975, has continued to ignore it.

Reorganizing Consumer Goods and Services

With the Ninth Five Year Plan the regime decided to emphasize the supply of consumer goods by increasing the overall turnover by 35-40 percent. As in the case of housing it has been the basic responsibility of local governments to supply most consumer goods and services. Light industries and cooperatives manufacturing for local consumption were usually placed under urban jurisdiction. The regime provided only minimal capitalization for these industries and local governments had little capital of their own. As a result the industries had a low level of mechanization and the products were generally of low quality. Nevertheless, the profits from these enterprises provided some income for the cities and gave cities some flexibility in budgeting.

For food supplies the city has depended primarily on the collective and private farm plots of the local region. The collective and state farms deliver their produce to the city's warehouses, which in turn distribute it to the population through city-operated retail stores. A major supplement to this system has been the collective farm market. In these markets the city rents space to individual farmers and collective farms so that they can sell their surpluses directly to the population.

Thus the basic supply of consumer products has been very localized. Neither the transportation nor the wholesale distribution system to import goods from beyond the local *oblast* has existed. At best, local governments with their limited capital and resources have been able to supply minimal benefits. As a result, state enterprises under Stalin, as a means of attracting and retaining their workers, used their superior resources to open additional retail outlets and services for their own employees. Thus most enterprises in addition to constructing much of their own housing opened their own restaurants and commissaries, where scarce items could be secured, and provided day care centers and special recreational facilities for their workers. Some even made available transportation facilities for their workers to and from their homes and to the city center.

Theoretically the whole system of consumer welfare even under Stalin was overseen and controlled by ministries at the republic level. These ministries were afforded few resources, however, and were confined to issuing numerous decrees aimed at raising standards. Since the conditions varied from city to city and the responsibility at the local area was diffused between industry and the various urban developments, there was little coordination or control. Thus at the end of the Stalinist era the manufacture and distribution of consumer goods and services and the production of food supplies were, compared to heavy industry, still underdeveloped and haphazard.

Stalin's successors sought to increase the resources in the food and light industrial sectors, and almost immediately increased the amounts of consumer goods and food, supplementing the meager and poor-quality domestic supply with imported goods. But the regime's allocation of new capital to those sectors proved sporadic and uncoordinated, and in the long run improvement was uneven and unsystematic, except in the field of housing. Not until the Ninth Five Year Plan was concerted attention given to these sectors, but more than one five-year plan will be required. A comprehensive system of distribution and marketing for efficient national distribution of goods still has to be created. Changes in the status and improvement in the quality of local industrial outlets have to occur and research into methods of determining demand needs to be pursued. Most important is the need to find a way to reconcile and coordinate the goals and supervision decreed from Moscow with the republican ministries, the interests and possibilities at the local level, and the needs and demands of the populace. These sectors require comprehensive planning which will be much more complex than that in housing construction and even more dependent on the capabilities of local government.

Having learned from its experience in housing, the Soviet leadership, in reviewing and giving new emphasis to consumer priorities in the Ninth Five Year Plan, is resisting centralization and trying to expand the local base. The housing model and the record of the first years of the Ninth Five Year Plan suggest that it will take time, a couple of decades. Local administrators, except in the leading cities, have neither the skills nor the authority to take the initiative and bring about a major reorganization of planning and supply in spite of encouragement. Such conservative central bureaucracies as the Ministry of Finance and the banks which have traditionally supervised local administration refuse to give local administrators much leeway or independence. Furthermore, with continued scarcities and poor services, heavy industries have resisted turning over their retail goods and services business to local governments, and their continued control makes comprehensive and efficient planning impossible. Finally, there is reason to doubt how far the shift to consumer production has really gone. Significantly in 1972, a generally bad year for the Soviet economy, light industry suffered a more serious setback than heavy industry, although according to the plan its output was to have increased more rapidly. This would seem to imply that the influence of heavy industry is still dominant, regardless of the leadership's intentions, and is able to command absolute priority over other sectors.

More than anything else it would seem that the cities need a sound financial base from which to construct and maintain a new consumer system, one that does not depend on the whims and fluctuating allocations of the central planners. Thus far cities have been forced to keep the prices for their services minimal. For example fares for public transport are only 3 to 4 cents for trams, 4 to 5 cents for trolley-buses, and 5 to 6 cents for subways and buses. This allows for little or no profit margin. In 1964 local governments were able to finance only 63.8 percent of the building and maintaining of new communal services from their own resources. For housing the situation has been even worse; cities have been able to finance only 8 percent of the cost of constructing and maintaining public housing.[25] Beginning in 1964 the financial position of local governments began to improve slightly in that they were allowed to keep more of their income from local industry. Then beginning in January 1972 enterprises were required to turn over 5 percent of their capital investments intended for housing to the city for the construction of trade and catering services.[26] Against these increases, however, are 1) the need for local governments to subsidize housing management and capital repairs by over a billion rubles a year; 2) a rapidly expanding housing fund; 3) the growing demand for improved roads, parks, and transport; 4) a declining income from public services because of rising costs and more or less stable rates.

If local governments are to have an adequate and steady income, they will have to be permitted to collect and keep more taxes or be allowed to increase significantly the prices they charge for consumer services. In the case of housing, doubling or even tripling of rents would not seem unreasonable or a great hardship since the average rent and utilities paid by a Soviet worker amount to less than 4 percent of his wages.[27]

Summary

During the Stalinist era the Communist Party and central government took over the training and socialization of the workers, while the city governments were given the task of housing and feeding these workers. With the help of industry, cities somehow managed to fulfill the minimal physical needs of their inhabitants, even during and after the devastation of World War II. During the post-Stalin era Soviet leaders have attempted to rearrange responsibilities in order to accommodate a shift in priorities toward improving gradually the standard of living of the masses. The reorganization of roles has proved much more formidable than might have been expected in a highly authoritarian system. First, no comprehensive precedent existed to guide the sharing of roles between the central authorities and local administration. Second, for all its experience in planning, the Soviet system has not developed adequate techniques for comprehensive planning at the local level. Third, powerful groups within the bureaucracy have resisted change. These groups include the various branches of heavy industry, the financial agencies such as Gosbank, and the ministries of finance and their supporters in the Party. Fourth, it has been necessary to train a new cadre of local administrators capable of dealing with the complex problems of comprehensive planning. While significant progress toward comprehensive planning has been achieved in new housing construction, the regime is only beginning to study and experiment with the production and distribution of consumer goods and services and has chosen to bypass and ignore the growing problem of housing management and maintenance.

Notes

1. Examples of the decline of urban population:

	1917	1920
Leningrad	2,500,000	722,000
Moscow	1,701,264	925,255
Novgorod	148,130	105,918

Rabochaia zhilishchno-stroitelnaia kooperatsiia (Moscow, 1925), p. 50.

2. For example, in 1921 one-quarter of the apartments in St. Petersburg stood empty, the number of public baths declined from 88 in 1916 to 21 in 1921, and the number of tram cars in service (the main mode of transport at this time) declined from 724 in 1918 to 227 in 1921. N. Manakov and N. Petrov, *Gorodskoe khoziaistvo Leningrada* (Leningrad, 1949), p. 57.

3. By 1924 the average amount of housing space per person in Moscow was almost

25 percent less than in 1912, and 36.7 percent of the city's population was living more than two to a room. *Rabochaia zhilishchno-stroitelnaia kooperatsiia*, p. 50.

4. In housing the rents for the RSFSR were established in 1924 with minor revisions to 1937, when the present basic schedule was established. Rents were calculated so that no worker would have to spend more than 10 percent of his income on rent. This provided the cities with very limited resources to maintain their housing, much of which was in a state of poor repair.

5. In Leningrad gas for cooking and heating was halted in 1920 and was not again available until 1935. Tram lines were not fully restored until 1928, at which time the system was carrying twice as many passengers as in 1917.

6. Rough estimates put the destruction in the cities at more than seventy million square meters, or one-sixth of all urban housing space. At least another sixth was damaged. N. Grigorev, *Zhilishchnaia problema budet reshena* (Moscow, 1963), p. 30.

7. In 1962, among the 1,039 largest urban areas in the RSFSR, only 718 city governments had significant housing funds, 37 had none, and 284 had an insignificant amount. For example, in Magnitogorsk, 98.5 percent of housing was run by organizations other than the local government; in Sverdlosk, 84.7 percent and in Chiriki, 92.4 percent. E. I. Ianovskaia, *Khozraschet v zhilishchno khoziaistve i puti evo dalneishevo ukrepleniia* (Moscow, 1964), p. 2; B. M. Kolotilkin, *Dolgovechnost zhilikh zdanii* (Moscow, 1965), p. 104.

8. In the case of Moscow 46 construction trusts and 190 departments were brought together. These 250 organizations previously had been subordinate to 44 different ministries and departments. *Zhilishchnoe stroitelstvo*, 1967, no. 7: 8.

9. New housing constructed by local governments (square meters of general usable space): 1960: 14.6 million; 1961: 12.4 million; 1962: 10.7 million. *Ekonomika zhilishchno-kommunalnovo khoziaistva* (Moscow, 1965), p. 54.

10. In 1963 construction by small, middle-size, and large cities:

	Population		
	50-151,000	*151-350,000*	*Over 350,000*
New housing (square meters per person)	.30	.35	.43
Percentage prefab housing	23.2	36.4	40.8

Zhilishchnoe stroitelstvo, 1965, no. 9:7.

11. In February 1967 construction was divided functionally into four ministries: the Ministry for Construction of Heavy Industrial Enterprises, the Ministry of Industrial Construction, the Ministry of Construction, and the Ministry of Rural Construction. Gosstroi, the State Committee on Construction, coordinates their activities.

12. One study of Glavmosstroi in Moscow showed that the introduction of mass-produced large-panel housing from 1954 to 1964 had reduced costs by twenty rubles per square meter of housing space, or 13 to 15 percent, and the amount of labor expended by 7 to 9 percent. *Ekonomika stroitelstva*, 1965, no. 4: 15.

13. See table, note 10 above. While 51 percent of new housing construction in Moscow was large-panel prefab, panel prefabs accounted for only 8.5 percent in Belorussia, 11 percent in Uzbekistan, and 8 percent in the Ukraine in 1964. *Ekonomika stroitelstvo*, 1965, no. 1: 34.

14. A study of plan fulfillment for Leningrad in the early 1960s indicates how serious the problem had become:

	New Nurseries and Creches			Store Outlets		
	Planned	Fulfillment	Percentage Fulfilled	Planned	Fulfillment	Percentage Fulfilled
1960	42	24	57	25	2	8
1961	30	13	43	19	6	31
1962(6 mos.)	23	13	62	19	3	15

Voprosi proizvoditelnosti truda i sebestroimosti v zhilishchnom stroitelstve (Leningrad, 1962), p. 90. See also report on Fifth All-Union Architects Congress in *Pravda*, October 22, 1970.

15. During the *sovnarkhoz* reform, 1957-1964, much of local industry was taken away from local government. In 1955 about 25 percent of the contribution to the budget of the municipal governments came from local industry, but by 1959 this had been reduced to about 18 percent. The rate of profitability to income for consumer services decreased from 37.6 percent to 30.8 percent in 1954-1964. *Ekonomika zhilishno-kommunalnovo khoziaistva* (Moscow, 1965), p. 26; L. N. Goltsman, *Ekonomika kommunalnovo khoziaistva, uslugi, tarifi* (Moscow, 1966), p. 53.

16. The architectural journals have constantly complained about the inadequacy of city planning. Thus, as one Soviet architect complained, "The national economic plans often say one thing, while the general plans for development of cities say something altogether different. . . . Often cities are planned in isolation from the long-term plans for developing the entire area, i.e., they are planned unscientifically." Another editorial complained that Lenproekt, the institute in Leningrad which was planning for several Siberian cities, did not have sufficient knowledge of local conditions, particularly Siberian climatic conditions, to do an adequate job. *Arkhitektura SSSR*, 1966, no. 6: 2.

17. E. Levina and E. Syrkina, "Reflections on the microdistrict," *Zvezda*, 1966, no. 10: 150-56, translated in *Current Digest of the Soviet Press* 19, no. 3 (1967): 35.

18. The Party has traditionally operated in the same way. The local Party secretaries of the major cities are appointed by the central Party apparatus and are responsible to it. They work closely with the local authorities and wield tremendous power over them as the local agents of the Party leadership. See Richard Hough, *The Soviet Prefects, The Local Party Organs in Industrial Decision-Making* (Cambridge, Mass.: Harvard University Press, 1969).

19. About 1960 there were only 64 architects per million of population in the USSR compared to 364 in England, 240 in Sweden, 130 in the United States, 312 in Bulgaria, and 154 in Hungary. Furthermore, out of 10,462 Soviet architects in 1965, 3,640 were in Moscow and another 1,248 were in Leningrad.

20. The rate of investment in housing was reduced from 5.5 billion rubles in 1963 to 4.7 billion in 1965. I. B. Martkovich and V. R. Skripko, *Kvartirnaia plana* (Moscow, 1965), p. 4.

21. In 1967, 35,000 rural apartments were constructed and 73,300 received major repairs. This was two times the number the previous year. *Arkhitektura SSSR*, 1968, no. 10: 48.

22. While it costs local soviets about 3.75 rubles to maintain and repair each square meter of usable housing space, income from the apartment buildings amounts to only about 2.62 rubles per square meter. Kolotilkin, pp. 102-03. It was estimated in 1965 that there was a need for 1.5 to 2.0 times the number of workers then employed in current housing repairs. One reason is that as far as prestige and wages are concerned, housing maintenance and repair personnel are at the bottom in every category. The salary of workers in housing repairs in 1962 was 43 to 63 rubles per month, at a time when the minimum wage for urban workers was 40 rubles per month. The low level of

skills is exemplified by a study in Moscow in 1963 where among 2,000 technical inspectors in housing management and repairs only 450 (23 percent) had higher or middle education, and 1,200 had worked as inspectors less than five years. *Ekonomika zhilishchnovo khoziaistva* (Moscow, 1962), p. 47; N. M. Emelianov, *Organizatsiia zarobotnii plati v zhilishchno-kommunalnom khoziaistve* (Moscow, 1963), p. 40; *Gorodskoe khoziaistvo Moskvi*, 1964, no. 8: 29. One study of 609 apartment buildings in the 1960s showed that 64 percent needed roof repairs in four years, 90 percent in eight years, and all in 10 years, although the roofs were supposed to last 30 years. Another investigation in Leningrad reported in the same article that one series of new apartments after three or four years needed a capital repair expenditure of 9.9 to 14.2 rubles per square meter of housing space. *Arkhitektura SSSR*, 1968, no. 6: 22.

23. *Zhilishchnoe i kommunalnoe khoziaistvo*, 1969, no. 2: 21.

24. One study reported that in Moscow between 1960 and 1963 the cost of capital repairs of some buildings reached 122 rubles per square meter of housing space and some even reached 188 rubles at a time when new housing space cost 116 to 118 rubles a square meter for structures of similar construction. Another study in Leningrad found capital repairs reached 117 to 150 rubles a square meter of housing space. On an average in Moscow in 1963 capital repairs were costing 105 rubles and in Leningrad 92 rubles per square meter. In other cities the cost was even higher. *Gorodskoe khoziaistvo Moskvi*, 1964, no. 3: 27; no. 8: 45. *Zhilishchnoe i kommunalnoe khoziaistvo*, 1963, no. 12: 22.

25. The percentage of income from housing and the communal economy to total expenditures in housing and communal economy:

	1953	1964
A. *Including* appropriations for capital construction		
Housing and communal economy	77.0	24.8
Housing	36.3	8.0
Communal economy	111.0	63.8
B. *Excluding* appropriations for capital construction		
Housing and communal economy	141.0	98.8
Housing	64.7	40.6
Communal economy	211.0	170.0

Goltsman, p. 67.

26. *Pravda*, January 30, 1972.

27. Average rents in Leningrad:

	Average Rent per Square Meter of Housing Space (Rubles)	Percent of Average Wage	Percent of Average Wage, including Average Cost of Utilities
1939	1.09	2.7 (1940)	5.4 (1940)
1948	1.27	1.6 (1950)	4.4 (1950)
1956	1.32	1.3	3.7

Gorodskoe khoziaistvo (Leningrad, 1957), p. 30.

THE NEW MOSCOW CITY PLAN

B. M. Frolic

For over a decade Moscow planners and officials worked on a new master plan for Moscow, to develop a comparable replacement for the 1935 plan. In 1960, V. Kucherenko, a leading planner and head of the State Construction Committee (Gosstroi), noted that "work was currently being done on a new Moscow 20-year plan."[1] In 1963, the Moscow city Communist Party organization and the executive committee of the Moscow city soviet submitted the basic indices of the prospective plan to the central Party and government organs for their approval. In 1965, when I was in Moscow interviewing municipal officials, planners, and architects, the plan's basic outlines had not yet been approved because of a debate over future restrictions on industrial expansion within Moscow's boundaries. The planners had submitted a document limiting the size of Moscow to 6.6-6.8 million inhabitants, and forcefully restricting future industrial expansion within the city. They also asked that $250,000,000 of previously approved though still unbuilt industrial construction be immediately halted. This was opposed by Gosstroi, Gosplan (the USSR State Planning Committee), and other top ministries, who argued that without industrial expansion economic productivity in Moscow would seriously decline. The Central Committee of the Party at this point apparently stepped in and supported the planners, permitting public criticism of Gosstroi and the ministries' position.[2] A 1965 decree of the USSR Council of Ministers announced that excessive concentration of factories was not permissible, and V. F. Promyslov, the chairman of the executive committee of the Moscow city soviet, in a speech later that year attacked "the ambitions of those who insist on expanding Moscow's industrial facilities." In 1966, a draft plan was published, though the draft was not finally approved until 1971.[3] In the interim, significant compromises had been made. The city's population limit was raised from the envisaged 6.6-6.8 million to a realistic 7.5-8.0 million, and the ministries had persuaded the Party to allow them to build most of the disputed new industrial construction.

According to Promyslov, the new document "is a model for the solution of the basic problems of urban development. It is a clear example of the utilization of the advantages of the socialist system. It reflects trends and the scientifically substantiated forecasts for technical progress; it earmarks the most effective means for the advancement of modern urban construction."[4] Promyslov is convinced that unlike its 1935 predecessor the new plan is attainable "because it is the logical extension of what we have been doing in Moscow up to now. There are no real surprises here; no big break with the past such as in the thirties. This is a pragmatic program which will make Moscow the model Communist city."[5] The plan assumes that the Moscow region will have over 50,000,000 inhabitants by the year 2000. Ties between the city and the region will intensify, and Moscow can expect 2,000,000 commuters every day, requiring further development of the city's railways, airports, waterways, and high-speed expressways. Eight million inhabitants will reside within the city boundaries, and an additional million will live in the Green Belt, which will continue to be the main recreation area for Muscovites.

In central Moscow, all industrial expansion is to cease. New industries must locate in the suburban zone beyond the Green Belt, and existing heavy industries will be forbidden to expand in size. The planners hope that the city's industries will become more specialized, stressing precision skills and quality craftsmanship. According to Promyslov, "Moscow will develop, first of all, industry requiring highly skilled labor—precision machine-building, instrument manufacturing, machine tool manufacturing, radio engineering, electronic, and electrical engineering industries, as well as high quality consumer goods." Service industries also will increase their volume and quality of production, so that by 1980 over 50 percent of the working force will be employed in the service sector (the present Moscow ratio is 57 percent for industry and manufacturing, and 43 percent for service sector employees.

The old monocentric planning structure of the city is being replaced by eight planning zones, each with a population of a million inhabitants. "The central hub concept is no longer valid in a city of eight million spread over a large area," said N. Ullas, one of Moscow's top planners. "By decentralizing the planning of Moscow, we reduce the problems of metropolitan complexity, while taking advantage of big city life. Apart from the Sadovoe Koltso, we expect to develop other subcenters to help decentralize the city." The eight planning zones will be broken down into planning districts (*rayony*), each with a population ranging from 250,000 to 400,000. These *rayony* in turn will be divided into a number of residential districts, each with 30,000 to 70,000 inhabitants. Each residential district will contain all the required services, sports, and cultural facilities for everyday usage. Population in the Sadovoe Koltso will be reduced from 600,000 to 250,000 to 300,000, and small factories and administrative buildings are to be removed from central Moscow. The number of employees in institutions and enterprises in the Sadovoe Koltso is to decrease from 500,000 to 250,000. "Thus," according to Ullas, "the city center will become a real cultural-administrative focal point, along with the main Moscow shops, plus some residential housing such as now already exists in Kalinin Street. We intend to build new parks, widen streets, and provide better facilities for residents, pedestrians, and shoppers."

The provision of adequate housing is a key element in the new plan. "Every year we have to relocate 500,000 people in Moscow," observed Promyslov. "So in the current twenty year period [1961-1980] we will build 2.2 million apartment units. As of 1970, we had already put up 1.3 million apartment units." In 1980 every Moscow family will have its own apartment with a separate room for each family member, and average per capita housing space is expected to reach 12 to 15 square yards. Yearly

The Twentieth-Century City

housing construction is to average 3,500,000 square yards, almost all of it prefabricated, large-panel construction. New buildings will have to be at least nine stories high, and in some areas residential buildings will reach twenty-five stories. "The main factor in the future," says Promyslov, "is better distribution of land use. By raising the heights of individual buildings we can reduce their per unit cost. The density of the residential area will not increase because the buildings will be spread out farther from each other. Economically, the nine story building is sound under Moscow conditions, but twenty-five stories is the maximum limit, given Moscow's climate." By 1980, only a small percentage of Moscow's total housing space is expected to be in buildings below nine stories; the old wooden one- and two-story houses will have long vanished from sight, and Moscow will be a city comprised exclusively of high-rise apartments and tall office buildings.

Massive housing construction is to be accompanied by large-scale development of public utilities, sociocultural services, and trade facilities. Industrial and personal water consumption will double to 240 gallons per capita per day in 1980. The Vazuza River system will be developed through the construction of large dams and reservoirs, providing Moscow with water from the Volga, the Moscow River system, and the Vazuza. Large capital investments are being made in the sewage system, and by 1980 enough treatment facilities will exist so that raw sewage will no longer be dumped in the Moscow River. The supply of electricity will quadruple, and the central heat supply which comes from the power generating process will reach 95 to 98 percent in the housing sector, and 80 to 85 percent in industry. Gas supply and usage will increase 3.5 times over 1960. According to the plan, "Gas will practically displace all other kinds of fuel, with the exception of those necessary to special technological needs and an emergency reserve." Gas will be piped to Moscow from western Siberia and Central Asia and stored in huge underground storage tanks with a capacity of 5 to 6 million cubic yards. An attempt will be made to provide Muscovites with enough telephones, putting an end to the long waiting period. "The installing of telephones in Moscow and the Green Belt is to occur at the rate of 45 per 100 inhabitants. This will provide every apartment with a telephone. . . . there should be over three million telephone listings by 1980."

As the population continues to grow, collection, removal, and neutralization of waste, summer and winter street cleaning, and maintenance of roads and parks have become major problems. The planners recommend converting wastes at present buried in dumps into secondary raw material for reuse and also into organic fertilizer. Moscow's greenspace will increase from the current per capita average of thirty-three square yards to forty square yards (including the Green Belt). The city is consolidating and preserving "green wedges," strips of parkland radiating outwards to the Belt Highway and the Green Belt, and developing the banks of the Moscow River system for parkland and natural forests. Since the Green Belt has become so important to Muscovites for their recreation, they advocate limiting private dacha construction in this area, and only a small increase in the permanent population of the Green Belt will be permitted. Market gardening facilities in the Green Belt will be expanded "so that Muscovites can have fresh fruit and vegetables twelve months of the year," and hostels, camping grounds, and other recreational facilities are to be developed close to transportation facilities.

Transportation is another vital element in the plan. Ullas claims, "It may be the most important aspect of the whole plan. Without efficient transportation the regional concept of development breaks down; the central city gets clogged with traffic and pollution, and people have to spend too much time getting to and from work." Since the number of passengers is to double by 1980, public transportation will have to be greatly expanded. The famous Moscow subway will be increased from its present length of approximately 120 miles to 200 miles, and construction will begin on a second circle linking the radial lines now being built. Streetcar, trolley bus, and bus line mileage will double. The share of passengers carried by the subway will rise to 38 percent. It is planned that subway and suburban railway lines will connect to each other wherever possible, so traffic can be moved in and out of the region. According to the plan, "It is also necessary to pay attention to the construction of new kinds of transport such as monorail and the rapid street car to connect the peripheral districts of the city and places of mass recreation." Other possible solutions under consideration include converting the circular railway line now used for freight traffic into passenger service, and constructing a central Moscow railway station, so that through passengers don't have to change stations inside Moscow. Iu. G. Saushkin, a leading Soviet geographer and specialist on the city of Moscow, cites London's experience as an example: "London's problem has been solved by the addition to the underground system of overland suburban connecting lines: changing platforms in two-three minutes at an underground station, a passenger soon finds himself traveling overland amidst a sea of cottages, gardens, and Greater London's industrial areas. . . . there is nothing like it in Moscow."[6] The planners expect that Muscovites will spend no more than 30 to 40 minutes on any trip inside the city, no more than 1 to 1½ hours to reach recreation areas within the Green Belt, and no more than 2½ hours to places located in the region.

"In five years," says Promyslov, "Moscow will have over a million cars." There may be 1.5 million cars in 1980, three times the number currently in Moscow. So planning for cars is an integral part of the new plan. "We try to minimize the effect of cars on the city by planning in advance." Radial routes are being widened and extended through the city center to the Belt Highway which rings the city. This should move traffic through the city at good speeds. Work has started on some of these projects (Metrostroievskaia, Volkhonka, Piatnitskaia), and proposals have been made to build roads joining the radial routes further out from the central city, so that traffic will not always have to go through the center to get from one district to another. Another recent proposal recommends immediate construction of high-speed freeways for buses and cars cutting across the city, along the shortest possible routes. Saushkin observes, "While the city's two circular routes well serve their purposes, they are hardly a short cut to anywhere. This calls for motorways, like those in Warsaw, Chicago, Toronto, and other major cities."[7]

Planning for the automobile age will not be easy, but so far Moscow has seriously tried to control the use of cars. First, the planners created a public transportation system that is as good an alternative to private cars as any existing public transportation system. Second, they constructed wide roads which have the capacity for handling increased motor traffic while containing congestion and pollution. Third, cars are deliberately made a scarce and expensive commodity, and it can take up to five years to buy a car after you have applied through normal channels. Finally, traffic is being encouraged to flow in a reverse direction from Moscow to the suburban area and beyond by improving main arteries, by constructing service areas on the Belt Highway, and by building motels. (It is rumored that an American chain will open and manage one of these motels in the near future.)

The projected increase in automobiles has evoked concern over pollution. Despite past Soviet claims to the contrary, Moscow is not pollution-free, though it has probably suffered less than comparable modern industrial cities. A decade ago Saushkin noted "a haze, consisting of smoke, ash, dust, the exhaust fumes of cars and aeroplanes and various industrial particles. Like a gigantic greyish umbrella that can usually be seen from a great distance, this pall hangs over large industrial cities, including Moscow."[8] A Soviet acquaintance complains that the Sadovoe Koltso is now a gray highway full of noisy trucks and cars, a vivid abuse of Moscow's environment, with greenery and birds having been permanently driven out by an endless cavalcade of noisy vehicles. Yet I find Moscow cleaner, quieter, and less polluted than any other large industrial city with the exception of Peking, which has practically no motor traffic and no comparable industry. The plan calls for removing polluting industries from the city; continuing to convert to gas, which is relatively cleaner; and facilitating rapid movement of traffic through the city center to prevent any concentration of exhaust emissions due to slow-moving heavy traffic.

Compared with its 1935 predecessor, the new plan is more

modest and therefore more likely to succeed. Much will depend on whether the Soviet government can find the resources to build the necessary housing while simultaneously providing new occupants with a full range of sociocultural services. If the development of the expanded transportation network lags, Moscow will be in serious trouble because the city can easily strangle itself if the large population cannot be moved economically and quickly. More importantly, after having failed for forty years, will planners finally be able to control the size and the movement of Moscow's population? There is again talk of enlarging current boundaries in order to reduce rising population densities. In the 1930s and 1940s, even when funds for urban development were made available, plan fulfillment was hampered by inexperienced planners and administrators. Now thirty years later, has the USSR managed to develop a competent corps of administrators and planners who, under Party direction, can execute the plan's provisions effectively? Promyslov is quick to reply "Yes." He says, "We have money. We have authority. We have everything. . . . All the designing is in the hands of the Moscow soviet and Moscow has its own construction industry. The Moscow soviet is master of this city." Compared to 1935, Moscow administrators in the 1970s do have more expertise, more power and authority to perform tasks which are more realistic in their goals. Still, in the light of forty years of Soviet failures to meet previous city planning goals, one must be cautious in evaluating even a relatively modest urban development program such as the new Moscow plan.

An Evaluation

Recalling the history of Moscow's development since the Revolution, one must be impressed by the way in which the planners have reshaped the physical structure of the city from a backward tsarist "big village" into a modern metropolis. Yet one also feels that the bigness of contemporary Moscow, the complexity of her technology, and the massive scale of the city's physical transformation have produced a city which, surprisingly, has diminished the human element that once was the primary concern of planners and officials. What seems to be missing in the recent plan is the intense social concern of town planning which characterized the debates over urban development in the 1920s, and which was to be the main criterion for urban life under socialism. Gone are the fanciful attempts to restructure human life in industrial cities, the communal kitchens, the search for a revolutionary architecture, and the attempts to develop small urban villages inside Moscow. Rather, the current plan seems designed mainly to cope with the problems of managing bigness. It is more an administrative document than a guide to revolutionary town and social planning. The key to the development of Moscow is management, as Promyslov notes in discussing the future economy of Moscow: "The extensive use of mathematical methods and computers is a major trend in the development of the city. . . . a Main Scientific Research Computer Center to manage the work of the branch automated management systems . . . will deal with current and long-range planning tasks, capital construction and the development of all sectors of the city economy; it will provide forecasts in all fields."[9]

Soviet planners and politicians contend that it is possible to manage a big socialist urban agglomeration and still provide the humanized sociopsychological setting that Marx sought over a century ago. "To compare Moscow today with our post-1917 expectations is unfair," observed one sociologist. "The proper comparison ought to be with nineteenth-century Russia on the one hand, and with capitalist cities such as New York and Tokyo on the other hand. That would put Moscow's development in a better perspective, removed from the ideological excesses of the 1920s. Then one could better see just how well we have prepared the basis for a truly fulfilling life in a giant city environment."

If we evaluate performance in terms of stated goals, however, it is fair to conclude that Soviet town planning performance has not measured up. This should not necessarily be taken as an adverse criticism, but as an acknowledgment that Moscow planners and politicians, like their counterparts throughout the Soviet Union, have always been too impatient to transform society overnight.

They have set impossible goals which could not be met because economic and human resources have turned out to be inadequate. The current plan is more realistic in this respect; its goals are more modest and its prospects of success are better. It seems that planning goals are more realizable if they involve physical rather than social restructuring. This is the lesson of the 1930s and of various later attempts at social experimentation. Postponement of social objectives for more pragmatic goals of street widening, public transportation, and tree planting may be a necessary strategy of socialist urban development, as long as this postponement is only temporary and is perceived as such by all those concerned.

The process of urbanization once set into motion is difficult to control and almost impossible to direct. Despite possessing the best resources of the Soviet state, and no matter how progressive their values and goals, Moscow planners and politicians have been powerless to alter the basic thrust of urbanization. They have managed to apply cosmetic surgery to this process, but have been unable in the short run to stop population growth or to provide adequate housing, consumer services, and public utilities. In the long run, they may have created the basis for a better human environment, but it has taken several generations to get to this point, despite central planning and an ambitious master plan. Ullas admits that "urbanization is a nonreversible process," and that large cities have many disadvantages. "People have to travel too far to get to work. They are alienated from nature. Sanitary and health conditions rapidly deteriorate. The cost of providing an infrastructure for a large city is enormous. But," he argues, "we can regulate and control urban development. There are advantages as well, including maximum access to choice of leisure and work."

It turns out that Moscow's planning experience has been one of attempting to regulate, but being unable to control, urbanization. Moscow sociologists recognize the existence of some conflict between universal urban values (urbanism) and socialist policies, referring to urbanism as "a type of culture, a social psychology intimately tied to conditions of life in all modern urban agglomerations."[10] Moscow social scientists are conducting surveys and research to see why there is a gap between social planning ideals and the realities of urban life. These social scientists conclude that the increased individual mobility, heterogeneity, and anonymity of modern big-city life basically contradict the group norms of socialism. Socialist policies may have failed because it is the nature of urbanism to make them fail, and the communal kitchen, whether it is ideologically correct or not, may have to be forced into the dustbin of history. Central planning does not solve everything and Soviet planners have made their share of mistakes. Planning is not enough when funds are lacking to carry out the plan, or when administrators and technical experts are unable to execute plans properly. Thus, as long as economic and political considerations have first priority, town planners cannot function successfully. This has been the case in Moscow, where town planning has always taken second place to the factory and to the politician. Planners are also fallible. They have made mistakes in estimating population growth and in several construction projects (the Belt Highway was practically obsolete from the time it was built). To state the obvious, socialist planners make mistakes because no one can predict the future accurately.

While Moscow is the Soviet capital and the model for all Soviet cities, the rest of the more than 2,000 Soviet cities are not simply smaller replicas of Moscow. We must remember that Moscow is a model, representing the best achievements of Soviet urban development. Per capita capital investment is lower in almost every other Soviet city. No other city has built as much new housing or possesses such a well-developed transportation system. Just travel thirty miles outside Moscow and you are in primitive towns and cities, walking on muddy streets, past wooden houses with outdoor plumbing, looking at empty shelves in small shops. Moscow is a "Potemkin Village" behind whose walls stand less privileged, less developed Soviet cities. Almost every social and planning experiment is first applied in Moscow, and no other Soviet city has Moscow's resources or her powers. No other city has Moscow's unique relationship to the central Party and government. A succession of Soviet leaders from Lenin through Brezhnev has emphasized this special status. At the twenty-fourth Party Congress, Brezhnev again announced that "We must strive to make Moscow a model city for communism." Moscow is the pace-setter—the example of what other Soviet cities may be like in the future.

From a broader perspective, Moscow's experience has limited relevance for the developed "capitalist cities" because Moscow's planning experience is based on public ownership of land and on central planning, two concepts which are anathema to the ideology of capitalism. While Moscow's experience can be useful for those responsible for developing Cairo, Lagos, Djakarta, and Peking, it is too late for capitalist cities. We cannot conceive of giving so much power to a plan and to planners to regulate our lives, and it would be folly to try to convert to public land ownership in our present society. Nor would we permit the fundamental political and administrative changes required to make central planning effective and to secure adequate financing for metropolitan development. Apparently we do not care for the Soviet concept of citizen participation—involvement in the administration of policies but not in their formulation. But once we push aside fundamental systemic differences, we can profit from specific features of Moscow's physical reconstruction in several ways. For example, we might do well to study Moscow's experience in the industrialization of high-rise apartment construction. The ratio of new apartment construction is rapidly rising in our large cities because of the high cost of land. We may have to employ similar methods of prefabricated construction. Indeed, several Western specialists have visited the USSR to observe the prefabricated construction process in action. We should also take another look at the way in which Moscow intends to move commuters from the suburbs and the region into the central city, by extending radial subway lines over long distances and establishing a single fare subway system with monthly unlimited travel passes. Whether we like it or not, we may have to revise and centralize municipal financing in the future, perhaps abolishing the property tax as a municipal revenue source. Moscow's example of reliance on centralized revenues and budgeting is also relevant here.

Moscow evokes strong attachments from those who have lived there. This jumble of architecture, wide empty streets, and crowded stores is a beautiful, fascinating combination of old Russia and new Soviet society. Moscow has a charm that buries itself in the heart. It also contains a promise of a better life to come for its inhabitants. There is yet optimism in Moscow that man can control his urban environment through centrally planned urban development. Only fifty years ago Moscow was a big village full of illiterate peasants. Today the city is one of the world's great capitals. The new plan seeks to develop tomorrow's Moscow, more modestly and pragmatically, into a modern socialist metropolis. Perhaps we should therefore suspend our judgment of Moscow's planning experiment a while longer to give Moscow planners, politicians, and citizens still more time to catch up with their ideals.

Notes

This is part of a larger study on Moscow currently in process. Interviews referred to in the text were conducted by the author in Moscow in 1965 and 1969, and by Dan Dimancescu and Crocker Snow, Jr., in 1971. My thanks to Dan Dimancescu, Wentworth Eldredge, Jane Mosher, Hans Blumenfeld, and Lev Kogan for their advice and assistance. Special thanks go to the Russian Research Center of Harvard University for their generous support of my research.

1. V. A. Kucherenko, "On the State of Urban Development in the USSR and Measures for Improving It," *Pravda*, June 1, 1960.

2. See William Taubman, *Governing Soviet Cities: Bureaucratic Politics and Urban Development in the USSR* (New York: Praeger, 1973), chapter 10.

3. See "O generalnom plane Moskvy," *Stroitelstvo i arkhitektura Moskvy* 11 (November 1966); "Generalny plan razvitii Moskvy," *Pravda*, June 10, 1971; V. F. Promyslov, "A Matter of Honor for the Entire Soviet People," *Kommunist* 4 (March 1972): 26-39.

4. Promyslov, p. 28.

5. From transcripts of interviews with Dimancescu and Snow in 1971. Unless specially cited, all other comments by Promyslov are taken from these interviews.

6. Iu. G. Saushkin, *Moscow* (Moscow, 1966), pp. 139-40.

7. Ibid., p. 141.

8. Ibid., p. 38.

9. Promyslov, p. 31.

10. Institut konkretnykh sotsialnykh issledovanii AN USSR, i sovetskaia sotsiologicheskaia assotsiatsiia, *Sotsiologicheskie issledovaniia goroda*, Informatsionny biulleten 16 (Moscow, 1969), p. 1.

PART IV
CONCLUSION

MODERNIZATION AND URBANIZATION IN RUSSIA: A COMPARATIVE VIEW

William L. Blackwell

In a populist utopian fantasy written at the end of the Russian Civil War, it was imagined that the peasant party would gain control of the Soviet government in 1934 and proceed to dismantle the cities, until after half a century Moscow would have been reduced to 100,000 permanent inhabitants.[1] Populists everywhere usually have opposed large-scale urbanization; but their Russian Marxist opponents have held an ambiguous view of the city. Some Soviet planners have wanted to deurbanize; others, perhaps closer to the views of Marx and Engels, have been willing to live with modern supercities provided they could be limited and controlled. Neither plan has yet succeeded. The Soviet Union is, for some rather compelling reasons, "a land of large cities."[2] Moscow has now become a "world city" of eight million inhabitants, ringed with suburbs, highways, and satellite towns.[3] In the 1930s, the Soviet Union experienced the most spectacular urban transformation in world history. Only three other urban migrations could be compared to this phenomenon—the massive influx of people into American cities from 1880 to 1930 and after World War II (which it exceeded); and, in the same postwar period, the urban explosion in Japan (which surpassed it). Although now on the level of Brazil and Italy rather than the United States, Japan, and England in terms of large cities, the population of the USSR is expected to be 75 percent urban by the end of the twentieth century.[4]

The background of this momentous process is a rich urban

history that is a thousand years old; yet the study of Russian urbanization is hardly under way. Indeed this collection of essays is a beginning: it is the first book to be written outside the Soviet Union (where the study of Russian urban history has been pursued for some years) that concerns itself with the urbanization of that society in broad historical perspective, particularly the period prior to 1917. Sources are scarce: beyond the valuable information presented in the essays themselves, much of it based on published and archival documents, studies of Russian urban history other than for the most recent period are fragmentary, almost exclusively Russian, and predominantly Soviet. General and comparative historical studies of world urbanization make only the barest passing reference to Russian cities.

Therefore, in this concluding essay, I have aimed at a discussion of the problems of research in this new field, and have tried to provide suggestions for future investigation rather than definitive conclusions, which must await the accumulation of a much more substantial body of scholarship. My method has been not only to summarize and comment on the essays but also to sketch in issues that have not been presented. I have focused on the period before 1917, about which the least has been written. Recently, a few studies of Soviet urbanization have appeared as articles, books, or unpublished dissertations, and these have been used along with other materials to provide a brief introduction to some of the problems of urbanization of this most recent period, with which I will conclude my essay.[5] It should also be noted that although sociologists, geographers, and political scientists have contributed to the collection, as well as historians, I am commenting as one of the latter. Therefore, events and personalities enter more substantially into my account of the history of Russian cities. It also seemed appropriate for a concluding essay to provide a comparative dimension—necessarily a selective one—for Russian urbanization. The parallels and contrasts with the urban experience of the United States, Europe, and the Middle and Far East in particular are significant.

Three general questions may provide a way of entering this very large subject: How is Russian urban history to be periodized? What is the most useful conceptual and interpretative framework in which to place it? How does the Russian experience compare and rank with urbanization in the history of other peoples?

Russian urbanization requires first of all a scheme of periodization. One possible scheme, widely accepted for other societies, might use industrialization as a key to stages of urban development. Many scholars, from Adna Weber onward, have seen the passage from the preindustrial to the industrial city as a major transition in urban history.[6] This scheme could be applied to Russian urban history, because rapid urbanization and industrialization in Russia began at about the same time, in the late nineteenth century.

The concept of the industrial city has limitations for describing the nature of Russian urbanization in the past century, however. Although industrialization has been a central element in Russian urbanization, with a substantial proliferation of smaller cities functioning primarily as industrial centers, in the industrial push of the 1930s the most significant urbanization took place in other kinds of cities; and the largest and most numerous of the major Russian cities are not exclusively industrial or transport centers in their genesis and function. The broader process of modernization may be more appropriate for a historical definition of urbanization in Russia since the mid-nineteenth century, because modernization embraces not only the industrial, technological, and transport revolutions, but also political, social, and cultural development so crucial for an understanding of Russian history and particularly the relationship of the state and city in that process.*

Modernization, not industrialization alone, has forged the major

*For the purposes of this essay modernization may be defined briefly as "the impact on societies of the scientific and technological revolution that has transformed existence in the last three or four centuries" (Cyril Black). Modernization thus is not limited to the effects of this revolution on the economy through the transformation of agriculture and the development of industry, but includes also the social impact of the scientific and technological revolution as reflected in the stability or instability of the political and social order, changes in values, and the emergence of new institutional and social forms. Historically, modernization began to accelerate dynamically in western Europe and the United States in the mid-nineteenth century, and in Russia and Japan in the succeeding

Russian cities of today. Moscow, the brain and will of this dynamic system, is essentially the center of administration—of planning, science, education, and culture—for a superstate where the government has nearly total control of the economic and political process. Although Moscow is the largest industrial center in the USSR, her numerous industries are oriented toward consumer goods and services and engineering: the older textile industry and the newer electronics, machine, and automobile firms, establishments catering to the needs of the capital. White collar workers are almost as numerous as industrial laborers. The capitals of the republics and of the regions within them—the largest cities in the Soviet Union—are smaller copies of Moscow. This is not to minimize the importance of Russia's equally numerous more purely industrial cities. Without the regional clusters of concentrated industrial production in smaller centers, the administrative cities would not have grown as they did.

In view of this, Russian urban history might be periodized by identifying the 1860s as the turning point between the premodern and the modernizing Russian city. In this decade the two capital cities of Russia began to grow rapidly, a number of new industrial and commercial cities appeared, a railroad network connecting

---

generation. By the mid-twentieth century, it had become a global process and a recognized field of scholarship.

As applied to the city in history, definition of the process of modernization, since it takes place very largely in cities, must be rigorously limited to urban problems. Fundamentally, modernization has caused the appearance of new types of cities, or the transformation of older ones, in the past 150 years. The main types include industrial, administrative, and trade and transport centers. Change in these cities during modernization has involved, 1) political development: adjustments and reform of urban administration, planning, the changing relationship of the municipality to central state authority, and the consolidation or breakdown of urban political order; 2) economic development: the effect of industrial, commercial, and financial institutions on urbanization; 3) technological development: the effect of machinery and electronics, particularly new means of transport and communication, on urbanization and urban life; 4) social development: migration, changes in social organization, and social disorientation; and 5) cultural development: the emergence of a new type of urban culture and new habits and values. For the historiography, a bibliography, and general discussions of modernization, see Cyril E. Black, *The Dynamics of Modernization* (New York: Harper, 1966); and Samuel P. Huntington, "The Change to Change: Modernization, Development, and Politics," *Comparative Politics* 3 (1970-1971): 283-322.

cities and markets was built, and the first comprehensive urban administrative reform was promulgated (1870). Since 1861 is widely accepted as a turning point in Russian social and economic development by both Soviet and non-Soviet historians, it might be convenient to view the same year as symbolic of the transition from the premodern to the modern period of urbanization, understanding that political decisions and events, such as those of 1861 or 1917, although dramatic, are not necessarily congruent with the broader patterns of social and economic history. Thus, although the events of 1917 certainly prepared a foundation for the massive urbanization that later occurred, urban growth did not begin to accelerate significantly until the late 1920s.

The period from the revolution of 1917 to the opening of the Stalin first plan era was actually one of urban stagnation, destruction, and even deurbanization, particularly during the first hectic years of the Civil War; and the early 1920s were essentially a period of recovery from this disaster for the cities. Thus, in the periodization of Russian urban development, the period 1861-1914 actually constitutes one unit: a long period of growth. This was followed by a second phase, characterized by urban decline and reconstruction and by a political consolidation of the new regime comparable to the political consolidation of the old regime in the 1860s. The next major turning point in Russian urban history after that of 1861 came with the collectivization drive of 1929. This agrarian revolution was accompanied not only by an industrial take-off but by an urban revolution as well, one unprecedented in human history.

The urban revolution of the 1930s was followed by a new whirlwind of war even more devastating to Russian urban life than the Civil War: more than 1,700 cities, towns, and villages were destroyed, according to one estimate, not to mention the battering of Leningrad, Kharkov, and other major urban centers.[7] The destruction of cities in wars and civil wars was hardly a new experience for Russian urban dwellers, any more than Napoleon's incendiary destruction of their capital was a unique catastrophe for Moscovites. Great conflagrations and plagues depopulated the city upon numerous occasions of its early history. The Mongol invasions and the Time of Troubles brought with them other waves of urban destruction. To be sure, Russia, in the twentieth century particularly, is not alone in seeing her cities ravaged by war. Japan, Germany, Poland, Holland, England, and Southeast Asia have all suffered deurbanization (and sometimes urbanization) by bombardment. But no assessment of the pace and scope of Russian urban development can avoid considering the grim fact that during the first three decades of the new regime, from 1917 to 1945, at a time when most of the cities of the world were growing undisturbed, the cities of the Soviet Union were suffering frequent and extensive destruction. The years 1945 to 1973, on the other hand, brought a new phase of urbanization, characterized by the emergence of large metropolises and by the attendant problems of size. As with other countries that have reached the more advanced stages of modernization, urbanization in the Soviet Union is increasingly becoming less a matter of growth and more one of control and integration.

Within the framework of this scheme of periodization my essay will attempt to describe Russian urbanization with particular emphasis on the process of modernization and on a comparison of the Russian experience with that of modernizing cities in other societies. At the beginning, however, I shall make a comparative analysis of the Russian city prior to modernization, for tradition everywhere, and notably in Russia, has had a great effect on urbanization in the period of modernization. Tradition and modernization—these are the two keys to understanding the city in Russian history.

The Premodern Russian City

Kievan Rus' was known to the Vikings as a "land of cities." Rather dramatically, as Tikhomirov describes it, in the tenth to twelfth centuries at least one hundred of what Soviet scholars by a conservative estimate would accept as truly urban settlements came into being.[8] Apart from ancient Greek colonies in the south, they were a new experience for Russians. The origins of these first Russian towns were not different in the main from the origins of towns elsewhere. The same convergence of resources, institutions, and skills, as well as of economic and military necessities, occurred here as it did in most other parts of the ancient and medieval world in Europe and Asia. There was a similar development of political and religious organization, technology, and agricultural resources capable of supporting and supplying from the surrounding area a concentration of people not engaged exclusively in agriculture. More important, there came about at the same time the same conjuncture of fortress and market, when merchants and craftsmen attached themselves permanently to a fortified estate, that marked the beginning of town life.[9] The strength of the commercial impulse has been debated by Russian historians since the time of Kliuchevsky. Clearly, it varied from place to place. Some towns were essentially the stockades of chieftains who extracted tribute from the surrounding countryside and also traded with merchants; others were mainly rural marketplaces; and others were important Eurasian trading depots situated on the river highways. The number of cities increased perhaps threefold in the Kievan period, and new types of cities evolved. By the twelfth century, two national political-commercial-religious centers of much greater size and sophistication had emerged: Kiev and Novgorod.[10]

Russian towns came into being at about the same time as those of western Europe and performed similar functions. As Lawrence Langer has pointed out in the first essay here, in terms of size and population they did not differ greatly from their European counterparts during the thirteenth to fifteenth centuries, except for the much larger Italian cities. However, the institutional and social evolution peculiar to the medieval European towns, which has been described by Max Weber, Henri Pirenne, and their numerous followers, seems not to have characterized city growth in Russia. The medieval Russian town, it is frequently asserted, developed little sense of community and few autonomous institutions, with a consequent stifling of freedom and growth. This view has been challenged, but without success; and Langer's conclusion that "the models of medieval urban development constructed by Pirenne and Weber are not applicable to Russia" would seem to be supported by most historians not preoccupied with attempting to prove the identity of Russian and western European medieval institutions. On the other hand, the assertion of the uniqueness of medieval European urban life as contrasted with Russian and oriental development is not free from the distortions of Europocentristic thinking, as well as, it may be suggested, of antimodernist romanticization of the traditional European society of the Middle Ages, of which the towns were seen as an outstanding feature.[11]

Comparison also should be made between the premodern Russian city and the premodern oriental city, as Gilbert Rozman has shown in discussing China and Japan. It is clear from his comparative analysis that in terms of percentage of population in cities and of urban networks, urbanization in Russia was at the same stage as that in China and Japan in the late eighteenth century. In terms of the percentage of urban dwellers in the total population, the premodern urbanization of Japan was exceptionally great by contrast with Russia, although premodern urbanization in the Middle East probably exceeded that of Russia at the end of the eighteenth century, as that of Europe certainly did.[12] Nevertheless, Rozman concludes that the quantitative gap between urbanization in Russia and that in western Europe was much narrower at that time than has been assumed.

This highlights the question of the nature of this urbanization in Russia. Was it a hesitant and partial recapitulation of European urban development during the early industrial revolution, as some Soviet scholars suggest,[13] or was it closer to a premodern kind of urbanization, as in the Far and Middle East? The reasons adduced by Issawi for extensive Middle Eastern urbanization during a process of cultural and political decline in this very same period are instructive: the absence of castles and other rural strongholds; pilgrimages; the residence of large numbers of the military and ruling elite in urban areas; the flight of peasants to towns from villages made insecure by brigandage; and inland trade.[14] These factors, in varying but significant degrees, were operative in seventeenth- and eighteenth-century Russia, but little research has been devoted to them.

In their lack of municipal self-government as well as in their subordination to a centralized administration for the purposes of control and extraction of taxes, the experience of the Russian cities of early modern times can be compared to that of both Asian and European societies wherever centralized national or imperial power developed. The *hsien* cities of China offer a striking example of an elaborate and enduring network of planned administrative centers which could provide revenue, grain, labor, and troops for war and public works. Commerce and crafts soon came to thrive in these cities, but the function of traditional Chinese urban society remained primarily to serve the needs of a centralized empire.[15] The urban administrative system of Catherine the Great was a faint shadow of this formidable structure, but the function of cities as units in a large, centralized fiscal and administrative system was the same for both societies. As J. Michael Hittle has summarized in his essay, "The Russian city can be understood only as an integral part of a polity dominated by a powerful, centralized state."

Most of the cities of Europe were undergoing this experience with the consolidation of nation states and multinational empires in early modern times, but it was in Russia and Prussia that the subordination of city to state was furthest advanced. The similarities in this process are instructive, and also noteworthy because they occurred almost simultaneously. It is a history that goes back to the emergence of the Grand Duchy of Muscovy and of the Margravate of Brandenburg as expanding states in the fifteenth century, and culminates in the harnessing of the cities of Russia and Prussia to a rationalized bureaucratic power by Peter the Great and Frederick William I. The key to the process in both cases, as pointed out in the essays by David Miller and J. Michael Hittle, was the view of the city as a source of revenue for the state. The townsman was a "service" townsman, just as the noble served the state as a soldier or bureaucrat and the peasant met his labor and tax obligations to the landlord and the state. In Russia, the towns, like the peasant communes, supported the war machine through communally apportioned direct taxes and through indirect taxes on trade and liquor. In Prussia, similar indirect taxes (*akzise*) levied on the townsmen for grain, beer, and other items of consumption provided the largest part of the state war chest.

The period from the reign of the Great Elector to that of Frederick William I saw the gradual subordination of any independent urban government to the *Steurkommissar*, originally (1688) a collector of the war tax appointed by the central *Kriegskommissariat*.[16] Military people were used widely in these local administrative posts.[17] Similarly, in seventeenth-century Russia, administration, justice, and taxation in the towns were turned over to the local military commander, the *voivoda*, to whom elected town officials were subordinated. The system was far more disorganized than in Prussia, and the *voivoda* often shared power with a host of other government officials: *namestnik, gorodnichi, prikashchik,* and others.[18] The reforms of Peter the Great and later of Catherine the Great, as detailed in the essays by Hittle and Miller, achieved some rationalization of this haphazard chain of command, as well as a broadening of the administrative functions of the cities, while maintaining the primacy of the tax obligation. Such a system invited corruption and favoritism, which was long characteristic of urban administration in both Prussia and Russia. Such intrusion and exploitation were not accepted obediently by townsmen in either country: urban disorders were not frequent but were noticeable. Hittle has recorded the Moscow uprising of 1648, in which taxes and concessions were the main issues. Rebellions in Berlin and other Prussian towns date back to the very early days of the Hohenzollerns in the fifteenth century. In the seventeenth century, vigorous opposition by the merchant guilds to new administrative and fiscal measures was crushed by Frederick William.

Unusually prominent in the urban history of Russia, compared to other centralizing national states and empires in Europe and

Asia in the early modern period, has been the role of the capital city. Long before the advent of modernization, Moscow dwarfed all of the hundreds of other towns of Russia. As early as the sixteenth century, a third of the urban population was concentrated there. Moscow combined many of the functions of the world's traditional capital cities. Like Berlin or Constantinople, it was first and foremost the administrative center of a dynamically expanding state, the peak of a hierarchy of hundreds of local and (by the early eighteenth century) provincial administrative centers. More and more, the aristocracy as well as the gentry took up residence there. Moscow became the home of military regiments and of officials administering an emerging empire, as well as of the people who catered to them. This brought the development of parade grounds, barracks, and offices, as well as town houses and palaces. And, like medieval Rome and Jerusalem through the ages, Moscow from its early years became a holy city: a city of churches, pilgrims, miracles, and holy objects—a national shrine. Moscow was and always has remained a center of Russian nationalism. Unlike cosmopolitan St. Petersburg, foreigners were not welcome here; if they came they were segregated in special quarters, in Moscow's first term as Russia's capital city, before 1721, as well as in its second during the Soviet reign.

Seventeenth-century Moscow was also becoming, in addition to its role as an administrative and ideological center, the focal point of another hierarchy, an economic one. A Russian national market was forming there, as well as an international commercial center that brought together merchants of Europe, Russia, and Asia. Wealthy merchants were settling in its commercial quarter, the Kitai Gorod, and the business of buying and selling was being dispersed along streets as well as in the rows of shops and stands constituting the permanent urban market of the Gostinnoi Dvor.[19]

Unlike Moscow, St. Petersburg did not experience a gradual metamorphosis over several centuries into a commercial, religious, and administrative center. It was created overnight, as Toynbee puts it, "an extreme case of the deliberate choice of a peripheral site for a capital . . . conjured up *ex nihilo* in the swamps at the mouth of the river Neva." The peculiar location of St. Petersburg was chosen for both strategic and cultural reasons: to control the Baltic and to import goods and ideas from the West.[20] Less like Moscow and other cities of the Russian interior, and more like the great port cities of Africa and Asia in the era of imperialism, St. Petersburg was a cosmopolitan complex with a large foreign colony. These foreigners were not so much segregated as in Moscow, nor did they have the power and the privilege that Europeans enjoyed in the great imperial depots that have developed into many of the leading cities of the world. But the social process observable in St. Petersburg was comparable to that of a city like Cairo: the foreigners and the upper classes, associating socially and speaking Western languages, isolated themselves from the servants and the poor who spoke the native tongue.

St. Petersburg became, even more than Moscow, the capital of a rapidly expanding and increasingly centralized empire. By the end of the eighteenth century it greatly exceeded the old capital in size, population, and the scale of its monuments. It was the home of the autocrat and the imperial court, the hub of a sprawling bureaucracy, and the garrison for the elite units of the armed forces. This concentration of the most powerful courtiers, administrators, and military officers in one large capital city, the nerve center of a centralized empire, gave rise to a type of urban-based political revolution which became characteristic of Russian political life almost from the founding of St. Petersburg to the 1917 revolution. This type of coup d'état or palace revolution in an imperial capital, frequently termed "praetorian" revolution from the experience of ancient Rome, where similar conditions existed, could also be observed in medieval Cairo, in early modern Constantinople, in nineteenth century Paris ("the mecca of revolutions"), and in many capital cities of the world in the twentieth century. The techniques were essentially the same everywhere: 1) the forming of an organized secret conspiracy in the capital city; 2) planning for the elimination of the head of state and seizure of the main centers of command and communication located in various parts of the city; and 3) marshalling of armed forces, recruited usually from military units stationed in the capital. The praetorian revolution did not usually enlist mass support, either from the military or the civilian population of the city, but was carried out by a much smaller force, usually two or three regiments. In 1917, Bolshevik forces in Petrograd, consisting largely of military personnel, numbered about 25,000, according to Trotsky. The praetorian revolution was thus characteristic of both the premodern and the modernizing periods of Russia's capital cities. Modernization made it more sophisticated; instead of the nocturnal galloping of mounted guards officers through empty streets from barracks to barracks, revolutionary task forces quietly and systematically seized the telephone exchanges, telegraph stations, armories, banks, and railroad terminals, all of the nerve centers of a modern city, while its millions provided the praetorians with the invaluable neutrality of sleep.

There was no massive and rapid urbanization in Russia until the late nineteenth century: the dividing line between premodern and modern urbanization, as suggested earlier, is 1861. Nevertheless, the early nineteenth century must be recognized as a period of preparation for the emergence, after the Great Reforms, of the modern Russian city, just as the stage was set in the preceding generation for Russia's first industrial revolution of the post-Reform period.[21] The urban population, although small compared to that of the late nineteenth century, continued to grow. Permanent urban markets were replacing the great fairs of the Ukraine and Central Russia. New, more modern types of cities appeared. Although few in number, they prefigured what was to come. Odessa, founded at the end of the eighteenth century, was one such new city, whose history has been detailed in Frederick W. Skinner's essay above. Odessa was a commercial port city, the main outlet during the early nineteenth century for the burgeoning grain export crop. Its growth was spectacular for the time and place, the population expanding to 119,000 in the first seventy years. Ivanovo was another new city—Russia's first purely industrial city of any significance. Situated 200 miles east of Moscow in the forests of Vladimir province near the Volga River and its canal systems, the so-called "Manchester of Russia" was essentially a frontier boom town in the early nineteenth century, where bears, wolves, and outlaws were still as much a part of the environment as the new factories and shops. But it was in these cotton printing factories and shops that the technological potential of the Russian peasant craftsman was first proved.

The two capital cities were developing an industrial character in the early nineteenth century, and it is interesting to compare their social and economic growth. The Moscow of the churches and boyars was becoming a Moscow of factories and industrialists. But one industry dominated—textiles, an industry developed largely by Russians. Russia's first authentic industrial bourgeoisie and factory working class were recruited at this time from among the Old Believers, who had come to constitute a large part of the population of Moscow and the surrounding villages. Intensely religious and patriotic, these new classes perpetuated in modernized form throughout the subsequent urbanization of Moscow in the tsarist period the city's traditional role as a center of Russian national feeling.

St. Petersburg in the early nineteenth century, like Moscow in the Soviet period, was becoming not just an industrial center but a cosmopolitan headquarters of industry, commerce, and finance, a role more appropriate to the city that served as the administrative hub of the empire and as its westernmost port. A cotton textile industry developed in St. Petersburg, as in Moscow, but it was dominated by foreigners, most of them Englishmen, capitalizing on the advanced technology they brought with them. The most sophisticated Russian industry of the time was centered in St. Petersburg: the manufacture of industrial machinery and locomotives, again dominated by foreigners. Foreigners also controlled much of the import-export business, and were involved with the nascent banking and financial institutions. It was in St. Petersburg before 1861 that most of the business, engineering, technological, and polytechnical schools were founded. The imperial capital possessed at the same time the most substantial middle class of all

the Russian cities, but far more cosmopolitan and heavily bureaucratic than in Moscow. Thus, it was already clear in the early
nineteenth century that St. Petersburg was to be the brain center
for Russian modernization during the last part of the tsarist
period.

One can conclude that by 1861 Russia had a well-developed
premodern system of local and regional administrative centers and
markets, capped by two large capital cities. This system was
comparable to the premodern urban systems developed in western
Europe and the Far East.[22] St. Petersburg and Moscow—at this
time among the most highly developed of the premodern type of
city with a combined population approaching a million inhabitants—had begun to assume an industrial character in the early
nineteenth century, at a time when new types of industrial and
commercial cities were emerging in other parts of the empire.
Despite these foreshadowings of change, comprehensive modern
urbanization did not make its belated appearance in Russia until
the late nineteenth century. From that time on it was facilitated,
as in Japan, by a well developed and long-standing tradition of
centralized political order.[23]

The First Urban Transformation, 1861-1914

The year 1861, generally recognized as a turning point for Russian
economic and political development, when extensive agrarian and
administrative reforms were initiated, also marks a new era in the
history of Russian cities. It was at this time that the tsarist
government embarked on a new course, a program of modernization. At the same time, the influx into Russia of foreign capital,
enterprise, and technology began to increase significantly. Russian
industrial and commercial capitalism also began to grow at a much
faster rate. And the tempo of Russian urbanization significantly
quickened. Many new industrial and commercial cities appeared,
and the population of cities generally expanded greatly. It was
clear that Russia was experiencing her first modern urban transformation; but it was not to be the only one.

The tsarist modernization drive, however, was a partial and sluggish push to modernity. It provides a classic example of political institutions failing to keep pace with social and economic change, resulting in stagnation and instability as much as dynamic growth and orderly change. Industrial development was disproportionate: the agrarian sector remained economically stagnant and politically unstable. The intrusion of foreign capital and the growth of Russian capital were both insufficient. The development of a native technology was retarded.

Russian urbanization in the late nineteenth and early twentieth centuries reflected this mixed process of dynamic modernization and breakdown. On the one hand, there was the dynamism of rapidly expanding cities, with large numbers of workers and factories, a burgeoning municipal bureaucratic apparatus, and a new and sophisticated urban culture among the professional and intellectual elites; on the other, urban misgovernment and oppression, a deepening fiscal crisis, poverty, slums, social disorientation, and increasing political instability.

During the same period, an alternative modernizing leadership was forming in the cities of Russia among disaffected intellectual elements who had located in them. The breakdown of the tsarist political order, accelerated by war, permitted this new leadership to consolidate its power during a decade of revolution and civil war as well as intense rivalry and struggle within its ranks. With political order reestablished by the late 1920s, a second urban transformation, which was both more comprehensive and more painful than the first, began in Russia.

Dynamic urbanization of the modern type first occurred in Russia in the last third of the nineteenth century, considerably later than in England, the population of which was 50 percent urban by 1850, and the United States, where the rapid growth of modern cities began in the 1830s and where nearly 20 percent of the population was urban by 1860.[24] Not until 1913 did Russia come just short of achieving the same proportion of rural-urban population, while still lagging behind Germany, France, and the Low Countries, as well as the United States and England. Nevertheless, Russia can hardly be considered a latecomer to world urbanization, and must be ranked with Japan, western Austria-Hungary, northern Italy, and Scandinavia as precursors to the rest of the world in the business of spawning modern cities. The average annual rate of urban growth in tsarist Russia after 1867 (2.3 percent) contrasts markedly with the slower rate of urbanization of the early nineteenth century (1.5 percent), as well as with the world average for the last half of the nineteenth century of 1.5 percent, as cited by Robert A. Lewis and Richard H. Rowland in their essay, above. There is a smaller gap between the annual growth rate of the last half century of the old regime and the higher rate of 2.8 percent for the first fifty years of the Soviet period.[25]

The reasons for this spurt of urbanization in late nineteenth-century Russia can be found not just in the fact that Russia began to modernize comprehensively in this period, but also in the way Russia was being modernized. Two features of this modernization were important: the prominent role of the Russian state and the even greater impact of foreign influences—industrial, financial, technological, and political. In contrast to the largely autarkic Soviet method of modernization, the tsarist program was closely bound up with the world economy. Its dynamics were state fiscal and commercial policy. What resulted from this combination of factors was commercial expansion, particularly of the grain trade, extensive railroad building, and the growth of industry. This in turn determined the kind of urbanization that took place. As in the United States in the mid-nineteenth century, there was extensive development of predominantly commercial cities: rail centers such as Kharkov or Chicago, river ports such as Rostov-on-the-Don or St. Louis, seaports such as Odessa or New Orleans.[26]

As in England, continental Europe, and the United States, although on a much smaller scale until the Soviet period, purely industrial cities appeared in Russia in the late nineteenth century. As elsewhere, these cities were located near the raw materials and fuels used by their industries, which were largely extractive: Baku near oil, Yuzhovka near coal and iron. The latter, and fifty-two other cities of New Russia, as has been detailed by Roger L. Thiede in his essay above, represent the closest approximation of tsarist Russian industrial urbanization and that of the English Midlands. By World War I, industry in New Russia played a greater role than trade in the urbanization process. Thus, it is clear that industrial urbanization occurred in some regions of Russia, particularly in the provinces specializing in industry of an extractive type, most notably in the Ukraine and the southwestern provinces of the Empire, but much less significantly elsewhere until Soviet times. Moreover, the most important of these cities were developed by foreign capital and enterprise, and used foreign technology. In addition they were not yet defined as cities in official statistics.

This administrative oversight of thickly populated industrial centers was of course ridiculous, but in fact the largest and most dynamically expanding cities in Russia in this first stage of rapid modernization were the administrative ones. These did not include the many administrative centers that were hardly more than villages, nor did it apply to agricultural administrative centers, such as Tambov, that were enlivened by the expanding grain trade and would decline in Soviet times. The cities that continued to predominate were the old national administrative centers: the two Russian "capitals" (St. Petersburg more than Moscow), Kiev, Tiflis, Riga, and others.[27] This was a feature not typical of the United States and England (despite London, the commercial and administrative seat of a vast empire), but, as Adna Weber noticed long ago, was characteristic of the more centralized and bureaucratized European states and empires: France's Paris, Germany's Berlin, the several old capitals of Austria-Hungary, and the administrative centers of Northern Italy, the Low Countries, and Scandinavia.[28]

The changing social structure of the cities in the last decades of the old regime also provides evidence of the same as well as other peculiarities of Russian modernization. In this area, the essay by Richard Rowland is instructive. Peasants were pushed off the land by the hardships of rural life and were attracted by better prospects for making a living in the cities. There is evidence that the more capable of the rural populace left the village,[29] but despite the rapid industrial development of the last years of the nineteenth century most of these in-migrants were not absorbed by urban industry. The majority, according to Rowland, went into domestic service and day labor. This would suggest that many were part of the service force catering to the needs of the large and growing nonindustrial population of the administrative cities, performing functions ranging from shopkeeping to various kinds of semiskilled household labor and unskilled manual labor. The growth of a "downtown" and the sophistication of Moscow's various markets sketched in the article by Robert Gohstand suggests this. The Khitrov Market district in Moscow, before it became a skid row in the last years of the old regime, served as a labor exchange, where new arrivals from the countryside, skilled and unskilled, could muster for jobs.[30] And in the main Russian cities of the same era, as in many oriental cities today from Calcutta to Cairo, a *lumpenproletariat* of unemployed peasants was forming. There is evidence that some kept body and soul together by working for the government at rough manual labor on excavations or shovelling snow. Industrial work there was, to be sure, and Rowland's observation of the low proportion of female in-migrants in Russia compared to most other urbanizing countries tells us something about the extensive winter residence of males in factory barracks.

Another significant migration into Russian cities during the last decades of the old regime that until recently has been given less attention than that of the peasants was that of the nobility. The Soviet historian L. Ivanov has indicated recently that by the end of the nineteenth century 48 percent of the nobility had come to live in cities. Some were officials in the central government, and others lived in town houses supported by the incomes of their estates, as the nobility traditionally had done. Some became industrialists. But after 1861, a large number also abandoned their estates to embark upon new ways of life offered by the modernizing capital and other large administrative cities—city administration, the professions, or a *rentier* existence.[31] Here again, we have a pattern of gentry migration and metamorphosis that can be likened to many parts of eastern Europe, particularly Poland, and contrasted to the United States, with its massive urban influx of lower class foreign immigrants. The important foreign migration into Russian cities in the nineteenth century was of the middle class—industrial entrepreneurs, engineers, merchants, and bankers. In any case, the many levels of the new urban society emerging in Russia in the late nineteenth century, and the prominence of different types of cities suggest a much more complex process than industrialization.

In 1904, a Russian journalist, E. Matrosov, published in the *Historical Herald* an article on "American Slums." Observing the slums of the Lower East Side of New York, he remarked: "This Russian-Jewish part of the city appears to be one entire slum of a completely unique character, which at once transports us mentally to the most thickly populated quarters of Vilna, Minsk, Bobruisk, or Berdichev."[32] Matrosov's comparison of urban America and urban Russia of 1904 was limited to comparing the slums of New York to the Jewish cities of Russian Poland and he did not attempt any comparison of American slums with those that were already well developed in the main Russian cities. The rapid urbanization in Russia during the last third of the nineteenth century soon brought not only a massive in-migration of rural people but also the social deterioration that European and American cities had been experiencing since the early 1800s—overcrowding, filth, disease, crime, and rioting. Russians had observed these developments in foreign cities and had hoped that their unique traditions would enable them to avoid such consequences of rapid urban growth, but in St. Petersburg as early as the 1860s the signs were unmistakable.[33] Little is known about the social disorganization that occurred during this first period of rapid urbanization. Overcrowding was probably as severe as in mid-century London or in Vienna of the succeeding generation. Adna Weber cites the comparative figures of Bertillon, which estimate for 1895 the percentage of urban inhabitants living in dwellings where the number of persons exceeded double the number of rooms: in London, 21 percent; in Berlin and Vienna, 28 percent; and in St. Petersburg, 46 percent.[34] Despite the unreliability of some of Bertillon's figures, other evidence would show that there definitely was great overcrowding in St. Petersburg just before World War I, where like Berlin of the late nineteenth century thousands lived in unventilated cellar rooms. If about half the population of the Russian capital lived at least two to a room, this was certainly less than the crowding of Budapest in the same period, with its notorious incidence of people living in trees in the public parks, or the four-to-a-room Soviet average of the late Stalin period.[35]

Both Moscow and St. Petersburg did have slum areas, which from the few descriptions we have were a combination of working class district and skid row. The Haven and Maiden Field districts of St. Petersburg, where Father Gapon began his work among the urban poor, were slums adjacent to the Neva and Baltic wharves. Here were situated many factories, but also open fields, which served as garbage dumps and homes for the impoverished, for derelicts, and for thieves.[36] The Khitrov Market district of Moscow was originally a point of reception and hiring for rural immigrants, which soon degenerated into a slum where the unemployed, tramps, and criminals lived permanently. Dwellings in both the Haven and the Khitrov Market, like the flophouses of the New York Bowery and the Berlin *Mietskasernen*, were ramshackle dormitory-like affairs where the destitute could obtain a night's lodging.[37] The Khitrov way of life was dramatized by Maxim Gorky in his *Lower Depths*.

Although the damp, frequently flooded, and generally undesirable riverfront area lent itself to the growth of these two slums, as in the waterfront area of many of the world's ports, the location of the railroads, as Lewis Mumford has noted, provided another physical basis for producing slum conditions.[38] In the Russian cities of the late nineteenth century, as almost everywhere else, the railroads were hacked into the center of town. There seems to have been no consideration at that time by the tsarist authorities of the social costs of railroad construction, just as the social cost of the automobile in this century has little concerned Soviet (or other) urban planners. Yet in many other respects the 1860s marked the beginning of modernization in urban policy and planning. As Frederick Skinner has shown in his essay on planning in nineteenth-century Odessa, the modernization program had two phases: first, a period of "external development," of construction—public buildings, monuments, squares, avenues, commercial, cultural, and industrial facilities, and banks. Then, as urbanization accelerated and social problems emerged, policy shifted "from an emphasis on the outward appearance of cities to the more fundamental problem of the condition of life within the community. . . . toward the modernization of the structure itself through the improvement of water supply, sanitation, street lighting and paving, municipal transportation, and the other systems and services that are essential for the maintenance and indeed the very survival of modern urban life." This is a sequence that was recapitulated in the other Russian cities to a greater or lesser degree, as in European and American cities of the late nineteenth century. If the splendid opera house of Odessa is a worthy emulation of those of Vienna and Paris, the modernization of "structure and system" that took place in late nineteenth-century Odessa recapitulates Emperor Franz Joseph's rebuilding of Vienna in the 1860s and 1870s, and—less successfully—Karl Lueger's later social reforms, which made Vienna an international model of municipal administration.[39]

The 1870 Municipal Statute provided the basis for the modernization of urban government in Russia, as is evident from Walter Hanchett's detailing of the legislation, by involving for the first time the leaders of local community and urban governments in the wide range of activities essential to the organization of the new kind of urban life—planning, municipal economy, food supply, sanitation, business development, the provision of cultural institutions, parks, roads, lighting, banks, and services for public health, safety, and education. The crucial problem not solved by the 1870 statute, or thereafter by the tsarist regime, which vitiated this reform, was that of establishing a relationship between the Russian city and the central government that would facilitate modernization. Restrictive regulation surrounding many of the provisions of this statute, particularly the law of 1892, effectively precluded the development of any significant urban self-government in Russia. This is probably the main reason for the political apathy of the few citizens who were permitted participation in urban local government, although there may be other causes for this indifference.

The stifling of local initiative also was a factor in the breakdown of urban modernization that set in during the last two decades of the old regime. More crucial in this breakdown was the difficult and deteriorating financial relationship between the Russian municipality and the central government, an issue that Michael Hamm has summarized with particular forcefulness in the beginning section of his essay, and his main points deserve reiteration and comment. The period from the urban statute of 1892 to the collapse of the tsarist municipal system in 1917 was one of an accelerating breakdown of urban modernization, characterized by a deterioration in the quality of life on the social level, and on the administrative plane a deepening fiscal plight. The poverty of the Russian municipalities was attributable to a number of conditions, all of which could be traced ultimately to the unwillingness or inability of the central government to come to the aid of the ailing cities: the inability of the municipal governments to obtain cheap and readily available credit, grave restrictions on their taxing powers, excessive financial obligations to the central government, exemption of state property from local taxation, niggardly state spending in cities, and delays in the delivery of such small funds as were appropriated. This catalog of shortcomings was hardly unique to Russia, or to the tsarist period of Russian history, or to the same period in the history of European and American cities. But Hamm's point is well taken that to the other afflictions of the old regime in Russia that have long been recognized—the agrarian and nationalities problems, the war, the corruption and decrepitude of the central government—must be added that of an intensifying urban crisis.

If the intensifying crisis in Russia's cities during the last twenty-five years of the old regime makes it plausible to fit the problems of the Russian cities into the general picture of the decline of imperial Russia, it should be noted that the same period witnessed a different and significant social and cultural history in the great cities. These cities were magnets not only for ambitious bureaucrats and desperate peasants, but also for a growing bourgeoisie and intelligentsia. The latter—new classes spawned by modernization—flocked into the cities to build a modern urban elite culture. Russia was experiencing what has been called by Berdiaev and others a renaissance. St. Petersburg and Moscow, the springs of this cultural and social movement, must be ranked with Vienna, Berlin, Paris, and London, among other great cities of the same period, as centers of the new urban artistic, scientific, and professional life. The intellectual elites of the modernizing European capitals are now being studied in depth, particularly those of Vienna and Berlin; the cultural history of their contemporary Russian cities remains largely unexplored. Numerous subjects and problems suggest themselves for research. Most obscure is the history of the professions—medicine, law, and education—as they emerged and matured in the cities after the Great Reforms. Not much more is known about the scientists and engineers nourished in the urban environment of the last years of the old regime. The "World of Art" is best known, although incompletely—the Moscow industrialist art collectors, the patrons and creators of the theater and ballet, and the philosophical and literary circles of St. Petersburg. The poets and novelists of this period, notably Briusov and Biely, had much to say about the "wingless dragons" (recalling the former's poetic image), the new monster cities that were their home. The intellectual movements of the great cities of Russia at the turn of the century included urbanizers and antiurbanizers, modernizers and antimodernizers. One recalls the city planner Enakiev, discussed by S. Frederick Starr, who wished to restore and revive eighteenth-century St. Petersburg and at the same time to provide for the traffic and other phenomena of a modern city.

Another cadre among the intellectual elites of Russia's modernizing cities during the same period was the revolutionary underground. Revolutionaries also migrated like other classes of Russians, not to the villages, forests, and mountains, as earlier revolutionaries in Russia had done and as later revolutionaries in Latin America and Asia were to do, but to the big cities. Here, like many of their counterparts in Europe and America, they lived in an underground world of slum communes, cafes, clandestine printing establishments, and explosives laboratories. They developed a plan of urban revolution, a revolutionary struggle that was to occur in large cities, led by urban intellectuals and staffed by urban factory workers organized into councils and armed detachments. From these urban islands the revolution would then spread to the ocean of peasants surrounding them, rather than the opposite process of the rural revolutionary masses overwhelming the cities, as had been imagined earlier in the populist phase of the Russian revolutionary movement. One reason for the emergence of this urban revolutionary tactic in fin-de-siècle Russia was the growing influence of Marxist city-centered thinking. But the construction of such a tactic also reflected a substantial degree of urbanization, which had indeed occurred as the collapse of the old regime loomed larger on the horizon.

Urban Disintegration, 1914-1929

The period from 1914 to 1921 in Russia's cities, as in most other areas of Russian life, witnessed what can legitimately be called a catastrophic breakdown of modernization. Urban disintegration was in evidence in the form of a growing fiscal and social crisis during the two decades prior to World War I. The war put new strains on the municipalities which could only intensify this crisis, given their untenable relationship with the rest of the system. With the collapse of the old order came the October Revolution, perhaps the most successful urban-based seizure of political power in history. The grim civil war that followed, however, not only accelerated the deterioration of conditions in the cities, but resulted in a massive deurbanization. Although political order was established by the new regime by 1921, it would take almost a decade merely to repair the damage. This period of recovery in the 1920s, in the cities as elsewhere in Soviet society, was not essentially one of modernization, although there was much discussion and planning for the future. With the consolidation of a totalitarian political order by Stalin at the end of the decade came a dynamic resumption of modernization and with it a new urban transformation.

Initially, World War I did not precipitate the type of disintegration and depopulation that was to characterize urban life during the Civil War or World War II. Except in the western provinces, there was little destruction through bombardment. Refugees from this area flooded into distant cities, intensifying problems of sanitation, hygiene, and feeding, but not to crisis proportions. The fiscal situation of the municipalities deteriorated rapidly, but here also adjustments were made by local authorities and some aid was rendered by the central government. Michael Hamm has indicated in his essay the revival of local leadership prompted by the wartime pressures. Existing programs of modernization had to be curtailed or abandoned, but it is clear that the various new municipal organizations were preparing to exercise an initiative as instruments of "social and economic modernization," as well as acting to expedite wartime problems. But it was too late: these problems intensified, particularly that of food supply with the running down of the Russian transport system, and in the wake of dwindling rations came growing political instability. It is interesting to note that at the time when the urban masses finally went into the streets in full force in February 1917, they were shouting "bread!"[40] in a city where food shipments had long been curtailed by hundreds of railroad carloads.

The Russian Revolution of 1917 was of course as much a peasant revolution—in the villages and in the army—as it was an urban one, and much of it was decided outside the cities. The cities, nevertheless, were the centers of political and economic power, and it was the cities, in the view of the revolutionists, where the revolution was to occur. They were right: in February

1917, and without their planning or prompting, the revolution came, not to the front lines or the villages (this would begin some months later) but to the capital city, Petrograd. There were numerous reasons for the collapse of the old regime which pertain solely to military, economic, and dynastic matters; but the situation that triggered the chain reaction of the collapse of authority in Petrograd was the fact of concentration there of hundreds of thousands of impoverished, hungry, and embittered people, many of them from the new classes of industrial workers and intelligentsia, in addition to a bloated and desperate wartime *lumpenproletariat*. Suddenly they left their jobs and lodgings in droves and flooded into the streets, a mass of rebels who then thronged from the industrial suburbs across the river bridges into the administrative heart of the tsarist empire in the center of the city. Here they were joined by tens of thousands more who constituted most of the military garrison of Petrograd. This human flood then spilled over into the headquarters of the new government in the tiny Taurida Palace, jamming its halls and assembly rooms, thereafter influencing the revolutionary course of events.

The city of Petrograd remained the main theater of the Russian Revolution until October 1917, when another kind of urban revolution was made. The theory of this revolution, as we have seen, was that state power could be seized, not with the active intrusion of the urban masses but on the contrary through their benevolent neutrality or indifference. The method, which had been employed many times before in Russia's capital city, was for a much smaller group, well organized along military lines, to seize the machinery of state intact by overpowering its high command and to gain control of the nerve centers of a modern city—railway and telegraph stations, telephone exchanges, banks, printing presses, all of the technical and administrative machinery necessary for the normal function of urban life, without the control of which the capital city and hence the whole structure of state would become paralyzed.

The Bolsheviks performed this seizure of Petrograd with remarkable proficiency on the night of October 24, 1917; and this performance with somewhat less smoothness and more bloodshed was soon repeated in Moscow and all the major cities of Russia. But now the Bolsheviks stared out of their urban bastions and saw not only the regrouping armies of their political enemies, but even more ominous a spectacle, the millions of potentially hostile peasants. The Reds faced the Whites; but also modernized urban Russia confronted premodern—indeed antimodern—rural Russia. A state of siege set in for the Communist cities, not directed by the White and Interventionist forces, which were never really able to penetrate the urban core of European Russia, but established by the peasants, who, as they became estranged from the new regime and its impositions, began to starve out the cities by withholding grain. Detachments of urbanites sent out to the villages to obtain supplies by force only intensified the plight of the starving cities. Ultimately, Russia's cities began to disintegrate. Some people, mainly those connected with the old government apparatus in Petrograd, emigrated for political reasons; others died of starvation and disease; still others fled to the countryside in large numbers to avoid this fate. Thus Petrograd shrank from a population of 2,500,000 in 1917 to an incredible 706,000 in 1920, most of the contraction taking place during the Civil War.[41] Because of the fuel shortage the capital city was disappearing not only in human but in material terms as well: it is estimated that one-fourth of the wood-frame houses were torn down during the Civil War to provide firewood. According to David Cattell, most other cities declined in population by a third or more in this same period.

It took six years for the repopulation and rebuilding of Soviet cities after this disaster. Thus the period from 1917 to the late 1920s must be considered one of rather marked decline, both in terms of urban growth and, again referring to David Cattell, in terms of modernization—housing, public transport, utilities, sanitation, and most of the amenities that are needed to preserve the quality of urban life. Urbanization in Russia was not much farther along by 1929 than it had been in 1914, and living conditions in the cities had deteriorated. After the worst was over—the Civil War period, in which many urban facilities broke down completely—the emphasis, as in most other areas of Soviet society, was on recovery and reconstruction of the prewar plant, and little was or could be done to realize the more ambitious goals of modernization, given the immense scope of seven years of destruction followed by a devastating famine. As S. Frederick Starr has described it, the 1920s for Russia and her cities were a "moment of suspense . . . when dreams for the future assumed a greater clarity and vividness than did any practical steps taken in the uncertainty of the present." Nowhere were the numerous futuristic dreams of the Soviet 1920s more vivid than in the area of urban planning.

These plans are interesting first, as Starr has shown, because of their continuity with the two most vigorous planning traditions of the late tsarist period, the classical revival and the garden city movement. One can add to this a larger continuity with tsarism—rigorous state control of urban planning. Just as Catherine the Great insisted that all of the early Russian urban plans had to be approved personally "by the hand of the Imperial Majesty," so, as Milka Bliznakov has pointed out, the Council of People's Commissars, beginning in 1918, was to approve all plans for larger cities. Vesenkha, the NKVD, and other agencies also had a hand in supervising urban planning. The urban plans of the 1920s are interesting also because of the conflict they reveal between those planners who wished to modernize large cities along traditional architectural lines, and those who advocated more radical architectural styles, whose formula for modernization entailed deconcentration or cities of limited size, and who were opposed to the supercity or even to cities themselves. The latter group had their day in the 1920s, at least on paper; but it was the former who soon after triumphed, as Russia at the end of the decade embarked on a new modernization drive, a modernization with large cities.

The Second Urban Transformation

In the late 1920s, Russian cities once again began to grow and multiply at a pace unprecedented in history, an urban transformation which continues to this day. Chauncy Harris's recent book

Cities of the Soviet Union[42] and the essay by Robert Lewis and
Richard Rowland in this collection provide a detailed geographical
and demographical analysis of this dynamic process, from which
the most significant figures can be summarized here: From 1926
to 1967, Russia's urban population increased by just over 100
million, or a number almost four times as large as the 26.3 million
urban dwellers of the mid-1920s. By 1967 urban dwellers constituted more than half of the total population. The most rapid
urbanization took place in the 1930s, exceeding all previous urban
growth in Russian or world history. The average annual growth
rate was 6.5 percent in this period, as compared to 2.3 percent for
the last fifty years of the tsarist period, and 2.43 percent for the
late 1960s. Well over half of this increase in the urban population
was derived from migration out of the villages. In the late 1930s,
the most significant urban growth came to the older cities of
European Russia and the industrializing regions of the Ukraine.
After World War II, dynamic urbanization shifted to the interior
of the USSR, to the Volga, the Urals, and the central Siberian
region, where new industries and particularly oil fields were being
developed. In most recent years, however, according to Lewis and
Rowland, there has been a resurgence of urban growth in European Russia, which has enjoyed a prolonged period of peace,
improved transport facilities, readily available fuels, and proximity
to the West at a time when trade with Western countries is expanding.

Almost all of this urban growth has taken place in cities of more
than 50,000. There are now over 200 cities of more than 100,000
inhabitants, and six cities—Moscow, Leningrad, Kiev, Baku, Tashkent, and Novosibirsk—of over a million. It is clear from Harris's
findings that two types of cities predominate in the urban revolution that has taken place in the Soviet Union since the 1920s:
industrial cities, specialized manufacturing centers located near
their resources, of which there are 136, and an almost equal
number of diversified administrative cities. The latter constitute
by far the most important manifestations of recent Soviet urbanization, comprising the 30 largest cities of the land. The more

purely industrial cities tend to be much smaller than the administrative cities, ranging between 50,000 and 250,000 in population, although they have grown more rapidly than the administrative centers, particularly when, as with Magnitogorsk, they have been built from scratch.

The causes of the overwhelming predominance of large administrative cities in the contemporary Soviet urban structure can be found once again in the two keys to the understanding of Russian urbanization presented at the beginning of and throughout this essay: tradition and modernization. The most important cities of the Soviet Union are enlarged versions of the old capitals and administrative centers, some of which declined in the early Soviet period but most of which have been rebuilt and restored to their traditional function. Harris cites the example of Yerivan, the capital of Armenia, where 60 percent of the Republic's urban population was already concentrated by 1959: the "capital city, the focus of the cultural, political-administrative and economic life of Armenia, the Soviet home of the Armenians."[43]

It was cities like Yerivan that became the administrative brain centers of Soviet modernization. Elsewhere Harris suggests this in his discussion of the role of industrial and administrative cities in Soviet urban development: "The overwhelming predominance of these two types reflects the nature of the Soviet economy as a command economy, directed by the party and government apparatus, owned by the state, and administered by government organs with the result that the political administrative structure operated through the urban hierarchy plays a key role in directing and coordinating the entire economic life of the country."[44] It was characteristic of Soviet modernization that while factories were multiplying, a sizable administrative machine was being constructed just as rapidly: the economic apparatus which included the proliferating industrial ministries, the numerous bureaus of the planning organization, financial and inspectional agencies, a veritable army of statisticians, another network of research institutes and schools, and the extensive party, police, and state agencies which concerned themselves everywhere with the industrialization drive. This bureaucratic mass, the precise extent of which would be difficult to determine but which must have been enormous, invaded the administrative cities, followed by another uncounted horde of people required to service it. Such urban growth was practically inevitable, given the bureaucratic nature of Soviet political life. Factories could locate in rural areas, a feasible if expensive and frequently avoided move; the bureaucracies could not. They grew rooted, as it were, to the central cities.

Urban bureaucratization was one feature of the Stalinist method of modernization, but this did not mean necessarily the modernization of the rapidly growing cities of the USSR. The basic principle of Stalinist modernization, as has often been recognized, was the disproportionate reallocation of resources to foster breakneck development of some areas of the economy at the expense, through neglect or even exploitation, of others.[45] Those who paid the highest bills for the construction of Soviet heavy industry and the war machine through taxation and deprivation were the peasants, the consumers, and, for a while, the railroads. The cities also paid, heavily and in a very direct way, for the development of Russian industry. This was done essentially by forestalling their modernization at a time of rapid urban growth. The cities were placed on a low rung in the ladder of Soviet priorities. They were consigned an equally humble position in the power structure. Thus, both the resources and, as Cattell points out, the capabilities for the implementation of urban planning were absent. The result was a recapitulation of tsarist urbanization and of the experience of rapidly urbanizing societies in Europe and America in the nineteenth and twentieth centuries: haphazard growth and slum conditions. On top of this came the catastrophic urban desolation of World War II.

Local government during the Soviet urban revolution was theoretically in the hands of the local soviets. Actually, the soviets were and are subordinated to a "large and many sided network of higher control agencies."[46] The several central agencies that held most of the purse strings for the local soviets were niggardly in the dispersal of funds. Centrally determined needs dictated their diversion elsewhere. In addition to this conflict of local and central power, so common to the history of urbanization in modern times, a second and equally destructive conflict developed, one also not unique to Soviet experience. This was the struggle between municipality and industry. Usually when a conflict of interest developed between urban needs and the objectives of local industrial management, the latter won out. The industrial bureaucracy at all levels was naturally attracted to the cities, where facilities had already been established and the costs of location and operation were thereby diminished. The local administration might not have a veto over the decision of an industry to establish itself in a particular city or even the location within the city of the industrial installations, particularly if the industry was one that had power and pull. And as industries proliferated in the cities, they appropriated local power by assuming responsibility for the construction and maintenance of facilities that the municipalities could not afford. We have an interesting sketch, in the unpublished dissertation by William Taubman, of the experience of the new Stalinist steel city of Magnitogorsk, where the Metallurgical Combine, which ran most of the city's industries, also came to control the fuel and power systems, public transport, and most of the housing. The local soviet was rendered powerless at times against this concentration of economic, administrative, and technological power, as when the Combine would cut off electricity to the homes whenever extra kilowatts were needed for the factories.[47]

One result of the conflicts of the Soviet city with the state and with industry, and of the impotence and poverty of the municipal governments combined with general inexperience in the organization and administration of urban expansion, was unplanned, fortuitous growth. Few urban plans were formulated in the Stalin era, the notable exception being the Moscow Plan of 1935. As late as 1960, 60 percent of the main cities of the Russian Republic were without plans. Industries were located haphazardly in residential and park zones. There was an uncoordinated proliferation of private dwellings, as Robert Osborn describes it in his dissertation, "from year around dachas to shacks."[48] The ambitious Moscow

Plan of 1935, the first major Soviet urban plan to be implemented, although substantially improving many public facilities, failed in its major goal of limiting the size of the capital city. Moscow's Kremlin, in other ways omnipotent, could not or would not prevent the migration of industries into its own back yard.[49]

In Moscow, as in other Soviet cities, the drastic curtailment of investment in housing and public facilities characteristic of the Stalinist modernization drive, at a time of incredibly rapid expansion of the urban population, resulted very quickly in the appearance of slum conditions. There was a sharp curtailment of housing construction: the building of individual dwellings in the mid-1930s dropped to not much more than 20 percent of that of the late NEP period. Although public housing increased almost tenfold, it could not keep pace with the hectic tempo of urbanization. This can be seen in the decrease in the average square meterage per capita in urban areas, which dropped from 6.45 in 1923 to 4.09 in 1940 and 3.98 in 1950. This means that the average density of occupancy per room increased from 2.6 persons in 1923 (roughly equivalent to 1913), to 4.02 in 1950, or well over twice the density defined as overcrowding in Western countries.[50] It was only by 1964-1965, as Cattell points out, that the 1923 average of square meters per capita in Soviet cities was surpassed, and then only by .35 of a square meter. In over forty years, the ordinary Soviet urbanite had accrued about an extra square foot of living space, although the increase from the suffocating densities of the late Stalin period was significant. The minimum sanitary standard of nine square meters per capita, a frustrated goal of Khrushchev's, was still 1.4 square meters short of attainment in 1972.

Sacrifice of the quality of urban life during the period of crash industrialization can be seen also in the greatly diminished construction of public facilities, except for stadiums, public halls, monuments, and other types of more spectacular urban architecture. The Soviet Union had inherited primitive urban services from tsarist Russia. Many large cities had no public sewerage or water supply systems. By 1939-1940 this situation had changed little. Of 174 cities with above 50,000 population at that time, only 140 had sewerage systems, and only 20 percent of all Soviet cities had water systems.[51] Electrification was somewhat more advanced in the larger cities, but plumbing everywhere was inadequate. Many of these deficiencies had not been remedied as late as 1960, when only 35 percent of the housing units in the Soviet Union had sewers, and only 38 percent had running water. In specific localities, the same backwardness of the urban structure was observable. The heat, water, and sewerage systems of Magnitogorsk were still inadequate by 1961.[52] In the spring of the same year, this author observed numerous unpaved dirt roads in residential districts of Kharkov.

One cannot avoid the conclusion that, compared with the United States, Japan, and western Europe, the Soviet Union is still coping with an earlier stage of urbanization; the communist authorities are dealing with many of the same problems of sanitation, power, and water that the tsarist cities faced. New problems of advanced modernization indeed have appeared, but only the early warning signs, compared to the crises of the supercities of the West and Far East. The problems of megalopolis, of size, are still in embryonic form in the USSR. Although this problem has been on the minds of Soviet planners since the 1920s, as has been described at length in several of the essays in this collection, it has been viewed until recently essentially in terms of the old populist dream of deurbanization. The deurbanization plans of the 1920s were shelved in the Stalinist period, and large cities continued to grow, despite periodic condemnations of megalopolis by party leaders, and equally feckless limitations on bigness written into urban plans. The utopia of the small community, with a lineage as venerable as Chernyshevsky, continues to be dreamed by Soviet writers, most notably S. G. Strumilin, with his vision of tiny urban clusters of self-contained communes. Experimentation in the 1960s with a more practical version of the small community, the microrayon, has taken place in a few localities near Moscow, but its large-scale application is "still a pipe dream."[53]

The thrust of recent planning, on a theoretical as well as a practical level, as B. Mitchell Frolic has evaluated it in his study of the current Moscow city plan, is not for the re-creation of small cities but for improved organization of large ones. The vision of the supercity of automated industry and forested parks with 200- to 300-story apartment buildings that some Soviet writers paint[54] may not materialize, but the silhouette of more modest 25-story office and residential buildings that already is beginning to scrape the sky of Russia's capital would seem, according to Frolic, to be in store for Moscow, 1980.

Pollution has become a serious problem in the Soviet Union, but it is essentially the older type of pollution resulting from dumping industrial wastes and raw sewage into rivers and lakes, or the air pollution caused by urban and rural factories rather than automobile exhaust, plastic waste, and other more "modern" forms of despoilment of the environment. Paper mills may have poisoned Lake Baikal, as they have been polluting the rivers of New England for a century; Tbilisi, like Los Angeles and Trent, may be smog-bound by the surrounding hills; and the pine forest of Tolstoi's Yasnaya Polyana may be dead because of fumes from the chemical combine built nearby, but motor vehicles are not yet sufficiently numerous in the big Russian cities to create the vast traffic-clogged and smog-laden urban sprawls that have overtaken large parts of the United States, Europe, and Japan.[55]

More than a century ago Prince V. F. Odoevsky, the Slavophile, foretold the emergence of the Russian megalopolis in his fantasy of the future, *The Year 4338*, if I may conclude as I began with another of the interesting prophecies of Russian utopian fiction. As projected by Odoevsky, the St. Petersburg and Moscow of the fifth millennium would be the western and eastern sides of one huge city—megalopolis would have come to Russia.[56] Odoevsky's vision would seem to be far removed from the realities of today. When one leaves contemporary Moscow by train bound for Leningrad, almost within minutes he enters a Russian countryside pretty much the way it was a century ago. The bears and eagles observed by the American engineers who helped build the railroad at that time may have disappeared, but it is still a different world from the Boston-to-Washington supercity of contemporary America and its equivalents in Japan and western Europe. Will this also occur in the Soviet Union?

Students of Soviet environmental problems have tended to conclude that an exploitative attitude toward the natural environment and an industrial strategy that discounts "social costs of production" in terms of both pollution and urban blight are no less characteristic of Soviet industrial bureaucrats than of the private entrepreneurs of capitalist countries. Soviet urban government has long been ineffective in its efforts to thwart the "metal eaters" and indeed, until recently, had a vested interest in pollution.[57] However, the central government of the Soviet Union, if it cannot and will not make the return to premodern rural Russia most recently urged by the exiled writer Solzhenitsyn, could, nevertheless, with its vast power, act more decisively than the governments of the consumer market countries to control all the problems of massive urbanization. Most crucial of these is the private automobile and the highway placed at the disposal of an expanding urban-suburban population enjoying the higher standard of living brought by modernization. It is the private automobile that is the greatest despoiler of the contemporary inner cities of the West, choked by traffic and air pollution, as well as the spawner of endless suburbia, their expressways lined with industrial and commercial sprawl.[58] If the automobile achieves the same dominion in the Soviet Union as it has in the most advanced modernized countries elsewhere, then Moscow and Leningrad may well become one city long before the year 4338.

Notes

1. Ivan Kremnev, *Puteshestvye moego brata Alekseia v stranu krestianskoi utopii* (Moscow, 1920), pp. 14-16.

2. As Chauncy Harris opens his recent and definitive geographical study, *Cities of the Soviet Union*, Monograph No. 5, Association of American Geographers (Chicago: Rand McNally, 1970), p. 1.

3. Peter Hall, *The World Cities* (New York: McGraw-Hill, 1966), pp. 158-81.

4. Kingsley Davis, *World Urbanization, 1950-1970*, Population Monograph Series, No. 4 (Berkeley: Institute of International Studies, University of California, 1969),

Table A, pp. 57-82; Harris, pp. 3-4. Harris defines "urban" as cities and towns of more than 10,000 population (p. ix).

5. In addition to the works of Harris and Hall already cited, one should note the article by B. Michael Frolic, "The Soviet City," *Town Planning Review* 34 (1964): 285-303; the earlier study by Maurice Frank Parkins, *City Planning in Soviet Russia* (Chicago: University of Chicago Press, 1958); and the Columbia University dissertations by Robert J. Osborn, "Public Participation in Soviet City Government" (1963), and William Chase Taubman, "Politics of Urban Development in the Soviet Union" (1969).

6. Most recently, Gideon Sjoberg, *The Preindustrial City* (Glencoe, Ill.: Free Press, 1960).

7. B. Kerblay, "La ville soviétique," *Annales economies, sociétiés, civilisations* 25 (1970): 897.

8. M. N. Tikhomirov, *Drevnerusskogo goroda*, 2nd ed. (Moscow, 1956), pp. 9, 32-53. Lawrence Langer, in the first chapter above, discusses the problem of numbers.

9. The most authoritative works dealing with the premodern city in a comparative way, whose definitions I have drawn upon here, are Sjoberg, *The Preindustrial City*; Max Weber, *The City* (Glencoe, Ill.: Free Press, 1958), especially chapter 1; Lewis Mumford, *The City in History* (New York: Harcourt, Brace and World, 1961); and Arnold Toynbee, *Cities on the Move* (New York: Oxford University Press, 1970). Toynbee gives the best comparative account of the various types of traditional capital cities. All of these works, however, give no more than passing reference to Russian cities.

10. My thanks here to Gilbert Rozman of Princeton University, who allowed me to read in manuscript chapter 2 of *Urban Networks in Russia, 1750-1800, and Premodern Periodization* (Princeton, N.J.: Princeton University Press, forthcoming). Rozman's work provides a new perspective on the complexity of premodern urban development in Russia as compared to other societies where urbanization was extensive in earlier times. My thanks to Gilbert Rozman, C. E. Black, and S. Frederick Starr for their critical readings of this essay.

11. See Reinhold Bendix, "Tradition and Modernity," *Comparative Studies in Society and History* 9 (1967): 294-313, for observations on this reaction and its influence on later thought.

12. Charles Issawi, in *Middle Eastern Cities*, Ira Lapidus, ed. (Berkeley: University of California Press, 1969), pp. 102-04.

13. See Iu. R. Klokman, *Sotsialno-ekonomicheskaia istoriia russkogo goroda, vtoraia polovina XVIII veka* (Moscow, 1967), pp. 314-16.

14. Issawi, pp. 106-07.

15. Glenn T. Trewartha, "Chinese Cities: Origins and Functions," *Annals of the Association of American Geographers* 42 (1952): 69-93.

16. See Gustav Schmoller, "Das Städtewesen unter Friedrich Wilhelm I," *Deutsches Städtewesen in Alterzeit* (Bonn and Leipzig, 1922). Schmoller's monograph, first published in 1873, remains the classic study of the subordination of the Prussian city to the state. For a recent brief treatment of this problem, see Mack Walker, *Community, State and General Estate in Germany, 1648-1871* (Ithaca, N.Y.: Cornell University Press, 1971), pp. 21-26; also Sidney Fay and Klaus Epstein, *The Rise of Brandenberg-Prussia to 1786*, revised ed. (New York: Holt and Co., 1964), pp. 57-83.

17. Hans Rosenberg, *Bureaucracy, Aristocracy and Autocracy: The Prussian Experience, 1660-1815* (Cambridge, Mass.: Harvard University Press, 1958), p. 65.

18. N. D. Chechulin, *Goroda Moskovskago gosudarstva v XVI veke* (St. Petersburg, 1889), pp. 341-43.

19. Again, my thanks to Gilbert Rozman for materials from his unpublished manuscript for materials utilized for some of the statements in this paragraph.

20. Toynbee, p. 142.

21. See my *Beginnings of Russian Industrialization* (Princeton, N.J.: Princeton University Press, 1968), particularly chapter 4.

22. This theme is fully developed by Rozman.

23. This is one of the important conclusions of the manuscript "Modernization of Japan and Russia," by Cyril E. Black, Marius Jansen, Herbert Levine, Marion J. Levy, Jr., Henry Rosovsky, Gilbert Rozman, Henry D. Smith II, and S. Frederick Starr. My thanks to these scholars for permitting me to read the manuscript and participate in the seminar devoted to it at Princeton, July 1973.

24. Blake McKelvey, *American Urbanization: A Comparative History* (Glenview, Ill.: Scott, Foresman, 1973), p. 26. My thanks to Professor Bayrd Still of New York University for calling my attention to this chapter of McKelvey's new book, and for his careful critical reading of this manuscript.

25. Harris, p. 231.

26. See ibid., pp. 243-55, 269-71; McKelvey, pp. 34-38.

27. Harris, pp. 243-52, 408-09.

28. Adna Weber, *The Growth of Cities in the Nineteenth Century*, Columbia University Studies in History, Economy and Public Law, no. 11 (New York, 1899), pp. 74, 91-92, 100, 110, 113, 115-18.

29. One of the findings of Barbara A. Anderson, "Internal Migration in a Modernizing Society: the Case of Late Nineteenth Century European Russia," Ph.D. dissertation, Dept. of Sociology, Princeton University, 1973.

30. P. V. Sytin, *Proshloe Moskvy v nazvaniiakh ulits* (Moscow, 1948), p. 125, note.

31. L. Ivanov, "O soslovno-klassovoi strukture gorodov kapitalisticheskoi Rossii," *Problemy sotsialno-ekonomicheskoi istorii Rossii, sbornik statei* (Moscow, 1971), pp. 318, 336.

32. E. Matrosov, "Amerikanskiia Trushchoby," *Istoricheskii vestnik* 95 (1904): 1074.

33. See Reginald Zelnik, *Labor and Society in Tsarist Russia, 1855-1870* (Stanford, Cal.: Stanford University Press, 1971).

34. Weber, p. 416, note 1.

35. Allan Janik and Stephen Toulmin, *Wittgenstein's Vienna* (New York: Simon and Schuster, 1973), pp. 50-51.

36. G. A. Gapon, *The Story of My Life* (London, 1905), pp. 59-60, 63-64.

37. See the descriptions by Henri Troyat, *Daily Life in Russia under the Last Tsar* (London: Allen and Unwin, 1961), pp. 57-62, 90-91. On Berlin, see Gerhard Masur, *Imperial Berlin* (New York: Basic Books, 1970), pp. 49, 68.

38. Mumford, p. 461.

39. Janik and Toulmin, pp. 41, 55.

40. For a detailed eye-witness account of the February Revolution in Petrograd by a police official, see A. I. Spiridovich, *Velikaia voina i Fevralskaia revoliutsiia 1914-1917 r.r.* (New York: Vseslavianskoe izdatelstvo, 1960-1962), vol. 3. On "bread," see pp. 77-79.

41. Harris, p. 255. See also the essay above by David Cattell.

42. Harris, especially pp. 1, 4, 80, 90, 210, 292-98, 302-03, 313, 368-69, 401-02, 408.

43. Ibid., pp. 309, 340.

44. Ibid., p. 61.

45. See my *Industrialization of Russia: An Historical Perspective* (New York: T. Y. Crowell, 1970), "The Stalinist Method of Industrialization," pp. 98-130, and bibliographical essay, pp. 177-90.

46. Osborn, pp. 94-95.

47. Taubman, pp. 95-100, 179, 196, gives a good exposition of the conflict of factory and local soviet.

48. See Osborn, pp. 28-30, on unplanned urban development in the Stalin era. Soviet urbanization in the 1930s is a subject about which much more needs to be written.

49. See Parkins, pp. 37-44, for a discussion of the Moscow Plan of 1935 and its implementation.

50. Figures from Timothy Sosnovy, *The Housing Problem in the Soviet Union* (New York: Research Program on the USSR, 1954), appendix 2, chart 5, p. 269; chart 6, p. 270; chart 12, p. 276; table 7, p. 73; p. 98.

51. Ibid., table 25, pp. 136-38.

52. General figures in Marshall I. Goldman, *The Spoils of Progress: Environmental Pollution in the Soviet Union* (Cambridge, Mass.: M.I.T. Press, 1972), p. 106; on Magnitogorsk, see Taubman, p. 96.

53. Frolic, p. 303. Frolic details the utopias and the practical application of the Soviet small community idea in the 1960s.

54. The architect G. Gradov, cited in E. D. Mordzhinskaia and Ts. A. Stepanian, eds., *Budushchee chelovecheskogo obshchestva* (Moscow, 1971), p. 348.

55. See Goldman, passim, for a discussion of these various cases and of the emergent air pollution of Moscow.

56. V. F. Odoevsky, *4338-i god, fantasticheskii roman* (Moscow, 1926), p. 19.

57. See Goldman, especially pp. 1-5, 36-39, 57-75; and Philip R. Pryde, "Victors Are Not Judged," *Environment* 12, no. 9 (1970): 30, 32, 36.

58. See John B. Rae, "Metropolis on the Fairway," in *The American Automobile: A Brief History* (Chicago: University of Chicago Press, 1965), pp. 219-36.

SELECTED BIBLIOGRAPHY

The Preindustrial Russian Town

Russian Language

Artsikhovskii, A. V. "Gorodskie kontsy v drevnei Rusi." *Istoricheskie zapiski* 16 (1945): 3-13.

Aseev, Iu. *Drevnii Kiev (X-XVII vv.)*. Moscow, 1956.

Bakhrushin, S. V. "Moskovskie vosstanie 1648 g." *Nauchnye trudy* 2 (1954): 46-91.

Bernadskii, V. *Novgorod i Novgorodskaia Zemlia v XV veke*. Moscow-Leningrad, 1961.

Chechulin, N. D. *Goroda Moskovskago gosudarstva v XVI veke*. St. Petersburg, 1889; reprinted, The Hague: Mouton, 1969.

Chistiakova, E. V. "Moskva v seredine 30-kh godov XVII v." In V. A. Aleksandrov et al., *Novoe o proshlom nashei strany, pamiati akademika M. N. Tikhomirova*. Moscow, 1967.

Ditiatin, I. I. *Stati po istorii russkago prava*. St. Petersburg, 1895.

——. *Ustroistvo i upravlenie gorodov Rossii*. St. Petersburg, 1875.

Goroda feodal'noi Rossii. Moscow, 1966.

Ianin, V. L. *Novgorodskie posadniki*. Moscow, 1962.

Kafengauz, B. B. *Drevnii Pskov*. Moscow, 1969.

Kizevetter, A. A. *Gil'diia Moskovskago kupechestva*. Moscow, 1915.

——. *Gorodovoe polozhenie Ekateriny II. 1785 g.* Moscow, 1909.

——. *Posadskaia obshchina v Rossii XVIII st.* Moscow, 1903.

Klokman, Iu. R. "Gorod v zakonodatel'stve russkogo absoliutizma vo vtoroi polovine XVII-XVIII vv." In N. M. Druzhinin et al., *Absoliutizm v Rossii (XVII-XVIII vv.)* (Moscow, 1964), pp. 320-54.

Klokman, Iu. R. *Sotsial'no-ekonomicheskaia istoriia russkogo goroda*. Moscow, 1967.

Man'kov, A. G. "Bor'ba posada a feodalami vo vtoroi polovine XVII v." *Istoricheskie zapiski* 64 (1959): 217-32.

Nikitskii, A. I. *Istoriia ekonomicheskogo byta Velikogo Novgoroda*. Moscow, 1897.

Novosel'tsev, A. P. "Goroda Azerbaidzhana i vostochnoi Armenii v XVII-XVIII vv." *Istoriia SSSR* (Moscow), 1959, no. 1: 87-108.

————, and Pashuto, V. T. "Vneshniaia torgovlia drevnei Rusi (do serediny XIII v.)." *Istoriia SSSR* (Moscow), 1967, no. 3: 81-108.

Polianskii, F. Ia. *Gorodskoe remeslo i manufaktura v Rossii XVIII veka*. Moscow, 1960.

Rozhkov, N. A. *Gorod i derevnia v russkoi istorii*. St. Petersburg, 1913.

Ryndziunskii, P. G. *Gorodskoe grazhdanstvo doreformennoi Rossii*. Moscow, 1958.

Sakharov, A. M. *Goroda severo-vostochnoi Rusi XIV-XV vekov*. Moscow, 1959.

Serbina, K. N. *Ocherki iz sotsial'no-ekonomicheskoi istorii russkogo goroda: Tikhvinskii posad v XVI i XVII vv*. Moscow-Leningrad, 1951.

Smirnov, P. P. *Posadskie liudi i ikh klassovaia bor'ba do serediny XVII v*. 2 vols. Moscow-Leningrad, 1947-1948.

Soloviev, S. M. "Russkii gorod v XVII veke." *Sovremennik* 1 (January 1853), sect. 2:1-20.

Tikhomirov, M. N. *Klassovaia bor'ba v Rossii XVII v*. Moscow, 1969.

Tverskoi, L. M. *Russkoe gradostroitel'stvo do kontsa XVII veke*. Moscow-Leningrad, 1953.

Voronin, N. N. *Zodchestvo severo-vostochnoi Rusi*. 2 vols. Moscow, 1962.

Zaozerskaia, E. I. "Moskovskii posad pri Petre 1." *Voprosi istorii* 9 (1947): 19-35.

Zasurtsev, P. I. *Novgorod, otkrytyi arkheologami*. Moscow, 1967.

Zimin, A. A. "Sostav russkikh gorodov XVI vv." *Istoricheskie zapiski* 52 (1955): 336-47.

English Language

Baron, Samuel H. "The Town in 'Feudal' Russia." *Slavic Review* 28 (March 1969): 116-22.

Langer, Lawrence N. "V. L. Ianin and the History of Novgorod." *Slavic Review* 33 (March 1974): 114-19.

Murvar, V. "Max Weber's Urban Typology and Russia." *Sociological Quarterly* 8 (Autumn 1967): 481-94.

Schmitt, Albert J. "William Hastie, Scottish Planner of Russian Cities." *Proceedings of the American Philosophical Society* 114 (1970): 226-43.

Thompson, M. W., ed. *Novgorod the Great.* New York: Praeger, 1967.

Tikhomirov, M. *The Towns of Ancient Rus.* Moscow: Foreign Languages Publishing House, 1959.

Vernadsky, George. *Kievan Russia.* New Haven: Yale University Press, 1948.

The Nineteenth-Century Russian City

Russian Language

Ashukin, N. S., ed. *Ushedshaia Moskva: Vospominaniia sovremennikov o Moskve vtoroi poloviny XIX veka.* Moscow, 1964.

Astrov, N. "Iz istorii gorodskikh samoupravlenii v Rossii." In *Mestnoe samoupravlenie: Trudy obshchestva dlia izucheniia gorodskogo samoupravleniia v Chekhoslovatskoi respublike* (Prague, 1925), pp. 9-42.

Chicherin, B. N. *Vospominaniia: Zemstvo i Moskovskaia duma.* Moscow, 1934.

De Ribas, Alexander. *Staraia Odessa. Istoricheskie ocherki i vospominaniia.* Odessa, 1913.

Giliarovskii, V. A. *Moskva i moskvichi.* Moscow, 1968.

Karzhanskii, N. *Kak izbiralas i rabotala Moskovskaia gorodskaia duma.* Moscow, 1950.

Lander, K. I. "Gorod i gorodskoe samoupravlenie v Pribaltiiskom krae." In *Istoriia Rossiia v XIX v.*, 9 vols. (St. Petersburg, n.d.), 4: 29-43.

Punin, A. "Idei ratsionalizma v russkoi arkhitekture vtoroi poloviny XIX veka." *Arkhitektura SSSR* 11 (1962): 55-58.

Semenov, D. D. *Gorodskoe samoupravlenie: Ocherki i opyty.* St. Petersburg, 1901.

Semenov Tian-Shanskii, V. P. *Gorod i derevnia v evropeiskoi Rossii.* St. Petersburg, 1910.

Shchepkin, M. P. *Obshchestvennoe samoupravlenie v Moskve: Proekt gorodovogo polozheniia.* Moscow, 1906.

Shreider, G. I. "Gorod i gorodovoe polozhenie 1870 goda." In *Istoriia Rossii v XIX v.*, 9 vols. (St. Petersburg, n.d.), 4: 1-29.

———. "Gorodskaia kontr'-reforma 11 iiunia 1892 g." *Istoriia Rossii v XIX v.*, 9 vols. (St. Petersburg, n.d.), 5: 181-228.

Vegner, I. A. *Gorodskoe samoupravlenie v Rossii.* Moscow, 1906.

English Language

Blackwell, William L. *The Beginnings of Russian Industrialization, 1800-1860.* Princeton: Princeton University Press, 1968.

Blumenfeld, Hans. "Russian City Planning of the 18th and Early 19th Centuries." *Journal of the American Society of Architectural Historians* 4 (January 1944): 22-33.

Fox, David J. "Odessa." *Scottish Geographical Magazine* 79 (April 1963): 5-22.

Gliksman, Jerzy G. "The Russian Urban Worker: From Serf to Proletarian." In Cyril Black, ed., *The Transformation of Russian Society* (Cambridge, Mass.: Harvard University Press, 1960), pp. 311-23.

Haimson, Leopold. "The Problem of Social Stability in Urban Russia, 1905-1917." *Slavic Review* 23 (December 1964): 619-42; 24 (March 1965): 1-22.

Hooson, David J. M. "The Growth of Cities in Pre-Soviet Russia." In R. P. Beckinsale and J. M. Houston, eds., *Urbanization and Its Problems: Essays in Honour of E. W. Gilbert* (Oxford: Basil Blackwell, 1970), pp. 254-76.

Leasure, J. William, and Lewis, Robert A. "Internal Migration in Russia in the Late Nineteenth Century." *Slavic Review* 27 (September 1968): 375-94.

Lincoln, W. Bruce. "N. A. Miliutin and the St. Petersburg Municipal Act of 1846: A Study in Reform under Nicholas I." *Slavic Review* 33 (March 1974): 55-68.

Puryear, Vernon J. "Odessa: Its Rise and International Importance, 1815-1850." *Pacific Historical Review* 3 (1934): 192-215.

Thiede, Roger L. "Urbanization and Industrialization in Pre-Revolutionary Russia." *Professional Geographer* 25 (February 1973): 16-21.

Vucinich, Alexander. "The State and the Local Community." In Cyril Black, ed., *The Transformation of Russian Society* (Cambridge, Mass.: Harvard University Press, 1960), pp. 191-209.

Zelnik, Reginald E. *Labor and Society in Tsarist Russia: The Factory Workers of St. Petersburg, 1855-1870.* Stanford: Stanford University Press, 1971.

The Soviet City

Russian Language

Baranov, N. W. *Sovremennoe gradostroitel'stvo: glavnye problemy.* Moscow, 1962.

Gabrichidze, B. N. *Gorodskie Sovety deputatov trudiashchikhsia.* Moscow, 1968.

Gradov, G. Z. *Gorod i byt.* Moscow, 1968.

Institut konkretnykh sotsialnykh issledovanii AN SSSR. *Sotsiologicheskie issledovaniia goroda.* Moscow, 1969.

Kogan, L. B. "Urbanizatsiia—obshchenie—mikroraion." *Arkhitektura SSSR*, April 1967, pp. 39-44.

————; Akhiezer, A. S.; and Ianitsky, O. N. "Urbanizatsiia, obshchestvo i nauchno-tekhnicheskaia revoliutsiia." *Voprosy filosofii*, February 1969, pp. 44-53.

Listengurt, S. "Perspektivnye izmeneniia gorodskogo naseleniia

SSSR." *Izvestiia AN SSSR, seriia geograficheskaia,* June 1969, pp. 59-68.

Poliak, G. *Biudzhet Moskvy.* Moscow, 1968.

Posokhin, M. V. "Gorod budushchego sozidaetsa segodnia." *Arkhitektura SSSR,* October 1964, pp. 1-9.

Safarov, R. A. *Nauchnye prognozy razvitiia i formirovaniia sovetskikh gorodov na baze sotsial'nogo i nauchno-tekhniicheskogo progressa.* 2 vols. Moscow, 1968-1969.

――――. *Raionnye sovety deputatov trudiashchikhsia v gorodakh.* Moscow, 1961.

Shirkevich, N. *Mestnye biudzhety SSSR.* Moscow, 1965.

Svetlichnyi, B. "Gradostroitel'stvo i planirovanie." *Arkhitektura SSSR,* March 1966, pp. 28-32.

――――. "Nekotorye voprosy perspektivnogo razvitiia gorodov." *Voprosy ekonomiki,* March 1962, pp. 58-69.

Valentei, D. I., et al. *Problemy urbanizatsii v SSSR.* Moscow, 1971.

English Language

Cattell, David T. "Leningrad: A Case Study of Soviet Local Government." *Western Political Quarterly* 17 (June 1964): 188-99.

――――. *Leningrad: A Case Study of Soviet Urban Government.* New York: Praeger, 1968.

DiMaio, Alfred John, Jr. *Soviet Urban Housing: Problems and Policies.* New York: Praeger, 1973.

Frampton, Kenneth. "Note on Soviet Urbanism, 1917-1932." *Architects' Yearbook* 12 (London, 1968): 238-52.

Frolic, B. Michael. "Decision Making in Soviet Cities." *American Political Science Review* 66 (March 1972): 38-52.

――――. "Municipal Administrations, Departments, Commissions and Organizations." *Soviet Studies* 22 (January 1971): 376-93.

――――. "The Soviet City." *Town Planning Review* 34 (January 1964): 285-306.

――――. "The Soviet Study of Soviet Cities." *Journal of Politics* 32 (August 1970): 675-95.

————. "Soviet Urban Political Leaders." *Comparative Political Studies* 2 (January 1970): 443-64.

Gordon, L. A., and Klopov, E. V. "The Social Development of the Working Class of the USSR." *Soviet Review* 14 (Spring 1973): 3-35.

Gordon, L., and Levin, B. "Some Consequences of the Five-day Week in Social and Daily Life in Large and Small Cities." *Soviet Review* 10 (Summer 1969): 22-27.

Gutnov, Alexei, et al. *The Ideal Communist City*. Translated by Renee Neu Watkins. New York: George Braziller, 1968.

Harris, Chauncy D. *Cities of the Soviet Union*. Chicago: Rand McNally, 1970.

————. "City and Region in the Soviet Union." In R. P. Beckinsale and J. M. Houston, eds., *Urbanization and Its Problems: Essays in Honour of E. W. Gilbert* (Oxford: Basil Blackwell, 1970), pp. 277-96.

————. "Ethnic Groups in Cities of the Soviet Union." *Geographical Review* 35 (July 1945): 466-73.

————. "Urbanization and Population Growth in the Soviet Union, 1959-1970." *Geographical Review* 61 (January 1971): 102-24.

Herman, L. M. "Urbanization and New Housing Construction in the Soviet Union." *American Journal of Economics* 30 (April 1971): 203-19.

Kopp, Anatole. *Town and Revolution: Soviet Architecture and City Planning, 1917-1935*. Translated by Thomas E. Burton. New York: George Braziller, 1970.

Krupyanskaya, V., and Rabinovich, M. G. "The Ethnography of the City and the Industrial Settlement." *Soviet Sociology* 3 (Fall 1964): 13-19.

Leasure, J. William, and Lewis, Robert A. "Internal Migration in Russia in the Late Nineteenth Century." *Slavic Review* 27 (September 1968): 375-94.

————. "Internal Migration in the U.S.S.R.: 1897-1926." *Demography* 4 (1967): 479-86.

Lewis, Robert A., and Rowland, Richard H. "Urbanization in

Russia and the USSR, 1897-1966." *Annals of the Association of American Geographers* 59 (December 1969): 776-96.

Mellor, Roy E. H. "The Soviet Town." *Town and Country Planning*, February 1963.

Osborn, Robert J. *Soviet Social Policies: Welfare, Equality, and Community*. Homewood, Ill.: Dorsey Press, 1970.

————, and Reiner, Thomas A. "Soviet City Planning: Current Issues and Future Perspectives." *Journal of the American Institute of Planners* 28 (November 1962): 239-50.

Osipov, G. V., ed. *Town, Country, and People*. London: Tavistock Publications, 1969.

Parkins, Maurice Frank. *City Planning in Soviet Russia*. Chicago: University of Chicago Press, 1953.

Pchelintsev, O. S. "Problems of the Development of Large Cities." *Soviet Review* 7 (Winter 1966-1967): 15-23.

Ruzavina, E. "Economic Aspects in the Urbanization Process." *Soviet Review* 11 (Spring 1970): 82-93.

Shidlovskii, Oleg A., comp. *Building in the USSR, 1917-1932*. New York: Praeger, 1971.

Sosnovy, Timothy. "Housing Conditions and Urban Development in the U.S.S.R." In *New Directions in the Soviet Economy*, Part II-B. Joint Economic Committee, Subcommittee on Foreign Economic Policy, 89th U.S. Congress, 2d Session (Washington, D.C.: Government Printing Office, 1966), pp. 533-53.

Starr, S. Frederick. "Writings from the 1960s on the Modern Movement in Russia." *Journal of the Society of Architectural Historians* 30 (May 1971): 170-78.

Taubman, William. *Governing Soviet Cities: Bureaucratic Politics and Urban Development in the USSR*. New York: Praeger, 1973.

Zile, Zigurds L. "Programs and Problems of City Planning in the Soviet Union." *Washington University Law Quarterly* (February 1963): 19-59.

Russian Language

Akademiia nauk SSSR, Institut istorii. *Istoriia Moskvy.* 6 vols. Moscow, 1952-1959.

————. *Ocherki istorii Leningrada.* 5 vols. Moscow, 1955-1967.

Gol'denberg, P., and Gol'denberg, B. *Planirovka zhilogo kvartala Moskvy XVII, XVIII, i XIX vv.* Moscow-Leningrad, 1935.

Larina, V. I. *Ocherki istorii gorodov Severnoi Osetii (XVIII-XIX vv.).* Ordzhonikidze, 1960.

Saushkin, Iu. G. *Moskva-Geograficheskaia kharakteristika.* Moscow, 1964.

Sergeev, V. "Pervye Sibirskie goroda, ikh voennoe, ekonomicheskoe i kulturnoe znachenie." *Vestnik istorii mirovoi kultury* 3 (21) (1960): 113-24.

Shelikhova, N. M. *Istoriia Kieva.* 2 vols. Kiev, 1958-1959.

Smol'ianinov, K. *Istoriia Odessy.* Odessa, 1853.

Zykov, S. S. "Voprosy razvitiia gorodov Sibiri." *Izvestiia Sibirskogo otdeleniia Akademii nauk SSSR, seriia obshchestvennykh nauk* 1 (1964): 63-69.

English Language

Gutkind, E. A. *Urban Development in Eastern Europe: Bulgaria, Romania, and the U.S.S.R.* New York: Free Press, 1972.

Hall, Peter. "Moscow." In Peter Hall, *The World Cities* (New York: World University Library, 1971), pp. 158-81.

"Turkmenistan: Urban Development." *Central Asian Review* 2, no. 1 (1954): 76-84.

CONTRIBUTORS

Michael F. Hamm is Assistant Professor of History at Centre College of Kentucky.

Lawrence Langer is Assistant Professor of History at the University of Connecticut.

David H. Miller is Assistant Professor of History at Rutgers University.

J. Michael Hittle is Assistant Professor of History at Lawrence University.

Gilbert Rozman is Assistant Professor of Sociology at Princeton University.

Walter Hanchett is Professor of History at the State University of New York, College at Cortland.

Richard H. Rowland is Assistant Professor of Geography at California State College, San Bernadino.

Roger L. Thiede is Assistant Professor of Geography at the University of Georgia.

Frederick W. Skinner is Assistant Professor of History at the University of Montana.

Robert Gohstand is Assistant Professor of Geography at California State College, Northridge.

Robert A. Lewis is Professor of Geography at Columbia University.

S. Frederick Starr is Assistant Professor of History at Princeton University.

Milka Bliznakov is Professor of Architecture at Virginia Polytechnic Institute and State University.

David T. Cattell is Professor of Political Science at the University of California, Los Angeles.

B. M. Frolic is Associate Professor of Political Science at York University.

William L. Blackwell is Professor of History at New York University.

INDEX

Cities, Russian (*continued*): franchise in, 92-101, 108-12, 186-88, 191, 194-95; general characteristics of, 1-3, 5, 35, 91, 116, 125-27, 129, 297-98; general quality of life in, 141-42, 146-47, 151-56, 182-92, 195-98, 224, 227, 230-31, 257-62, 266-71, 277-88, 306, 310-14, 316-19, 324-27; and historiography, 2-3, 11-13, 27-28, 69-79, 83-84, 126, 292, 297-98; mortality rates in, 42, 117, 147, 152, 182, 210, 217; and peasants, 12, 26, 41, 43-44, 57, 62-63, 93, 96, 100-101, 108, 117-22, 177-78, 196, 213, 237, 268, 300, 304, 308-09, 318; and police, 105, 150, 185; problem of definition of, 75-79, 125-27; problem of fire in, 42-44, 141, 198, 224, 295; problems of health and sanitation in, 105, 141-42, 146-47, 151-55, 182-86, 188-89, 196-98, 224, 230, 257-58, 266-67, 279-80, 285, 316, 324-26; and provision of service for the state, 31, 35-37, 40-41, 54-58, 61-67, 299-300; and question of voting curiae, 92-95, 100-101, 108-12, 194-95; and revolutionaries, 313-14, 316-17; and serfdom, 30, 40-41, 50, 83; social stability in, 4, 29-30, 39-40, 56, 190-93, 197, 300, 310, 316; as source of tax revenue for state, 31, 34, 36-42, 46-50, 54-60, 183-86, 299-300; violence in, 29-30, 39-40, 56, 197, 300, 316; and Western cities, 3, 12-14, 18, 24-25, 30, 56, 100, 141, 147, 178, 182-86, 196-98, 228, 235, 281, 284, 287, 291, 296-98, 299-301, 306-15; 325; and Western influence, 145, 150, 164-65, 174-75, 223-40, 246, 253. *See also* Architecture; Bureaucracy; Cities, medieval Russian; Communist Party; Housing; Municipal Statutes; Planning, city; Reform; State, Russian; Transportation; Urbanization; *individual cities by name*

Civil War, Russian, 4, 306, 315, 318

Collectivization, and urbanization, 4, 203, 295

Cologne, 14

Communist Party, Soviet, and city planning, 222-23, 236-40, 243-46, 252-72, 276, 283-84, 286-87

Constantinople, 21, 301-02

Crimea, cities in, 19-22, 181-82, 195-96, 213, 235

Dadonov, V., 233

Deurbanization, 38, 44; and Civil War, 4, 203, 257, 295, 315, 318; fantasy about, 291, 325; and Ivan IV, 30, 36; and plague, 26, 42, 49-50; proponents of and plans for, 243-52, 325; and tax levies, 36-37; and World War I, 316

Dmitri Donskoi, 29-30

Duma (council), municipal: and All-Russian municipal movement, 193, 195; apathy of, 187, 313; assertiveness of, 150, 316; functions of, 92-95, 99-101, 109-12; and municipal newspapers, 193-95; and Municipal Statute of 1892, 109-12, 153, 183-88; in Odessa, 149-58; revitalization of, 192-95; state control over, 105-11

Dvinsk, 184, 197

Ekaterinburg, 235

Enakiev, F., 228-29, 313

Engels, Friedrich, 237, 244, 291

Fialko, Ivan, 238

Finland, cities in, 109, 185

Fomin, Ivan, 227, 229, 235, 238, 244

France, 186, 223, 306

Frankfurt-am-Main, 14

Frederick William I (Prussia), 299-300

Garden city movement, 196, 223, 230-38; and Russian state, 236

German cities: and garden city movement, 231; and Russian cities, 14, 18, 185-86, 299-301, 306

Ginsburg, Moisei, 238, 243, 249-51, 253

Gor'kii, 213

Gorky, Maxim, 213, 311

Gorodskoe delo (St. Petersburg), 194, 233

Great Siberian Migration, reversal of, 215

Green city, design for, 251

Gron, Jan de, 45

Guerin, Charles, 226

Guilds, absence of, 24-27

Hanseatic trade, 16-19, 31
Haussman, Baron, 228
Hilbersmeier, Ludwig, 246
Historiography, of cities, 2-3, 11-13, 27-28, 69-79, 83-84, 126, 292, 297-98
Housing, urban (in Russia): and central planning, 244-46, 259-72, 285, 323-24; and city government, 186, 190, 196-97, 257-65; condition of (pre-Soviet period), 152, 155, 182, 186, 190-91, 196-97, 224, 227, 310-11; condition of (Soviet period), 230, 237, 257-60, 311, 318, 324; and current Moscow plan, 278-79; and development of central business district, 175, 178-80; and garden city movement, 230-31, 233-35; and industrial enterprises, 196-97, 224, 234-35, 259-61, 269, 271, 322-23; maintenance of, 267-68, 271-72, 274-75 n. 22, n. 24; prefabricated, 260-61, 273 n. 10, n. 13, 279, 287; rent for, 191, 196, 257, 267, 271, 273 n. 4, 275 n. 27; shortage of, 258-68, 271-72; space per person in, 196-97, 257-59, 266-67, 272-73 n. 3, 278, 310-11, 324; superblock, 244, 254-55, 323-24; theories about (20th century), 227, 234-40, 244-45, 247-52, 254-55, 284
Howard, Ebenezer, 231-37

Iaroslav Iaroslavich, 28
Iaroslavl', 42-44, 49
Industrialization: and energy, 216, 255, 264; and foreign trade, 216; and garden city movement, 231-33; and handicraft industry, 212-13; and Moscow, 160, 252, 276-78, 304; and numbers of workers by region, 211-12; and planning, 224, 231-33, 240, 250-58, 276-78, 326; regional variation in, 212-17; and urbanization, 121-23, 125-37, 160, 203, 211-17, 255-56, 293, 303, 305-09, 320-23
In-migration. *See* Urbanization
Irkutsk, 194
Italy, 14
Ivan III, the Great, 22, 25
Ivan IV, the Terrible: and Moscow's trade,

162-63; and urban administration, 31; and urban depopulation, 30, 36
Ivanovo, 303-04

Japan: urbanization in, 71; urbanization compared to Russian, 78, 80-84, 291, 298, 305, 307, 325-26
Jerusalem, 301
Jews: and municipal reform, 195; and Municipal Statute of 1892, 111, 186-87, 195; and urban poverty, 197, 310

Kabuzan, V. M., 74-75, 77
Kadet Party, 191
Kafa, 19-22
Kaganovich, Lazar, 252-54
Kakhanov, M. S., 108
Karasev, K., 236
Katkov, M. N., 108
Kazan, 56
Kerch, 195-96
Kharkov, 193, 235, 261, 295, 307, 325
Kherson, 155
Khrushchev, Nikita: and urban housing, 259-67
Kiev: arts in, 23; as cultural center, 140; early trade in, 20; city duma, 192, 194-95; garden city movement in, 235; general development of, 158, 297, 308, 320; municipal congress of 1913 in, 193, 195; municipal journal of, 194; special status of, 261
Kievan Rus': absence of guilds in, 24; cities in, 12, 296-97; and commerce, 20; and slavery, 25-26; and urban crafts, 23; and *veche*, 27, 31
Kishinev, 194
Kostroma, 13, 27, 49
Kosygin, Alexei: and urban consumer, 267-72
Krizanich, Iurii, 45
Kropotkin, Prince Peter, 231
Kucherenko, V., 276
Kursk, 49

Ladovsky, Nikolai, 243, 252-53
Langeron, Count Alexander de, 144
Lansere, N., 228
Law Code (*Ulozhenie*) of 1649, and townsmen, 40-45, 49-50, 57

Le Corbusier, 239, 246
Lenin, Nikolai, 213, 245, 286
Leningrad: classicism in, 238; depopulation of, 257, 272 n. 1; industrialization in, 252; and megalopolis, 326-27; planning in, 252, 262-63; size of, 320; special status of, 261; and World War II, 295. *See also* Saint Petersburg
Leonidov, Ivan, 248-49
Linear city, 238, 251-52, 256
London, 14, 186, 281, 310-11, 314
Lübeck, 14
Lugansk, 137
Lukomskii, Grigorii, 226

Magnitogorsk, 261, 321, 323, 325
Maiat, V., 236
Mangu-Temir, 16-17, 20
Marx, Karl, 70, 84, 244-45, 284, 291
Mayor, city: function of (19th century), 92, 99-100, 109
Microrayon, 255, 263
Middle East, urbanization in, 298-99
Mikhail Fedorovich, Tsar, 37-38
Miliutin, N. A., 94
Miliutin, Nikolai: and linear city, 238, 251-52, 256
Minsk, 238, 310
Modernization, urban, 158, 198; breakdown of, 154-55, 182-98, 306, 313-16, 318; and Municipal Statute of 1870, 96, 107, 152, 182, 312-13; and Municipal Statute of 1892, 154-55, 183, 195, 313; in Odessa, 142, 149-51, 154-58; and praetorian revolt, 303; of trading establishments, 164-65, 175-79; and urbanization, 293-96, 305-27
Moldavia, 213, 215
Monasteries: as anti-cities, 37-38; and Black Death, 26; competition with cities, 44; loss of influence of, 42; and taxation, 36-37, 42; and trade, 22-23, 25
Mongol invasions: and urban life, 13-23, 30-31; and *veche*, 27-28
Morosov, Boris, 39-40
Moscow: administration of, 91-92, 94-95; and All-Russian Union of Towns, 193; attempts to improve automobiles in, 280-33, 326; changing appearance of,

160-66, 175-80, 238, 283-84, 288; and chiliarchate, 29; city planning in, 179-80, 196, 252, 262-63; and city plan of 1935, 276-77, 282-83, 323; commercial pattern in, 161-64, 169-80; commercial rivalry in, 175; current city plan of, 276-88, 326; depopulation of, 42, 272; finances of, 189-92; fire in, 42; and garden city movement, 234-37; geography of trade in, 160-80; growth of (19th century), 89-90, 160; as holy city, 301; housing in, 272-73 n. 3, 278-79, 283, 287, 324; and industrialization, 160, 252, 276-78, 304; limitation in size of, 276-77; medieval population of, 13; and megalopolis, 326-27; and Mongols, 15; and municipal congress of 1910, 193; and municipal journal, 194; and Municipal Statute of 1870, 107; and Municipal Statute of 1892, 109-11, 186-88, 194; and nationalism, 301, 304; and Novgorod, 18; pollution in, 282, 326; projected population of, 277; quality of life in, 186, 191-92, 272-73 n. 3, 311, 314; relationship to other Russian cities, 158, 192, 277, 286-87, 294, 300-302, 308; relative size of, 79, 91, 139, 301, 320; riot of 1648 in, 40, 301; and self-government, 94-95, 98, 101, 186-92, 194, 235, 283; significance of trade in, 166-69, 301; special status of, 261, 277, 286-87, 294, 301-05; strike movement in, 190; and suburbs, 172-73, 179-80, 191, 234-35, 277, 287; types of trade establishments in, 161-66, 174-80; uprising in, 29-30; urban crafts in, 23-24; and *veche*, 27-28; and World War I, 189-92
Moscow Architectural Society, 235
Municipal Statute of 1846, 92-95
Municipal Statute of 1862, 95
Municipal Statute of 1870, 96-108, 112, 149-50, 182-83, 195, 224, 295, 312-13; historical significance of, 97-98, 103, 107, 182, 295, 312-13
Municipal Statute of 1892, 108-13, 182-83; and city finances, 153-55, 183-86, 188, 192, 195-96, 198, 313; and franchise, 110-13, 186-88; impact

on city life of, 112-13, 152-57, 182-83, 195-98; and World War I, 188-89, 192
Murom, 15, 21
Muthesius, Hermann, 233

New Russia, urbanization in, 125-37, 307-08
New York city, 186, 310
Nicholas I: and urban development, 141, 146-48, 182
Nicholas II, 112-13, 153
Nikolaev, 155, 197, 214
Nikon, Patriarch, 42
Ninth Five Year Plan, 268-69
Nizhnii Novgorod: depopulation of, 49; economic importance of, 21; medieval size of, 13; and Mongols, 16; urban crafts in, 23; urbanization of, 213; and *veche*, 27
Nobility: and migration to cities, 301, 309-10; participation in city government, 187-88
Northeast Russia: and medieval cities, 13, 27, 31; and Mongols, 16-22
Novgorod, 297; depopulation of, 30, 272 n. 1; liberties of, 28; medieval political institutions in, 17-18, 27-31; medieval population of, 13, 35; and Mongols, 15-17; and Moscow, 18; and trade with West, 17-19, 22; and Tver, 18; urban crafts in, 23; urban factions in, 28-29
Novosibirsk, 253, 320

Octobrist Party, 194-95
Odessa: architecture in, 145-46, 150; compared to other Russian cities, 140, 184, 188; cultural life in, 139; finances of, 147-50, 153-55, 184; growth of, 131, 139-40, 143-44, 154, 213-14, 303, 307; mortality rate in, 147, 152; and municipal congress of 1910, 193; and Municipal Statute of 1870, 107, 149-50; and Municipal Statute of 1892, 109, 152-57, 184, 187; planning in, 139-58, 311-12; quality of life in, 142-58; self-government in, 94, 148-58, 184, 187; and shipping, 139, 144, 150-51, 154-55; and the state, 145, 147-58
Odoevsky, Prince V. F., 326

Okhitovich, Moisei, 249
Ol, A., 236
Old Believers, 304
Ordin-Nashchokin, A. I., 45-46
Ostroumova-Lebedeva, Anna, 226

Paris, 14, 186, 228, 302, 308, 314
Paul I, Tsar, 143
Peasantry. *See* Cities, Russian: and peasants
Peking, 282
Peretiatkovich, M., 228
Peter I, the Great, 299; and city planning, 141, 222; and urban reform of 1699, 47-50, 53, 57-60; and urban reform of 1721, 60-62
Pirenne, Henri, 12, 30, 298
Pisa, 14
Planning, city (in Russia): absence of, 197, 323; and city government, 148, 151, 154-58, 188, 245, 253, 259-65, 270-72, 312-13, 322-23; and commercial development, 179-80; and Communist Party, 222-23, 236-40, 243-46, 252-72, 286; and consumer services, 257-72, 277-80, 285, 322; and deurbanization, 243-52; and dissolution of the family, 245, 247, 249, 284; and environment, 326; goals vs. realities in, 284-86; and industrialization, 224, 231-33, 240, 250-58, 276-78; and local coordination, 259-72, 274 n. 16, 278, 323; and Marxist ideology, 233, 237-39, 243-46, 251-52, 284; in Moscow, 179-80, 196, 252, 276-78; in Odessa, 140-58; and problems with data, 263, 270, 284; and professional organizations, 252-54; in St. Petersburg (Leningrad), 223-30, 234, 252; and scarcity of planners, 263, 266, 270, 283; and the state (pre-Soviet), 140-43, 147-48, 152-53, 155-57, 222, 319; theories of (20th century), 222-40, 243-56, 284, 314, 319; and the West, 141, 223-40, 246, 253, 281-82, 287, 312
Pobedonostsev, K. P., 108
Pogorelko, A., 193
Poland, cities in, 109, 192, 310
Pollution, urban, 282, 326-27
Polotsk, 18-19

Strumilin, S. G., 325
Suburbs: and commerce, 172-73, 179-80; and garden city movement, 231-32, 234-35; quality of life in, 146, 152, 155, 196, 287. *See also Posad*

Tambov, 308
Tashkent, 194, 320
Taut, Bruno, 246
Tbilisi (Tiflis), 308, 326
Tokyo, 82
Tolstoi, Count D. A., 108
Trade. *See* Central Asia; Moscow; Novgorod
Transportation, urban: and current Moscow plan, 277, 280-83, 287; and planning theories, 143, 231-32, 234-35, 247-48, 251, 254, 285, 311-12; problems of, 142, 146, 148-49, 151-52, 154-55, 172-73, 178, 186, 189, 191, 196, 257-58, 262, 271, 285, 311-12
Tuchkov, P. A., 94
Tula, 235
Tver': and chiliarchate, 29; and Mongols, 15-16, 19-20; and Novgorod, 18, urban crafts in, 23-24; and *veche,* 27

Ukraine, cities in, 184, 213-15, 232, 255-56, 303, 308, 320. *See also* Kharkov; Kiev; New Russia; Odessa
Ullas, N., 278, 285
Ulozhenie of 1649. *See* Law Code of 1649
Union of Architects-Urbanists (ARU), 252-53
Union of Soviet Architects, 253-54, 266
Union of Towns, All-Russian, 188, 193, 234
United States, 291, 306-07, 310, 325
Uprava (city administrative board), 99-100, 104, 108-10
Urals (region), 213, 215
Urbanization, in Russia: and age, 119; approaches to the study of, 69-79, 83-84, 117-23, 209, 211; and birthrate, 4-5; and city finances, 185-86; and city growth, 206-09, 255-56, 296, 307; and city planning, 141-43, 147, 156-57, 255-56, 285; and collectivization, 4, 203, 210; and commercial development, 175-79, 305, 307; compared to urbanization elsewhere, 71, 73, 75, 78-84, 116-19, 121, 197-98, 203, 206-08, 216-17, 291, 296-312, 322, 325-27; contemporary problems of, 4, 215-16; definition of, 206; in eighteenth century, 69-84; and emancipation of serfs, 120, 177, 180, 294-95, 303; and energy, 216, 320; and growth of industrial labor force, 197, 211-14, 255-56, 304; and historical periodization, 293-327; and historiography, 69-79, 83-84, 292, 297, 314; and industrialization, 121-23, 125-37, 160, 203, 211-17, 255-56, 293, 303, 305-09, 320-23; and job opportunities, 119-23, 214, 309; and megalopolis, 325-26; and modernization, 182-83, 195-98, 293-96, 305-27; and Mongols, 15-16, 30; and mortality rates, 14, 117, 210, 217; in New Russia, 125-37, 307-08; in 19th century, 89, 115-23, 125-37, 160, 177, 206-07, 293; and peasants, 117-22, 177, 213, 308-09; projected rate of, 291; and quality of urban life, 182-83, 185 86, 195-98, 210, 322; rapidity of, 89, 160, 203, 206-08, 319-20; regional comparisons, 80, 205-06, 211-16; and reversal of Great Siberian Migration, 215; and serfdom, 83; and service sector, 120-22, 214, 258, 322; and sex, 117-21, 309; and state policies, 83-84, 210-11, 215-16, 255-56, 305-08; in 20th century, 4, 89, 203, 205-18, 291, 303, 318-20; and urban in-migration, 115-23, 160, 179-80, 206, 209-10, 308-09, 320; and urban network approach, 79-84; and urban reform, 48-50, 84, 96; and urban self-government, 69-71; and World War II, 210, 215, 291, 295, 320, 322
Ustiug Velikii, 40

Valuev, P. A., 96-97
Vandervelde, Emile, 231
Veche, 27-28, 31
Vernyi (Alma-Ata), 232
Vesnin, Alexander, 234, 236, 243, 248
Vesnin, Leonid, 243, 248
Vesnin, Victor, 243, 248
Viatka, 253

This book has been set in Aldine Roman on the IBM Composer by the University of Kentucky Printing Services.

Lettering by Calvert Guthrie

Design by Jonathan Greene

Printed and bound by NAPCO Graphic Arts, Inc.